Archives of Labor

# Archives of Labor WORKING-CLASS WOMEN AND LITERARY CULTURE IN THE ANTEBELLUM UNITED STATES

*Lori Merish*

Duke University Press • Durham and London • 2017

© 2017 DUKE UNIVERSITY PRESS. All rights reserved.
Printed in the United States of America on acid-free paper ∞.
Cover design by Matthew Tauch; interior design by Courtney Leigh Baker.
Typeset in Garamond Premier Pro by Graphic Composition, Inc.

Library of Congress Cataloging-in-Publication Data
Names: Merish, Lori, [date] author.
Title: Archives of labor : working-class women and literary culture
in the antebellum United States / Lori Merish.
Description: Durham : Duke University Press, 2017. |
Includes bibliographical references and index.
Identifiers: LCCN 20216047425 (print)
LCCN 2016051069 (ebook)
ISBN 9780822362999 (hardcover : alk. paper)
ISBN 9780822363224 (pbk. : alk. paper)
ISBN 9780822373315 (ebook)
Subjects: LCSH: Working class women—United States—Social conditions—
19th century. | Working class women in literature. | Literature and
society—United States—History—19th century. | Women textile workers—
Massachusetts—Lowell—History—19th century. | American literature—19th
century—History and criticism. | Social classes in literature. | Race in literature.
| Popular culture—United States—History—19th century.
Classification: LCC PS217.W66 M47 2017 (print) | LCC PS217.W66 (ebook) | DDC
810.9/352209034—dc23
LC record available at https://lccn.loc.gov/2016047425

Cover art: Tintype of two women holding bobbins. Courtesy of American Textile History
Museum, Lowell, MA.

To the memory of my grandmother and my mother,
*Agnese Dagradi Riccardi* and *Elsie Riccardi Merish*

And for Sophia

Acknowledgments • ix

Introduction • 1

*One*. Factory Fictions: Lowell Mill Women
and the Romance of Labor • 33

*Two*. Factory Labor and Literary Aesthetics: The Lowell Mill Girl, Popular
Fiction, and the Proletarian Grotesque • 73

*Three*. Narrating Female Dependency: The Sentimental Seamstress
and the Erotics of Labor Reform • 113

*Four*. Harriet Wilson's *Our Nig* and the Labor of Race • 153

*Five*. Hidden Hands: E. D. E. N. Southworth and
Working-Class Performance • 180

*Six*. Writing Mexicana Workers: Race, Labor,
and the Western Frontier • 219

Postscript. Looking for Antebellum Workingwomen • 247

Notes • 251    Works Cited • 285    Index • 303

ACKNOWLEDGMENTS

This book was years in the making; I have accrued far more debts than I can possibly rehearse—but with pleasure I acknowledge a few of them here.

A Mellon Postdoctoral Fellowship at Stanford University enabled me to cultivate this project in its earliest stages. At Georgetown University, Junior and Senior Faculty Research Fellowships provided much-needed releases from teaching to draft early chapters and revise the entire manuscript. A National Endowment for the Humanities Research Fellowship during 2007–8 was crucial, supporting archival research that changed the course of the project.

I tested the book's ideas in many conference presentations and invited lectures. I am especially indebted to audiences at the following for feedback and suggestions: the American Studies Department of the University of California, Santa Cruz, and the English departments at the University of California, Davis, Miami University, Brown University, Johns Hopkins University, and Carnegie Mellon University. A year as a Beatrice Bain Fellow at UC Berkeley provided an invigorating feminist community for debating the book's theoretical approach and critical claims.

The expert assistance of staff at the Library of Congress, the American Antiquarian Society, the American Textile History Museum, the Center for Lowell History at the University of Massachusetts, Lowell, the New York Public Library, and the Bancroft Library helped me locate relevant materials. I am indebted to Judith Ranta, historian and librarian at the Center for Lowell History, whose painstaking efforts indexing and creating bibliographies of factory women's writings aided me in navigating archives and identifying sources for my first two chapters.

Although I didn't start this book while I was a graduate student, if it hadn't been for UC Berkeley I'm pretty sure I wouldn't have written it. The inspiration and example of many teachers, especially Carolyn Porter, Michael Rogin,

Susan Schweik, David Lloyd, Barbara Christian, Cathy Gallagher, Tom La-
queur, Janet Adelman, Mitch Breitwieser, and Elizabeth Abel, made it seem a
project worth doing. They also modeled a kind of accessibility, care, and passion
that made being an academic seem both attractive and possible. Having grown
up in a working-class town, this made all the difference for me. State support for
public education—especially California's, which is ever at risk—made this path
feasible for me, among many others. Graduate student friends at Berkeley—the
list is huge, and some names appear below, so I'll single out for mention Scott
Dykstra, Mary Caraway, Jane Garrity, Karen Jacobs, Cindy Schrager, Bruce Bur-
gett, Franny Nudelman, Irene Tucker, Frann Michel, Lauren Muller, and Yvonne
Vowels—fostered an astonishingly lively, intellectually generative community.
Even when we can't see one another, the fellowship and camaraderie of these
friends have sustained my work over the years in more ways than I can count.

This project was first envisioned when I was an assistant professor of English
at Miami University. I am grateful to students in my graduate courses on class,
who are now esteemed colleagues: Cara Ungar, Jennifer Thorington-Springer,
Jill Swiencicki, Malea Powell, and Tim Helwig. The early support of my fan-
tastic chair at Miami, Barry Chabot, helped launch the project. Conversations
with Kate McCullough during our commute from Cincinnati to Oxford were
a weekly touchstone, providing critique and encouragement in equal measure.
Conversations with other Miami friends and feminist colleagues, especially my
draft group (Susan Jarratt, Vicki Smith, Laura Mandell, Alice Adams) moved
the project forward. Mary Jean Corbett's critical brilliance and expertise in Victorian studies and working-class writing enlivened this book since it was a gleam
in my eye; I am indebted to her for that, and for her abiding friendship.

A Mellon Fellowship at Stanford supplied the time and space to begin the
project in earnest. For their collegial generosity at Stanford, I thank Sharon
Holland, Rob Polhemus, Suvir Kaul, Paula Moya, Patricia Parker, and the late
Jay Fliegelman; graduate students, especially Patricia Roylance, Joel Burgess,
and Joe Shapiro, were lively interlocutors.

The English Department at Georgetown has provided a stimulating, sup-
portive intellectual environment in which to draft and revise this book. The
early support of Lucy Maddox, Gay Cima, and the late Michael Ragussis helped
me maintain my focus while adjusting to a new job. I am grateful to present and
former colleagues, especially Ann Cubilie, Lyndon Dominique, Jennifer Fink,
Leona Fisher, Lindsay Kaplan, Dana Luciano, Mark McMorris, Angie Mitchell, Patricia O'Connor, Patrick O'Malley, Sam Pinto, Henry Schwarz, Steve
Wurtzler, Joy Young, and Paul Young, for intellectual exchange and friendship.
Past and present chairs in the department, Joe Sitterson, Penn Szittya, Kathryn

Temple, and Ricardo Ortiz, provided steady support. Since my arrival Pam Fox has been an extraordinary colleague, interlocutor, and friend; writing this book would have been far lonelier without her. Although we work in different fields, the ongoing support of Sarah McNamer has been invaluable. Conversations about shared interests with Christine So have enriched my life and work over more than a decade. Although she arrived at Georgetown only a few years ago, Sherry Linkon has energized class studies on campus; her gift at community building and belief in this book have been a boon. I am grateful to Joe McCartin, director of the Kalmanovitz Initiative for Labor and the Working Poor, for his support; the KI provides a warm home for faculty and students working on labor and class issues on campus. Fellow organizers of Georgetown's Lannan Symposium on Economic Precarity, and those who participated in the event, gave this book a welcome boost.

My students at Georgetown were in the trenches with me as I worked through these ideas. Students in my graduate and undergraduate courses on class in U.S. literature challenged and enriched my textual readings. Students in my women's and gender studies courses on class in the contemporary United States, and especially the extraordinary group in my 2013 justice and peace studies course Economic Justice, pushed me to clarify this book's theoretical bearings and political stakes.

For reading drafts, sharing ideas, and offering feedback at key points, I am grateful to Tom Augst, Bill Andrews, David Anthony, Giulia Fabi, Beth Freeman, Anne Goldman, Sandra Gunning, Dori Hale, Gordon Hutner, Gavin Jones, Katie Johnson, Amy Schrager Lang, Andrew Lawson, Bob Levine, Jennifer Luff, Lucy Maddox, Tim Melley, Marianne Noble, Dana Nelson, Sam Otter, Paula Rabinowitz, Judith Rosen, Shirley Samuels, Xiomara Santamarina, Jacqueline Shea-Murphy, Gillian Silverman, Margit Stange, Katherine Stubbs, Lynn Wardley, Cindy Weinstein, and Liz Young.

At Duke University Press I am immensely grateful to Ken Wissoker for his wise counsel, good humor, and patient, abiding support of the project, and to Elizabeth Ault and Lisa Bintrim for cheerfully shepherding the book through the publication process. The enthusiastic support of Russ Castronovo and the two anonymous readers helped me stay the course; their acute suggestions for revision strengthened the book. The meticulous research assistance of Eujin Kim, who pored over microfilms of Spanish-language California newspapers, and Emily Coccia, who worked through countless final details, helped get this into print.

In New Jersey, the Merish, Riccardi, and Soules families, especially my sister Nancy, have long sustained me with their love, support, and irrepressible humor.

In California the Rose clan's passion for great food and outdoor adventure have kept me fed in mind, body, and spirit. In D.C. the Berman-Nienstadts have been like a treasured second family; your generosity is epic, and I will never forget it. I have counted on dear friends, especially Deborah Altamirano, Judy Berman, Julie Buckner, Patty Enrado, Laura Fejerman, Liza Kramer, Michael Morris, Becky Pizer, Linda Tam, and Lori Varlotta, for just the right combination of inspiration and distraction.

The loving childcare of Leanne Auyong made many hours of worry-free writing possible.

Most of all I thank Charles Rose for intellectual companionship and steady support on the home front, especially for carving out space for my regular weekend writing sessions at the café, and to Sophia for putting up with them. Thanks, Charles and Sophia, for helping me remember me why I do this work—and reminding me to play.

Earlier versions of portions of chapters 2 and 3 originally appeared as "Fictions of the Factory: Popular Narrative and Workingwomen's Desire in the 1840s," *Arizona Quarterly* (Fall 2012): 1–34; "Story Paper Weeklies, 1830–1920," in *U.S. Popular Print Culture, 1860–1920*, edited by Christine Bold (Oxford University Press, 2012), 43–62; and "Representing the 'Deserving Poor': The 'Sentimental Seamstress' and the Feminization of Poverty in Antebellum America," in *Our Sisters' Keepers: Theories of Poverty Relief in the Work of 19th-C American Women Writers*, edited by Debra Bernardi and Jill Bergman (University of Alabama Press, 2005), 49–79.

*T*he *Aristocrat and Trades Union Advocate*, an 1834 pamphlet poem by a "working woman of Boston," offers a striking commentary on the meaning of industrialism and its much trumpeted "progress" for working people. One of the first works of trade-union imaginative literature published by an American, the poem initiates the tradition of antebellum working-class women's writing examined in this book. Dedicated to members of the Boston Trades Union, the poem purportedly records a conversation overheard between the parties named in its title during a Fourth of July procession—a frame that positions the working-class woman writer as a witness to male politics, a medium, and a scribe of male voices. The poem thus could be seen as allegorizing the gendered (and racialized) politics of class during the antebellum period, when working-class dissent, linked to a recently enfranchised white working-class manhood, was predicated on feminine subordination and silence.[1] However, the text also affirms, in complex ways, female discursive and literary authority. Using a lengthy preface—a frequent feature of poetry of this type—to register her relation to the class conflict here cast as masculine dialogue, the poet immediately converts the seemingly auxiliary position of spectator or listener into a stance of political affiliation and engagement: "Do not imagine," she charges her Unionist readers, "that I acted the part of a vile listener. . . . Long before the gentlemen began to speak, I had chosen my position and resolved not to give it up for man, woman, or child."[2] Claiming a political initiation that "long" precedes the masculine debate that is her poetic subject, the poet signals the existence of a robust political discourse among antebellum women, one corroborated by recent scholars.[3] But here feminine political autonomy and agency are specifically located in a collective body of *working-class* women. Observing that Unionist readers will doubtless wonder, "as [the recorded dialogue] did not pertain to household affairs or matters of dress, but to topics of political bearing, how could it be interesting to a working woman?" (iv), the poet avers that the political opinions expressed by the advocate "resemble[d] [those] of our working women." "That there were certain customs and practices creeping in among us contrary to a republic," she states with remarkable force, was "discussed by our working women long before you thought of forming a 'dangerous combination'" (vi). Later in the preface she anchors this oppositional oral culture in the historical countermemory of "our mothers and old fashioned aunts," who possess an intimate knowledge of the decline of republicanism and the degradation of the laboring class in the early nineteenth century (vii). For this writer, "republican motherhood" is a locus of working-class power and produces not only "republican sons" but activist, working-class daughters.[4] The oral (counter)knowledge of "our [plebian] mothers" at once unsettles the primacy of the masculine voice of class protest the poem ostensibly records and serves to anchor and authorize workingwomen's textual expression.[5]

The female agency of listening assumes concrete form in the poet's transformation of political discourse into verse. While disparagingly attributing her conversion of everyday speech into rhyming couplets of iambic pentameter to a "defect in early education," a mere "few months [of] instruction" at the age of three, she designs to filter male speech through the medium of feminine literary imagination (v).[6] Workingwomen, she shows, have an unquestioned stake in antebellum print culture. Asserting boldly that "women will read the papers" (vi), she establishes herself as an avid consumer of the emerging transatlantic working-class culture of letters, referencing papers as diverse as Cobbett's *Political Register* and the London *Times* (28–29). The poem itself contributes to the body of working-class political verse associated with the contemporaneous Chartist movement.[7] Armed with such literary competencies, the writer is attuned to the power of words, especially their significance as tokens of class contest. Thus, she observes, industrial "improvements" do not in reality benefit all (as Whigs contend) but depend upon the degradation and exploitation of labor; the "expansion of . . . national industry" (xi) has widened the gap between rich and poor while generating increasing "pride" among the "gentry" (ix). The "dangerous combination[s]" are not the unions and "clubs" of the "lower orders" (24), as the *Aristocrat* professes, but the chartered corporations and "factio[ns]" of elite professional men ("Judges and Lawyers") who monopolize economic and political power; while the "age of intellect" (the title of a widely circulated Cruikshank print from 1828 and a phrase bandied about by middle-class organizations such as the Societies for the Diffusion of Useful Knowledge) is erected on workers' ignorance.

But the poet is particularly attuned to how gender, in David Montgomery's words, "profoundly shaped the everyday experience of class."[8] Capturing the perspective of a female domestic worker, the poem opens with an epigraph attributed to Shakespeare that is actually a clever rewriting of lines from *Othello*:

> Rude am I in speech,
> And little blessed with the phrase of schools,
> For since these arms of mine had ten years pith
> Until these few last hours they have used
> Their dearest action in the busy kitchen:
> And little of this great world can I speak,
> More than pertains to feats of broils and stews;
> And therefore little shall I grace your cause,
> Yet, unions, by your gracious patience,
> I will a plain unvarnished tail [*sic*] deliver.

Cannily revising Othello's speech—warrior is transformed into maid, "feats of stews" replace Shakespearean "feats of battle," and "tented field[s]" become a "busy kitchen" as the setting of the speaker's literary exile—the poet again appropriates a male voice as a vehicle for feminine poetic agency. Further, in adapting Othello's words the poet performs a cross-identification that is racial as well as sexual: in a fascinating instance of "love and theft" by a working-class woman (specifically a servant, with all of that term's racial connotations in the antebellum era), Othello's "rude . . . speech" is an enabling condition of poetic discourse and a textual frame the author repeatedly unsettles. For one thing, the conventional apologia is undone by the poet's treatment of Shakespeare as cultural capital and literary currency, gestures that ironize her assertion of poetic "rudeness."[9] Indeed, the grounds of gendered class contest in the poem are at once political and aesthetic: her language will be "plain" and "unvarnished," she declares, repudiating the "grace[s]" of conventional literary arts. Forging her working-class aesthetic, the poet resists the silence imposed by an endless round of household tasks and the "increasing pride of the gentry" (ix) who "impress on the minds of independent women" a sense of class inferiority (xi). Like the Lowell worker who reveals how servants are consigned to silence unless "some question is put to them,"[10] the poet notes that feelings of deference and gratitude, rather than "independence and equality," are expected psychological traits of household workers (x). These constraints on working-class female speech are reinforced by workingmen's gendered expectations: the view of workingwomen as "mere" domestic servants infects workingmen's view as well. After all, it is male Unionists the poet takes to task for their assumption that workingwomen "are not to meddle with matters" outside domestic affairs (v); hastening to conclude her preface, she predicts that her readers' "patience with me is about gone" (xiii). An intensification of feminine "servitude," the author implies, is a direct consequence of industrial "improvement."[11] Invoking while repudiating the gendered, racialized meanings of both servitude and dependency in U.S. political discourse by the 1830s, the poet exploits an identification with Othello as the site of miscegenous desire and an enabling condition of poetic possibility. Her servitude is a position at once inscribed within and undone by the form of the poem itself.

Published twenty years later, at the opposite end of the period covered in this book, Lucy Ann Lobdell's extraordinary autobiography, *The Female Hunter* (1855), envisions what might be described as a more extended performance of cross-gendered vocalization. Indeed Lobdell's narrative literalizes what Engels and others called a "struggle for the breeches" in the working-class household.[12] The wife of a farm laborer, Lobdell leaves her abusive, improvident husband to pursue a career of female self-support, first as a "female hunter" who hunts game to feed herself, her infant daughter, and her aging, feeble parents, and later as an itinerant laborer who dresses as a man to secure "skilled," better-paid work. Lobdell's itinerancy is motivated by both the threat of her husband's return and her family's extreme poverty: "My father was lame, and in consequence, I had worked in-doors and out; and as hard times were crowding upon us, I made up my mind to dress in men's attire to seek labor, as I was used to men's work. *And as I might work harder at house-work*, and get only a dollar per week, and I was capable of doing men's work, and getting men's wages, I resolved to try . . . to get work away among strangers."[13] Male disability and its devastating economic effects in a male breadwinner economy here enable an unsettling of emerging liberal-capitalist norms of able-bodiedness and gendered embodiment. While slave narrators frequently envision the vulnerability of the master's body (the mortality and therefore inadequate protection even a benevolent master could afford) as a weak point in proslavery ideology in a capitalist order, working-women envision the "protection" afforded by a male breadwinner as more wishful thinking than fact. Lobdell's subversive assertion that she "might work harder at house-work" than "men's work" is reinforced by the strikingly detailed account of poor women's "double burden" with which the narrative concludes. Should she remain at her father's house,

> I should be obliged to toil from morning till night, and then I could demand but a dollar per week; and how much, I ask, would this do to support a child and myself.... Woman ... toils from morning till night, and then the way her sorrows cease is this—her children are to be attended to; she must dress and undress them for bed; after their little voices are hushed, she must sit up and look after the preparations for breakfast, and, probably nine, ten, eleven, or twelve o'clock comes round before she can go to rest. Again, she must be up at early dawn to get breakfast, and whilst the breakfast is cooking, she must wash and dress some half a dozen children. (42)

Appealing to men's concern for their daughters' future, Lobdell asks that her male readers endeavor to "secure to [woman] her rights" to equal wages; otherwise, she demands in barely constrained anger that they "permit her to wear the pants, and breathe the pure air of heaven, and you stay and be convinced at home with the children how pleasant a task it is to act the part that woman must act" (45). Coupling cross-dressing with images of escape and transcendence (the pants-wearing woman breathes "the pure air of heaven"), Lobdell contributes to a burgeoning political discourse of the female breadwinner and the value and productivity of domestic labor that, we shall see, echoed through the feminist periodical press of the 1850s.

Lobdell's powerful indictment of the economic privileges of masculinity is reinforced by another published account of the female hunter: a letter by a peddler, Mr. Talmage, that appeared in "many different papers" (38) (gaining Lobdell some notoriety) and was reprinted in *The Female Hunter*. Encountering Lobdell hunting in the woods sporting male hunting garb while a "good looking rifle" rests on her shoulder and a "formidable hunting-knife" hangs in phallic suspension from her waist (37), Talmage is invited inside the Lobdell home. "The maiden-hunter instead of setting down to rest as most hunters do when they get home," he pointedly notes, "remarked that she had got the chores to do" (37). Lucy, Talmage learns, has taken charge of all the farm chores as well as the household work since her father has been "confined to the house with the rheumatism" (37), and this particular day's activities are not unusual.

After stabling, feeding, and watering the farm animals and chopping wood for the evening, "her next business was to change her dress, and get tea. . . . After tea, she finished up the usual house-work, and then sat down and commenced plying her needle in the most ladylike manner" (37). The evening concludes with Lobdell bringing out her violin, playing and singing "in a style that showed that she was far from being destitute of musical skill" (38). In Talmage's letter, as throughout *The Female Hunter*, Lobdell's defiance of antebellum gender codes is marked both sartorially and economically: her bodily performances transgress the "law" of dress and the gender division of labor. Depicting this defiance of gender norms, *The Female Hunter*—like the treatments of "female Amazons" common in antebellum pamphlet fiction—stresses Lobdell's singularity; many readers will find her, the narrator acknowledges, a type of gender prodigy, a "strange sort of being" (46).[14] But like many early nineteenth-century socialists, including Fanny Wright (who herself habitually wore bloomer-like trousers), Lobdell emphasizes androgyny and sexual nonconformity as the basis of what one Owenite termed the entire reorganization of the "social and domestic system."[15] When her husband, accusing her of "spreeing," attempts to destroy Lucy's reputation through an elaborate charade meant to "expose" to the community her inattentive housekeeping, one can glimpse how closely the discipline of domesticity and working-class female "respectability" were becoming intertwined, during this period, in a discourse largely fashioned by men.[16]

Autobiographical narratives by free African American women similarly reveal the struggles of the female breadwinner and the economic debilities suffered by "domestic" women. For example, Harriet Jacobs charts a course "from slavery to poverty" in Linda Brent's narrative trajectory; mapping continuities from slavery to "free" domestic service, it foregrounds the indispensability of black women's reproductive labor in both the northern and southern economies. The Marxist feminist Sylvia Federici argues that under capitalism the female body was defined as a type of commons for men, a "natural resource, laying outside the sphere of market relations," and that women's unpaid reproductive and sexual labor have served as primary means of capital accumulation under "capitalist patriarchy."[17] Jacobs's *Incidents in the Life of a Slave Girl* suggests that the forced seizure of the black female body is consigned to unspeakability, placed outside the bounds of the literary itself. In struggling against Lydia Maria Child's editorship to cast her story in terms comprehensible to the "delicate ears" of middle-class readers, Jacobs reveals those discursive constraints to be as stifling as the prison-like space Brent inhabits for nearly a decade. In both the South and the North, black female productive and reproductive labor is revealed to be the source of white wealth; in *Incidents* that labor is also materially and symbolically claimed by black women as the basis of black physical and cultural survival. Similarly, Sojourner Truth's *Narrative* shows how class and labor shape narrative possibilities of gendered identity. In particular, Truth's *Narrative* "instructs [readers] in nineteenth-century working-class realities" while revealing the "overlap[ping]" experiences and cultures of white and black workers in the antebellum North, a period of abolition and racial uncertainty especially in northern cities.[18] We are now well acquainted with the nativism and racism of white workers in the Jacksonian era; less familiar are the forms of racial transgression and liminality—what Shane White calls the "fluidity of racial categories" as well as the interracial relationships and sexuality—common especially in poor urban neighborhoods.[19] In some sense, the miscegenous production of Truth's (auto)biographical narrative—dictated to Olive Gilbert, fellow resident of the Northampton Association—exemplifies the "biracial egalitarianism" of the Northampton Association and the miscegenous desires evident in poor neighborhoods and working-class cultural forms.[20] Truth, who grew up a slave laboring alongside Low Dutch mistresses renowned (as she would become) for their physical prowess and who, once free, worked alongside white female reformers in the Magdalen Society and New York's notorious (and interracial) neighborhood of Five Points, figures physical strength and spiritual sanctity as equally treasured personal gifts. Her autobiographical narrative—as fully as Lobdell's—reveals workingwomen's pressure on antebellum discourses of gendered embodiment and identity. For example, her mystical sense of a "union existing between herself and . . . Jesus, the transcendentally lovely as well as great and powerful," inspires her to imagine "surprising comparisons" between "herself and [the] great of this world" (68). While her repudiation of urban capitalism's "great system of robbery and wrong" (98) fuels her rebirth as "Sojourner," her determination to rely on the hospitality of others and her subsequent residence among various utopian communities (including the Northampton Association), while attesting to her "independence of character" (109), generate a startling range of race and class identifications. Incorporating rhetorics of radical abolitionism, millenarianism, and working-class socialism, Truth's *Narrative* opens up for us an enriched antebellum vocabulary of class. In particular the *Narrative*, like the writings of Fourierists and Saint-Simonians that inspired the antebellum communitarian movement,[21] mobilizes an affective vocabulary of solidarity and universal love in excess of standard interpretations of antebellum sympathy as "disciplinary intimacy" and middle-class affect.

Taken together these texts introduce issues central to this book and the body of workingwomen's literature examined within it. First, they foreground workingwomen's access to "the class-based, racially segregated, gender-exclusive slugfest of the Jacksonian public sphere."[22] Challenging the purportedly masculine character of class dissent and an image of workingwomen's silence—familiarly emblematized by the mute paper mill women in Melville's "Tartarus of Maids" (discussed in chapter 2)—they alert our attention to a vital, diverse archive of texts. These texts reveal how the expanding wage labor market in the antebellum period and forms of political discourse and activity associated with that expansion were sites of gendered cultural contest, materializing women's subordination while generating new forms of social identity, agency, and desire. Laboring women record especially the ways class relations are *gendered*, constituted by gendered processes of production and distribution that are justified and represented in discourse, including cultural discourse. Disrupting the hegemonic image of the white male industrial laborer as the "quintessential worker," they fashion new fictions of labor and working-class subjectivity.[23]

Crafting such fictions, working-class women writers necessarily engage with the representational status of working-class women in midcentury cultural and political discourse; in particular, they address ways in which the female worker was positioned to *represent* the condition of class exploitation, subjection, and economic suffering. In a host of texts—court documents and legal transcripts; petitions, testimonials, and "poverty narratives" collected by almshouses and bastardy courts; working-class men's writings about industrialism; and reports by urban and social reformers—poor and working-class women were expected to bear the "burden of poverty" both culturally and socially: they were tasked with representing forms of "social suffering" associated with poverty, excessive labor and bodily violation, physical compulsion (including sexual compulsion), and abuse.[24] According to Adrienne Siegel, women and children came to signify the degradation of the urban labor force in antebellum popular fiction: story paper, pamphlet, and serial fiction was "saturated . . . with the plight of two working-class groups, women and children."[25] The representational division of labor through which poor and workingwomen came to represent the trauma of poverty and economic exploitation certainly limited the cultural imagination of female economic subjectivity and restricted workingwomen's narrative plots; as we shall see in chapter 3, it aligned workingwomen with the tragic mode and conscripted them into what became naturalism's "plot of decline" while distancing them from narratives of individual or collective "progress," including the narrative of the American dream.[26] As one New England mill woman put it, women "have no share in that American privilege which sets in full view of the poorest white male laborer a growing income, a bank account, the possibilities of an Astor, and every office within the gift of the Republic if he have the brain and the courage to win them."[27] Challenging the reduction of working-class women's experience to inarticulate suffering and sorrow, working-class women writers reinflected the sign of the working-class woman, contesting her reiterated appearance as the very type of the dependent worker.

Of particular importance to my study is the role of the home in working-women's writings as an explicit locus of cultural contest, anchoring both gender subjection and class privilege. As Lobdell and the author of *The Aristocrat and Trades Union Advocate* differently suggest, antebellum workingwomen's social identities are often at odds with—but always defined in relation to—the domestic sphere and its increasingly hegemonic gender norms. This entailed refashioning cultural definitions of reproductive as well as productive labor. For example, rather than aligning women with the reproduction of cultural capital, as in domestic fiction—or pathologizing poor and working-class women for their purported role in the reproduction of poverty's moral and material degradation, as in the debates examined in chapter 2—texts such as the *Aristocrat* tie working-class women to the reproduction of a culture of class resistance, a culture transmitted, in part, by written texts.[28] According to one social historian, domesticity's "process of redefinition [of gender] . . . led to a denial of the more radical gender meanings—including greater political awareness and economic independence—implied in the experiences of poorer women who had sacrificed so much during the course of the [Revolutionary] war."[29] Mobilizing these "radical gender meanings" (in the *Aristocrat* these are lodged in the communal memory of plebian women), women workers drove a wedge in masculine, familial definitions of class, both conservative and oppositional, instituted in the early nineteenth century and with us to this day. Contesting the emerging norm of the family wage, these authors envision the family less as an image of class unity than as a site of class struggle; many foreground the gendered nature of class power and exploitation within and outside of the family. Their writings thus illustrate how, in the words of the theorist Joan Acker, "processes and practices [of] gendering and racialization are integral to the creation and recreation of class inequalities and class divisions, emerging in complex, multifaceted, boundary-spanning capitalist activities"—precisely at a moment when a new definition of gender was being installed as socially normative.[30] Working-class women's literature thus brings into clearer view the material and ideological stakes of the domestic model of gender that has received substantial critical attention in the field of antebellum women's writing. Their texts illuminate cultural definitions of class while contributing crucially to our understanding of nineteenth-century U.S. literary and cultural history.

The first book-length study of antebellum working-class women's literature, *Archives of Labor* examines textual representations of a diverse group of working women: Lowell mill women, African American "free laborers," Mexicana mission workers, urban seamstresses, and prostitutes. The book aims to address a significant absence in the critical literature about class in nineteenth-century U.S. cultural studies: although a number of recent works—by, most notably, Shelley Streeby, Gavin Jones, Amy Schrager Lang, and Eric Schocket—aim to address what Michael Gilmore in 1994 called a general silence about class matters in nineteenth-century literary studies,[31] none focuses expressly on working-class women. Indeed nearly all work on class in antebellum America overlooks working women. While scholarship on women's class identities has focused on the middle class and the role of domestic womanhood in securing middle-class hegemony, studies that address the formation of the working class and working-class subjectivities (including the ways in which, in Eric Lott's terms, class has been *staged* through race in the United States) have examined working-class *men* and the construction of class-inflected masculinities.[32] Delving into previously unexplored archives of working-class women's culture (including pamphlet novels, theatrical melodrama, and literature published in story papers and labor periodicals), *Archives of Labor* recovers working-class women's vital presence in antebellum America as both writers and readers. The book argues that antebellum popular literature both represents and helps shape working-women's subjectivity; challenging what Carolyn Kay Steedman and Cora Kaplan describe as the widespread attribution (in scholarly and other discourses) of a kind of psychological simplicity to working-class subjects, I emphasize the complex, often contradictory forms of antebellum workingwomen's subjectivities and desires.[33]

As the author of *Aristocrat* suggests, working-class women's literary texts are sites of class memory, archives that preserve and transmit popular languages of social class, democracy, and economic justice. I argue in chapter 2 that they can be envisioned as part of what Oskar Negt and Alexander Kluge term a "proletarian public sphere" in which working-class and poor women's concerns, experiences, and desires are given cultural expression.[34] As David Montgomery has demonstrated, by the 1840s, with the rise of universal white male suffrage, class was largely removed from the domain of politics and insulated from democratic control;[35] such depoliticization has worked not only to privatize the operations of the economy but also to naturalize racialized, gendered forms of political and economic privilege. The workingwomen's writings I examine here disrupt liberalism's separation of "*class politics* . . . from *identity politics*";[36] they help us see the ways that class—in the antebellum era, as today—is fundamentally a *gendered* as well as *racialized* relation. For example, the activist Lowell women discussed in chapter 1 invoke the figure of the female breadwinner to challenge emerging models of female economic and political dependency and the gendered exclusions of the workplace; popular fictions about factory women and seamstresses (examined in chapters 2 and 3, respectively) explore the feminization of poverty in the capitalist era and the delimitation of "benevolence" and welfare support that attended the rise of wage labor and the normalization of the family wage. These texts illuminate "intricate imbrications of relations of race, gender, sexuality, and class in the institutions of capitalist modernity" and their historically changing modes of economic distribution and production; they reveal how class operates through "status" categories of race and gender "at every stage of its historical development."[37] Attending to ways that class is actually *lived* through gender, race, and sexuality enriches and complicates our sense of the class past while enhancing our ability to imagine possible class futures. Writing in an era of social reform and utopian socialist experiments (such as those in which Sojourner Truth participated), when the inextricability of gender, class, and sexuality was powerfully theorized, workingwomen crafted languages of class and versions of class identity that remain visionary and politically generative. I see the value of restoring a sense of this tradition as both historical and genealogical: in addition to enabling us to see working-class women as writers and readers—thus shifting our sense of the literature of this period—it recuperates the importance of antebellum activist working-class women for the history of "material feminism" recovered by Dolores Hayden and for the evolution of what Dorothy Sue Cobble has termed "labor feminism" and the "other women's movement."[38]

Part historical recovery project, this book aims to restore an important chapter in American women's literary history, while its multiethnic focus enables an interrogation of the racially hegemonic (white) terms in which class identities, especially working-class identities, have often been defined. And while asserting the national import of this tradition (thus interrupting the myth of classlessness in the United States), I insist on its transnational reach. Like abolitionism, with which it overlapped, labor reform was part of a literary "culture of reform" with transnational, particularly transatlantic coordinates.[39] Not only did activists and their texts crisscross the Atlantic—Chartists, land reformers, and utopian socialists from Britain, Germany, and France emigrated to the United States, while Orestes Brownson's "Laboring Classes," a flashpoint in antebellum political discourse about industrialization, was published first in Britain—but discourses about class were forged in a transatlantic context. The nativist class icon of the Lowell mill girl was itself defined in the shadow of Manchester; strikingly, when one former millworker, Harriet Robinson, wishes to describe the Lowell mill girl's life circumstances, she refers her readers to Elizabeth Gaskell's *Mary*

*Barton*.[40] British debates about Chartism and the expansion of the franchise, reform of the poor laws, the dangers of "combination," and the benefits and liabilities of industrialism were reproduced and followed in the U.S. press and to some extent were mirrored in U.S. policy debates. *Archives of Labor* thus argues for the importance of the transatlantic in understanding antebellum working-women's literary culture. This is perhaps especially true of the field of popular literature; in the absence of U.S. copyright laws, the penny press was dominated by pirated stories, many from Britain, signaling how, in the era of the "American 1848," class wishes, aspirations, and fears were forged in a transnational context.[41] The struggle against the capitalist organization of ownership and productive and reproductive labor was transnational in scope, a fact taken up in my last chapter. In tracing these transnational coordinates, the prominence of class in British cultural studies is salutary, for this work can attune us to class accents and possibilities in nineteenth-century U.S. writings. For example, the entire humanist tradition explored by Raymond Williams's *Culture and Society*, which centered on nineteenth-century debates about literature as a repository of humanizing feeling in the industrial era, is largely absent from critical discourse about U.S. sentimentalism, which has often been dominated by a Foucauldian reading of sympathy as an ideological formation that reinforces middle-class hegemony—a theoretical frame that negates the complex cultural and political history of sentimentalism and the nuanced political valences of literary sympathy. Transatlantic work on class, sentiment, and affect (such as Bruce Robbins's important work) can help disrupt the exceptionalist notion that America was exempt from sustained class conflict and enliven our understanding of the class meanings embedded within a range of antebellum texts.

Antebellum workingwomen wrote and published in a variety of forms; some—exemplified by author of the *Aristocrat*, Lobdell, and Truth—published poetry and autobiographies; some published articles and sketches in the new labor periodicals; others published fiction. Several chapters in this study focus on fiction, especially cheap fiction published in story papers and other periodicals and in pamphlet form. Popular fiction is a crucial terrain for bringing workingwomen's subjectivities into critical focus. As several historians have noted, the emergence of the industrial working class in antebellum America coincided with the rise of a popular, democratic journalism and literature directed toward and sometimes produced by the lower classes, including the development of the penny press in the 1830s and the explosion of paperback novels in the 1840s, developments that signal the importance of print culture for the constitution of working-class subjectivities during this period.[42] I argue that working-class women were an important readership for the popular, sensational fiction that flooded the literary market after 1830 (I discuss examples of this literature in chapters 1–3.) Occasionally this audience was made explicit. For example, in 1871 the *New York Weekly* expressly linked publishing stories about women sewing machine operators with seeking them as an audience, while periodicals published by and for Lowell factory women regularly contained advertisements for cheap fiction (see chapter 2). At other times this working-class audience remained implicit. But it is my contention that even where it is commodified, popular literature operates in a dynamic interrelation with its working-class audience and encodes and facilitates forms of class desire and identification.[43]

## ANTEBELLUM LITERATURE AND
## THE MATTER OF CLASS

Broadly speaking, what Fredric Jameson terms the "dialogical" is the critical frame through which workingwomen's texts will be interpreted. "Refocus[ing]" the "individual cultural artifact" as the "irreconcilable demands and positions of antagonistic classes"—for Jameson the primary manifestation of ideological contradiction in cultural texts—the dialogical allows us to read individual texts as "utterance[s]" in "the vaster system, or langue, of class discourse." [44] Such an interpretive effort requires challenging any illusion of literary "autonomy" while recollecting what V. N. Volosinov first termed the historical "materiality" (the "live social intelligibility" or "accents") of the discursive sign. It involves a double move, both the "rewriting" of literary "masterworks" to their proper place within the "dialogic system" as "the voice of a hegemonic class" and the "restoration or artificial reconstruction" of a voice "opposed" to hegemonic utterance but marginalized, stifled, or "scattered to the winds." [45] Although one must challenge Jameson's description of a singular voice of working-class opposition, whether "restored" or "reconstructed" (and this book contends that working-class voices are indelibly marked by differences of race, gender, and sexuality), the value of this dialectical hermeneutic is to restore a sense of literary texts as sites of live and uneven social struggle—a perspective sorely lacking in nineteenth-century American literary studies.[46]

To grasp the challenge workingwomen posed requires radically historicizing their vision, a project that enables us to glimpse the rich imaginative possibilities, including (re)articulations of democracy and nation legible in their writings. In the antebellum period the ascendancy of the capitalist industrial and market system was decidedly not inevitable; the vast majority of the population remained agrarian in economic orientation and minimally integrated into a market system, and there was, even among Anglo Americans, a strong tradition of resistance to private property, free market ideology, and an industrial division of labor, from expressions of a "moral economy" inherited from English popular traditions to the agrarian republicanism of Jefferson and the humanism of an Emerson or Thoreau.[47] Writing broadly about the history of class dissent in the capitalist West, Eric Hobsbawm notes, "Looking back on the 1840s it is easy to think the socialists who predicted the imminent final crisis of capitalism were dreamers confusing their hopes with realistic prospects. For in fact what followed was not the breakdown of capitalism, but its most rapid and unchallenged period of expansion and triumph. Yet in the 1830s and 1840s it was far from evident that the new economy could or would overcome its difficulties which merely seemed to increase with its power to produce larger and larger quantities of goods by more and more revolutionary methods."[48] Neither was the domestic ideal that anchored middle-class power an inevitable development. As Mary Poovey observes in her study of Victorian England, middle-class womanhood was "both contested and always under construction; because it was always in the making, it was always open to revision, dispute, and the emergence of oppositional formulations."[49] To cite one relevant example, emerging expectations of a family or breadwinner wage—a rallying cry for workingmen in the 1830s and 1840s—reflected how "public authorit[ies]" have used thoroughly historical expectations of fairness, custom, and social roles (especially gender roles) to justify their intervention in and regulation of the labor and wage market.[50] Reading texts by and about antebellum women workers allows us to glimpse the formation and contestation of these categories as live historical process; these writings pose challenges to normative formations of gender and sexuality, and to the capitalist organization of the labor system, at a crucial moment in the history of American capitalism.

Working-class women waged class warfare on the discursive terrain of gender, race, and sexuality. Indeed it is only when the dialogic nature of this class struggle over gender is restored that we can fully grasp what has often been called the politics of domestic and sentimental fiction. I read domestic sentimental texts as encoding a hegemonic reappropriation of the ethical basis of much working-class and popular discourse, reformulating traditional concerns with social interdependency in ways hospitable to the emerging capitalist wage system. One cannot understand the crucial ideological aspect of sentimental texts, their promotion of benign paternalism through the combined "influence" of domestic femininity and commercial expansion—twinned centerpieces of Whig political discourse—without considering the social meanings that these texts were both reformulating and privatizing. Similarly, female wage labor was a key site of ideological contest: the cultural ideal of sentimental domesticity was inseparable from constructions of feminine leisure and the devaluation and ideological erasure—what Jeanne Boydston terms the "pastoralization"—of female labor in the home.[51] If the ability (and right) to care for dependents at once defined "civil citizenship" and constituted male independence and power, the female wage worker—especially the female industrial worker, with her much-heralded bank account—was an uncanny figure, troubling the very ground of male power. Due to the suturing of *worker* and *citizen* in democratic discourses during the antebellum era, the construction of women as nonworkers had clear political implications, underwriting their political invisibility.[52] Read dialogically and dialectically, constructions of domesticity are inseparable from constructions of female industrial and wage labor: sentimental and domestic texts are haunted by—and arguably work to exorcize—versions of female agency, enterprise, and individual and collective desire imaged by women workers. Workingwomen's writings allow us to glimpse an entire complex of gendered discourses and identities, and attendant political possibilities, not usually visible to us.

The dialogic framework described by Jameson for understanding class in or as literature can thus help revise our understanding of both familiar and unfamiliar antebellum literary texts. Although I focus on working-class texts, I briefly consider here how canonical nineteenth-century American texts might be reconsidered in light of this dialogic model. Specifically I argue that Hawthorne's *The House of the Seven Gables* should be read as performing what Jameson calls a hegemonic "re-appropriation and neutralization" of popular materials—in this case antebellum challenges to property ownership (especially the attack on hereditary property) posed by radical workingmen such as Thomas Skidmore and Orestes Brownson.

As some fine work on Hawthorne has demonstrated, he was a writer supremely sensitive to the politics of class and invested in the cultural work of the emergent middle-class familial ideal.[53] In *The House of the Seven Gables* he delineates a class antagonism projected back into the Puritan past: a conflict between the Pyncheons and the Maules, a family of "aristocrat[s]" and another from the "lower classes," that involves the questionable seizure of Matthew Maule's small "homestead," "hewn out" of the forest by "his own toil," by the "prominent and powerful" Colonel Pyncheon for erection of a "family mansion," an appropriation enabled by personal connections and "the strength of a grant from the legislature."[54] The novel interrogates the American myth of a radical break from a prerevolutionary social order, when "the great man of the town was commonly called King, and his wife . . . Lady" (63), and postrevolutionary egalitarianism and "union" (an ideal figured in images of boundlessness, a "mighty river of life" and "surging stream of human sympathies" [165]), documenting the persistence of class distinctions in a democratic order. That persistence is of course symbol-ized by the house (called a "gray, feudal castle" [10]), that emblem of ancestral genealogy and the "prejudice of propinquity" in consolidating and transmitting wealth (23), whose lasting material presence seems to naturalize class power. As the narrator states, "There is something so massive, stable, and almost ir-resistibly imposing, in the exterior presentment of established rank and great possessions, that their very existence seems to give them a right to exist" (25). The contradictory presence of class is also embodied in the character of Jaffrey Pyncheon, whose great wealth and numerous "deeds of goodly aspect, done in the public eye," are metaphorized as a "tall and stately edifice" (229). The text highlights, in the narrator's words, "how much of old material goes to make up the freshest novelty of human life" (6).

*The House of the Seven Gables* is obviously concerned with inheritance in all its spiritual, moral, psychological, and social complexity; but it explicitly casts this preoccupation in the antebellum idiom of class conflict. Whereas the Pyn-cheons "cherish, from generation to generation" a sense of "family importance," a "kind of nobility" (19), the "poverty-stricken" Maules are "always plebeian and obscure; working with unsuccessful diligence at handicrafts; laboring on the wharves, or, following the sea, as sailors before the mast; living . . . in hired tenements," before finding their "natural home" in the almshouse (25). The text's depiction of the "controversy" over ownership in the language of natural "right[s]" (7, 19) and the invocation of a labor theory of value situate this con-troversy in discourses of class in the industrial era, as does the metaphoric de-scription of Colonel Pyncheon as "iron-hearted" (15) and animated by "an iron energy of purpose" (7). The "public memory" (19) of his act of illegitimate ap-propriation and "proprietorship" (7) is cast from the start as historical counter-memory, the product of oral "tradition" (7) and the common gossip of old women (10)—knowledge "obliterate[d]" (7) by "mouldy parchments" (19) and the authoritative textuality of the law, which, for instance, bury "the [original] appellation of Maule's Lane" (6) under the more "decorous" name of Pyncheon-street (11).[55]

In a classic reading Walter Benn Michaels argues that the novel is indeed centrally preoccupied with questions of property as they emerged "during the years of Jacksonian democracy." However, he contends that the text invests in a bourgeois fantasy of inalienable property freed from the violent fluctuations and social instability of the antebellum market, an ideal exemplified by the "title of the hereditary noble," the "land for the landless" movement that culminated in the 1862 Homestead Act, and the fiction of property expressed by abolition-ists such as Harriet Beecher Stowe. Michaels sees this conception of inalienable property as fundamental to Hawthorne's idea of romance as nonmimetic representation. For Michaels the novel "by no means enacts a Jacksonian confrontation between the 'people' and those who sought to exercise a 'despotic sway' over them." Instead it evinces "the appeal of a title based on neither labor nor wealth and hence free from the risk of appropriation."[56]

I would argue, of course, that *The House of the Seven Gables* indeed "enacts" just such a "Jacksonian confrontation" and that its fictive resolution of this conflict and the fiction of ownership that enables it are inseparable from its treatment of gender—of little import in Michaels's reading. In this novel, as in so many eighteenth- and nineteenth-century novels, class conflict is undone by domestic desire: femininity converts a violent (and racialized) class antagonism into what antebellum writers called a "harmony of interests" between the classes. Marginalizing gender, Michaels's reading marginalizes Holgrave (while indirectly calling attention to Holgrave at several points). A Maule by blood, Holgrave speaks out not in support of his family's claim to rightful ownership but against the principles of inheritance and transgenerational familial identity—indeed genealogy—altogether. Holgrave is a reformer who lives by "a law of his own" (85). Hepzibah recalls with distaste "a paragraph in a penny-paper" that describes a "wild" speech he delivered "at a meeting of his banditti-like associates" (84). Speaking with Phoebe midway through the text, Holgrave states with great earnestness:

> Shall we never, never get rid of this Past? . . . It lies upon the Present like a giant's dead body! In fact, the case is just as if a young giant were compelled to waste all his strength in carrying about the corpse of the old giant, his grandfather, who died a long while ago, and only needs to be decently buried. . . . A Dead Man, if he happen to have made a will, disposes of wealth no longer his own; or, if he die intestate, it is distributed in accordance with the notions of men much longer dead than he. . . . Whatever we seek to do, of our own free motion, a Dead Man's icy hand obstructs us! . . . We must be dead ourselves, before we can begin to have our proper influence on our own world, which will then be no longer our world, but the world of another generation, with which we shall have no shadow of a right to interfere. (182–83)

It is the ownership of real estate that comes under particular censure: "We shall live to see the day, I trust," Holgrave continues, "when no man shall build his house for posterity. . . . If each generation were allowed and expected to build its own houses, that single change, comparatively unimportant in itself, would imply almost every reform which society is now suffering for" (183–84). Although Phoebe is made "dizzy" by such talk of a "shifting world," Holgrave continues more strongly, "To plant a family! This idea is at the bottom of most of the wrong and mischief which men do!" (184–85).

If much of this sounds Thoreauvian, it resembles still more closely the arguments of radical workingmen, especially Skidmore and Brownson, who challenged the era's legal consolidation of absolute private property rights by marshalling traditional and natural rights arguments about communal claims to ownership. Holgrave's language echoes Skidmore directly: arguing boldly in *The Rights of Man to Property* that "all men should live on their own labor, and not on the labor of others" and thus that men of "enormous property . . . have no just title to their possessions," Skidmore proposes to abolish hereditary property altogether, imploring his fellow citizens to pull "down the present edifice of society, and . . . build a new one in its stead." Like Holgrave, Skidmore is especially troubled by the authority that the "law of property" vests in the "rights of dead men," enabling a "posthumous dominion over property" that exerts a gothic power over the living.[57] The critique of private property, articulated most strongly in *The House of the Seven Gables* by Holgrave, is echoed by Uncle Venner, that representative of "the very lowest point of the social scale," who has "seen a great deal of the world" in kitchens and backyards, on street corners and wharves (155, 82). His accumulated wisdom, Holgrave notes, has something of "the principles of Fourier" in it (156). Uncle Venner speaks particularly for the traditional claims to charitable, public care; had he devoted his life to the labor of accumulation, heaping up "property upon property," he tells the group, "I should feel as if Providence was not bound to take care of me; and, at all events, the city wouldn't be" (156). The narrative as a whole, in venturing to differentiate between a "moral" and a "legal" right to ownership (20), treads upon the territory of the "moral economy," evoking traditional, customary limits on absolute private property ownership for what revolutionary-era writers termed the "public good." Such views, collectively considered, cannot be collapsed into the aristocratic ideal of inalienable property or the bourgeois model of market alienability that Michaels outlines—or the hybrid fiction of bourgeois inalienability that, for Michaels, represents the novel's fantasized solution to the text's dilemmas of inheritance. In fact that solution—what Michaels describes as the text's "anchoring" of property in "character," which gives ownership a "kind of psychological legitima[cy]"—depends entirely upon gender: while Michaels interprets Holgrave's eventual "legitimation" of property late in the text as exemplifying the transmutation of "accumulation" into inheritance, this reading of Holgrave's conversion entirely overlooks the agency of domestic desire.[58] In effecting Holgrave's conversion, the novel envisions a feminine tempering of masculine "grasping spirit," which redefines the "moral" right to ownership as the particular property of the virtuous, domestic woman. In Phoebe proprietary desire equates to (domestic) benevolence, and ambition—the desire to "seek [one's] fortune"—equates to "a self-respecting purpose to confer as much benefit as she could anywise receive" (*The House of the Seven Gables*, 74). That the novel, in what many view as an awkward application of the machinery of closure, transforms Holgrave from radical to conservative, incorporating him in its marriage plot, does not negate the oppositional force of his proclamations; rather, it makes the mechanics of bourgeois narrative, its incorporation and containment of popular materials, conspicuously apparent.

Like the domestic woman theorized by Nancy Armstrong, Phoebe is an agent of (self-)discipline and domestic desire: if she is "sweet," she is also "order-loving" (305). Emphasizing Phoebe's domestic charm, Hawthorne also stresses her limitations: her "essence," the narrator says, "was to keep within the limits of law" (85). A prominent part of Phoebe's "limit-loving" (131) nature is love of private property; baffled by Uncle Venner's views, she affirms that "for this short life of ours, one would like a house and a moderate garden-spot of one's own" (156). The discipline she works on Holgrave entails engendering an attachment to property. While she fears that Holgrave will "make [her] strive to follow you, where it is pathless," he replies with "almost a sigh," "I have a presentiment, that, hereafter, it will be my lot to set out trees, to make fences—perhaps, even, in due time, to build a house for another generation . . . to conform myself to laws, and the peaceful practice of society" (306–7). In the end Holgrave's transformation is complete; admiring Judge Pyncheon's country house, Holgrave wonders that the Judge "should not have felt the propriety of embodying so excellent a piece of domestic architecture in stone, rather than in wood," for the "impression of permanence" (314–15). If Hawthorne ironizes the concluding vision of domestic happiness, as he surely does (his couple declare their love in the garden, "transfigur[ing] the earth, and ma[king] it Eden again," while the Judge's corpse rots in the house [307]), his is the irony of a fatalist; Hawthorne invests Holgrave's conversion with the increasingly normative force of domestic desire.

In *The House of the Seven Gables* the domestic woman secures masculine consent to the law of property and the course of social reproduction; it is his spontaneous love of Phoebe that fosters Holgrave's desire to "plant a family" and build a stone house as love's enduring legacy. In a similar way the reformer Orestes Brownson acknowledged that conventional ideas of "family love" are thoroughly entangled with—and often serve to justify—the "law of property"; like Skidmore, Brownson envisioned a redistribution of property and questioned the role of the family in its consolidation and transmission. In two controversial articles published in 1840, "The Laboring Classes" and "Defense of the Article on the Laboring Classes," Brownson argues for the abolition of hereditary property as an inherently antirepublican, monopolistic, oppressive institution. In the tradition of Tom Paine, he advances a plan for redistribution that involves reappropriating each citizen's property at the time of his death, so that each citizen will receive, as a national birthright, a certain portion when he (or, more radically, she) attains adulthood. Brownson demonstrates how sympathy for a man's dependents was used to defend private property and a wage and inheritance system that itself disadvantaged women and children essentially by producing the very dependency it was enlisted to remedy. In the "Defense" he identifies one "objection" to his plan he "had not anticipated": it "would bear exceedingly hard upon the widow and the orphan. As soon as a man dies, the state takes his property, and the widow and the orphan must be sent to the almshouse"; this argument, Brownson acknowledges, "appeals to our sensibilities." However, according to his plan, children would be "provided for in the school, where they fare the same [as] they would were the father living," while apropos the widow, Brownson boldly argues, "in the reappropriation, the distinction of sex should not play the important part it does now. In all that concerns property, woman should share equally with man, and like him be an independent proprietor, a relation which marriage should not [affect]." Powerfully, Brownson asserts that "the idea of dependence should never necessarily attach to the one more than to the other. Marriage . . . should never be regarded as a marriage of estates, but of persons, and hearts. Each should have the means of living independent of that relation." To the inevitable concern that his "proposed reforms will break up the family relation," Brownson, while admitting "great respect" for "the family feeling," argues for a reformation and expansion of social sentiment in accord with a truly democratic social order: "We have been taught by our religion, and by our philosophy, that the family is subordinate to Humanity, and that, though it is the centre of our affections, and the sphere in which lie our special duties, still it is in our love and action always to give place to mankind at large, and to universal justice."[59] Like many of the workingwomen I discuss in this study, Brownson proposes a reformation in social sympathies, boldly imagining a new erotics not governed by a Victorian gender binary of masculine independency and feminine dependency.

## CLASS AND SEXUALITY

I argue throughout this book that antebellum workingwomen's interventions into discourses of class took shape in a highly visible way across the cultural terrain of sexuality. This is in part because, as Armstrong and others contend, middle-class cultural texts disseminated a particular, sexualized model of class power; Armstrong's *Desire and Domestic Fiction* demonstrates that the ideal of femininity and the "sexual contract" *constituted* middle-class authority and a form of social power rendered all the more effective because of the force of ideological (mis)recognition—that is, because it purportedly operated at a remove from politics and thus appeared no force at all. Armstrong argues that the domestic woman, written into existence in the voluminous conduct literature of the seventeenth and eighteenth century and elevated into cultural common sense in domestic fiction, came to epitomize the new middle-class self; in particular, she embodied the self-regulatory, supervisory techniques that characterize disciplinary society and constitute middle-class power. Radical workingwomen such as Sarah Bagley recognized the class power embodied in the domestic ideal; as chapter 1 shows, factory women recognized the ideological power of femininity and feminine "delicacy" to privatize the identity of female factory operatives, specifically to mark politicized female speech as deviant and to contain workingwomen's class dissent. Lowell women's disruption of the "Romance of Labor" entailed uncoupling factory work from the domestic norms that would render female bodily labor invisible and positioning workingwomen outside the sexual contract that legislated feminine economic dependency and defined a willing submission to male authority as a desirable—indeed the only legitimate—form of female power.[60] Countering mainstream depictions of the "beauties of factory life," radical Lowell women challenged the aestheticization of female factory work that would efface the pains of the female laboring body and euphemistically construe female labor as feminine leisure.[61] The cultural struggle to feminize workingwomen traced in these pages—and workingwomen's resistance to these efforts (especially in gestures of what Christine Stansell calls "antidomesticity")[62]—highlights the special ability of workingwomen to disrupt and contest what was an increasingly hegemonic formation of class and gender.

As a public, visibly social form of labor, female factory work was a hotly contested sign. As chapter 1 demonstrates, the female factory worker assumed an iconic presence in the discourse of industrialization, with many writers contrasting the virtuous, cultured American mill girl with her degraded British counterpart. Such idealistic accounts ignored the observations of workingmen such as James Burn, who claimed that, like the Lancashire factory girls he had known in England, American factory women "are neither fitted for wives by a due regard for the feelings and wishes of their husbands, nor a knowledge of the simple rudiments of housekeeping. . . . They will not be instructed by their husbands; and as proof of their obstinacy, one of their common remarks to each other when speaking of their husbands is that they would like to see a man who would boss them."[63] They also ignored the words of Lowell women themselves, such as the writer who argued that long hours of factory labor "destroy all love of order and practice in domestic affairs . . . so that by the time a young lady has worked in a factory one year, she will lose all relish for the quiet, fireside comforts" of domestic life.[64] Lowell women took special pleasure in exposing contradictions in industrial propaganda about Lowell women; writing in the *Voice of Industry*, Bagley notes that, while factory defenders are fond of "talk[ing] about the 'virtuous and puritanical daughters of the New England farmers'" who supposedly populate Lowell, claiming that supervision is "so vigilant that it is hardly possible for an operative to be vicious," they at the same time protest the prospect of a ten-hour workday because "the time allowed to the operatives, would be spent in vicious indulgence."[65] Although Lowell women aimed to complicate this account, many antebellum depictions of them represent factory work as an apprenticeship in virtuous domesticity. The *Lowell Offering* was established, in fact, to display the superior cultural accomplishments and attributes of the American female factory worker—to display through her writing (especially poetry) that she possessed feminine sensibility. In the pages of the *Lowell Offering* the public nature of factory work was representationally contained by a thoroughgoing domestication; by depicting flowers and other traces of domestic decor in the factory, by describing factory women's good manners and other domestic graces, and by inscribing the supervisor as a benevolent paternal figure, the factory was portrayed as an extension of the home.[66] Celebratory renderings such as these positioned the mechanized order of the factory in opposition to—indeed as the imaginary corrective of—the disorderly, promiscuous (and interracial) mixing of bodies in working-class streets and housing depicted in the new, proto-sociological literature on the urban poor.

If, as Armstrong suggests, the self-regulated domestic woman was assigned the hegemonic cultural task of civilizing (domesticating) men and producing their consent (willing submission) to modern forms of power, then working-women's very subjectivity was an object of profound cultural concern; policing and re-forming that subjectivity was understood to be a precise form of labor discipline (securing workingmen's accommodation to the wage labor contract). In light of this reading, the debates about American factory women's femininity—Was factory work compatible with domesticity? Did factory work compromise women's manners, sensibility, or sexuality?—start to make a good deal more sense. Universalizing domestic womanhood was quite clearly a class tool. As the historians Anna Clark and Barbara Taylor have pointed out, some radical authors concerned with the capitalist reordering of economic life imagined a redefinition of social relations that included gender and sexual relations. Owenite socialists, for example, advocated an egalitarian society, challenged conventional sexual morality, denounced tyranny in marriage, organized women along with men, and demanded truly universal suffrage. Robert Owen rejected the central patriarchal tie of marriage, whose contractual origins signified to him its market origins. Referring to gender relations in the 1830s in Britain, Taylor writes, "All was plastic, all was possible." Such utopian visions of class and gender transformation—combining free love, a critique of the capitalist division of labor, and a commitment to common ownership—were well known in America; in *The Blithedale Romance* Hawthorne gives them canonical inscription. Other long-standing sexual traditions "from below," such as consensual union and betrothal, persisted even with the hegemony of domestic norms.[67] The power and meaning of those norms cannot be understood, I suggest, apart from the class and sexual traditions I describe. Workingwomen who emphasized the economic value of women's domestic labor and sexual services profoundly destabilized the domestic model by calling attention to forms of power typically masked by domestic norms. By desentimentalizing domestic labor and sexual relations—extricating them from norms of middle-class eroticism—workingwomen insisted upon the relevance of economic and political power to the construction of domesticity: specifically, they refused to separate women's sexual "consent" from relations of domination and exploitation.

The discourse surrounding Lowell women can thus be seen to specify ways gender helps to *constitute* class relations.[68] In chapters 1 and 2 I demonstrate that the category of gender was central to debates about industrialization and an American industrial system. Writers since Jefferson had expressed grave concern about urbanization and industrialization, fearing that wage labor would undermine (male) citizens' independence; as Richard Slotkin observes, women were viewed as a group of workers who could supply factories with necessary labor because their "natural" political dependency rendered them compatible with wage work, thus assuaging political fears and easing the contradiction between capitalism and democratic republicanism. Women's political dependency was thus imagined as inextricable from their economic dependency; indeed, the former both determined and justified the latter. By the 1830s domestic ideology inflected this gendered dependency with psychological and moral content so that women's dependency (their passivity, passionlessness, modesty) was seen as a *positive* attribute, a "natural and gratifying component of respectable femininity."[69] I have argued elsewhere that sentimental literature eroticized this dependency, constructing feminine dependency as both natural and desirable.[70] I argue here that workingwomen's dependency was a primary form of class discipline: dependency constituted a means to "civilize" male workers and configure their consent to forms of wage labor as a product of private desire, not public coercion and force. For example, an article in the *New York Post* suggested that the only way to make husbands sober and industrious was to keep women dependent by low wages.[71] As I demonstrate throughout this book, many working-class women understood the ideology of feminine dependency and the forms of eroticism that subtend it as a crucial psychological site for what we might call gendered "injuries of class."[72] While middle-class reformers tended to highlight workingwomen's dependency in fashioning a sympathetic vision of urban workers (see chapter 3), workingwomen resisted this construction in various ways, emphasizing their pragmatism and economic rationality in navigating heterosexual relations and stressing the value of female economic independence. Viewing the family as the institution through which the erotics of feminine dependency were both sanctioned and normalized, they presented thoroughgoing critiques of both domestic ideology and working-class family practices, problematizing the family as what Stansell terms "a controlling metaphor of class consciousness" and political unity.[73]

The discourse of the family wage brought capitalist processes of distribution and the reproduction of labor into harmony with these increasingly hegemonic domestic norms of desire. As Joan Acker explains, the wage is both "an aspect of production and a mechanism of distribution. It is the major way that production becomes the means of subsistence for the majority of adult males, and many adult females. At the same time, it is the wage relation that specifies the worker's connection to the means of production and to those who own and control industry and capital."[74] As the vehicle for converting labor into the "means of subsistence," the wage is a site where capitalist processes of distribution touch the bodies of class subjects, engendering requisite forms of (self-)discipline and desire. The whole discourse of wages was highly sexualized: many writers on working-class wages (such as Malthus) protested high wages for workers as the cause of both idleness and sexual and reproductive excess. The discourse of the family wage normalizes forms of female dependency and erotic (self-)discipline; reinforcing an image of women as nonlaborers, the family wage enables the reconfiguration of distribution as a sign of desire. This marked a departure from earlier forms of distribution characteristic of traditional (feudal) societies, in which an individual's right to support rested in a relation of entitlement, not market exchange.[75] In this way the rise of the domestic ideal displaced earlier models of economic entitlement or support, ushering in a distinct, (hetero) eroticized model of paternalism. This model of familial distribution expanded outward in antebellum discourses of charity; as chapter 3 demonstrates, the sentimental (fragile, meek) seamstress was the era's predominant example of the "worthy poor," a figure whose economic need was legitimated by her performance of normative domestic femininity.

Reconstructing antebellum literature as class dialogue involves contextualizing laboring women's texts in the era's dominant representations of working-class women, including available narrative possibilities for representing workingwomen's class experience. For instance, the very term *mill girl*, like the late nineteenth-century *working girl*, assigned the woman worker a kind of liminality by designating female labor as a transitory state; obviously serving the logic of capitalist exploitation, this construction cheapened female labor by severing it from adulthood, making the female breadwinner a conceptual impossibility. This is the version of female labor featured in many domestic novels, which plot labor (and female working-class status) as a developmental stage; thus in *The Wide, Wide World*, Ellen Montgomery's passage from urban comfort to the hard domestic labor of the rural home of Miss Fortune, in which female labor has a clear cash value, is cast as a spiritual trial, an intermediate narrative episode superseded by her class redemption (through marriage) and recuperation in proper domesticity. This is also the version scripted by George Lippard, who refers to the seamstress as a "girl-woman," a formulation that places the seamstress, like the mill girl, in a time-space at once dilated and transitory. This plotting of female labor along a temporal trajectory, as a stage to be outgrown, was underwritten by an evolutionary narrative already conventional in the antebellum era, in which women in "savage" or "primitive" societies (such as the Native American women in Fuller's *Summer on the Lakes* or Mexicanas on the California frontier) were cast as drudges and "civilized" women were properly valued for their affective, not physical labor—a working-class variant of the distinction between feminine (bodily) surface and (psychological) depth that Armstrong traces in British women's writing. Indeed, domestic fiction, in which girls learn to manage their bodily passions and transcend their savage, embodied (and laboring) pasts, can seem to both cite and enact this broader social narrative of individual and collective amelioration. This ascription imparted a certain racial instability to workingwomen's narratives, examined throughout this book. Overall it led to a conceptual and temporal containment of female wage labor, its melancholic encrypting in the social order; like domestic work it was assigned a kind of cyclicality, a going nowhere, outside time and outside social progress—a cultural vision that has certainly inhibited labor organizing among women workers as thoroughly as it has shaped literary fictions of female work. The working girl's perennial adolescence is thus tied to her economic and social immobility, barring her from scripts of both individual progress (or mobility) and ambition (a hallmark, according to Peter Brooks, of the nineteenth-century bourgeois novel) and collective transformation. This is the version of workingwomen's "stuckness" that the Lowell writer refers to when she complains that women "have no share in that American privilege which sets in full view of the poorest white male laborer . . . the possibilities of an Astor, and every office within the gift of the Republic." The texts addressed in this study register and at times contest the gendered class limits on workingwomen's stories; together they expand the narrative repertoire in which workingwomen's lives have been imagined and culturally defined.

In the antebellum cultural imaginary, workingwomen could signify women's economic possibility (best exemplified by Lowell women) and economic abjection (melodramatically epitomized by the seamstress). According to the feminist labor historian Annelise Orleck, through their words and activism antebellum factory women made wage work "respectable" for women, representing a usable past that Progressive Era labor reformers could draw upon in organizing and advocating for female workers.[76] Factory women's writings thus helped establish new economic and literary trajectories for women; these in turn helped constitute new forms of social subjectivity, embodiment, and structures of social and political desire. Looking back on antebellum Lowell from the late nineteenth century, one former millworker, Harriet Robinson, describes factory labor as a powerfully progressive force, transforming a woman from "a ward, an appendage, a relict" to an active social subject: "For the first time in this country woman's labor had a money value. She had become not only an earner and a producer, but also a spender of money, a recognized factor in the political economy of her time. And thus a long upward step in our material civilization was taken." Wages could transform women in "a condition approaching pauperism" from abject dependency to active agency; women who were "depressed, modest, mincing," with a "limp carriage and inelastic gait," were visibly re-embodied. "After their first pay-day came, and they felt the jingle of silver in their pockets, and had begun to feel its mercurial influence, their bowed heads were lifted, their necks seemed braced with steel, they looked you in the face, sang blithely among their looms or frames, and walked with elastic step to and from their work." In language that recalls Hepzibah's invigoration through trade in Hawthorne's *The House of the Seven Gables*, Robinson depicts the industrial element as a force that animates and strengthens women's very bodies: "It seemed as if a great hope impelled them,—the harbinger of the new era that was about to dawn for them and for all women-kind." Such women were enabled, in Herculean fashion, to "lift" a mortgage from the family homestead.[77] The transformative power Robinson describes, and the shift in women's narratives that it enables, is legible in the texts I discuss.

Workingwomen's texts thus reworked the "plots and plausibilities" of antebellum women's narratives.[78] As noted earlier, a concern with the condition of poor and working-class women was a primary focus of social reformers (especially labor and urban reformers) in the antebellum United States; such a concern shaped factory debates in England and America as well as sociological studies of urban life. In courtrooms, charitable institutions, and cross-class encounters on urban streets, laboring and poor women were asked to provide moving testimonies of economic suffering. Such accounts pressured literary discourse in complex ways. For example, a range of midcentury fiction and nonfiction literary texts (including Lydia Maria Child's *Letters from New York* and George Foster's *New York by Gas-Light*) include scenes in which a wealthy man or woman encounters a female stranger who recounts a "poverty narrative," firsthand experiences of economic deprivation; explicitly challenging the reformer Charles Loring Brace's claim that "the poor *feel*, but they can seldom speak," these works depict scenes in which poor women come to voice and articulate moving if attenuated life narratives.[79] Such a repertoire made poor women's narratives a conventional part of antebellum oral and written culture but radically simplified their stories, creating exceptionally narrow frameworks for representing poor and workingwomen's lives. As we shall see, both radical workingmen and middle-class feminists came to find in working-class women's experience an important literary and political resource, but both routinely spoke *for* working-class women, defining working-class women's experience according to their own needs and interests. This book will ask not only to what uses workingwomen's stories were put but also what uses they defined for themselves.

At times working-class women labored to gather and reshape these oral narratives. Jennie Collins, a one-time mill girl and the author of one of the first book-length works by a white U.S. workingwoman, is especially intent upon recording everyday acts of kindness and generosity by poor and working-class people, for "it often happens that the most charitable are never heard of by the world."[80] Collins affirms the findings of twenty-first-century studies that poor and working-class people give a greater percentage of their earnings to charity than do the wealthy, although it is the wealthy donors of huge sums who are known for their philanthropy and whose benevolent acts are "noised abroad" (144) and "emblazoned on the banners of worldly praise" (142). Like Harriet Wilson in *Our Nig* (discussed in chapter 4), Collins insists upon the moral authority of the "kitchen-girl," for it was commonplace for people in need of food to come to the kitchen door of large houses; thus were female servants best positioned to hear the stories of the poor. Collins recounts several such kitchen encounters with "poor beggar-wom[e]n" (19) and men and relates the "simple stor[ies]" they tell (20), enlightening her readers with the narrative wisdom of the kitchen-girl: "Ah, ye drawing-room beauties . . . ye cannot see the phases of life which the kitchen-girl sees. . . . If you would but go to the kitchen door in the cold winter mornings when that hesitating, gentle rap comes upon the panel . . . and would look into the little pleading faces as they tremblingly ask for food, you would find a field of useful work" (21). The kitchen is thus an incubator of sympathy, a school of "generosity and kindness" (85); the "infection" with which domestic servants were frequently associated is here envisioned as at once affective and morally beneficial. While the kitchen-girl meets these pleas with unheralded acts of benevolence and generosity, Collins describes how wealthy men routinely "turn a deaf ear" to supplicants' "touching" stories (28). Complaining that women are often faulted by men for being "unkind" and malicious toward one another, Collins reveals workingwomen to be "exceedingly charitable towards those of their own sex" (65). Indeed, Collins argues that precisely because men have the opportunity for advancement and can benefit materially by aligning with capitalists—thus becoming "a fit tool for tyranny, and hence an 'excellent overseer'" (123)—they are less reliable instruments of class benevolence, less effective in preserving the kitchen-girl's moral economy of feeling. Preserving that feminine ethic is critical, for in this "age of bargains and contracts" the "good old days of generous hospitality, of friendly assistance, and of mutual good-will have passed into history as a thing that existed once, but can never come again" (87). Collins imagines the workingwoman's text as a kind of archive, one that memorializes and preserves a social ethos of "hospitality" in the kitchens, in the "friendly treatment" of the poor toward one another, in the sisterhood of shop girls, the abiding "attachments" (105) and loyal friendships forged in the "community" (89) of the factories and workshops, and the solidarity of the unions. Reflecting her interest in spiritualism, Collins depicts writing as a form of mediumship, a gesture of communion with the dead:

> They are sad tales indeed which I have to tell. Too full of sorrow and suffering, defeats and discouragements, oppression and cruelty to be sought by the gay, and too true to attract the novelist. Yet I must write them. The world shall hear them, though the recollection brings tears and the repetition a shudder. Sad faces! How they crowd upon me now that I open

the gate of memory! Lonely wives, oppressed daughters, tearful toilers at needle and loom, broken-hearted victims, and lifeless suicides.

Must I live it over again? Must I look once more into those tearful eyes, and see those outstretched hands? . . . Yea, I will tread fearlessly back along the thorny path of my short life; and the shades of the hungry, toil-killed, and heart-shattered men and women shall tell their tales to the world in death, as they told them to me in life. (11)

Writing during the Depression, the proletarian author Meridel Le Sueur described her work as "epitaphs marking the lives of women who . . . leave no statistics, no record, obituary or remembrance."[81] Like Le Sueur—and like the author of the *Aristocrat*, who locates workingwomen's literary authority in the historical countermemory of "our mothers and old fashioned aunts"—Collins imagines her writing as a bearer of class memory, a means of honoring, preserving, and transmitting the voices of the dead while preserving a female moral economy of class feeling.

As Collins's writing suggests, workingwomen's rearticulation of sympathy was crucial to their feminist working-class politics. Workingwomen's texts contribute forcefully to our understanding of the politics of sympathy in the antebellum era; indeed, they remind us that sympathy *had* a (class) politics. As Brownson's essays and Truth's *Narrative* indicate, *sympathy* was a keyword in socialist debates, in the work of Owenites and especially Fourierists and Saint-Simonians; hegemonically defining the meaning of *sympathy* was thus essential to the operations of class power. Describing this process in Britain, Poovey has argued that sentimentalism, with its doctrine of innate and spontaneous humanitarian benevolence, anchored the moral authority of the bourgeoisie; as an economic strategy its "paradigm" of innate benevolence "sanctioned . . . and helped underwrite" the laissez-faire individualism that gradually transformed England from a paternalistic hierarchy to a modern class society while allowing the bourgeoisie to usurp from the aristocracy the role of England's moral conscience.[82] In bourgeois society this benevolence was largely circumscribed within the nuclear family, thus domesticating and privatizing traditional forms of social benevolence associated with a paternalist social order. As demonstrated in chapter 1, Lowell women responded forcefully to the class parameters of bourgeois sentimentality, particularly as it was increasingly localized within the domestic sphere; they especially objected to the ways antebellum sentimental literary texts domesticate sympathy and gender it feminine while using it to underwrite novel but supposedly natural versions of female subjectivity. Exposing the ideology of corporate benevolence as a sham, Lowell women at once protested the constriction of sympathy to the familial realm, denaturalized sentimentality as a regulatory norm that privatizes femininity, and exposed the ways that norm could legitimate, by masking, an exploitative economic relation between the sexes. Workingwomen's texts, I argue, thus contribute a critical if unremarked chapter in the history of sentimentality. In particular, in contesting the normalization of domestic sentimentality, their writings made legible other versions of sympathy as class affect, at once marking and memorializing, mobilizing and preserving structures of feeling marginalized in the liberal-capitalist social order.

### STRUCTURE OF THE BOOK

Chapters 1 through 3 focus on women in the textile and garment industries. Marx describes the female army of factory laborers as the "mass of cheap human material" to match the supply of "raw material" in the textile industry. The first to industrialize, textile manufacturing was a major employer of (cheap) female labor in the antebellum era, as in today's global economy.[83] Taking up depictions of the New England factory girl during the 1830s and 1840s, in chapter 1 I examine periodicals edited by mill women, especially the *Voice of Industry* and the *Factory Girls' Album*, as formative cultural sites for the production of workingwomen's subjectivity and discourse. Continuing this analysis of the mill girl as a contested sign in early industrial discourse, in chapter 2 I analyze popular fiction about Lowell women from the 1840s. I argue that working-class and popular fiction exploits emerging urban discourses of the subliterary, especially the gothic and sensational, to register often inchoate longings, affinities, aspirations, and social tastes; these works thus fashion an alternative, popular discourse of female working-class experience.[84] Turning to writings by and about needlewomen, in chapter 3 I examine the construction of the "sentimental seamstress," a stock figure in discourses of class in the 1840s. Countering the oppositional class accents of factory girl fiction (and the real militancy of activist needlewomen), crafters of seamstress narratives fashioned an influential—and highly problematic—image of antebellum workingwomen.

Chapters 4 through 6 foreground a problematic central to this study: the racialization of class and the contested cultural and political association of "unfree labor" with people of color in the antebellum United States. Additionally all three chapters focus on class (as) *performance*, proposing new ways to read workingwomen's literature in relation to working-class oral and performance cultures. Published on the brink of the Civil War, both Wilson's *Our Nig* (the subject of chapter 4) and Southworth's *The Hidden Hand* (discussed in chapter 5) are Bildungsromane of sorts, fictional records of working-class girlhood as it pressures the contours of working-class womanhood; both highlight the insistent, historically charged ways that class was refracted by race in the watershed years of the 1850s.[85] Replacing northern free labor with black and white servitude and framing the narrative of a mixed-race daughter with that of her (precariously) white working-class mother, Wilson's tale of miscegenation figures oft-unspoken racial complexities of antebellum working-class life. Tracking rich exchanges between print and performance cultures in the antebellum era, in chapter 5 I consider how popular performance—a crucial site of working-women's culture—shapes (and is shaped by) *The Hidden Hand*; in particular, I explore how the "transmission of [lower-class] interracial affiliations" in and by antebellum vernacular performance leaves a clear imprint on Southworth's novel.[86] Chapter 6 extends the book's analysis of the dialectic of race and class, resituating it within the frame of U.S. empire building and territorial expansion. I focus on the Californio *testimonios*, first-person narratives by Mexicanos/as living in Mexican California during annexation to the United States, collected by Hubert Howe Bancroft in the 1870s. Central to my analysis are narratives by Apolinaria Lorenzana and Eulalia Pérez, domestic workers in the missions, which shed critical light on relations of gender and labor in Alta California, constituting an invaluable archive of Mexican (American) working womanhood. Taken together these chapters focus the book's gendered class lens on the unmistakably racial and imperial coordinates of the "American 1848."

## *One.* Factory Fictions

LOWELL MILL WOMEN AND THE
ROMANCE OF LABOR

Two popular texts supply a telling frame for my consideration of factory women's writings; each maps the unsettling presence of laboring women in urban space. *The Mysteries of Lowell*, a pamphlet novel published anonymously in 1844, is by the prolific Osgood Bradbury.[1] An example of the literature of urban exposé initiated by the work of Pierce Egan and Eugène Sue, Bradbury's text devotes significant narrative attention to hidden crimes perpetrated by purportedly "virtuous" elite men. But in one passage Bradbury locates the primary mystery of Lowell in the very subjectivity of his protagonist, a millworker named Augusta Walton: "The greatest mystery is the female heart.... Geniuses ... of the most brilliant powers of imagination, from Fielding to Eugene Sue ... [have] taxed their powers to the utmost ... [but] the female heart remains a great mystery. Scarcely the title page of this mysterious book is yet understood, and its contents are yet sealed up from the world" (10). Casting himself less as a knowing author than a baffled suitor, Bradbury figures the female heart as a sealed book that defies (male) literary disclosure, using a sensational rhetoric distinct from middle-class sentimental codes in which feelings are easily read on the body. Paradoxically, what renders Augusta's heart sentimentally illegible is, it seems, her spectacular publicity: Bradbury compares Augusta's arrival in the factory to "a comet [that] first makes its appearance in our solar system"; "observed of all observers," her beauty, on public display, draws admirers like a "magnet."

My second text is George Foster's *New York by Gas-Light*, a collection of sketches first published in 1850. For Foster uncontrolled female sexuality in the form of "public prostitution" is the steamy center of the urban underworld, and streetwalking's ground zero is the working-class (and interracial) neighborhood Five Points, "the very type and physical semblance ... of hell itself."[2] Illicit female sexuality is an object of obsessive fascination, that which must be made visible and controlled by discourse. But it is also something alarmingly generative and potentially uncontainable. Foster's narrative aims are revealed in the opening: "To penetrate beneath the thick veil of night and lay bare the fearful mysteries of darkness ... the festivities of prostitution, the orgies of pauperism, the haunts of theft and murder, the scenes of drunkenness and beastly debauch, and all the sad realities that go to make up the lower stratum—the under-ground story—of life in New York!" (69). Again we find a sexualized language of unveiling to denote urban mysteries, the same fantasy of penetration—though here the narrator's discoveries disgust and horrify as well as titillate. This ambivalence is legible in phrases like "*festivities* of prostitution" and the startling "*orgies* of pauperism"; signaling a new liberal consensus equating poverty with vice, Foster's metaphors yoke economic marginalization to images of pleasure and self-indulgence. New York's "lower stratum" is a realm of transgressive desire as well as class suffering; while paupers and prostitutes were cast as class victims in antebellum discourses of moral reform, Foster locates them in an urban carnivalesque. Prominent within this "underground story" of the "lowest type of human degradation" is the "public prostitute"; Foster warns his readers against the "frightful phalanx of female depravity" that is the "curse of an enfeebled and depraved civilization" (83).

In *New York by Gas-Light* the ambiguously racialized working-class female body comes to define what Foster terms the "lower stratum" of social life, the object of obsessive fascination and equally obsessive repudiation.[3] As I argue in chapter 2, that prominence was registered in discourses about popular literature itself: the antebellum era's rapidly multiplying body of popular literature—"common" literature—was routinely described as a metaphoric extension of the prostitute's body, spreading its noxious, contaminating influence and the "infection" of illicit desires throughout the body politic.[4] The "class horror" generated by this literature (and that body) had political motivations and referents; the languages of popular literature were reproduced in and at times drawn from political discourse.[5] Sensational narratives of working-class labor and life, like the shocking parliamentary reports (Blue Books) discussed by the British feminist Anna Jameson, often "teem[ed] with graphic narratives and discoveries of horror."[6] Foster portrays urban prostitutes as a "frightful *phalanx* of female depravity," a reference to Charles Fourier's socialist model of sociosexual organization; female sexual disorder and economic upheaval are here—as elsewhere—explicitly conjoined.[7] The compulsive cultural interest in working-class women's sexuality, voiced by Bradbury and Foster, could articulate Malthusian anxieties about working-class female reproductive power (and debates about birth control were ongoing in the U.S. radical workingmen's press),[8] or it could connote general anxieties about urbanization—the teeming life of cities and seeming impenetrability of urban spaces.

In this chapter I unpack the gendered class fantasies evident in Foster's and Bradbury's texts, situating them in antebellum discourses of class. The sensational construction of female working-class subjectivity and desire, I argue, registered the very real challenge working-class women presented to an increasingly dominant formation of gender and class. The inscrutably desiring working girl in Bradbury's text, like the prostitute in Foster's, creates a sensation because she stands for a particular kind of "gender trouble": she troubles the distinction between erotic or affective activity and the economic life central to the emerging liberal definition of separate spheres.

I focus my first two chapters on mill women for several reasons. One is the abundance and availability of textual materials, itself an index of the class politics of literary production and archive formation; because of the national(ist) import of the Lowell experiment, a substantial amount of writing about Lowell, some of it by factory women themselves, was published and preserved in and as the national archive. A highly visible symbol of the reorganization of economic life, the factory was a "concentrated metaphor for hopes and fears about the direction and pace of industrial change."[9] And depending on one's perspective, the factory could represent antebellum gender trouble or a benevolent institutionalization of male authority and female virtue; it could signify the harmonious workings of a well-oiled machine or a dangerous subversion of social order. Such meanings were forged in a transatlantic discourse in which Manchester, England, signified the unnecessary evils of industrialization, while the virtuous American "mill girl" emblematized industrialism's ambiguous promise. Most early American manufacturers visited Manchester, while English and European visitors interested in social questions flocked to Lowell. Transnational industrial tourism fueled an awareness of Lowell as public spectacle, a showcase mill town, informing a particular industrial aesthetic that developed around Lowell, one operatives would vigorously contest. That aesthetic involved policing factory women's racial identification, stabilizing the precarious whiteness of poor and laboring women; as we shall see, part of the function of the aestheticized mill girl was to manage the racial intimacies of the cotton textile trade, the social proximity of female factory workers to the institution of slavery that produced the raw materials of industrial production.[10] For Marx the collectivized nature of factory work both served the optimization of capitalist exploitation and enabled the *evolution* of the social: the socialization of labor in the factory could foster class consciousness and the formation of a collective laboring subject.[11] Fears as well as hopes about the latter are envisioned in the writings I discuss.

The spectacle of female labor at Lowell was in a dialectical relation with emerging configurations of both class and gender. Judy Lown writes that factory debates in England took place largely between manufacturers and landowners, with some input from working-class men, over "who should control women and what form this control should take."[12] As many foresaw, industrialization could profoundly transform social relations, including gender relations; new technologies could undermine the supposedly natural difference (in bodily stature and physical strength) between the sexes, a distinction upheld in much Enlightenment social thought. Owenites and other utopian thinkers (and Marx himself) understood that mechanization could profoundly transform the social body.[13] However, Perry Anderson notes, "the early capitalist mode of production inherited and reworked [the] millennial inequality [between the sexes], with all its myriad oppressions, at once extensively utilizing and profoundly transforming it."[14]

The widely publicized experiment at Lowell emphatically made gender what the labor historian Ardis Cameron calls a "component" of industrial organization. The factory was organized to subordinate the workforce in general and women in particular: men managed the payroll, bossed the floor, supervised the "hands"; deference was expected from every worker, but from women it was expected "sooner and in greater quantity." At the point of production, women confronted a world that promoted a "specific psychology of female subordination," enhancing men's "ability to define [the women's] womanhood and to control their labor power." Simultaneously, however, women were positioned to experience "contradictions between the reality of female economic importance and worth and shop floor policies" that devalued their labor and expected their "feminine" compliance with male overseers and superiors. The factory and boardinghouse engendered sites of subterfuge, autonomous social spaces where women could foster alternative socialities and develop an independent sense of

*Fig 1.1.* Early tintype, c. 1860, American Museum of Textile History, Lowell, Massachusetts. As this chapter demonstrates, such alternative socialities are abundantly evident in literary as well as visual depictions of factory women.

worth.[15] In the antebellum decades the Lowell mill girl, with her (reputed) *feme sole* status, famed bank account, and well-publicized labor protests and walkouts (prompting at least one commentator's fears of "gynecocracy"),[16] represented a visible instance of the feminization of economic independence and the political autonomy that might usher from it.

What I describe in chapter 2 as the "sensationalizing" of the Lowell mill woman—specifically the association of female wage labor with nonnormative affect and illicit sex—is one sign of the gender trouble she generates. The factory girl constituted a highly visible challenge to the particular, state-sanctioned model of capitalism under formation in the 1830s and 1840s and organized around the heterosexual nuclear family; specifically, she posed a challenge to the normalization of "domestic desire" and the constriction of love associated with the rise of the middle class. Tied to the increasingly hegemonic cult of domesticity, this model of capitalism was transmitted and reinforced through the family wage; as what Alice Kessler-Harris calls a "social rather than theoretic construct" that contains a "system of meanings" that influence both "expectations" and "behavior," the family wage is a primary means through which this new political economy of gender touches the bodies of individuals and (re) produces its norms of desire.[17] The gendered and sexualized meanings of the wage are emphasized in the Lowell seduction narratives, examined in chapter 2, where the wage appears as a tool of seduction, an image that crystallizes the interpellative force of the wage, its power to engender subjects and organize erotic life. Intensifying domestic affect, the family wage especially narrowed a sense of kinship, curtailing feelings of social responsibility toward those outside the nuclear family and limiting sympathy for nonfamilial dependents.

That the wage is a means of erotic regulation was an idea handed down from none other than Adam Smith, progenitor of classical economics. Smith asserted that the market in free labor was entirely compatible with the customary dependencies of the household. "Especially in the lower ranks," he writes, the wife owed her "maintenance . . . intirely to her husband, and from this dependance it is that she is thought to be bound to be faithfull and constant to him." Tellingly merging the language of bondage and the language of "constan[cy]" and love, Smith baldly presents economic dependency as affective and erotic discipline (engendering the "bonds of love") and envisions economic dependence as that which *produces* feminine virtue, especially among the "lower ranks." The gendered wage structure endorsed by Smith, it would seem, helped underwrite the shift, often noted by scholars, from the conception of female carnality and excess so prominent in American Puritan writings to the view of white women as maintainers of piety and morality widespread in Victorian America.[18] Smith identifies the hireling as "free" because the sale of his labor ensures his property in his domestic dependents, and he defines this proprietorship (enabled by the wage's gender dimension) as that which distinguishes wage worker from slave. Sanctioned by the family wage, domesticity here serves a fortified whiteness, a means of policing what Martha Hodes calls the "mutability" of poor and working-class women's racial identifications and desires.[19]

By the 1840s industrialists and workingmen shared an investment in "feminizing" women workers; both rhetorically constructed a factory girl whose independence as worker was undercut by the "natural" dependency of gender and a primary identity as domestic being.[20] In various ways Lowell women challenged this construction; wage labor offered possibilities of economic autonomy and what Margaret Fuller terms female "self-dependence" that unsettled feminine dependency and domestic norms.[21] Those possibilities are envisioned, narrated, and sometimes foreclosed in political representations and popular fiction about Lowell women.

## FACTORY WOMEN IN WORKINGMEN'S DISCOURSE

The American factory system was initially confined to a few locales in one region, New England, and employed a small proportion of America's labor force. But given the numerous advantages to the capitalist, there was good reason to expect that the merchant princes of Boston—the Cabots, the Lowells, the Appletons, the Jacksons, who had invested their commercial fortunes in the creation of New England factories and factory towns—would soon have innumerable imitators. Advocates of Henry Clay's "national system," political economists, and factory owners were optimistic about practically every aspect of the new system; they anticipated great benefits, including the improved lot of labor by lowering prices and increasing demand, stimulating production and reabsorbing temporarily displaced labor into the economy. A small minority of men would become rich, but the "standard of living of the mass" would rise simultaneously.[22]

While early endorsers of manufacturing such as Tench Coxe celebrated the new mechanical technology as a sublime invention, workingmen saw things differently.[23] Most understood the course of English industrialism in terms drawn by Dickens and Carlyle, Engels's *Condition of the English Working Classes*, and the parliamentary investigations of the Sadler Committee and Lord Shaftsbury; they saw factories as "dark, satanic mills" in which laborers of all ages and both sexes were shamelessly overworked and underpaid under abysmal conditions. The British factory debates were reported in labor periodicals throughout New England, and their imagery was reiterated by British labor radicals, such as the Chartists who immigrated to America during this period to escape criminal prosecution and were active in the American labor movement.[24] Convinced that the grim situation in England was industrialization's inevitable result, male labor leaders countered the rhetoric of American exceptionalism, depicting Lowell, Waltham, and Fall River in language associated with English industry.

Gender figured prominently in industrial discourse. The years of labor activism in the United States leading up to the economic crisis of 1837 have been identified as a period when workingmen were "open in new ways to solidarity with women," their sexist distrust of women workers momentarily relaxed.[25] Yet if workingmen at times saw women as partners in a shared struggle, their rhetoric drew heavily on melodramatic imagery of female inferiority and passivity, recycling representations of helpless, dependent factory workers common in the British debates; here, as elsewhere, female workers were tasked with figuring labor's subjection and "bear[ing] witness to the suffering of the people."[26] This was certainly not the only way to script female factory work: when female factory workers in Pittsburgh broke down fences and factory walls to expel strikebreakers, the *Pittsburgh Journal* called them "factory Amazons" and portrayed their victory in an extended military metaphor.[27] Activist factory women themselves recognized the growing public concern about their agitation, proudly declaring, "Our influence"—a force distinct from the celebrated moral influence of middle-class women—"[is] felt and feared."[28] But depictions of factory women as industrial victims were widespread, generating stereotypes to which women workers necessarily responded.

Antebellum workingmen used the language of popular fiction to emphasize the purity and vulnerability of factory women and the horrifying conditions they faced; they portrayed workingwomen as emphatically embodied and as victims of distressing forms of compulsion and force.[29] Linking factory women and slaves, these texts signal the compromised whiteness of wage-earning women while revealing a wish to police racial boundaries through fantasies of domestic rescue. Charles Douglass represents Lowell women as "dragging out a life of slavery and wretchedness. It is enough to make one's heart ache, to behold these degraded females" and "mark . . . their woe stricken appearance. These establishments are the present abode of wretchedness, disease and misery; and are inevitably calculated to perpetuate them—if not to destroy liberty itself."[30] William English wonders, "Who but a tyrant could drag her, 'the pride and ornament of our race,' forth from 'domestic retirement to the performance of manual labor'?" Apparently agency-less, Lowell women are depicted by English as domesticity's "bright ornament," "borne away" by inhuman factory owners to a life of "toil, poverty, and degradation."[31] Using similar images of coercion, Douglass stresses the misery and suffering of Lowell women, while English characteristically contrasts domestic "retirement" and ornamental femininity with "the performance of manual labor" in the factory—an opposition that negates the physically demanding aspects of household labor while imposing a middle-class ideal on working-class families.[32]

Gendered imagery was acutely evident in the speeches and writings of Seth Luther. Called by Philip Foner "perhaps the most enlightened labor leader of the period on the issue of women workers," Luther could view workingwomen as industrial allies; in an 1834 address he warned his fellow workers, "Unless we have the female sex on our side, we cannot hope to accomplish any object we have in view."[33] However, Luther consistently used the pejorative gendered imagery common in workingmen's texts. His *Address to the Working-Men of New England* established him as the region's leading unionist and became an important rallying cry for the entire labor movement.[34] Skillfully deploying gothic and sensational imagery, Luther describes cotton mills as places "where cruelties are practised, excessive labor [is] required, education [is] neglected, and vice [is] . . . on the increase" and accuses corrupt politicians and avaricious factory owners of "using all means to keep out of sight the evils growing up" within the system (17). A striking image of daughters of mill owners listening to music that "floats from quivering strings" while the nerves of female factory workers "are quivering with almost dying agony, from excessive labor" encapsulates Luther's economic theory (his subscription to a labor theory of value) and aesthetic practice (29). Through repetition and parallelism he expressly contrasts the passivity, leisure, and pleasure of the daughters of mill owners, idle consumers seemingly suspended above the world's cares, and the excessive activity, labor, and pains of female workers. However, by metaphorically linking "quivering strings" and quivering nerves, the material artifact of a musical instrument and the bodies of female workers, Luther not only makes palpable the artifact's existence as a product of living human labor; he also materializes the aesthetic, tying the etherealized (feminized) realm of the aesthetic (the music "float[s]" above the listening women) to the laboring body itself. In his sequence of images workingwomen's bodies dissolve into quivering strings, and rich women's pleasures signify, indeed seem to necessitate poor women's pains. Invoking forms of parasitism often featured in anticapitalist writings, Luther represents (feminine) aesthetic sensibility as something violent, even vampiric.[35] His visceral imagery vividly captures the bodily nature of labor. However, by invoking female nerves—a newly gendered bodily property in medical discourse and other writings tied to "a distinctively middle-class notion of femininity"[36] —Luther references women's bodily vulnerability and weakness, not their agency and strength. If workingwomen have quivering nerves, workingmen presumably have muscles; capitalists may "carry" women away, but workingmen can bring them back home. In accounts such as Luther's, the mill girl requires the "protection" of an interventionist state or male domestic authority.[37]

Luther repeatedly invokes the cruelty of the English factory system to deconstruct the opposition between Old World and New; Lowell might easily become the "Manchester of America," and the defense of the factory system represents a vast deception: "We see the system of manufacturing lauded to the skies [by] senators, representatives, owners, and agents.... Cotton mills ... are [misleadingly] denominated [by John Quincy Adams] 'the principalities of the destitute, the palaces of the poor.'" In truth, for scant reward American operatives worked even longer hours than their English counterparts, and education and moral "improvement" inevitably suffered. The result was a caste system in America dividing rich and poor, undermining the democratic ideals of the founding fathers, and serving the interests of the wealthy alone, a group Luther sarcastically denominates "we, the aristocracy" (17, 28). Such antirepublican tendencies, Luther argues, are due to an acquisitive lust—"avarice," an "evil passion" (7)—once confined to Europe but now pervading American manufactures, especially the cotton mills. Avarice transforms men into unfeeling monsters: "It hardens the hearts, sears the conscience, and deafens the ear to the cry of suffering humanity" (7). Again Luther utilizes oral imagery and the language of cannibalism to sensationalize capitalism's economic depredations: men "gorge ... an insatiate appetite for gold" by exploiting the poor, who are "lawful prey" (7, 31). The factory is a system for transferring wealth and bodily energies from poor to rich; paternalist arguments about providing "means of subsistence" to the poor through labor are, Luther argues, a mere cover for parasitic consumption. "While [the higher orders] are boasting that they 'can take care of themselves'; while they are dependent on you every moment for . . . that property, which they have obtained from your *bones*, and *sinews*, and *heart's blood*, they are using it in an attempt to starve you into submission" (26).

The reversals central to Luther's discourse—the refined pleasures of music are predicated on violence; the idealized Lowell system manifests the cruelty of English factories; "benevolent" elites are predatory cannibals—reveal twinned features of his rhetoric: a "technique of demystification" borrowed from Paine, a seminal influence on plebian radicals during this period,[38] and reliance on visceral, sensational images to denote industrial "reality." Attacking the dazzling idealizations and "misleading" euphemisms of industrial advocates such as Adams, Luther maps a class politics of the aesthetic. According to Peter Stallybrass and Allon White, the authority of the "literary" was defined (albeit ambivalently) in the late eighteenth century by its "elevat[ion]" above and distance from the demands (and attractions) of the bodily "low."[39] Against the idealization of what one Lowell mill woman astutely termed "romances of factory life,"[40] Luther mobilized a representational strategy sensationally centered on the worker's body, with important cultural and political effects. As Nicholas Bromell observes, the historical experience of manual labor has seemed to resist representation and has gone largely unwritten—partly because such experience was not considered to constitute true knowledge, partly because the skills involved in manual work have been passed down orally and experientially, not transmitted through texts.[41] Luther's images of dismemberment, wounding, and pain evoke the central presence of the body in factory work, thus assigning value, economically and representationally, to bodily labor.[42] He uses sensational bodily imagery to make visible the primacy of the body as what David Harvey calls an "accumulation strategy" under capitalism, exposing forms of labor magically erased by commodity fetishism and capitalist exchange.[43] However, while foregrounding the laboring body's primacy and presence, workingmen such as Luther simultaneously aspired to what has been called the "disembodiment" of political citizenship.[44] That contradiction was largely resolved through the language of gender: the condition of emphatic embodiment associated with factory work could be displaced and projected onto women.

## DISMANTLING "ROMANCES OF FACTORY LIFE": FACTORY WORK AND INDUSTRIAL AESTHETICS

Portraying the factory's extraction of bodily energy as a monstrous violation, Luther debunks the "myth of Lowell" promoted by supporters of American industrialism. Casting that myth as a species of what Walter Benjamin terms the capitalist "phantasmagoria" — the dream of progress in a capitalist system at the expense of the suppression of traces of labor[45] — Luther employs a "technique of demystification" throughout his text, demonstrating that false representations mask a hidden, exploitative reality. Labor leaders like Luther understood that aesthetic distinctions carried class meanings. In the Lowell labor press Washingtonians defended their practice of "common speech" against charges that their discourse was "crude and coarse," distinguishing their speech practices against the "polished," "soft words [culled from the] dictionary" and the "gentle milk-and-water addresses" of the "educated or professional classes."[46] Such distinctions were embedded in social definitions of knowledge. As the novelist John Neal observed in his 1838 address before the Maine Charitable Mechanics' Association, while education undoubtedly "makes the difference between one class and another," what counts as education is not self-evident: "the few," educated at "colleges and universities," who have "spent their lives in the acquisition of learning [through books]," have agreed "to call a particular learning, knowledge" and to call those similarly "acquainted with this particular sort of learning . . . the educated," thus discrediting knowledge "obtained in the streets and thoroughfares, the high-ways and the workshops of the world. . . . Is not the accomplished blacksmith, or shipwright, or fisherman, or tailor, or shoemaker, an *educated* man?"[47] Centering his text on the counterknowledge of manual workers, Luther maps a class hierarchy of the senses: the visual sense, predicated on distance and associated with the illusions of theater and spectacle, frames the perspective of industrial propagandists; other senses, especially the tactile and the oral/aural, convey the immediacy of workers' bodily certainties.

Luther redirects Paine's "technique of demystification" away from the "master-fraud" of monarchical government toward the new industrial forces of economic power.[48] He not only lays bare the conditions of labor and the economic relations they signify; he addresses the construction of Lowell as a textual commodity, a spectacle to be consumed. While industrial propagandists idealize factory conditions abroad, Luther represents that "splendid example" as public theater: "It has always been the policy in imperial and kingly governments, to talk much about National glory, National wealth, and National improvement. The splendid victories, high titles and refinement of the 'higher orders' are sounded forth by the governments and their parasites. . . . Under such governments, the subjects are amused with carnivals, masquerades, military parades, imposing and splendid religious ceremonies, and national songs" (9). Such spectacles are intended to distract and intimidate the "lower orders," to "keep [them] from *thinking*, from *reasoning*, from watching the movements of Emperors, Kings, Dukes, Lords, and other villains, who are fleecing the poor" (9). Such practices are widespread in Europe, and, Luther contends, "we shall find, notwithstanding all our *boasted liberty* and *freedom*," that American factory owners and their political allies use similar forms of "splend[or]" to confound the public (9). The "dazzling lustre" of industrial wealth should not be celebrated because "in the exact ration of the increase of the power and wealth and glory of all *nations* as such, so is the *misery* of the *poor* increased" (9). Luther's aim is to expose the bodily suffering, the rank corruption, concealed within the system: "We propose to draw aside the veil [and] dissipate the enchantment which distance lends to the view" (9). Countering industrial spectacle with a language of material proximity and utilizing graphic physical imagery, he insists on the materiality of factory production: the injuries and permanent deformities suffered by workers; the physically taxing, repetitive tasks; the forms of physical constraint and corporal punishment, including beatings and whippings, practiced in the mills. He also foregrounds the bodily realities of poverty—the hunger, physical pain, overcrowding, and unhealthy living conditions—endured by operatives. Foregrounding a language of embodied experience, Luther labors to startle workers out of their own industrial enthrallment and to force otherwise comfortable readers to feel something of the operatives' pain.[49] Critiquing both factory practices and capitalist representational norms, he profoundly calls into question the "romances of factory life" written by factory defenders. Like the mill women's writings examined later in this chapter, Luther's *Address* suggests that antebellum definitions of the literary and norms of literary taste were fundamentally shaped by class.[50]

Luther's account of the propaganda of mill owners and their class allies echoes the work of abolitionist writers and slave narrators, who similarly employ gothic language to call attention to the hidden corruption and bodily horrors within the southern system. While slave narrators such as Harriet Jacobs describe how southerners conduct elaborate charades to charm northern visitors,[51] Luther reveals how mill owners prepare for visits from illustrious industrial tourists: "The men, girls, and boys, are ordered to array themselves in their best apparel. Flowers of every hue are brought to decorate the mill, and enwreath the brows of the fair sex. If nature will not furnish the materials from the lap of summer, art supplies the deficiency" (18). When the "Honorables" arrive, "smiles are on every brow. No *cowhide*, or rod, or '*well seasoned strap*' is suffered to be seen" (19). Once again the aesthetic ("If nature will not furnish the materials . . . art supplies the deficiency") equates to mystification and duplicity; featuring the attractions of workers' "best apparel," floral adornments, and appealing smiles, factory work becomes a kind of industrial pageantry, whose deceptive staging only reiterates industrialists' control over workers' bodies.

Strikingly, Luther calls attention to the intense sexuality of the factory: part of the "romance of labor" is a sexual romance.[52] Indeed the myth of Lowell and the visitor's "enchantment" by what he sees derive in part, Luther suggests, from an expressly erotic pleasure. It is as if the display of poor and laboring female bodies in various sites in the antebellum era—from slave markets to the new "model artist" shows described by Foster and others—is here reprised as the spectacle of industrial labor.[53] The "honorable Senator's" response to Lowell is visceral:

> [He] views with keen eye the "clockwork." He sees the rosy faces of the Houries inhabiting this palace of beauty; he is in ecstasy . . . he enjoys the enchanting scene with the most intense delight. For an hour or more (not fourteen hours) he seems to be in the regions described in Oriental song. . . . [He] retires, almost unconscious of the cheers which follow his steps; or if he hears the ringing shout, 'tis but to convince him that he is in a land of reality, and not of fiction. His mind being filled with sensations, which, from their novelty, are without a name, he exclaims, "'tis a paradise." (19)

In this remarkable passage Luther's rhetoric certainly reveals workingmen's outrage at the ways millwork provides elite men sexual access to "their" workingwomen.[54] But the eroticism Luther identifies is a quality of industrial writings acknowledged by contemporary scholars; examining Dickens's and Disraeli's descriptions of factory women and similar accounts in parliamentary reports, Frank Mort concludes that such texts' "detailed descriptions of the girls' physical appearance . . . tell us much about the sexual desire of these professional men."[55] In Luther's passage the "scene" of female factory labor transports the "honorable Senator" to an exotic world of sexual enchantment and "ecstasy": the public display of so many young women, overwhelming in its "novelty," evokes an Orientalist fantasy (the women are "Houries," the factory a "palace of beauty"), associations that "delight" the senator as thoroughly as they incense Luther. The senator's "enchantment" depends on brevity of exposure; brilliantly signaling a difference in class perspectives, Luther notes that the visitor is present "an hour at most (not fourteen hours)," while his gratification requires that the voices of Lowell women—the "cheers" at his departure and the reality of class conflict they express—be suppressed. These male (sexual) fantasies were understood, and responded to, by Lowell women themselves. But here I want to emphasize how, in insisting elite men's interest in workingwomen is overwhelmingly (if unconsciously) sexual, Luther further refutes claims of aesthetic and moral "disinterest," pointing again to the body politics of factory labor.

Luther illuminates a particular aesthetic at work in reports such as the "honorable Senator's": like many abolitionist writings, his text raises questions of aesthetic judgments at work both in inscribing the female laboring body and in dictating what is or should be seen or unseen, represented or not represented, deemed aesthetically pleasing (and appropriate) or disgusting. Such aesthetic judgments were part of an emerging vocabulary of gender. Examining British literary representations of labor, Nancy Armstrong and Leonard Tennenhouse have argued that "aesthetic judgments," involving a "culture- and class-specific form" of aesthetic valorization or revulsion, and the aestheticization of the female body specifically, were prominent in eighteenth- and nineteenth-century representations of female labor, working to differentiate the appropriately gendered feminine body from the (normatively masculine) laboring body. Generating forms of feminine "delicacy" that had aesthetic as well as moral significance, the language of aesthetics comprised a "well-established poetics of gender" during this period and effected the definition of productive labor as masculine practice.[56] Extending Armstrong and Tennenhouse's argument, this "poetics of gender," constructing the female body as an aesthetic object rather than a means of productive labor, marginalized female productivity in the larger economy while rendering invisible women's productive work in the domestic sphere.[57] This "poetics of gender" and its codes of feminine delicacy were registered as well as challenged in industrial fiction in both England and America. In particular, in several industrial novels (including Elizabeth Stuart Phelps's *The Silent Partner*) the factory owner's daughter appears as a central character and readerly surrogate, enabling the author to make visible aesthetic norms that circumscribe cultural representations and to reveal how aesthetic tastes were under (class) contest. For example, in Frances Trollope's *The Adventures of Michael Armstrong, the Factory Boy* (1840), "no one speaks of the factory in the house of the manufacturer. Be this as it may, the fact is certain, and Mary Brotherton, like perhaps a hundred other rich young ladies, of the same class, grew up in total ignorance of the moans and misery that lurked beneath the unsightly edifices, which she just knew were called factories, but which were much too ugly in her picturesque eyes for her ever to look at them, when she could help it." Here, taste is an attribute of gender; Mary Brotherton's "picturesque," beauty-seeking eyes and an aestheticizing gaze demand the erasure, or at least avoidance of the "moans and misery" of factory workers.[58] In another British factory novel, Charlotte Tonna's *Helen Fleetwood* (1841), Helen's guardian is reprimanded for "introducing such improper subjects [as factory conditions] in the presence of a young lady, whose ears ought not to have been assailed by discourse so unfit for a delicate mind."[59] The language of delicacy construes feminine sensibility as a vulnerable bodily property that requires protection, transferring the locus of socially significant suffering from factory to home.

Feminine sensibility and delicacy not only mandate the spatial segregation of home and workplace and the invisibility of exploitative conditions; they are also invoked—notably by men—to legitimate the policing of discourse. During a period when feminine sensibility, as moral and aesthetic authority as well as socializing force, performed crucial social labor, protecting and appropriately forming the female psyche was a charged cultural task. Predictably the mill owner's daughter became a prominent target in workingwomen's discourse; for example, in the debate over the editorship of the *Lowell Offering*, Sarah Bagley accuses the editor Harriet Farley of behaving as the mill owner's favorite rather than as "poverty's daughter" and a laboring sister. As Bagley understood, the textual disappearance of the laboring body was effected not just by political economy but by the production of gender, especially the emergence of literary "tastes" lodged within an increasingly influential feminine reader.

Taking aim at those tastes, Luther unsettles the valorization of the mill girl and the mystifying idealizations of the bourgeois aesthetic, constructing factory life and labor in gothic, sensational terms. But in his sensational counter-aesthetic, the horrors of industrial exploitation are problematically localized in the female body. Signifying workingwomen's special vulnerability as laborers and their need for male protection, the abject female body renders the working class vulnerable to and penetrable by "aristocratic" power while delimiting possibilities for unity and collective action between working men and women.

## FEMINISTS AND FACTORY WOMEN

If workingmen used the mill woman to represent what Barbara Taylor calls "the rape of class by class,"[60] first-wave feminists were drawn to the mill woman because she troubled the emerging political economy of gender. The unmarried factory woman was an object of intense feminist interest, for she publicized the possibility of what feminists termed women's "economic emancipation." While radical workingmen foregrounded the class nature of factory women's exploitation, scripting factory work as a violation of patriarchal rights within the family (and specifically their own benevolent control or protection of workingwomen), antebellum feminists emphasized how factory women's plight helped make visible the *gendered* nature of economic exploitation, publicizing often invisible relations of domination within the family. As one Lowell activist complained, the same economic motives affected work in the kitchen and the factory; thus for women the sphere of exploited labor was virtually impossible to escape. Particularly in the radical feminist press of the 1850s—in such journals as the *Una* and the *Lily*—there developed a robust discourse about female labor, women's wages (by law the property of their husband), and what one writer tellingly described as the "delicate" subject of women's unpaid household labor. The exploited but valiant mill girl contributed significantly to the emerging feminist discourses about female labor and what were increasingly designated women's economic and "pecuniary" rights.

Feminists engaging the "bread question" were particularly influenced by utopian socialists and Fourierists, who maintained the inseparability of labor reform and the restructuring of gender and sexual relations. Associationists and socialists assailed the "selfishness" of what the era's most prominent American Fourierist, Alfred Brisbane, identified as the "isolated family system" that accompanied the capitalist system of industrial organization, a system that reduced universal love to domestic sympathy and produced intense suffering for the majority of the "human family." At the centerpiece of Brisbane's proposal was the collectivization of household labor, which would liberate most women from household drudgery to pursue other professions while granting household workers a "just remuneration" for their labor. These ideas were broadly publicized in the 1840s, especially through Brisbane's widely reprinted weekly column in the New York *Tribune* during 1842–43 and a prominent debate between the *Courier and Enquirer* and the *Tribune* in 1846, which addressed the merits and failings of the "isolated family as divinely-appointed form of intimate relationship."[61]

Nancy Isenberg observes, "Feminists versed in the socialist theories of Charles Fourier readily recognized the similar 'antagonisms' between classes and the sexes"; while labor activists attacked the "avaricious MONOPOLIST and purse-proud ARISTOCRAT," woman's rights supporters attacked husbands for acting the part of "lords and barons."[62] In their writings the household, far from being a sanctuary from the market, was in fact a mirror image of the factory, identifying wives with exploited workers, "upper servants," and "hirelings," with complex political effects. As a number of historians argue, the moral and spiritual idealization of the home associated with the rise of the "cult of domesticity" was predicated on the erasure of female domestic labor. "Ironically," Nancy Folbre observes, "the moral elevation of the home was accompanied by the economic devaluation of the work performed there."[63] Charting the evolution of this process beginning in the eighteenth century, Jeanne Boydston explains that many cultural commentators (ministers, authors of advice texts, and political writers) dropped an earlier formulation that "praised wives as 'fellow labourers'" and began to describe wives in a way "that emphasized their *freedom* from labor," framing their contribution to the family in emotional and psychological (rather than economic) terms; "true females," by this account, were leisured and delicate and "betrayed no sign of toil."[64] By the antebellum decades this construction of feminine delicacy and leisure was positioned within civilizationist ideologies and racializing narratives of progress; whereas in "primitive" societies, the argument ran, women were treated as "drudges," valorization of women's "refinement" ("cultural capital") and subjective and emotional assets characterized "civilized" societies. In feminist writings the embodied factory woman served as a vehicle for repudiating the aesthetic erasure of female labor; depicting factory and home as parallel sites facilitating a transfer of wealth from female body to male owner or capitalist, these writers theorized a gendered relation of class.[65]

Amplifying a strand of Lowell women's own discourse, antebellum feminists expose feminine "delicacy" as class regime. Detecting a "narrow class-feeling" in the "gallantry of man to the other sex," a writer in the *Lily* describes how a gentleman will rush to pick up the dropped glove of a "lady" but will readily permit "any waiting-maid in the house to descend and pick it up for him." Similarly he will rush to save "the lady 'of his order'" from exerting herself as she passes from front door to carriage, but "he is not at all shocked when the maid-servant runs out to bring his umbrella."[66] Strongly echoing Sojourner Truth's "Ain't I a Woman" speech, a writer in the *Una* observes, "A *poor* woman is not out of her sphere sawing wood, picking rags in the gutters, peddling fish in the street, in short doing any hard drudgery which will give her a subsistence. She may plough in the field, yoked with the bullock . . . work on the quays, act as porter, and fight her way through, for she has the physical strength, the bone and muscle to conquer, and 'might makes right.'" According to such writers, the construction of feminine delicacy is politically disabling, negating the reality of women's physical strength and competency and rendering "unseemly" realities of female bodily life. Protesting that claims of "tenderness and regard for the sex, and its delicacy and infirmity . . . [are] made to cover [women's] pecuniary wrongs," Paulina Wright Davis argues in the *Una*, "the conservators of female purity and decorum, make no objection to her employment in the menial occupations of the household, the exhausting toil of the needle, and the ill paid labor of the cotton factory. This sort of labor is permitted, and tenderness for the sex does not prevent a heavy discount upon its wages." Construing capitalist economic "progress" as a history of loss (of women's economic agency and opportunity), not gain, writers on the bread question turn civilizationist ideology on its head. Davis depicts the factory as a sign not of a general degradation of labor (as in workingmen's writings) but of a specific degradation of female labor; feminizing the artisanal critique, she suggests that the factory deskills female labor, depresses its value, and diminishes women's control over their work. Further, "the civil subjection of the past was bad enough, but it was mitigated by our social, domestic, and industrial consequence. All this is gone, or going," and women are offered only "genteel pauperism and dependence, under pretty names."[67]

Those "pretty names" define women's economic contribution to the family as "a delicate subject to touch upon":

> When woman toils alike with man, day after day, to support and sustain her family, very likely works more hours and passes more sleepless nights in discharging the duties which devolve upon her, he seems not to realize that she earns any thing—that her labor is of any account—but it's MY FARM, MY MONEY, and he doles out to her with a sparing hand the mite, for which in great emergencies she ventures to ask, and very likely accompanies it with "I don't see what you do with so much money—it was only last week I gave you fifty cents."[68]

Claiming that domestic labor is indeed "of [some] account," the article insists upon the cash value of women's invisible labor. Like contributors to the *Factory Girl's Album*, early feminist writers countered the sentimental idealization of the home with depictions of its mundane economic dimensions, what one writer in the *Lily* termed "life in all its reality." In the article "The Every-day Life of Woman," the writer contends that marriage is less a romantic dream than an economic alliance for profit and capital accumulation. Here the husband's spirit of "avarice" changed "the woman of his love" into "his most devoted drudge," whose unpaid labor is a means to acquire more wealth. The wife is "broken-down . . . twenty years before [her] time," only to die without reward and to be replaced by a second wife; household work is as damaging to women's bodies as millwork, with wives as replaceable as factory workers. The exposé reveals wives' oppression from the "division of labor" within a relatively prosperous household: the "enterprising husband" is both a master of old and a capitalist who reaps profits from the labor of his wife.[69]

Like workingmen who see "lords of the loom" as parasites and cannibals, feminists exploring the bread question foreground the bodily nature of domestic exploitation. Several writers offer accounts of female invalidism, of wives' broken health because of overwork and an endless round of domestic duties and cares, emphasizing the physical demands of household labor and severely undercutting the myth of bourgeois women's leisure. The central figure of the satiric sketch "A Convention in the Inner Life" is a woman of "gradually declining" health who "was advised to employ someone to aid her in her domestic duties that she might have rest and spend some of her time in the open air" to restore her health. Uncertain what to do, she convenes an "assembly" of different interior voices (all, notably, male) to debate and decide her fate; Individuality, Self-Esteem and Common Sense are nearly overwhelmed by the sanctimonious recommendations of Acquisitiveness, Approbativeness (who recommends that she save money she would spend on a servant to keep her home sufficiently tidy), and—strikingly—Benevolence (who preaches usefulness to her family).[70] The antebellum critique of forms of servitude in the factory and in the household thus emerged in tandem with one another, and factory women were important relays in this discourse: the very public image of the mill girl helped advertise the ways emerging capitalist class relations were constitutively gendered and racialized.

READING MILL WOMEN'S WRITINGS

Invoked for varied purposes by industrialists, workingmen, and feminists, mill women asserted the authority of their experience, crafting their own analyses as discursive *subjects*, and forging new languages of class as well as gender. I now turn to factory women's own writings from the mid-1840s, focusing on selections from three periodicals published in or around Lowell: the well-known *Lowell*

*Offering*, the *Voice of Industry* (published in Lowell), and the *Factory Girl's Album* (published in Exeter, New Hampshire). Because of the factory speedups and lengthened workdays that followed the financial crisis of 1837, the mid-1840s were years of intense labor agitation and organizing among New England women workers; for example, this period oversaw the emergence of the first women's labor union, the Lowell Female Labor Reform Association (LFLRA), founded by a former operative, Sarah Bagley. Periodical literature played a key role in workingwomen's activism. While the *Lowell Offering*, an established periodical with close ties to the corporations, often reinforced dominant imagery about Lowell women, other periodicals, especially the *Voice of Industry*, founded in 1845, and the *Factory Girl's Album*, founded in early 1846, were published by factory operatives themselves and tended to challenge the public image of Lowell's labor idyll.[71] Refusing to "listen in silence to those who speak for gain, and are the mere echo of the will of the corporations," Lowell women writers also questioned the ability of workingmen to represent their interests, demanding that factory women "be permitted to speak for themselves."[72] The working-class feminist import of their writings is unmistakable; Bagley, for example, boldly exhorts her factory sisters in an 1846 editorial published in the *Voice of Industry*, "*On ourselves alone* rests the great responsibility of reforming [the factory system]." It was time to break with the nineteenth-century sexual contract and advocate for female self-reliance over dependency in the masculine realm of politics.[73]

In their efforts to reimagine gendered relations of labor, Lowell women were influenced by socialists as well as first-wave feminists. Although historians often emphasize the distinction between working-class labor activists and (often middle-class) Fourierists and socialists, there were important ties between them; Jama Lazerow notes that the writings of labor reformers were "'suffused' with associationist rhetoric."[74] Described as an "important intermediary" between Fourierists and labor groups, Bagley was acquainted with Brisbane, and her friendship and correspondence with the feminist and Fourierist Angelique Martin had a lasting influence on her activism. Martin evidently encouraged Lowell women to purchase the *Voice of Industry* so that they could exercise editorial control over their own journal and fashion their own public voice; Bagley later claimed that Martin's visit to Lowell and speech before the LFLRA in 1845 helped shape the organization's new "goal" of "women's rights."[75] Increasingly focusing on women's rights during this period, the *Voice of Industry* became an important source of what Annelise Orleck terms "industrial feminism."[76] Informed by utopian-socialist critiques of women's domestic servitude and "pecuniary dependence," Lowell women's critiques of the exploitation of factory women's labor were not only in dialogue with radical workingmen's discourses; they con-

*Fig 1.2.* The earliest known daguerreotype of a factory worker at a power loom, c. 1850, American Museum of Textile History, Lowell, Massachusetts.

tributed to broader, midcentury feminist discourses about sexual and economic relations of domination inside and outside the family.

Like their male peers, workingwomen contested the social distinctions that intensified under industrialism, employing a political critique of the class divide and an economic critique of capitalist exploitation. In important ways the women who wrote for Lowell labor periodicals drew upon contemporary languages of radical democracy to define a new set of rights for workingwomen. While most Whigs easily construed capitalist expansion and industrialization as emblems of progress, and Jacksonians less confidently envisioned an egalitarian society in which politically independent, vigilant (white) men could secure economic success, for factory women the democratization of economic life was an unrealized potential rather than an evident fact. Reinflecting a democratic-republican vocabulary—including such foundational terms as *justice*, *liberty*, and *equality*—while activating traditional, plebian conceptions of customary social obligations and interdependency, they extended the "egalitarian imaginary" of the Jacksonian era to address inequities of gender as well as class.[77] Arguing that workingwomen were burdened by "femininity" but reaped none of its so-called advantages (domestic protection, economic support), workingwomen took on the ideology of womanhood that was fundamental, they claimed, to their economic exploitation and political denigration.

Lowell women especially targeted the rhetoric of paternalism central to the writings of Lowell propagandists. Paul Johnson has demonstrated that traditional forms of paternalism associated with the patriarchal artisanal order, in which masters assumed economic and moral responsibility for their journeymen, were displaced by impersonal relations of wage labor, a transition aided by evangelical Protestant theology's emphasis on the free moral agency of individuals.[78] E. P. Thompson writes that capitalism's "harsh profit-and-loss purgatives voided the body politic of old notions of duty, mutuality, and paternal care."[79] This entailed narrowing the cultural definition of the family from the traditional model of what we would now term the household (blood kin plus servants) to a small group of immediate blood relations, a process that marked the cultural ascendancy of the middle class.[80] On the wane in actuality, paternalism was central to the Lowell ethos, thus helping to legitimate the new industrial order. Especially with the degradation of working conditions in the 1840s, Lowell women took on the ideology of benevolent industrial paternalism in all its forms. Often playing off a traditional conception of the family against its more modern, nuclear incarnation, factory women exploited contradictions in industrialists' as well as workingmen's versions of the family, thus unsettling the family as the locus of workingwomen's value and identity. In particular they unmasked male "benevolence" in the factory era as a cover for gendered class exploitation in both the workplace and the home.

Factory women variously asserted the power to interpret their own experience as embodied subjects of labor.[81] In a speech before the Manchester Industrial Reform Association reproduced in the *Voice of Industry*, the labor activist Mehitable Eastman claims the authority of experience in exposing labor's degradation: "Who can speak the truth on this subject, if the operative cannot, who has dragged out a miserable existence within the prison walls of a factory?"[82] For workingwomen publicly to voice these concerns *for themselves* required that they repudiate a politics of gender and class deference. In a speech before the New England Workingmen's Association in 1845 (later published in the *Voice of Industry*), Bagley observes, "For the last half a century, it has been deemed a violation of woman's sphere to appear before the public as a speaker; but when our rights are trampled upon and we appeal in vain to legislators, what shall we do but appeal to the people?" Announcing the Association's meeting the following year, the *Voice of Industry* implored, "Let no *false* delicacy prevent you from being present, and taking part in the plans for future progress and improvement." Such writers tackled the disabling ideology of separate spheres; others aimed to disassociate terms such as *popular* from the authority of elite opinion makers. One factory woman in the *Voice of Industry* recorded the following dialogue: "To-day a friend from Manchester said to me, 'Labor Reform is not popular; you don't see any great folks talking about Labor Reform.' I say 'tis popular according to the definition . . . suitable to the common people, familiar, plain, 'easy to be comprehended.' So I convinced him it was indeed popular."[83] Throughout the *Voice of Industry* terms such as *philanthropy*, *reform*, and *benevolence*—like *popular*—are divorced from middle-class definitions and imbued with workingwomen's meanings and values.[84]

Central to Lowell women's critique was the national icon of the Lowell factory girl and the discourse of American exceptionalism to which it was attached. Calling themselves "daughters of New England," factory women accessed the familial rhetoric of national genealogy and kinship conventional among male political writers, foregrounding the irony that the American factory system should become established in the cradle of the revolution.[85] One writer figured factory women's activism as a resurgence of the "spirit of 76," while the constitution of the LFLRA (reprinted in the *Voice of Industry*) states that it is each mill woman's "duty" to "assert and maintain that Independence which our brave ancestors bequeathed us."[86] Such texts employ revolutionary rhetoric to fashion factory women as "citizen workers," claiming title to full participation in the nation's economic and political spheres.

Using statistics to debunk the myth of New England labor, a writer in the *Factory Girl's Album* finds "no material difference in the circumstances of those who have to labor for their daily sustenance in this country and in England"; in fact American working conditions by the mid-1840s are worse than those in Manchester. New England mill women are required to work at least five hours more each week (seventy-four, at Lowell) than their English counterparts while "tend[ing] more looms than in England." Other articles point to growing evidence of status distinctions and class prejudice in republican America. Asserting, "There is far too much of an aristocratic feeling existing among our people," Bagley protests in the *Factory Girl's Album* that "[one] feature abounding in grievous wrong" is "the difference in caste which the employers create between their sons and daughters and the sons and daughters whom they employ to increase their wealth. We are opposed to this distinction. It is wrong; it is unjust to give the latter a supremacy in society over the former." Bagley suggests that these "difference[s] in caste" legitimate the economic injustices of the factory system: "[The factory girl's] industry is to be commended—she toils from morning until night at the loom, or on some portion of the work which goes to make up the whole. But does she receive an adequate reward for her services? Not so. Her pay is too little in comparison to the profits derived from [it]."[87] Both writers oppose the factory system to what they claim are fundamentally American ideals of political, social, and economic liberty.

While such articles challenged the myth of Lowell as an industrial utopia, one, titled "Female Labor," assailed the sexism embedded within the Lowell system of "benevolent paternalism" and reproduced in workingmen's discourse: "The labor of one person ought to command the same price as the labor of another person, provided it be done as well and in the same time, whether the laborer be man or woman." The writer continues, "The fit place and the proper employment, for male and female, are [those] for which they are best fitted by bodily powers, character, intellect, and education." Embracing the egalitarianism of such figures as Fanny Wright, the author uses Enlightenment rhetorics of universality and rationality to contest the discourse of woman's "sphere" and an emerging gender division of economic life.[88] In the *Voice of Industry* those languages were woven into a powerful discourse of plebian women's rights: protesting "regulations by which the operatives are governed" in boardinghouses and mills, one writer observes, "When they conflict with our rights as rational beings . . . then it would seem that we have a right to call them in question, and regard them as arbitrary, and call for a reform." And the freethinking author of "The Rights of Women" delineates five "inalienable right[s]" for women, including the right to equal respect with men in public and domestic life, the right to "freedom of [social] intercourse, and unrestrainedness of expression in language and address," and the right to "buy and sell" without interference in the marketplace.[89]

The author of "Female Labor" protested the discrepancy between a "female" and a "male" (or family) wage, calling attention to how a particular construction of gender was being installed in capitalist processes of labor and distribution. Importantly, many militant Lowell women focused on issues of distribution. The author of the poem "There Must Be Something Wrong" asks why "poor men's tables waste away" when "with surfeits one great table bends," appealing to traditional Christian arguments about mankind's common ownership of nature's bounty to question the justice of a system that allows for poverty and starvation. "An Operative" argues in the *Voice of Industry* that, although women

## Regulations

TO BE OBSERVED BY ALL PERSONS EMPLOYED IN THE FACTORIES OF THE

# HAMILTON MANUFACTURING COMPANY.

The Overseers are to be punctual in their rooms at the starting of the mill, and not be absent unnecessarily during working hours. They are to see that all those employed in their rooms, are in their places in due season, and keep a correct account of their time and work. They may grant leave of absence to those employed under them, when they have spare hands to supply their places, and not otherwise, except in cases of absolute necessity.

All persons in the employ of the Hamilton Manufacturing Company are to observe the regulations of the Overseer of the room where they are employed. They are not to be absent from their work without his consent, except in cases of sickness, and then they are to send him word of the cause of their absence. They are to board in one of the houses of the Company, and give information to the Counting Room, where they board, when they begin, or whenever they may change their boarding-place, and are to observe the regulations of their boarding-house.

Those intending to leave the employment of the Company are to give at least two weeks' notice to their Overseer, and their engagement with the Company is not considered as fulfilled, unless they continue faithfully in their employment during this time.

The Company will not employ any one who is habitually absent from public worship on the Sabbath.

A Physician will attend once in every month at the Counting Room, to vaccinate all who may need it, free from expense.

All persons entering into the employment of the Company are considered as engaged for twelve months, and those who leave sooner will not receive a regular discharge.

Payments will be made monthly, including board and wages, which will be made up the last Saturday but one in every month, and paid in the course of the following week.

These regulations are considered part of the contract with all persons entering into the employment of the Hamilton Manufacturing Company.

JOHN AVERY, *Agent.*

*Fig 1.3.* Factory rules and regulations posted by the Hamilton Manufacturing Company, c. 1850, American Museum of Textile History, Lowell, Massachusetts.

in the mills earn less than half of what men earn, their necessary expenses are not proportionately reduced: "A female pays for her board . . . as much as the gentleman. . . . Shall we take a newspaper? . . . Shall we buy ourselves books?— then we must pay as much as men."[90] Others describe the psychological burdens of the female wage. One writer observes that "hundreds of operatives who work in our mills, are scarcely paid sufficient to board themselves, and are obliged to dress poorly, or, run in debt for their clothing"; becoming "discouraged," they "lose confidence in themselves," and some "abandon their virtue to obtain favors" from men out of feelings of powerlessness. Although women, like men, "strive" to attain "the highest honor set before them," the obstacles placed in women's path stifle ambition and engender a sense of hopelessness. Such writers depict inequities of distribution as a key source of what we might call gendered "injuries of class."[91]

Like Luther and other workingmen, factory women asserted that the mainstream press idealized working conditions to protect the interests of the wealthy,[92] contending that laborers necessarily have a different, more accurate perspective on questions of labor. However, factory women rejected the authority of workingmen to define or defend workingwomen's interests, implicitly and at times explicitly questioning the familial unity of the working class. Workingwomen highlight two things absent from workingmen's discourse: that industrial magnates are not only aristocrats but *men* and that paternalism at Lowell intersects with, and is to some extent mirrored by, paternalism within the working-class family (and the larger working-class community, including social and political organizations). Workingwomen saw that industrialism benefits men and can reinforce male authority, for example, by imposing gendered distinctions in the classification of skilled and unskilled labor, gendered relations of management, and a family wage system. Workingwomen's writings simultaneously contest hierarchies of gender as well as class.

Writing in the *Voice of Industry*, Ellen Munroe takes on the protection of women that elite men "make such a parade of giving": "Protect them, do you? let me point you to the thousands of women, doomed to lives of miserable drudgery, and receiving 'a compensation which if quadrupled, would be rejected by the man-laborer, with scorn'; are they less worthy [of] protection because they are trying to help themselves?" Laboring women, Munroe argues, need not the specious protection of men but the help of the "strong and resolute of their own sex."[93] This lesson is confirmed by "A Lowell Factory Girl," who describes deleterious effects of speedups and pay cuts: "The pay of the operatives in the Lowell factories has been considerably reduced, for the reason, as declared, that the depression of trade is so great and the sale of goods consequently so limited, *they are running them at a loss!* If this be a fact, (though nobody believes it,) why do they not cut down the fat salaries of their Agents, who roll about this city in their carriages, living at ease in fine houses, with servants of both sexes to do their bidding?" Intensified exploitation, the writer asserts, is cloaked by a hypocritical performance of paternal "benevolence": the operatives are "very *pathetically* told that the factories are only kept running at all from motives of *pure charity towards them.*"[94] Distinguishing the professed religion of factory owners from the "*practical* religion of the corporations" was one way factory women called attention to the constriction of benevolence that accompanied the rise of the factory system.[95]

Other writers protest a constriction in social sympathies to the narrow confines of the middle-class family, exploiting a contradiction in paternalistic rhetoric between the benevolence exhibited toward the industrial "family"—the "daughters of labor"—and middle-class family members. In the *Voice of Industry*, "Olivia" questions "gentlemen's" assurances that factory girls are blessed with impressive opportunities and benefits, cannily invoking tropes of industrial "kinship":

> We are told by gentlemen both in this country and abroad that the Lowell factory operatives are exceedingly well off. Good wages, sure pay, not very hard work, comfortable food and lodgings, and such unparalleled opportunities for intellectual cultivation (why, they even publish a Magazine there!!) what more can one desire? Really gentlemen! would you not reckon your wives and sisters fortunate if they could by any possibility be elevated into the situation of operatives? When in the tender transports of first love, you paint for the fairest and fondest of mortal maidens a whole life of uninterrupted joy, do you hope for her as the supremest felicity, the lot of a factory girl?

Like Bagley, who complains that corporate agents "box up [their] benevolence," Olivia demands that mill owners distribute their sympathy (like their wealth) more equitably and imagine the mill girls as equal to, indeed part of, the same "family" as their own daughters. Professions of paternal "benevolence," another writer argues, mask the devaluation of female labor in both home and factory. Linking operatives and domestic servants, "An Operative" writes, "We hear much on the subject of benevolence among the wealthy and, so called, *christian part* of community. Have we not cause to question the sincerity of those who, while they talk benevolence in the parlor, compel their help to labor for a mean, paltry pittance in the kitchen?"[96] Such writings at once demystify the paternalism of mill owners and foreground the role of the family in the production (and reproduction) of class distinctions.

Workingwomen thus tackle various aspects of the "Myth of Lowell." "Amelia" suggests that the myth itself, by broadcasting fancy as fact, seduces women from farms, convincing the future mill girl to "wend her way toward this far famed 'city of spindles.'" Suggesting that workingwomen are deliberately misled by "romances of factory life," fictions of a "promised land of the imagination,"

Amelia, like Luther, exposes the (gothic) reality behind the "beautiful fea-ture[s]" of the "*glorious* [factory] system": excessive work hours, "tyrannous and oppressive rul[e]," and confinement in close, noisy rooms. Amelia reinterprets specific aspects of the paternalism of the Lowell system. Noting that during leisure hours, workingwomen are required to remain at their boardinghouses, subjected to strict curfews and unable to move about freely, she draws astute parallels between the forms of physical constraint targeting factory women in their working and nonworking hours: "When [the millworker] is at last re-leased from her wearisome day's toil, still may she not depart in peace. No! her footsteps must be dogged to see that they do not stray beyond the corpora-tion limits, and she must . . . be subjected to the manifold inconveniences of a large crowded boarding-house."[97] Employing sarcasm to debunk factory own-ers' cant, Amelia explodes the myth of the "fortunate" factory girl: the Lowell worker is afforded no compensatory domestic "haven" from the rigors of labor, no escape from the oppressive discipline of factory life.

FACTORY WOMEN AND THE DISCOURSE OF SLAVERY

In an article bluntly titled "Voluntary?" Bagley writes, "Whenever I raise the point that it is immoral to shut us up in a close room twelve hours a day in the most monotonous and tedious of employment, I am told that we have come to the mills voluntarily, and we can leave when we will." To the contrary, Bagley asserts, "the whip which brings us to Lowell is NECESSITY."[98] In significant ways Lowell women engage discourses of slavery; as with male workers, representa-tions of female workers and mill workers' own self-representations inevitably drew upon a vocabulary of race and slavery. The comparison between southern slaves and northern workers was particularly resonant for Lowell women be-cause of the industry in which they worked; slave-picked cotton was the raw ma-terial used by Lowell spinners and weavers. These links were ratified by popular usage; by the mid-1840s the black wagons driven by Lowell factory recruiters throughout rural New England were widely known as "slavers," while proslavery southerners expressed fears of the "Lowellizing" of the laboring classes (black and white), by which they meant development of the militant, antipatriarchal tendencies of free laborers.[99] The racial intimacies of the cotton trade were at times embraced, at others disavowed, by Lowell women themselves.

Those intimacies were especially visible in the mid-1840s, with changes in the demographic composition of the Lowell workforce and the influx of "not quite white" Irish immigrant women into the mills. Thomas Dublin demonstrates that the earliest Lowell workers were largely Yankee women from relatively prosperous and propertied farm families; following the depression of 1837–40, when many New England farmers lost their farms, and especially with the influx of Irish immigrants into the mills during the 1840s, workers were markedly less affluent, and married women with families numbered increasingly among them.[100] According to Norman Ware, "As the New England farms disappeared, the freedom of the mill operatives contracted. . . . A permanent factory population became a reality."[101] Lowell women writers registered these changes; one observed in the *Voice of Industry* in 1845 that workers in the mills included "a large share of poverty's daughters, whose fathers do not possess one foot of land, but work day by day for the bread that feeds their families. . . . Many are foreigners who are *free* to work . . . according to the mandates of heartless power, or go to the poor house, beg, or do worse."[102] Unsettling the whiteness of the iconic mill girl, these changes could fuel nativism and racism; some Lowell women's efforts to reinflect the meanings of *benevolence* were intended to harness middle-class abolitionist sympathies in the cause of (white) labor reform. But these changes also marked new possibilities of interracial class solidarity in mill women's texts.

Depicting mills as "prison[s]," Lowell women emphasized forms of coercion endemic to mill life. Many protested restrictions placed by corporations (and enforced in the courts) on workers' ability to contract freely with employers. For example, through the corporate blacklist, and corporation regulations that compelled a worker who accepted a situation to remain in that place for twelve months, even if she had not understood this rule or her employer's promises about wages were not realized, the "voluntary" nature of "free labor" was severely undercut. One writer states that the hard-won document, a "regular discharge" releasing a worker from employment, "precisely" resembles that which "dealers in human flesh at the South [use in] the transfer of one piece of property from one owner to another."[103] Imagery of enslavement particularly enabled workingwomen to represent the factory as a site of rampant carnal desire.[104] One factory girl in Nashua, New Hampshire, reports the experience of a "sister operative" who, leaving one mill in search of a better opportunity, finds herself blackballed "because the overseer . . . of the mill she had left, had denounced her" as "a girl not worthy to be employed." Comparing overseers to "*driver[s],* in the southern term," the writer protests corporations' power over the good name and "character" of workers: "It is of no consequence what induces that opinion—bad temper, immoral conduct, or nothing, on the part of the girl, or private pique, the gratification of an envious favorite, revenge for disappointed lechery, or any other cause . . . if the overseer chooses to exercise his power over her destiny and her reputation." These "slaves" of Lowell are subject to "overseers of a dozen or two of cotton mills, who hold not only the bread, but the characters of those girls, in the palms of their hands, and can do with them as any passion may dictate or any caprice suggest, with perfect impunity of the law, and safety from all consequences to themselves."[105]

The rhetoric of enslavement in the mills was regularly employed in the *Voice of Industry* during the mid-1840s, when articles with such titles as "Some of the Beauties of Our Factory System—Otherwise, Lowell Slavery" peppered its pages. Editorials, articles, and poems linking the struggles against northern capital and southern slavery appeared with frequency; one antislavery poem, "North and South," includes the following lines:

Friends of freedom! heed the wail!
'Tis God's own cause,—ye cannot fail!
. . .
Remember, too, that wrong is here,
And give the north one pitying tear;
Oh! let the fruits of love go forth,
To free the South and bless the North!

While some articles equated mill work and slave labor, others supplied more nuanced representations. A letter from a factory girl from Rhode Island "encouraged workers to listen to the 'eloquent appeals' of Frederick Douglass and to realize that there 'is a depth in *slavery* beyond the reach of any, but those who have been made the recipients of its horrors.'" The writer directed readers to make necessary distinctions between factory work and chattel slavery: "Contrast the condition of the slave with that of your own; while you enjoy the liberty of conscience, and possess all the natural and enduring relations of human existence, the slave who is made in the image of God [is] bought and sold like cattle—families scattered, and hearths made desolate—infants torn from [their] mothers and sold by the pound." Another article reported that if the numerous Lowell women who signed their names to a recent "remonstrance against the extension of slavery" were to "join hand[s]," they "would stretch more than a mile"—evidencing their "heaven-inspired sympathy for the oppressed slave." Such writers aimed to refashion female working-class solidarity, reaching for a more effective medium of "sympathy" between white and black female laborers.[106]

## CHALLENGING WORKINGMEN'S PATERNALISM

The "romance of labor" took on one additional meaning in Lowell women's hands: it named an ideology of romantic love that undermined women's class consciousness. While the *Lowell Offering* often presented marriage—at times to the rich son of a mill owner—as a vehicle of class escape for the female worker, writers in the *Voice of Industry* frequently depicted marriage as continuing, indeed intensifying workingwomen's plight. Responding to an article by a Lowell physician published in the *Voice of Industry* that contended that factory women should reform not the system but themselves by utilizing opportunities for self-culture and improvement that arise when a woman first marries, one correspondent noted that while this might hold true for wealthy women "who have others to wait upon them," for working women domesticity affords not leisure but an intensification of labor's burden, especially because in such homes the wife *is* the servant: "Go into the abodes of the mechanic and workingman, *where a woman has all to do* and ask each one how much time she can spare to cultivate her mind" (emphasis added). Echoing arguments by feminist writers on the bread question, such writings emphasize the similarity, not opposition, between factory labor and women's domestic servitude.[107]

Thus in addition to exposing industrial paternalism as a sham—a project they shared with workingmen like Luther—factory women presented a critique of paternalism *within* the working-class family. A key forum for this was the *Factory Girl's Album.* While the *Voice of Industry* was dedicated to charting the progress of the struggle for a ten-hour workday, the Ten-Hour Movement (a major focus of the early labor movement), contributors to the *Factory Girl's Album* explored *social* aspects of workingwomen's experience, especially relations between working men and women, gender norms in working-class culture, and the social forms of the working-class family.

Sexual politics and working-class family life are primary topics in the *Factory Girl's Album.* There is a distinctly pragmatic tone to these writings: while some writers promote the cult of domesticity, such as those middle-class and artisanal texts the historian Mary Ryan discusses in *The Cradle of the Middle Class,* and sentimentalize family ties, the *Factory Girl's Album* presents the family more plainly as an economic institution.[108] Amid a succession of articles on the ten-hour system, the spirit of aristocracy among the capitalist class, deteriorating working conditions, the increasing gap between rich and poor, and the growing international competitiveness of the textile industry, there regularly appeared articles offering advice on courtship, marriage, and the battle of the sexes in the industrial age. For example, "Thoughts on Marriage," an excerpt from Margaret Fuller's *Woman in the Nineteenth Century,* outlined lower and higher forms of marital union, asserting, "Were woman established in the rights of an immoral being . . . she [would not] be perverted by the current of opinion that seizes her, into the belief that she must marry, if it be only to find a protector, and a home of her own."[109] Short fiction featured young women's independence in

marriage choices and especially their forceful resistance of the paternal prerogative in choosing a mate.[110] Articles also denaturalize American courtship practices by describing societies that afford women greater sexual autonomy. One
writer observes approvingly that Roman women are not bound by constraints
of "delicacy" and "modesty" that confine English and American women; when
a Roman woman encounters a man who pleases her, she "does not cast down
her eyes when he looks at her, but fixes them upon him long and with evident
pleasure"; she will then express her feelings openly "to a friend of the young
man's, 'tell that gentleman I like him.'" If the man returns her feelings, "in this
simple and unblemished manner commence connexions which last for years,
and which, when they are dissolved, plunge the men into despair."[111] It is hard
not to read this description as encoding a working-class (hetero)sexual revenge
fantasy: for Roman women, the sexual boldness for which factory women were
often morally maligned serves to increase rather than negate their sexual and
social power.

Misogyny and libertinism were traditional forms of workingmen's, especially
journeymen's, cultures. As Christine Stansell notes, in the "belligerent plebeian
heterosexuality" of the eighteenth century, "laboring men looked on women
as antagonists to be outfoxed and outmaneuvered." Such views persisted in the
nineteenth century; "seduction, even debauchery, remained sources of male
self-esteem into the antebellum years."[112] Although this plebian sexual ethos,
and especially the practices of libertines or "sporting men," are evident in popular literature, during the 1830s and 1840s sexual antagonisms were countered
in workingmen's rhetoric by a paternalist image of chivalrous manhood crafted
"to appeal to middle-class public opinion and also to gain working women's
support by promising that their husbands would behave better."[113] Anna Clark
observes of similar developments in Britain that the rhetoric of female domesticity enabled Chartist men to claim that in seeking to return women to the
home they were selflessly aiming to protect and provide for their womenfolk
rather than demanding a privileged position in the labor market for themselves.[114] The *Factory Girl's Album* challenged that image, contesting the ethical
appeal of workingmen's claims to a family wage as a way to "protect" working-
class women and children. The central figure in this project was the bachelor;
numerous articles assail what appears in the *Factory Girl's Album*'s pages to be
a veritable epidemic of single men, portrayed there as a strategy with which
workingmen utilize the family wage not to support dependents but to live a
fashionable, indulgent life.[115] While it was true that, in this era, journeymen
often had to delay marriage because of changes in the labor system, the *Factory
Girl's Album* depicts bachelorhood as an ethical evasion: workingmen reap the

benefit of male economic "independency" while opting out of its social responsibilities.[116] While the *Factory Girl's Album*'s discourse of bachelorhood as an unnatural state reinforces heterosexual, familial norms (even while calling attention to the existence of a homosexual working-class subculture and a cross-class urban culture of "sporting men"),[117] it also unsettles workingmen's claims to the gender entitlements of the family wage system. These gender and class accents are legible throughout the *Factory Girl's Album*.

The baldly titled "Bachelorism Unnatural" proclaims, "There never can be a paradise without some daughter of Eve within it; and home is only a place to eat and drink, and sit and sleep in, without the hallowing charm of a woman's presence." Other articles advise women to recognize suitors as sexual antagonists; professions of male chivalry notwithstanding, single men, these writers caution, are not to be trusted. For example, Dow Jr.'s "Short Patent Sermon" counsels women, "Be careful how you trust those deceitful creatures called men. Too many of them have their hearts in their pockets. Avarice eats big holes in their affections, and their love is but a brushwood blaze of passion that burns brightly upon the altar of Hymen; but, soon after, ends in smoke and ashes." By making love costly (for men), the writer cautions, the family wage economy threatens the very domestic affection it purports to support. Taking up issues of seduction and breach of promise that received extensive narrative treatment in popular fiction, the author addresses the sexual double standard according to which men were expected to be assertive, active agents in the sexual "market" while women remained passive objects of desire.[118] Although antebellum melodramas typically figure elite men as sexual predators and plebian women as their prey, most perpetrators of workingwomen's seduction were working-class men. In settled rural communities premarital sexual intercourse was viewed as a token of betrothal and the promise to marry was enforced by kin and neighbors, but in cities communal controls were largely absent, and premarital sex and pregnancy often resulted in a woman's abandonment.[119] The *Factory Girl's Album* registered an awareness of the forms of sexual danger faced by workingwomen that accompanied the freedoms of urban life and counseled distrust of workingmen's sexual fidelity and willingness to marry.[120] Another of Dow Jr.'s columns shows the bachelor as a reluctant provider: he advises young men, "Concentrate your affections upon one object, and not distribute them crumb by crumb, among a host of Susans, Sarahs, Marys, Loranas, Olives, Elizas, Augustas, Betsies, Peggies, and Dorothies—allowing each scarcely enough to nibble at." Metaphorizing affection as food, the author evokes a moral economy of distribution of the means of subsistence: because in a family wage economy women depend on men to survive, love's "hunger" could become literal, and a man's refusal to "concentrate" his affections could, literally, starve women—a reality that perhaps helps explain the strikingly frequent appearance of food imagery in the pages of the *Factory Girl's Album*. Articles such as "I Can't Afford It" scrutinize the financial excuses men make to justify marital avoidance, while a satiric poem proposes a bachelor tax to provide the needed incentive to marry.[121]

Entanglements of the wage and sexual markets are further emphasized in articles on the credit system. If, in civic humanist parlance, credit endangered republican virtue, the danger the credit system poses to the factory girls' virtue—like the form of dependency it engenders—is of an acutely sexual type. "The Credit System" playfully evokes the erotic entailments of credit in a family wage economy, as well as savvy women's ability to manipulate men's commercial and erotic expectations:

> A lady with a sweet face, and remarkably tempting pair of lips, entered one of our shops a few days since, and after examining some small articles, enquired the price of a nice little pair of mitts. The shopkeeper had almost lost himself in gazing at the ruby portals through which came the little musical voice. "Miss," said he, "you may have them for a kiss." "Agreed," replied the lady, the blush on her cheek eclipsed by the sparkle in her eye; "and, as I see you give credit here, you may charge it on your book, and collect it in the best way you can!" Smiling enough on the confused clerk to pay half the debt, she pocketed the purchase and tripped gaily out.

The sketch reveals workingwomen's recognition of the sexualization of commercial culture, a terrain in which sex was often, in Stansell's words, a "ticket of admission—the key to social [and consumer] pleasure."[122] The sketch provides further evidence of workingwomen's sexual pragmatism: they practice a "hermeneutics of suspicion" in examining the proposals of working- and lower-middle-class men (such as the "confused clerk") as thoroughly as elite men's sexual and economic promises.

## LOWELL WOMEN, WRITING, AND ANTEBELLUM LITERARY AESTHETICS

That hermeneutics of suspicion—a key feature of workingwomen's plebian skepticism—was directed not only at the charms of the (middle- and working-class) romance of labor but also at the uses to which Lowell women's literary labor was put. Mill women took on the class politics of the literary field, challenging aesthetic norms that, they saw, limited the content of their discourse.

They saw those limits on display especially in public debates over the *Lowell Offering*, the era's most acclaimed forum for factory women's literary expression.

There is arguably something quite peculiar about the *Lowell Offering*, a magazine dedicated to the literary productions of mill women—though it was initially edited by a Universalist minister and enjoyed the sanction and material support of mill owners. Gaining the attention of many observers and attracting a readership well beyond Lowell, the *Lowell Offering* was routinely invoked by defenders of the factory system for publicizing the "beauties" of the factory system. How should we interpret this spectacle of factory women's "literary" labor? Departing from the contemporary authorial ideal of romanticism, which affirmed a liberating imagination in opposition to the "mechanical forms of a new social order,"[123] the *Lowell Offering* represents a particular use of literature to publicize the humanity of a system of industrial production. This effort to utilize literature to placate republican anxieties about industrialism depended on the new model of domestic authorship as a legitimate and respectably feminine undertaking; drawing this link, Dickens asserted that the *Lowell Offering* "compare[s] advantageously with a great many English Annuals," or gift books.[124] Both developments owe something to the ideological uses of literature during this era as well as the role of what Armstrong terms "feminine writing" in the legitimation of middle-class power.

Raymond Williams tracks the historical distinction between the sense of literature as everything written and the more modern sense, dating from the late eighteenth century, of literature as particular kinds of writing (poetry, plays, etc.), entailing "a class specialization and control of a general social practice." He notes that literature was defined by the bourgeoisie as an expression of "'taste' or 'sensibility'" to embody the superiority of bourgeois "nature"; the category was mobilized not only against other kinds of (nonliterary) writing but against much of literature itself (e.g., "bad" writing, popular writing).[125] This view of literature as class-bound, written by and for the relatively privileged, was one the *Lowell Offering* at once advertised and opened to contest. In Britain, Jonathan Rose points out, the middle class found something menacing in working-class efforts at self-education; the public emphasis on the specifically *literary* proclivities of Lowell women—their investment in forms of literary "self-culture" that elevate, not degrade, with literature rather than politics—would have been deeply reassuring for many observers.[126] Here the mill girl's gender is crucial: the bourgeois specialization of the literary was largely effected, both Armstrong and Terry Eagleton demonstrate, by its feminization, a crucial means through which literature was established as a "specialized domain of culture where apolitical truths could be told."[127] Harriet Farley, who became the editor of the *Lowell*

*Offering* in 1842, affirmed this definition of the journal's aim, advising Lowell workers to remain above "sectarianism" because "with regard to politics we, as females should do, remain entirely neutral"; later, when editing that magazine's successor, the *New England Offering*, Farley admonished against such expressions of "unfeminine" emotion as "bitterness," "grumbling," or "whining," for all are "in shocking bad taste."[128] It is precisely this circumscription of the literary that activist Lowell women challenged. For them the *Lowell Offering* epitomized the process in which the beauty of their minds (their tasteful literary productions) as well as their bodies (the idealized image of the mill girl on the frontispiece of the *Lowell Offering*, the photographs and engravings of mill women circulated by factory recruiters) were pressed into service to advertise the humanity and progress of the industrial system.

Alongside workingmen such as Luther, Lowell women writers thus objected to the ideological uses of the aesthetic; they also pointed to the inadequacy of the received modes of the literary to represent factory women's work and lives. Acutely sensitive to the class politics of antebellum literary representation, these writers saw that neither the belles-lettrist tradition, often viewed as imitative of genteel British models and characterized by the polished detachment of a Washington Irving, nor the literary elevation and idealism (and emphatically masculine focus) of American romanticism were adequate to contemporary social realities. Lowell women were especially attentive to how the newly legitimized form of "feminine" writing—sentimental, domestic writing tethered to a domestic ideology and its class-based ideal of feminine delicacy, refinement, and taste—could inhibit serious engagement with the economic conditions of women's lives.[129] Lowell women's critique of the literary reveals an acute awareness of how the category was used to regulate the field of textual production and consumption and to marginalize evolving forms of popular and working-class culture, including popular literature.

Two examples from Lowell women's own writings help us understand what is at stake in the challenge mill women as literary *subjects*—in both senses—posed to antebellum literary culture. The first is the much publicized debate between Farley and Bagley over Farley's editorship of the *Lowell Offering* and that journal's definition of workingwomen's concerns. In 1845, at the height of the Ten-Hour Movement, the debate took place in speeches and print, initiated by Bagley's criticism that the *Lowell Offering* was a "mouthpiece of the corporations" rather than a forum for workingwomen's concerns.[130] In a widely reported speech at an Independence Day rally, Bagley asserted that "the Lowell Offering... was not the voice of the operatives—it gave a false representation to the truth—it was controlled by the manufacturing interest to give a gloss to their inhumanity, and anything calling in question the factory system, or a vindication of operative's rights, was neglected." Whereas defenders of industrialization pointed to the *Lowell Offering* as proof of the humanity of the Lowell system, Bagley contended that factory work "deprived [workers] of most human comfort[s]" and that the proposed extension of the workday to fourteen hours would intensify that deprivation and render Lowell women's celebrated self-culture virtually impossible. Bagley foregrounds the ideological use of Lowell women's literary productivity, suggesting that it is appropriated by the "manufacturing interest" as thoroughly as their factory labor: these literary texts about factory life, she suggests, misrepresent ("give a gloss to") the system's inhumanity, and the journal's commitment to literature rather than politics circumscribes its content, excluding any explicit political commentary about "the factory system, or a vindication of operative's rights."[131]

Defending her speech in the *Voice of Industry*, Bagley contends that the *Lowell Offering* "always has been under the fostering care of the Lowell Corporations, as a literary repository for the mental gems of those operatives who have ability, time and inclination to write—and the tendency of it ever has been to varnish over the evils, wrongs, and privations of a factory life." She demands that "the *Offering* stand upon its own bottom, instead of going out as the united voice of the Lowell Operatives, while it wears the Corporation lock and their apologizers hold the keys." Again Bagley uses class metaphors (operatives' writings are "gems," etc.) to align the literary with "polished" and "elevated" discourse, while her denomination of the *Lowell Offering* as a "repository"—a common name for middle-class literary journals and a word etymologically linked with *repose*—crystallizes this opposition between (feminine) literary discourse and workers' "unvarnished" truth. She attacks the effects of industrial paternalism—the "fostering care" of the Lowell corporations—on the factory and literary labors of workingwomen; she construes such care gothically, as bondage (a corporate "lock" binding the free expression of the operatives) that promotes the "evils, wrongs, and privations of a factory life." Turning to publication figures, she questions the class "authenticity" of the *Lowell Offering*: "We stated that the number of subscribers to the Offering among the operatives, was very limited; we were authorized to make such an assertion in conversation with Miss Farley a few months ago; and we would not charge her with telling an untruth either directly or *indirectly*, lest we should be deemed *unlady-like*."[132]

Bagley here identifies gender, and more precisely feminine "respectability" (a form of gender couched in class terms), as a crucial if often unspoken term in factory women's debates about literary aesthetics. This is acutely evident in Farley's response to Bagley, published in the *Lowell Advertiser* on July 15, 1845:

"I can bear very well to be misunderstood and misrepresented by the operatives, when I think they are, those, whose manner of advocating their cause must be more congenial to the promiscuous mass . . . whose kind sympathy is doubted, and whose most earnest endeavors in their behalf are attributed to an unwomanly love of notoriety."[133] Farley objects to Bagley's political involvement, cast here as a "manner . . . congenial to the promiscuous mass"—a likely reference to Bagley's 1845 speech before the Workingmen's Association.[134] She lodges her criticism in *psychological* terms, not only assailing Bagley's "unwomanly love of notoriety" but ascribing to her an insufficiency of "kind sympathy"—invoking norms of sentimental femininity and equating public aspirations with moral, subjective deficiencies. Farley rewrites the constraints of gender as the conditions of proper working-class female desire.

The debate over the *Lowell Offering* was thus fought on the terrain of feminine desire and taste. Defending the *Offering's* editorial practices, Farley states that she does not wish to "lowe[r] or degrad[e] the character of the *Offering* so as to have made it the medium of . . . complaint against the corporations"—phrasing that indicates how closely the avoidance of political controversy and a language of feminine refinement were intertwined.[135] Bagley responds, "I notice . . . that I have been favored with a specimen of *refined* literature, from the pen of one of the *geniuses* of the age, and feel myself highly honored with a passing notice from such a *high* source, although it comes in the form of personal abuse."[136] Bagley's use of italics aims to denaturalize the authority of the dominant, class-based vocabulary of literary valuation; responding not with feminine tact but with the directness (indeed sarcasm) characteristic of male political writers, she points to ways language itself is marked by a hierarchy of value. Bagley's refutation of the refinement of the *Lowell Offering* is positioned within a broader sociolinguistic struggle, when the Federalist literati of the early republic and their Whig successors, aiming to police the bounds of linguistic propriety, defended a neoclassical standard of "proper English" and the "purity of the English language" against the "barbarous phraseology" (Americanisms, slang, etc.) of the new (working-class) vernacular and popular press.[137] In Farley's editorial emphasis on workingwomen's literary "improvements," Bagley detects the accents of class and attempts to expose the political implications of Farley's "merely" literary choices. In Bagley's politicized discourse taste appears as a vehicle of class distinction as well as a means to police the bounds of female discourse and desire, while to Farley, Bagley's tastes are deviant, unwomanly. Indeed one burden of Bagley's rhetoric is to envision a female working-class subject that is not heterosexually or domestically defined and is not individual but collective: "The girls have united against this measure, and formed a society to repel this movement."[138]

This concern with the mystifications of the bourgeois literary aesthetic is similarly evident in mill women's commentary on the "beauties of factory life." The author of "Factory Life—Romance and Reality" sees the generic attributes of romance at work in what is a misleading, fanciful portrayal of the mills. This writer suggests that industrialists have created a Lowell myth, not unlike earlier myths of American abundance fashioned by imperial explorers, to entice travelers (workers and tourists alike) from afar: "Aristocratic strangers, in broad cloths and silks, with their imaginations excited by the wonderful stories—romances of Factory Life—which they have heard, have paid hasty visits to Lowell, or Manchester, and have gone away to praise, in prose and verse, the beauty of our 'Factory Queens,' and the comfort, elegance and almost perfection, of the arrangements by which the very fatherly care of Agents, Superintendents, Overseers, &c, has surrounded them."[139] Depicting "romances of factory life" as the work of "Aristocratic strangers" with little direct knowledge of Lowell, the author presents the Lowell myth as a self-generating web of literary misrepresentations. The depiction of industrial myth as aristocratic fiction invokes the class binary (laborers versus aristocrats) characteristic of radical discourse from this era to align the literary with the distanced gaze of the privileged class.

The idealization targeted by this writer encompasses what was seen to be the moral beauty of the paternalistic system: its display of class harmony and republican virtue. Such beautiful illusions, the writer suggests, appeal to elite men's narcissism, affirming their class and gender privilege by supplying a gratifying vision of chivalric manhood; the romance of factory life permits elite men to imagine that their class privilege and material gain are in the national interest. But here the phrase "romances of factory life" takes on an explicitly erotic, gendered cast: the author suggests that aesthetic valorization marks the sublimation of elite men's exploitative (sexual and economic) *interest* in the working-class female body—an interest scandalously legible in the many popular seduction novels about Lowell women (see chapter 2). "These lovers of the Romance of Labor—they don't like the *reality* very well—[they] see" the "blushing cheek and elastic motions of 'Industry's Angel daughters'" but not "the pale and emaciated ones. . . . They think little of the weariness and pain of those fair forms, as they stand there, at the loom and spindle, thirteen long hours, each day!"[140] Lowell writers variously assert that the Lowell myth obscures the physical, bodily realities of factory work; indeed, as Michael Newbury observes, the *Lowell Offering* included little mention of the working conditions of the mills and the labor women actually performed. In part this silence reflects "manual labor's resistance to verbal representation," a resistance with several sources.[141] But "Factory Life—Romance and Reality" attributes this invisibility not to epistemological distance but to forms of literary desire. The "picturesque gaze" skips over the vision of emaciated bodies and other signs of industrial "reality"; for the mind entranced by pleasing literary illusions, such images are both unseen and unwanted.

"Factory Life—Romance and Reality" elaborates how a particular industrial aesthetic defined cultural beliefs about Lowell while serving middle-class interests. Writing in the *Voice of Industry*, Juliana employs sarcasm to delineate the distance between workers' firsthand experience and familiar fictions about factory life: those who envision the factory as a "Garden of Eden" tell us that we are indeed "happy creatures [and] how truly grateful and humbly submissive [we] should be! Can it be that any are so stupefied as not to realize the exalted station . . . which [we] enjoy? If so, let them take a glance at pages 195 and 196 of [the Lowell propagandist] Rev. H. Miles' book, and they will surely awake to gratitude and be content." Dialogizing Miles's text, Juliana continues, "Pianos, teachers of music, evening schools, lectures, libraries and all these sorts are, says [Miles], enjoyed by operatives. . . . Very pretty picture that to write about; but we [who work in the factory know] the sober reality to be quite another thing altogether." Emphasizing that the "beauties of factory life" are a textual construction, Juliana identifies the literary as a tool of class power, crafting "very pretty picture[s]" that distract from rather than illuminate women's lived experience of factory life.[142] In the following chapter, I turn to antebellum popular fiction, examining texts that engage the aesthetic norms considered here and that—like Juliana—aim to dispel the charms of literary idealization. Rather than affirming the "beauties of factory life," the authors of popular fiction about Lowell labored to recast the literary field, drawing upon subliterary languages of the gothic, sensationalism, and melodrama to represent complexities of workingwomen's subjectivities and lives.

## *Two.* Factory Labor and Literary Aesthetics

### THE LOWELL MILL GIRL, POPULAR FICTION,
### AND THE PROLETARIAN GROTESQUE

Herman Melville's story "The Tartarus of Maids" (1855) both enacts and ironizes the phenomenon this chapter aims to explicate: the pervasive sexualization of antebellum working-class women in cultural representation. The story recounts the January visit of the male narrator, a "seedsman" who seeks supplies for his growing business, to a paper mill in the remote mountains of New England.[1] Melville's narrator "take[s] in" the "scene" with one "sweeping glance," and—as in accounts of male visitors to the Lowell mills—the scene is infused with eroticism; that the narrator's guide is called Cupid suggests Love's reign in the factory, while the first machine the narrator sees produces "rose-hued note paper" impressed with a "wreath of roses"—seemingly the stuff of "love-letters," perhaps the pink and white Valentines (often decorated with Cupid's image) mass-produced by the 1840s (327–29).[2] However, contrary to the "romance of labor" penned by factory celebrants, the narrator depicts factory work not in idealizing portrayals of "factory Queens" but in images of female servility and dehumanization. In "Tartarus" the factory appropriates the women's sexuality, draining the "blank-looking" women of erotic and reproductive vitality; the contrast between the "rosy paper" and their "pallid cheek[s]" captures the tragic reversals that for Melville mill work entails (328–29). Indeed the paper factory is explicitly designated a realm of perverse coupling: phallic, "piston-like" machines ("iron animal[s]") are tended by "passive-looking" women, "pale virgin[s]" who are the machines' "tame minister[s]" (328, 334). This motif culminates in a startling image of industrial reproduction: the papermaking machine is located in a "room, stifling with a strange, blood-like, abdominal heat," where the "egg-like substance" of pulp is "developed" into "germinous particles" of paper (331). But if the mill is a realm of sexual coupling and reproduction, it is seemingly devoid of female desire: Cupid, "gliding about . . . like a gold fish through hueless waves," is not the emissary of a voluptuous, impetuous goddess but an errand-boy among "unresisting" female servants (329). Remarking that "the human voice was banished from the spot," the narrator drives home the story's industrial critique: "Machinery—that vaunted slave of humanity—here stood menially served by human beings, who served mutely and cringingly as the slave serves the Sultan" (328). The constellation of figurative imagery—the paper mill is a "great whited sepulchre," mill work is a "fatal sentence," the women are their own "executioners," and their complexion signifies "consumptive pallors"—underscores the devastating effect of mill work on the female laborer (324, 330). At the same time, by figuring the mill women's slavery (albeit in Orientalist terms) while giving their whiteness an emphatic, hyperbolic presence, Melville at once evokes and contains the ways mill women's bodily presence could trouble the nativist icon of the mill girl (routinely opposed to her degraded counterpart in Manchester) and the discourses of respectable white working-class womanhood that gave that icon symbolic legibility.

In the "Valentine Offering," a "beautiful little sheet" issued by the Lowell Female Labor Reform Association for a special gathering on St. Valentine's Day 1846, Lowell women writers addressed the central irony of Melville's story.[3] However, while the remote, rural setting of Melville's story intensifies the women's isolation and the misery of their industrial "slave[ry]," in Lowell women's texts urban factory work, linked to a novel and vibrant female peer culture, gives rise to new forms of social subjectivity and collective life. And unlike Melville's mill women, who produce the raw material of epistolary and print communication but are consigned to silence (they speak not a word in "Tartarus"), Lowell writers are subjects of both discourse and desire. Playfully appropriating the tradition of sending Valentine notes to one's beloved, the Lowell women produce their "beautiful little sheet"—unlike the "pale sheets" Melville's mill women produce, with which they are metonymically identified—that emphasizes the power of women's love in the industrial age, calling for factory women's leadership in the reformation of social sentiment. Appealing to a millenarian language of universal charity, the author of "Valentinatory" proclaims, "Love never builds factories where beauty and health are sacrificed upon the altar of mammon." Inspiriting the female union of reformers bound together in the "holy Heavenly bonds of Love—love to god and love to man," this universal devotion will counter the "contemptible, aristocratic spirit" that "threatens to destroy all harmony and good feeling in the new world."[4] As in the writings of antebellum socialists, this utopian expansion of love is coupled with repudiation of the forms of heterosexual devotion conventionally associated with St. Valentine's Day.[5] The single Valentine note published in the "Valentine Offering," a letter addressed to a factory girl, Peggy Green, by a wealthy admirer, is replete with the language of romantic idealization; acknowledging that he is "almost an entire stranger" to the "angelic girl" but asserting "I have long known and adored you," while claiming that his "future happiness (and perhaps life)" hang on her response, the suitor wonders aloud, "Who that has a soul capable of appreciating true worth and real goodness, could behold so much shrouded in a form divinely fair, and not become entangled in the criss-cross net of love." The letter misses its mark, instead motivating the factory girl to affirm her class sympathies ("I could not . . . love one who [lives] on the hard-earned goods of the worthy laborer") and lecture her "aristocratic" suitor on his superficiality, idleness, and "vicious habits."[6] Like the activist Lowell mill women discussed in chapter 1 who critique the romance of labor, Peggy Green repudiates the language of courtly love and romantic idealization as well as the forms of erotic desire (love at first sight) over which Cupid traditionally presides. The mill women's rededication of Love entails a feminization of Cupid's aim; as the Lowell unionist Sarah Bagley writes, workingwomen will "kindle the spark of philanthropy on every heart till its brightness shall fill the whole earth."[7]

Taking up popular fiction about factory women, this chapter engages the problematic signaled by Melville's text and the "Valentine Offering": the place of working-class female *desire* in factory work and life.[8] In a pathbreaking essay in which she argues for a socialist feminist "rehabilitation of the [female] psyche in non moralized terms," Cora Kaplan points to the crucial role of literature, especially fiction, in registering the "relationship between female subjectivity and class identity" and the inseparability of the psychic from the social. For Kaplan "class is embodied in fiction in a way that it never is in bourgeois economic discourse or Marxist economic analysis"; "refusing the notion of a genderless class subjectivity," fiction registers the "immanence" and "psychic effects" of gender difference in the "social relations of class." Because fictional texts reveal the "powerful symbolic force of class and gender in ordering our social and political imagination" and shaping subjectivity, Kaplan incites us to read fictional narratives for the complex, often ambivalent and contradictory forms of desire inscribed within them.[9]

An emphasis on working-class female subjectivity and desire has rarely defined cultural criticism or working-class history. As Carolyn Steedman and Nan Enstad quite differently argue, the signs of working-class women's desire—for example, the desire for fashionable clothing, a clear preoccupation in the texts considered here—have not been dignified in the historical record; Steedman notes that her mother's desire for a "New Look" coat in the 1950s could not signify in the "official interpretive devices" through which the past has been made intelligible, while turn-of-the-century factory women's passion for French heels and fancy hats, Enstad argues, was suppressed in the historical record, partly because such desires were considered irrelevant to politics, partly because the figure of the mill worker as fashionable "lady" threatened the image of the serious, impoverished industrial worker that unions endeavored to promote.[10] (That fashionable dress had important *social* meaning and value for Lowell women and that mill women acutely understood how, in Steedman's words, decent clothing constituted a bid for social inclusion and respect is evident in many sources; a glance at magazines published by and for factory women, such as the *Factory Girl's Album*, in which advertisements for ready-made clothing, shawls, and other "foreign and domestic" dry goods predominate, suggests as much.) Popular fiction about Lowell women highlights diverse forms of workingwomen's desire—sexual and material desires, including investments in commercialized leisure and consumer culture; the affective intensities of the female peer culture of boardinghouse and workplace; the prospect of female economic and social "ambition"—associated with independent wage earning and novel pleasures of working-class urban life.[11] In my reading, popular literature is one among various forms of popular culture and commercial amusement that facilitated the social inscription and intelligibility of working-class female desire. Countering the proliferation of literary texts that aimed to (re)produce domestic womanhood and constituted a veritable discursive machinery of feminization, working-class and popular texts exploited emerging urban discourses of the subliterary, especially the gothic and sensational, to register often inchoate longings, affinities, aspirations, and social tastes; they thus fashioned an alternative, popular discourse of female working-class experience.[12]

This alternative discourse centered on the working-class female body. In an array of early nineteenth-century cultural and political discourses that body was

Fig 2.1. "Song of the Spinners," *Lowell Offering*, series 2:1, April 1841, 32, Widener Library, Harvard University. Songs such as this one expressed factory women's feelings of pride and independence in their work, as well as the pleasures of leisure. Working-class oral and performance cultures existed alongside and were often recollected within literary and print culture.

a site of sexual and textual excess; in particular the female laboring body was seen to challenge what Armstrong and Tennenhouse term an emerging "poetics of gender" and gendered norms of class taste.[13] As chapter 1 demonstrates, the aestheticized working-class female body had national(ist) as well as class import; the idealized construction of the Lowell mill girl in discourses about American industrialization suggests her iconic, public value as a gendered figure within what Lauren Berlant calls "national fantasy," a species of national idealization generically linked, Berlant suggests, with romance.[14] An emblem of American manufactory and economic "progress," one that drew upon the nationalist symbolics of garment manufacture of the Revolutionary War (when women wore homespun to protest British colonial authority), the "free," virtuous Lowell mill girl helped legitimate forms of economic protectionism (what became known as Henry Clay's "American system") in cotton manufacture that established a capitalist industrial system in the United States and the fortunes of an entrepreneurial elite. But this "poetics of gender" also had clear racial import: part of the function of the aestheticized mill girl was to manage the racial intimacies of the cotton textile trade, her emphatically white body and much noted chastity and respectability masking the all too real social proximity of female factory workers to the institution of slavery that produced the raw materials of industrial production.[15] Sites of public reading often infused with everyday life and saturated with "the presence of the present," popular fiction became spaces for envisioning new forms of social subjectivity and for registering the liberating as well as exploitative aspects of modern urban life. Emerging in tandem with and often borrowing from the "body-discourses" of working-class political journalism—especially the denigrated idiom of sensationalism—such fiction made culturally visible the embodied experience of women's factory work and working-class urban life.[16]

## MILL GIRLS AND THE "FICTION FACTORY"

The emergence of the story paper and pamphlet novel, like that of penny newspapers in the 1830s, bore the imprint of a revolution in print technology and the rise of a capitalist market in various kinds of commodities, including printed materials. As Michael Denning notes, these developments were fueled by the invention of the steam-driven cylinder press, the creation of an extensive rail and canal network to facilitate distribution, and the emergence of a mass reading public, including the artisans, mechanics, and factory girls concentrated in eastern cities.[17] Intended for mass consumption, antebellum popular literature benefited from the universal literacy movement and increases in literacy rates among the white and free black populations.[18] The cheap postal magazine rate for distributing newspapers—and later the emergence of distribution centers for newspapers and cheap fiction—also contributed to the commercial viability and success of these forms.

Working-class women were important as both subjects for and readers of popular fiction.[19] As I argue elsewhere, workingwomen were a significant, little studied readership of the era's cheap fiction; there were important links between female factory workers and the emerging "fiction factory"—popular texts that appeared in the penny press, story papers, and pamphlet fiction in the 1840s and 1850s. In their autobiographies and other writings laboring women such as the Lowell mill girl Lucy Larcom highlight the import of popular fiction for working-class women; later in the century Edward Everett Hale cited as evidence for the existence of a "sufficient" audience for American periodical literature that "a Boston publisher could say in 1841, 'We sell 1000 copies every month to the Lowell factory girls.'"[20] Indeed the unsettling presence of this population of working-class female readers was registered in the critical response to the startling proliferation of cheap fiction: what might be termed this era's "antipopular fiction" critical discourse was marked by a phobia about workingwomen's cultural (and bodily) presence. What happens when we read popular fiction, as well as contemporary critical discourse about it, with a focus on these "hidden hands"—the often occluded cultural presence of working-class women?

That focus is a valuable corrective for, if story papers and pamphlet novels were characterized as purveyors of the "low," they were also widely known as "boys' literature." The midcentury author of "What Our Boys Are Reading" contended that story papers featured stories "about hunting, Indian warfare, California desperado life, pirates, wild sea adventure, highwaymen, crimes and horrible accidents, horrors (tortures and snake stories), gamblers, practical jokes, the life of vagabond boys, and the wild behavior of dissipated boys in great cities," asserting that "there are no other stories."[21] But even in critical definitions of this literature, another audience is visible. In his well-known essay, "The Dime Novel in American Life" (1907), Charles M. Harvey at once invokes and (parenthetically) unsettles the "boys' literature" designation: "What boy of the sixties can ever forget Beadle's [dime] novels . . . conveniently shaped for the pocket, [which] became an inseparable part of the outfit of the boy (and to some extent of the girl also) of the period."[22] Writing in 1879 W. H. Bishop designates boys (especially elevator boys, street boys, and school lads) the "most ardent class of patrons" of cheap fiction. But he himself observes "a shop-girl on her way home from work; a servant from one of the good houses . . . and a middle-aged woman, with a shawl over her head and a half-peck of potatoes in a basket" purchasing story papers from a stationer's shop in New York City.[23] Similarly the author of "Disgraceful Hebdomadals," while bemoaning the "caliber and influence of the New York weekly press," identifies the "intended" readership of story papers as "chambermaids" and "washerwomen, as well as grocers' clerks" and "uneducated men and women" of any sphere.[24] But while the well-known genre of "working-girl fiction," which consolidated a female readership of shop and factory girls and appeared in publications marketed specifically to urban working-class women, didn't emerge until the 1870s and 1880s, working women were a significant readership of popular fiction from the outset; the regular appearance of advertisements for story papers in periodicals written for and read by Lowell factory women in the 1840s suggests as much.

Certainly the construction of dime novels and story paper fiction as boys' literature ignores the ways female readers might find in such literature of adventure rich forms of imaginative and social escape.[25] Workingwomen could actively engage with boys' literature, imaginatively appropriating its characters and plots for liberating alternatives to their own circumscribed identities and life narratives—thus capitalizing on what Engels and others envisioned as the "struggle for the breeches" in the working-class family produced by female wage work.[26] Notably, various genres of boys' literature embodied this cross-gendered address in transgressive female characters: cross-dressing swashbucklers, pirates, and soldiers; female frontierswomen, "Indian fighters," and hunters; female vagabonds and newsboys on the dangerous urban streets. As Henry Nash Smith long ago noted, antebellum popular literature was spectacularly populated by cross-dressing female "Amazons"; what was considered popular "street literature" was the very "home" of the antisentimental, antidomestic heroine.[27] E. D. E. N. Southworth's novels—anticipating Laura Jean Libbey's fiction later in the century—regularly thematized how working girls could appropriate forms of male agency (and ironize the feminine passivity) often featured in popular literature and culture.[28]

But it is crucial to recognize that working-class female readers found the unsettling possibilities of their own identities directly represented in cheap fiction. From the beginning there were countless stories published about working-class women, especially factory women, seamstresses, cigar girls, servants, prostitutes, and, after midcentury, the renowned "sewing machine girls." As Denning notes, "Though little collected and little studied, the working-girl novel is one of the major genres of the cheap stories, dominating a number of the major story papers and a host of cheap libraries." Writing two decades later, Sally Mitchell affirms that midcentury cheap fiction about workingwomen remains little studied.[29] The proliferation of popular narratives about factory women and seamstresses began in the 1840s; early issues of *Uncle Sam* and *Flag of Our Union*, for instance, featured stories of factory women's seduction and their sensational encounters with urban mysteries and dangers. Emerging alongside the first female industrial workforce, pamphlet novels and story papers increased the cultural visibility of working-class women as fictional protagonists and characters, while addressing these wage-earning women as a (potential) literary audience and market. The widely circulated image of Lowell women as avid consumers of frivolous goods, especially cheap clothing and cheap fiction, and the much discussed claim that their deposits in the Lowell savings bank had reached a hundred thousand dollars by the early 1840s, signaled broad awareness of factory women's economic agency and control over some quantity of discretionary income.[30] This audience may not have been consolidated until the second half of the century, when publishers explicitly identified workingwomen as a literary market. But that identity was marked out earlier, particularly by the iconic presence of the mill girl as a literary type. Historians of working-class readers such as Jane Greer argue—and available sources attest to this—that cheap fiction supplied working-class women readers with cultural materials to appropriate and improvise in imaginative and original ways; the publicness of this reading—especially the marked temporality of serial fiction, its status as a shared public event—intensified its communal import. Postbellum story papers such as *Girls of Today* included letter departments that published letters from readers, such as the "factory girl" who seeks advice on etiquette and how to "learn to speak very correctly," evidently taking inspiration from those working-girl heroines who are at once both workers and "ladies," a conflation both Denning and Enstad read for utopian political meanings.[31] For workingwomen cheap fiction provided meaningful sites of culture and community; read at home or at work and discussed in the workplace, boardinghouse, or spaces of everyday life, such texts could constitute the basis of communities with, in Greer's words, "enough social power to resist the imposition of middle-class standards of taste" by reformers and tastemakers.[32] Cheap fiction was interwoven with workingwomen's everyday lives and provided significant materials for their self-definition.

The increasing popularity of this fiction by midcentury met with a stiff critical response, the substance of which was fairly consistent. In articles with such titles as "Pen-Poison," critics objected to the dizzying proliferation of stories that differed from one another so little "the authors themselves could scarcely tell which was which," to immoral characters and sensational incidents, and to the "plentiful" use of "vulgar English" and "coarse and slangy expressions."[33] This response illuminates how the literary field constitutes a site of cultural and class struggle: critics, especially those self-appointed custodians of culture whose authority was threatened by new forms of pleasurable and popular reading, engaged in a struggle to authorize certain forms of literary competency while discrediting or containing others (including more radical or critical working-class literacies). Isabelle Lehuu explains, "A vernacular [print culture] that was cheap, sensational, and ephemeral mocked the long-established authority [and purported disembodiment] of print."[34] Critics were especially concerned with literature's ability to awaken "appetites" and uncontrolled emotions. While sensational exposés such as *New York by Gas-Light* envisioned the sexualized working-class female body as ground zero of the urban underworld, the threatening desires (and startling Malthusian fecundity) of the embodied working-class woman structured the critical discourse about story paper fiction. This literature's fantasized reader (and quite often its heroine) was the dangerously desiring working-class woman, whose unregulated reading practices and literary tastes were opposed to the virtuous reading and "literacy management" of the maternal purveyor of literacy, the proper(ly) domestic woman.[35]

In her study of the "carnivalesque tone" of antebellum popular print media, Lehuu writes, "From the miniature giftbooks to the mammoth [story] papers, all the new reading materials shared a festive and somewhat transgressive quality." She contends that a "bodily culture permeated the printed page": the "materiality of the text, both tactile and visual, and the tactile pleasure they warranted contested the well-established authority of the printed word," creating a "carnival" of and on the page. Lehuu notes that most new publications featured imagery of the cornucopia, with its fruits and flowers, emblems of femininity as well as abundance.[36] Critics of story papers invoked a threatening female reproductivity, aligned with both the female and the "low"; for example, Anthony Comstock's Society for the Suppression of Vice launched a campaign in the 1870s charging that the papers were "pregnant with mischief" and a "fruitful source of evil among the young."[37] A review of Southworth's *Shannondale* (1851) in the *Southern Literary Messenger* includes a striking example of this rhetoric; the reviewer describes the novel as one of "the inanities which, within twelve months past, have issued, like the heads of hydra, from previous critical decapitation, to the delight of milliner girls and the terror of editors."[38] If critical writing about the "fiction factory" borrowed metaphors of mechanized labor to depict new forms of literary production, it also featured metaphors of uncontrolled reproductivity—metaphors evocative of women's role as producers and consumers of this fiction. Despite efforts at critical "decapitation," this carnivalesque, prodigiously proliferating textuality was deemed especially threatening because of the new cultural import of middle-class women as purveyors and regulators of literacy. It defined, antithetically, the "virtuous" literacy practices associated with the proper "reproduction" of the middle class. Contemporary critical responses to sensation fiction in Britain similarly linked this literature to the "uncultivated, exaggerated appetites" of underclass women, bemoaning the possibility that middle-class female readers could be contaminated by this literature and the dangerous appeal of the low.[39]

If popular, sensational, and melodramatic literature, as Shelley Streeby suggests, constitutes "body genres" that materialized often unseen forms of bodily labor and discipline,[40] discourses about popular fiction also reveal particular *gendered* anxieties about working-class embodiment. And, as we shall see, popular fiction routinely explored, and sensationalized, lower-class female sexuality. From narratives of seduced and raped servant girls, seamstresses, and factory women to revenge narratives of the female "adventuress," such stories elaborate possibilities of workingwomen's erotic and economic agency and foreground the scandalous presence of working-class female embodiment, reproductivity, and desire. Such depictions are a counterdiscourse of the body and the bodily low that challenged middle-class literary tastes and cultural authority.

## EMBODYING THE MILL GIRL

As outlined in chapter 1, activist Lowell women mobilized a particular practice of gendered labor republicanism, constellated around authorial "anonymity" and the collective textual production of the periodical. This paradigm arguably pitted a residual republican, politicized (and, Michael Warner argues, anti-aesthetic) conception of print against a liberal model defined by the display of politeness and the management of esteem and distinction.[41] Coupling inscriptions of rationality with a focus on the embodiment of class, radical Lowell women devised authorial practices that had important affinities with the broad field of sensation fiction. Noting the allegorical relation between working-class women's bodies and mass-produced texts—a link evident in Melville's "Tartarus"—Lehuu writes that antebellum "popular publications were [regularly] associated with the negative metaphor of the 'public woman'"; that construction, Lehuu contends, challenges social boundaries (especially the gendered boundary between public and private) while creating space for a feminized public sphere.[42] Jennifer Doyle argues that "the rhetoric of prostitution is a permanent shadow of the ideology that imagines the aesthetic as removed from the concerns of the everyday, the personal, the libidinous, and the political"; the construction of popular literature as the whore's body avows "the sociality of art."[43] Against the sentimental construction of "maternal literacy," in which the text is envisioned as a maternal surrogate that extends feminine influence beyond the realm of bodily presence, the sensational text—mobilizing an association of publication with prostitution and metaphorized as the whore's body—disseminated not influence but "infection" in the grotesque realm of antebellum popular culture.

Activist Lowell women's class contestation of the literary evokes Stallybrass and White's account of the emergence of the literary as a mode of bodily "transcendence" and regulation.[44] It also accords with Grant Kester's description of the class operations of the aesthetic in the industrial era. Kester claims that, starting in the mid-nineteenth century, the bourgeoisie mediated their experience of the industrial order by regulating the visibility of the working class through spatial as well as cultural and ideological arrangements, thus foreclosing "the potential trauma of *seeing* the 'laboring classes.'" Central to the bourgeois "mode of perception" that contained the traumatizing visibility of labor and urban poverty was, Kester argues, the category of the aesthetic.[45] The class evasions of the aesthetic were routinely invoked by authors of the industrial novel, who (like activist mill women) aimed to redefine prevailing conceptions of the literary. For example, Elizabeth Stuart Phelps astutely registers what Kester calls the bourgeois "mode of perception" in *The Silent Partner*: the opening chapter, "Across the Gulf," elaborates the picturesque gaze of the wealthy protagonist, Perley, peering through the "white curtains" of her eyelids and viewing urban life as an "amus[ing]" and distant "picture" from the conformable recesses of her carriage—until the voice and touch of the factory girl Sip unsettles this "feminine" aesthetic complacency.[46] Here the touch of the factory "hand" across the class divide serves as a metonym for Phelps's own representational practice. Challenging the "beauties of factory life" and a literary aesthetic that would place their bodies, lives, and labor beyond the realm of cultural intelligibility, Lowell women similarly aimed to disrupt the repose of bourgeois aesthetic contemplation, unsettling the detachment of the gaze with the proximity of touch.

De-aestheticizing the mill girl, activist Lowell women disrupt aesthetic idealization through a representational emphasis on bodily life. The impaired physical and reproductive health of factory women, bodies permanently marked and deformed by the mechanized repetition of physical tasks (e.g., writers regularly reported an increase in workers' shoe size from the constant standing required to tend to looms and claimed that the right hand grew larger than the left from operating the machine), bodies wounded by industrial accidents, bodies starved as a consequence of overwork and underpayment—this body imagery was central to their repudiation of norms of feminine disembodiment as an aspect of industrial mystification.[47] Situated within the broad matrix of antebellum sensationalism, Lowell women's discourse of the body was a materialist strategy for making visible the female laboring body and revealing bodily injuries of class.[48] I read Lowell women's body discourse as an early instance of what Michael Denning and Tim Libretti, writing of the 1930s, call the "proletarian grotesque," a literary and epistemological mode that operates "in the construction of a working-class knowledge and consciousness from below to counter bourgeois abstractions" through "degradation and materialization of the prevailing bourgeois concepts of the world."[49] Countering the idealization of the mill girl and the specifically literary construction of the "beauties of factory life," images of factory women's physical harm, disfigurement, and violation are intended to disrupt the distance and repose of the bourgeois aesthetic and—by generating shock and outrage—push readers to action.

The emphatic presence of the body in these writings reveals the extent to which class is, as Bourdieu has shown, *embodied*—constituted in specific bodily dispositions, habits, and practices (the bodily "hexis") and materialized in specific forms of social subjectivity.[50] Recent social historians of the early national and antebellum periods have demonstrated the extent to which the bodies of poor and working-class people, women and men, were at once social texts to be read—conveyers of social meanings, upon which the record of class-based forms of suffering was strongly legible—and sites of profound social and economic contest. (This was an aesthetics of embodiment continuous with melodrama's "dramaturgy of excess and overstatement" in which affective and social meanings are converted into "somatic form" and the body, especially the "victimized woman's body," is the locus of determinate meaning.)[51] Simon Newman and others have noted that poor and working-class bodies bore signs of poverty, injury, and disease as well as the marks of labor, including the branding and whippings of slavery and indentured servitude.[52] The bodies of the poor and working class were disciplined and confined in institutions such as almshouses, reformatories, asylums, and prisons; targeted by a new regime of time discipline in capitalist and industrial labor processes; and subject to novel forms of moral regulation and control in a variety of leisure activities.

Poor and working-class bodies were, in a general sense, constructed as a kind of public property, at the disposal of those with greater social and economic power. The bodies of the poor could be held by almshouses in bondage to pay for their stay; the children of unmarried women were routinely seized and bound out as apprentices; debtors were legally imprisoned; the poor could be claimed (even exhumed) as objects of medical experimentation. And the notorious pauper auctions were still held in many rural villages—practices that illuminate relays between white and black bodies, working-class sensationalism and racial gothic. These practices often featured in sensational narratives about factory women, both "true crime" narratives and their wholly fictional counterparts. For example, in George Carroll's *The Manchester Tragedy* (1848), a nonfiction account of the seduction of Sarah Furber (a young worker in New Hampshire's Amoskeag Mills) and her death at the hands of an abortionist, her lover and doctor attempt to sell her body to the Medical College of Boston for purposes of dissection. The publicness of workingwomen's bodies—their construction as public property—was put on display in numerous sensational publications involving rape, murder, suicide, and botched abortions suffered by Lowell women. While visitors to the Lowell mills stood enchanted before the fairy forms of women workers, the many narratives about the murder of the pregnant mill girl Sarah Maria Cornell depicted (in varying degrees of detail) the horrifying sight of Cornell's body found hanging from a post and its mangling by medical examiners.[53] Constituted against the demure privacy of middle-class domestic (dis)embodiment, the poor and working-class female body was imaged as endangered and exposed, turned inside out in the pages of the grotesque world of the antebellum popular press. Defining a counterdiscourse of the bodily low, such depictions foreground the centrality of the working-class female body—its productive and reproductive labor—to the emerging organization of industrial production.

There were thus important links between Lowell women's working-class feminist deployment of the "proletarian grotesque" and the emerging field of popular sensational fiction. Both can be situated within what Oskar Negt and Alexander Kluge call a "proletarian public sphere," where issues "bracketed" within the liberal public sphere—questions of sexuality, labor, consumption, and the bodily nature of citizenship—could be brought into public and political deliberation.[54]

## THE USES OF MELODRAMA

Writers of Lowell fiction routinely turn to the plot of seduction, a popular format for representing the productive and reproductive "uses" of the female body. Exposing hidden forms of power operating within what factory defenders portrayed as the republican institution of the factory, these narratives warned workingwomen about the threat of workplace harassment and the predatory sexuality of upper-class suitors who pursue the "poor, unprotected" factory girl but whose class prejudices consign her to the status of mistress or whore, never wife. Revealing the corruption of love in the capitalist age, such texts recast the class politics of debauchery. Whereas bourgeois defenders of private property equated socialism with prostitution and what Rancière calls the "great phantasm of the community of women," seduction narratives present forced prostitution and sexual exploitation as the hidden agenda of the capitalist class.[55]

Despite Nina Baym's claim that the "disappearance of the novel of seduction" after 1820 was a "crucial event" in the history of American women's fiction,[56] the seduction narrative remained a staple of the popular press of the 1840s and early 1850s. In pamphlet and story paper fiction the seduction formula was put to new class use, and the class meanings of the Richardsonian model were repurposed for the industrial age. While bourgeois seduction novels such as *Clarissa* and *Pamela* devote substantial narrative space to the protagonist's inner, affective life, elaborating the process through which she comes to know her own heart and read the signs of love, factory tales portray seduction as overdetermined, an inevitable outcome of gendered and classed inequities of power in the factory town.[57] These narratives depict a class politics of sex shaped by industrialism as well as new ideologies about poverty that accompanied changes in poor relief and a hardening in attitudes toward the poor.

The seduction narrative formula was flexible and multivalent. In conventional melodramatic fashion many factory stories foreground workingwomen's sexual victimization, banishing the accents of independency and female labor republicanism evident in Lowell women's own writings. Other texts rewrite middle-class codes to provide narrative space for workingwomen's desire, independence, and agency. One of the first stories in the story paper *Flag of Our Union*, "The Lowell Factory Girl," portrays a mill worker whose sexual fall leads quickly to her marriage and respectable standing in the working-class community, thus registering the pragmatic, flexible working-class sexual ethos described by historians. As Pamela Haag observes of antebellum legal discourses of seduction and breach of promise, popular narratives of mill women's seduction contextualize extramarital sexuality within a broader account of relations of power and control.[58] Certainly many texts stage the "exposure of total hire,"[59] the absoluteness of workingwomen's dispossession, for workingwomen are robbed not only of their labor but also what is frequently figured as the "jewel" of their chastity and reputation. Other stories highlight ways workingwomen leveraged their sexuality and their desire to achieve certain kinds of agency, economic and otherwise. This is especially true of sensational texts such as *The Mysteries of Lowell*, examined later in this chapter. In such stories the working-class female body is positioned as an "accumulation strategy" but also as a territory of desire, a vessel of workingwomen's own class experience.[60]

First published in the cheap story paper *Flag of Our Union*, "Anna Archdale" illuminates the uses of melodrama to narrate the dilemmas of female labor. As a popular, working-class form, melodrama provided an influential vocabulary for representing changes wrought by the Industrial Revolution. However, as Martha Vicinus notes, while melodrama—particularly domestic melodrama, the most popular form by the 1840s, which focused on familial and sexual relations—was an aesthetic response to the traumas of industrialization, its social critique was fundamentally conservative; melodramas largely staged dramas of the restoration of traditional values, especially the restitution of the preindustrial, rural patriarchal family.[61] In "Anna Archdale" the conventions of melodrama were used to stabilize the meanings of the working-class female body and contain the threat of workingwomen's sexual "excess."

"Anna Archdale" follows the melodramatic formulae identified by scholars such as Vicinus and Peter Brooks. There is no character development, no "drama of consciousness" or record of psychic conflict, no detailed exploration or narrative elaboration of subjective desire. The narrative employs the conventionally heightened morality typical of what Brooks terms "the melodramatic imagination," and the evolution of the narrative entails less the psychological development of its principals than an externalization of their unchanging moral "nature."[62] But if "Anna Archdale" is conventionally melodramatic, it adapts melodramatic conventions to the factory girl's story. In particular, while Anna's decision to work at Lowell is coded as daughterly sacrifice, accents of a subversive female self-reliance are apparent. Anna is no shrinking melodramatic heroine: it is she who determines to work in the factory to save her father from financial ruin. Moreover the story's villain is not a would-be seducer but a jealous female rival, Mary Foster, who attempts to ruin Anna's reputation to reclaim her former lover, Dr. Corliss, for herself—a rewriting that gestures toward the affective intensity of female peer relations at Lowell. By splitting the figure of the mill girl into Anna and Mary, good and evil, the story both evokes and exorcizes the threatening prospect of female self-interest and ambition.

Anna is at once a moral exemplar, embodying filial gratitude and devotion, and an independent young woman. She decides to become a factory girl when her father, "having inherited a large fortune from his paternal parent," speculates rashly and is left "a bankrupt and comparative beggar" a month after losing "one of the best of wives, and when his daughter Anna had arrived at the interesting age of eighteen."[63] The story's class accents are clear: depicting the mill girl's fall from prosperity as a rich merchant's daughter, the story undermines the class elitism protested by Lowell writers, troubling the opposition between "mill girl" and "lady" by which women's class identities were defined. As in many antebellum narratives, speculation threatens republican stability and virtue; here it also renders bankrupt authority within the home. Paternal collapse is monetary, emotional, and physical: the "desponden[t]" father's melancholy ("I am a poor, broken-hearted and ruined man," he tells Anna) is produced by a series of devastating losses—loss of property (notably a paternal inheritance) and wife, male physical power and able-bodiedness, and especially the power to labor—that together undergird antebellum masculine power (7). Unsettling the binary of masculine "independency" and feminine "dependency," the text couples paternal "ruin" with the daughter's economic agency. Anna declares, "I can go to Lowell—get work in one of the factories, and earn enough to make both of us, at least, comfortable" (8). She even usurps his power of speech: "Don't say anything against it . . . for I am determined to make the trial" (8). Her "determin[ation]" to work for wages—clearly a novel occurrence in this family, as it was in many at the time—and to serve as the family breadwinner is legitimated in part, under the sign of filial devotion, as a means to restore the patriarchal family.

As in the domestic melodrama *Uncle Tom's Cabin*, the opening of "Anna Archdale" depicts the uncertainties of male power and authority in the market system. But the location of virtue in "Anna Archdale" is not the moral authority of the mother (as in Stowe's novel) but the economic autonomy of the daughter. While the father employs the language of pity ("Poor thing"), emphasizing his daughter's vulnerability and dependency, she repudiates such positioning: "I have nothing to ask of the charities of the world . . . so long as I am blessed with good health" (8). The novel prospect of female factory work fuels Anna's determination and agency. "Transformed" from Boston merchant's daughter to "humble factory girl" (8), she is established at Lowell, and the success she finds there redeems her father's economic decline.

The remainder of the narrative reveals Anna's virtue in this new urban context, attesting to the stability of character and the inevitable power of female virtue to be affirmed and recognized. Anna, the narrator assures us, "cheerfully . . . obtained employment amongst the looms and spindles of a New England cotton factory" and in three months "gained the good will and esteem of every one with whom she came in contact" (8). Her value is similarly evident in the marriage market: "By the power of her superior beauty, and the uniform gentleness of her manners, [Anna] gained the LOVE of a young physician, who had just commenced practice in the city" (8). The narrative's principal obstacle is the prospect of misrepresentation, which threatens the melodramatic economy of the story. Also in love with Anna's betrothed, Mary Foster sends Dr. Corliss an anonymous note instructing him to "watch closely" the front window of Anna's house one evening to witness her undue "familiarity" with a young man, thus attempting to "ruin Anna's character" by mobilizing the familiar association of factory women with illicit sex (9). However, the threatening possibility that Corliss's jealousy, as Mary hopes, will be sufficiently "arouse[d] . . . to . . . admit of no inquiry as to its cause" (10) is quickly foreclosed on. Corliss confronts Anna directly, and she and the young man explain the truth: he is her brother, a lawyer from Boston, visiting her at Lowell. The properly familial orientation of Anna's affections is confirmed: hers, we discover, is the chaste kiss of a sister.[64]

The story thus affirms melodrama's representational economy: Anna's constancy and chaste familial affection, deliberately misrepresented and potentially misread, are awarded proper social recognition. It also affirms the political limits of domestic melodrama as a frame for narrating female factory life. In "Anna Archdale" other women appear not as allies in work but as rivals for male affection; the story presents envy—rather than what Jennie Collins terms working-class "benevolence" or solidarity—as the predominant emotion among Lowell women, while mill women's anonymous writings are propelled by heterosexual competition, not sororal love. In Mary Foster working-class female ambition and the excessive nature of working-class female desire are presented as narrative possibilities, raised (albeit briefly) before being purged from the text. It is Anna who redirects the text's sensationalism at the end, vanquishing by exposing her rival. "That hand-writing is Mary Foster's. Now I can see the drift of the whole matter," she explains to Corliss (10). A second note confessing the scheme is retrieved from the dress pocket of the "drowned female" found floating in the canal—a conflation of body and text that cites the proletarian grotesque while protecting the working-class heroine from bodily (and moral) injury. (Notably the suicide here is not the victim of seduction but her would-be defamer and rival.) Mary, it turns out, cannot "ruin the character" of Anna: Restored as an agent of publicity, Anna regains control over her sexual story (10). Repudiating the power of sexual slander, "Anna Archdale" uses the conventions of melodrama to foil (female) virtue's misprision and to stabilize the proliferation of meanings attached to mill women's sexuality.

## WORKINGWOMEN'S DESIRE AND THE LANGUAGES
## OF EVANGELICAL PROTESTANTISM

Like "Anna Archdale," the anonymous pamphlet novella *The Factory Girl* restructures domestic fiction's narrative formula of maternal loss and domestic expulsion through the imperatives of the new industrial economy. But while in "Anna Archdale" the daughter's labor is defined as familial necessity, in *The Factory Girl* it is propelled by the heroine's desire in defiance of familial "duty" or prescription. Mary's economic ambition, unlike Anna's, is central to the narrative; Mary wants money to gain economic independence and especially to buy "things." Thus, whereas in "Anna Archdale," Anna works to restore the paternal home, in *The Factory Girl*, Mary's labor poses a significant challenge to the transmission of rural (and household) traditions, values, and identifications. *The Factory Girl* emphasizes labor as a crucial determinant of gender identity. Mary's labor is central to the family economy, so that the daughter's loss of family is also the family's (especially her mother's) loss of Mary's labor; the story emphasizes the centrality of labor to forms of female culture on the farm, where the reproduction of gender involves the transmission of labor practices. Mary's desire threatens those structures of gender, and as competing objects of Mary's affections at Lowell, the text juxtaposes Elizabeth, a maternal surrogate who embodies norms of feminine virtue and evangelical piety, and Sarah, a factory girl who pursues urban pleasures and encourages Mary to labor and spend for herself. Elizabeth's feminine influence and the force of her example (fortified, in sentimental fashion, by her death) help redirect Mary's desire, motivating her to renounce factory life and return, as a married woman, to the rural life she once escaped.

*The Factory Girl* is dedicated "to those who have been—especially to those who are, and to all those who think of becoming Factory Girls," and its working-class accents are unmistakable. The narrative incorporates political arguments employed by Lowell women, including defenses of the dignity of manual labor, critiques of emerging status distinctions unbefitting a democracy, and attacks on corporate practices and policies (e.g., blackballing), production speedups, and pervasive sexual harassment in the mills.[65] In addition the narrative devotes substantial space to detailing the working conditions in the factory. Recasting the languages of labor, *The Factory Girl*'s narrative structure is shaped by evangelical Protestantism, especially the conventions of the conversion narrative. In an important study of Lowell women, Teresa Murphy challenges an established view of the ascendancy of evangelicalism and moral reform among antebellum working-class communities; by that account, evangelical Protestantism, with its emphasis on free moral agency, legitimated the economic domination of capitalism over wage labor, disseminating middle-class values and suppressing labor militancy. Understanding religious language as "multiaccentual," Murphy finds instead that religion provided Lowell women with a "language of autonomy ... fundamentally at odds with the assumptions of paternalism," fueling women's "access to the public arena" and participation in the labor movement.[66] *The Factory Girl* confirms Murphy's assessment of religious language and its availability to working-class inflection: while the text's narrative structure of conversion might suggest a view of piety as class discipline, evangelical Protestantism supplies a nuanced language of affect and desire capable of registering complexities of factory women's experience. In particular the story maps new social relations enabled by urban factory life—especially forms of homosocial pleasure and desire, peer identification, and consumption—onto the structure of religious conversion. Unlike "Anna Archdale," which dramatizes its heroine's constancy, *The Factory Girl* details how factory life *changes* the subjectivity of its heroine. The conclusion—a reference to "the shuttle of time" marking workers' "factory days of toil and confinement"—signals its self-consciousness about the temporal dimensions of the mill woman's "story" (78).

*The Factory Girl* opens with a robust defense of physical labor. The girl named in the title, sixteen-year-old Mary, lives in the Granite State, where the "rocky soil" taxed the "energy of many a farmer or early working son" (7). Labor, the narrator insists, is the source of both moral virtue and political liberty: "though the inhabitants are compelled to labor," they are "as independent and unfettered in conscience, speech and action, as the free winds that roam their foliaged hills" (7). Nor does physical labor compromise workers' sensibilities: "Beneath their unpolished and unaffected exterior nowhere beat more generous and faithful hearts" (7). The contents of those hearts—their "warm gushing affections"—are most plainly expressed in the "home circle," where farm families gather during long winters to enjoy their "bountiful board [and] blazing hearth stone" (7). The pleasures of singing, reading, and "evenings spent in . . . sweet converse" define a rural home's "treasury of the heart" (8). Presiding over that treasury is the mother, the "central light" of home (8).

Domestic nostalgia is here inflected through the text of female individualism: factory work threatens the integrity of the (rural) home. Caring nothing for the "old proverbs" her mother quotes to her, Mary is seduced, the text suggests, by the language of progress (10). Initially in harmony with her surroundings, Mary is described in natural imagery: her cheeks resemble the "new-spread rose," and she is "radiant as the morning . . . and mild as the summer evening" (8–9). This pastoral idyll is disrupted by her "thinking" (9), which "shut[s]" out nature's sensory charms. "Thinking" is here code for "desire," fueling dissatisfaction with the commercial deprivations of rural life: "I haven't got anything—I can't *appear* like other girls—I'm ashamed to go into company—my thick shoes—my dress is faded—and my old bonnet looks so. . . . I think [it]'s strange I can't have things like other girls—I work hard enough" (10). Registering a number of class feelings (including shame borne of what Steedman identifies as the social importance of clothing for nineteenth-century girls and women), this passage, especially its concluding sentence, shows how the female individualism of factory work could trouble the purported collectivity of the farm economy. Mary's mother promises to "get her something real nice" (10) next summer, but "Mary had seen the Woodbury girls and heard their stories a little too long" (11). Mary's "dreams were full of factory—fine clothes—appearing like other girls—a great many attractions" (11). In *The Factory Girl* female desire is the primary narrative problematic: the fantasized "attractions" of the factory town—the commercial, social, and erotic desires mill life engenders—threaten the reproduction of rural familial norms. The mother's admonition, "Think [not] of going to the factory!" (10), is heard but not heeded; Mary "must be taught wisdom by experience" (47). The narrative trajectory proceeds by teaching Mary the wisdom of her mother's words, finally refocusing Mary's "dreams" within the family form.

The importance of "fine clothes" is emphasized throughout Lowell women's writings; clothing likely held special significance for these women because of the industry in which they worked.[67] As noted in chapter 1, the discourse of clothing in the *Voice of Industry*—in keeping with that journal's critique of "free-market" rhetoric—challenged an individualist construction of consumer "choice." Sarah Bagley, for example, complained that the requirement to dress respectably at church was yet another way elites decrease workers' pay and control workers' bodies.[68] In the *Lowell Offering* and *Factory Girls' Album* clothing could signify workingwomen's independence and enable women to mark out an identity beyond the family; in particular, fashionable dress connoted participation in social "progress" and differentiation from rural life.[69] Stories such as "Evening before Pay Day" thematized workingwomen's choice between the imperative to send money home or to use their wages to buy clothes for themselves.[70] Purchases were invested with gendered class meanings: buying clothing could affirm a "moral economy," demonstrating mill women's entitlement to the goods they helped produce; it could also be a means of asserting personal dignity, countering the women's experience of subordination and invisibility as industrial workers. Aspects of factory work described in journals such as the *Voice*—the exhausting, debilitating regime of industrial labor that destroyed workers' health and subordinated their physical, intellectual, and spiritual needs to the demands of capital—conveyed to mill women the message that the clothes they helped produce were worth more than they were themselves; asserting entitlement to clothing therefore strongly protested capitalism's perverse inversion of the relation between persons and things. Finally, as factory women well knew, fine clothes were material markers of distinctions in status that, Lowell writers regularly protested, were growing under industrialism. Purchasing and wearing fashionable dress could be a very public means of contesting the privileges of class entitlement and problematizing cultural oppositions through which class distinctions were legitimated and materialized.[71] For Mary in *The Factory Girl*, the investment in fashionable clothing, spurred by the Woodbury girls' example, fuels fantasies of subjective transformation, social respect, and pleasure. Fine clothes principally connote female economic independence, inspiring Mary to reinterpret the value of her own labor and shedding critical light on the gender and class constraints of the farm economy.

Once Mary arrives at Lowell, the factory is presented in an extended narrative intrusion, emphasizing the shock of urban experience. Depicted as a new world that defies rational comprehension, the mill provokes wonder as well as fear: "The first time I had a real vision of the factory's inside, I hardly knew where I was. There was such a click, click, click, and incessant rattle-te-slam-banging, I could scarcely see, hear or think" (17). Mary is especially struck by the sight of the largely female crowd: "On hearing bells she looked out and pouring from several buildings saw a host of girls; a few scattering men and boys; but the girls most like swarming bees from the hive. . . . She never saw so many before in all her life" (24). Experiencing the "revery of surprise" (21), Mary delights in the fashionable inn where she spends her first night: "Such nice chairs and sofas—large pictures, and glass—beautiful tables, and carpet—and all things so rich," she thinks (21). Although "novelty is always engaging" (21), Mary quickly recalls that she is "alone among strangers" (22) and spends the night in tearful memories of home (23). Even when she is settled at Lowell, she continues to oscillate between rural and urban, past and future, memory and desire—an ambivalence embodied by her two close friends, Sarah and Elizabeth.

Entering the factory Mary meets Elizabeth, a dedicated worker generous with assistance and encouragement, who becomes "the guardian spirit of [Mary's] first experience of the world from home" (75) as well as Mary's roommate in the boardinghouse. When Mary starts work, the text again takes pains to record her embodied experience; if rural work is portrayed as compatible with intellectual, moral, and civic freedom, at the factory Mary is subjected to the restrictions of industrial discipline so that time itself, divorced from its pastoral rhythms, becomes her "enemy" (32). "I never was so hurried back home," she complains, and Elizabeth responds, "Home and factory customs don't exactly agree" (31). Time discipline is enforced by bells signaling work and meal times, by the routinized movements of the machines, and by the requirement to labor efficiently to secure decent wages. Although she had lessons in weaving back home and anticipates little difficulty, during her first day Mary is "continually on [her] feet" tending to two looms and "fussing about little things," such as replenishing the shuttles and mending or untangling threads, all with the "constant expectation of trouble" from the machine (31). The machinery is an invasive presence: Mary is "stunned" by the noise and "frightened when the shuttle almost hit her, and when her dress caught in the machinery she thought—'I am gone—'" (30–31). Her body aches from the repetitive movements, an endless succession of putting in quills, breaking threads, tying knots, and listening to the "incessant clitter-clattering" (32). The "joy of deliverance from looms" (33) at day's end provides temporary exhilaration, while Elizabeth provides consolation in the "exchanging sympathies of congenial hearts" (36).

Interspersed within the narrative of Mary's departure from home and integration into the Lowell community appear passages of political commentary on the factory system. Like other antebellum women writers, the author of *The Factory Girl* uses her text as a platform for public persuasion. Elizabeth in particular voices strong political opinions, questioning especially the mill's corporate paternalism, lending support to Murphy's claim that, for Lowell women, piety and political radicalism often coexisted. Elizabeth explains to Mary that work is paid by the piece, by cut and quality, and that workers can be paid at different rates for the same work: "You 'tend six looms and possibly . . . receive only sixteen or eighteen cents a cut; but if two, you may get twenty or twenty-two cents a cut" (38). Elizabeth attributes such unfair practices to corporate efforts to attract new workers while reaping the greatest possible profits, as well as male overseers' attempts to exercise erotic leverage: "There may be corporation policy in it somewhere, if not factory girl policy" (38). Invoking the language of rights, she observes, "I've heard father say that corporations were apt to be exacting . . . because they had the power; and those dependent upon them are at their mercy. The rich always have the advantage over the poor, and the laboring and unfortunate are often cheated of their right" (38–39). Elizabeth acknowledges earning "more perhaps than I could at house work; they don't pay much for that; and then the wages are sure here. However this is not so much" (39).

Yet at Lowell the "botheration" of earning alternates with the pleasures of spending (39). One of Mary's first experiences with Elizabeth is a shopping expedition. Mary is initially overwhelmed in the shop: she "hardly knew what to buy; mother had always been her commissioner, and she felt a little queer buying things for herself" (38). In an intrusion the narrator notes, "Perhaps the reader may wonder at Mary, or more at the writer for noticing such little things in her story, but all such little events are thought of, and greatly estimated by the inexperienced" (38). Acknowledging the widespread trivialization of female purchasing—like female labor, it is generally beyond the bounds of literary representation—the narrator insists that this "little event" is psychologically and politically significant: "Elizabeth made good selections Mary thought, but she was of the most importance because *she* paid the money; and owned what was bought" (38). Purchasing here is a sign of working-class female independence, a means of publicizing workingwomen's desire within the social realm. Wage work—a structure of individuation that disrupts the daughter's "economic identification" with her mother—supplies a language of progress and urban enjoyment that competes with the text's (feminized) language of rural nostalgia and pastoral (re)union.[72]

Elizabeth's counterpart in the narrative and rival for Mary's affections is another young mill worker. Sarah's philosophy is pragmatic and hedonistic: "I think we girls should enjoy ourselves the best way we can; we have it hard enough any way" (39). *The Factory Girl* constructs Lowell as a new narrative space: an urban realm of female pleasure and homosocial as well as heterosocial "cheap amusements" of the sort described by Kathy Peiss in her study of turn-of-the-century New York workingwomen.[73] If Elizabeth is the factory girl as moral exemplar, Sarah represents an alternative type, the factory girl as consumer, immersed in the pleasures of urban commercial culture.⁷⁴ Sarah characterizes Elizabeth as "too sober [and] steady to enjoy much": "I never see her out any where; I should die confined as she is all the time" (40). For Sarah, Elizabeth is "old-womanish," embodying an outdated past (40). Denominating Elizabeth's pious self-control a species of feminine "depriv[ation]," Sarah contends that commercial "amusement" is as necessary to workingwomen as bread: "We *must* have amusement, or we should all die" (40).

Elizabeth's friendship with Mary, a "union" of "loving spirits" (41), symbolizes a return to domesticity; their room, "shut from the world," contains "an atmosphere of friendship and purity" (36). But in the factory the Woodbury girls and their stories are replaced by Sarah, whose words prompt in Mary new thoughts: "The word *pleasure* made enchantment, and awakened desire in Mary's heart" (40). Gradually Mary, through Sarah's influence, grows "acquainted with streets and stores," with "fashions and girls of the factory" (47). The narrative's elaboration of Sarah's perspective enables a revaluation of urban pleasure as well as normative femininity: domesticity here signifies confinement; "purity" and piety signify loneliness and deprivation.

The remainder of the narrative relates Mary's temporary "seduction," through Sarah's influence, by the "enchantment" of urban amusement and her subsequent "conversion" and reconciliation to the pious Elizabeth. A chapter entitled "The Wandering" moralistically relates how Mary, ignoring Elizabeth's warnings, "admit[s] to her heart" the "specious language of the other girls" (51), who convince her to attend the dance halls to enjoy the fruits of her earnings. Describing the nightly ball, Elizabeth aligns Lowell's urban youth culture with the uncontrollable forces of contagion and addiction: "A contagious disease is at work long before it is manifest. . . . We are gradually changed like [into] associated characters. We are also excited, once will not do, a second good time must be had" (48). While Elizabeth implores Mary to remember her mother's pious example, the other girls insist that the ball is an innocent pleasure: "Don't let Elizabeth deprive you of going. . . . She never goes anywhere to enjoy herself" (52). A struggle is waged over Mary's emotions: Elizabeth envisions virtuous attachments as silken bonds (54), while Mary's mother advises her to form attachments carefully so as to regulate dangerous influences ("Have few intimate friends, and make them not hastily" [14]). But Sarah speaks the language of more diffused social sympathies and "solidarity": describing Mary's attachment to Elizabeth as overly constricting, she justifies the girls' pursuit of public amusements, philosophizing, "We are social beings" (48). Sarah appeals especially to Mary's desire for social recognition and visibility: "You have nice clothes, and such beautiful hair—you will appear so well. I wish I was half as handsome, I guess I should attract some notice" (52). Mary's appearance at the dance hall confirms "the knowledge that she was beautiful" and produces the "boldness" and sexual self-confidence moralists often attributed to the factory girl, transforming the "modest" country girl into a "forward, boisterous," and "haughty" coquette (61). The combined effect of two experiences—a fainting spell Mary suffers while dancing due to tight lacing and the death of a fellow reveler from exhaustion (!)—restore Mary to Elizabeth; it turns out that "amusement," not deprivation, as Sarah would have it, is the true source of mortal danger. "Mary was really changed in heart, and the happy effects of piety upon her character and deportment were visible to all" (71). The contagion of virtue supplants the contagion of commercial pleasure; observing the change in Mary, Sarah too renounces the peer culture of urban amusements: "Sarah went no more to the *sinful* pleasures of youth—she had no heart for *such*," and "through her influence . . . a number of the factory girls made a [C]hristian circle—a happy band on the safe journey of life to the Paradise of God" (71).

In the end female "self dependence" through wage work is negated by the reproduction of motherhood. The text ultimately affirms what Lowell women sarcastically call the "romance" of factory life: Mary's piety and virtue enable her escape from factory work and the culmination of her story in marriage—notably to a lawyer and gentleman farmer. The novella concludes on a small, remote New Hampshire farm where Mary lives with her husband and children and performs "the duties of her household" (74). Her memories of factory life have distilled into Elizabeth's image, and she has named a daughter after her friend. Mary dedicates her labor to the reproduction of domesticity: "I should advise all girls who have a comfortable home . . . to stay there, for all of going to the factory. . . . I don't want my girls to go to the factory; and they never will, so long as I have a mother's heart or a mother's hands, and strength to use them" (77). Preaching the gospel of domesticity, Mary explains, "In the family circle, are fashioned and strengthened the characters of males and females, for all the business and stations of life" (77). The autonomy of wage labor and consumption and the forms of collective life engendered in the factory town are repudiated for the "queen[ly]" (77) authority of motherhood.

SENSATIONALIZING THE MILL GIRL

By the 1840s seduction narratives about Lowell women were a staple of the sensational press. Violating bourgeois taste by incorporating scenes of explicit sex and violence, sensational texts illuminate the gender and class body politics of antebellum industrial life. Sensational texts about factory women make visible an intensified misogyny toward poor women in an era of liberal political economy; they reveal a new hostility toward "dependents" that is the dark underside of the family wage in what Barbara Ehrenreich calls "the hearts of men." The highly determinist narratives of women's decline from seduction to unwed motherhood to prostitution and often death were structured by often unspoken institutional contexts, in which new discourses about poverty legitimated distrust of, even hatred toward, lower-class and poor women—especially sexually active women—and in which poor single mothers had reduced means of economic support. These narratives marked a constriction—representationally and materially—of public "benevolence" and sympathy toward the poor. In sensational texts lower-class female bodies become the site of illicit desires as well as forms of sexualized violence that are inseparable from, and sometimes mirror, the depredations of the industrial workplace.[75]

Less invested than bourgeois seduction novels in the psychological dynamics of the sexual fall—in the heroine's interiority and finely detailed subjective dilemmas, her struggle to interpret her lover's words and actions to know the feelings of her own heart—these texts focus on the inevitable physical fact of seduction, frequently conflating seduction with the bodily compulsion of physical abduction and forcible rape. These texts devote significant narrative space to the victim's story after her fall: her struggle to support herself, the loss of her position in the factory, her (invariably fatal) assent to her lover's plea to visit an abortionist in order to save her sexual "respectability," and what is often her decline into prostitution—a narrative arc that, for one thing, drew explicit links between the female labor market and an increasingly visible urban sex trade. As with the violated mill girl "pawned off," in one text, by her seducer-pimp as an innocent to an inexperienced greenhorn, the much trumpeted chastity of mill women functions in these narratives as little more than a lure to draw "sporting men" to the dance halls (in some cases owned by mill magnates) and increase the women's value as sexual commodities. For Marx the urban sex trade made baldly visible the dehumanizing, alienating effects of capitalist exploitation: prostitution is "a *specific* expression of the *general* [condition] of the *laborer*."[76] Reworking Marx's analogy, sensational texts about factory women drew narrative links between exploited sex and exploited labor, mapping their converging effects on workingwomen's bodies.

Seduction in these texts represented complex, explicitly gendered forms of class power. Specifically they highlight workingwomen's limited access to modern forms of economic and affective individualism; they suggest that a "free" market in both labor and sex could underwrite gendered inequities in power. Seduction's narrative emphasis on women's sexual disempowerment reflected a society in which the stigma as well as risks of premarital sexuality fell increasingly upon women. This reflected changes in social welfare discourses and practices in both Britain and America; debates about the poor laws in Britain during the 1830s were covered in the American press, helping to shape a new (transatlantic) understanding of the dangers of poverty and dependency. Reflecting a growing consensus around liberal economic principles and especially Malthusian population theory, British proponents of reform treated the growing poor population as a dangerous drain on the economy and faulted traditional bastardy provisions in the poor laws for enabling the poor to reproduce recklessly. While the less densely populated (and geographically expanding) United States never experienced the same anxiety about population, the rapidly growing welfare rolls in cities after 1815, especially after the Panic of 1819, effected a similar hardening in attitudes about poverty and changes in welfare policies. As in Britain, in the United States a number of scientific reports inquired into the causes of poverty and the identity, number, and condition of the poor, and a branch of the Society for the Prevention of Pauperism was established in every sizable northern city. Most branches recommended substantial changes in the distribution of poor relief, notably a shift from "outdoor relief" (cash pensions) to indoor relief (the almshouse and workhouse, with the stigma of shame that would serve as a spur to work), and were marked by a "deepening distrust" and growing "contempt" toward the "increasing throng" of the "dependent poor." Whereas colonials had accepted the idea that the poor must always be present and citizens are obliged to do what is necessary to help them, in the early nineteenth century, according to one historian of social welfare, "the influence of the classical economists . . . and the idea that public relief tended to pauperize and demoralize recipients" met "even more rigid acceptance in the United States than in England." Indeed the idea that in America poverty need not exist itself encouraged a "harsh and suspicious view of the poor."[77]

A central target of this new poverty discourse was the poor unmarried mother. Under the highly controversial Bastardy Clause of the British New Poor Law (1834), a single mother was prohibited from naming the father and from expecting the parish to extract money from the father or receive any cash payment; if she could not support her child, she would have to enter a workhouse. As Lisa Cody notes, Liberal and Whig supporters of the New Poor Law characterized single mothers as "pests of society," burdens, villains, strumpets, and cunning manipulators of men and charity. These discourses transformed poor women into deceitful calculators who became pregnant either to force their partner into marriage or to live idly on the relief the parish would provide in lieu of the father's support; the poor unmarried mother was a self-interested speculator whose womb was a kind of factory for the production of excess profit.[78] American poverty writers took up these themes as well. According to one commentator, extending relief to unmarried mothers as a regular stipend from the public purse "whenever the female cannot find a profitable father for her offspring" affords "countenance and encouragement" to vice and is thus (following the Malthusian logic) a "breeding ground" for pauperism. Several writers objected to women's "unblushing effrontery," "exacting as a *right*, what ought never to have been granted, even as a charity," in appealing for relief; since respectable poverty "shrinks from public view," the appeal for relief itself becomes a morally suspect performance.[79] The very notion that respectable poverty "shrinks from public view" affirmed the moralization of poverty, its construction as secret shame (a view evident in the pamphlet novel *Mary Bean*, discussed below). Several cities, including Boston and Philadelphia, crafted poor laws that mirrored British developments; by the 1820s poor women were expected to bear the responsibility—morally, socially, and economically—for premarital sexuality.

The Bastardy Clause enshrined a sexual double standard (one legible in antebellum cultural discourse more broadly): men were authorized to talk about their sexual exploits with impunity; women's sexual speech was shorn of legitimacy and power. The sensational seduction narratives I examine here are as concerned with the politics of textuality as with the politics of sexuality; specifically they suggest that male control over the circulation of sexual stories at once legitimated and mirrored male control over women's bodies. In the colonial United States, as in England, under existing bastardy laws the reputed father of a child was responsible for its maintenance. As Michael Grossberg observes, "Colonials had treated a woman's accusation [of a man for fathering her illegitimate child] as tantamount to conviction." But in the language of the New Poor Law, an illegitimate child and its father are "strangers" to one another: a mother's declaration has no legal standing, and the child becomes the responsibility of its mother and her family.[80] Examining early nineteenth-century Philadelphia, the historian Clare Lyons describes how the increasing refusal of the Guardians of the Poor (unpaid administrators of poor relief) to reveal fathers' identities, perhaps because of new middle-class sexual mores, installed poor women as the "public face of illicit sex," affirming class-based sexual stereotypes that further fueled the constriction of social benevolence.[81] Undergirded by the new bourgeois ideology of sexual respectability, this public censorship of cross-class sex *produced* seduction as sensational, subliterary material. It is in this context of a shift in public benevolence for poor women, the privatization of cross-class sex and reproduction, and the containment and delegitimation of poor women's words that sensational seduction narratives should be located.

The trope of seduction in these texts was thus invested with a number of different meanings. Deploying the trope of the industrial family, these texts unearth incestuous desires that could trouble industrial "kinship" and shadow the mill owners' and overseers' paternal care, thus drawing parallels between factory women and slaves and troubling mill women's ambiguous whiteness.[82] Additionally, sensational texts' constructions of labor and sex as parallel arenas of female subjection and exploitation drew upon the evolutionary discourses, discussed in my introduction, in which women's drudgery and rape were envisioned as features of "savage," barbarous societies, thus constructing the factory town not as pastoral ideal but as atavistic pocket in the midst of modern civilization. Popular stereotypes of lower-class women as hyperembodied and excessively sexual certainly shape these narratives. But the texts also critique the new urban sexual subculture, a culture of sporting men and sexual recreation, revealing ways that poor women could be disadvantaged—economically and ideologically—in or by the cash-based culture of urban anonymity.

Some narratives make the identification between labor and sexual exploitation explicit, highlighting the bodily nature of women's industrial "servitude." The 1856 pamphlet novel *Flora Montgomerie, the Factory Girl: Tale of the Lowell Factories* scripts a sensational economy in which women's labor (and the woman laborer) serves male pleasure: "wealth revels in exciting pleasures . . . from sensible to sensual," enabled by "the very money its victims have earned for the possessor" (7–8). The text's serial seducer is a cotton mill owner, Henry Richards, who preys on factory girls, including the story's eponymous heroine, whom Henry marries in a sham wedding and then casts off to pursue an heiress. The story conflates sexual and class warfare, pairing Flora's vow of revenge (she will be Henry's "bane" [57]) with a petition for higher wages by a group of workers who threaten to strike if Henry does not meet their demands. In such accounts sexuality extends men's power to command women's bodies; it redoubles women's class subjection.

Other texts comment on the sensationalizing of cross-class seduction, addressing the class parameters and exclusions of the "literary" that regulate the circulation of workingwomen's sexual stories. Echoing the activist mill women discussed in chapter 1, the author of *Ellen Merton, the Belle of Lowell: Or, the Confessions of the "G.F.K." Club* (1844) critiques the "false delicacy" and "overweening squeamishness . . . in regard to these matters" (4) that prevents a clear-eyed depiction of sexual abuses in the factory town. Policing the bounds of linguistic "respectability," these taste norms place clear restrictions on working-class female speech.[83]

*Ellen Merton* is ostensibly structured around the courtship and engagement of its eponymous factory girl heroine and a virtuous lower clerk in the mills,

William Walton; it is a narrative trajectory briefly interrupted by the attentions of the career seducer Harry Harford. But the titular factory girl is little more than a placeholder for male narratives of sexual "adventure" (23); most of the text recounts meetings of the G.F.K. Club, formed by young middle-class men as a forum for their tales of sexual conquest. Registering the seduced mill girl's transformation into an objectified text and mass-cultural "type," William imagines that one woman's sexual guilt is stamped in "living letters upon every lineament of her face" (5). *Ellen Merton* suggests that the mass reproduction of narratives of mill women's seduction—tales of sexual scandal "retail[ed] . . . about" (15)—is driven by masculine appetite; the commodification of the mill woman's laboring body is mirrored by relations of textual commodification over which, the text suggests, workingwomen exercised little control. The narrative's multiple seduced women are generally silent, "carrying [their] secret[s]" to the grave (12); their own stories are culturally irrelevant, because "once fallen," their words have no authority and "nobody will exonerate them from the blame" (10). The purpose of the club is to "communicate all new 'cases,'" pooling narrative resources for "coming it" over the women (16). In a kind of oral version of the "flash press," G.F.K. Club members catalogue their serial conquests in a succession of stories and anecdotes, signaling male control over sensational seduction stories and their circulation for male profit and pleasure.[84]

In the stories they tell, "ruin" connotes a state that is both economic and moral; the text's numerous seduced women find themselves not only abandoned by lovers but cast out by employers, dying in almshouses and prisons, driven from "respectability" to "wretchedness" (10). For example, one young servant, Ann, is compelled to leave her master's house once she is pregnant; after giving birth she works as a prostitute, is arrested and sent to the House of Correction, and, finally, is found lying sick in the almshouse. While the male (seducer) narrator conveniently attributes this outcome to class-based pathology—Ann is the "victim [of] her own unbridled passions" (11)—the text, highlighting his blatant disregard for her suffering, makes it clear that she is the victim of a class system in which poor women's access to benevolence and charity has been scandalously undermined. Foregrounding this absence of charity, the text mocks the discourse and rituals of religion: the recounting of sexual exploits is figured as "confession," seduction is a "baptism," and members authenticate their stories using the rhetoric of experience associated with the Washingtonians. (One club member belongs to both the Temperance Society and the G.F.K. Club [25].) In these mock confessions each man relates tales of serial seductions, the reproducibility of the narrative structure underscoring workingwomen's replaceability in Lowell's sexual and labor markets. The women's diminished social claims are legitimated through the language of credit and risk, language shaped in a context where bankruptcy has grown the commonplace. Male promises to marry have become "bankrupt" (13), and while in traditional courtship practices premarital sex was part of the marriage bargain (at times to prove a woman's chastity), in Lowell's commercial economy "no woman has a right to believe a lover's protestations," and a woman "is [not] to be pitied" if she "risks and loses herself" (13). Seducers, whose attentions are "general" and who accumulate sexual "conquests," bring capitalist rules of self-interest, temporary acquisition, and self-aggrandizement to the field of heterosexual relations.[85] Chastity alone—nonparticipation in the sexual/textual market—is a protection against male sexual license and the inevitability of female victimization; women's only defense is to be "chary of their charms," for if they "risk" and lose themselves they sacrifice any claim to pity (13). Narrating the extension of laissez-faire attitudes to the realm of sex, *Ellen Merton* underscores not only workingwomen's limited access to the "free labor" heralded by workingmen but also their limited access to the emotional, erotic autonomy associated with "affective individualism." Mill women in such stories need to learn the rules of social rank that determine that the authority granted female feeling in the discourse of modern love does not apply to workingwomen. *Ellen Merton* showcases the reality of class-based misogyny that perverts cross-class love, romantic or otherwise. In the era of the new liberal consensus about poverty, narratives of cross-class sex are an emphatically masculine currency, a species of libertine literature circulated among men for their erotic enjoyment.

The 1850 pamphlet novel *Mary Bean: The Factory Girl*, written by "Miss J.A.B. of Manchester," similarly features the perils of courtship in the factory age, when the economic and social risks of premarital sex intensify for women and "obtaining" a "good husband is like drawing a prize in a lottery, where all the tickets but one are blanks" (8). As with revolutionary-era seduction narratives, the story offers readers a kind of gender pedagogy, adapted to the conditions of antebellum industrial life. Mary is a country girl brought by her would-be seducer, George Hamilton, to the factory town (in this instance, Manchester, New Hampshire, not Lowell); here the passage to the factory town is not the prelude to but the vehicle of seduction, part of "the course which her *lover* had so ingeniously marked out" to promote her sexual "fall" and subsequent career as his mistress (17). The story exploits the seduced factory maid as a literary type: the title page describes her tale as "illustrating the trials and temptations of factory life," though the heroine's native village is, in fact, the place where George melodramatically "mould[s] [Mary] to [his] wishes" (10), and the factory tour, where Mary is "introduced" to "the pretty factory girls" (21), is a male plot device. Even Mary's labor is scripted under the sign of male desire: claiming that, due to failed investments, he "lacks the means" to provide her with "a maintenance becoming of [her] situation, and one worthy [of] the love" Mary bears him, George encourages her to seek a position in the factory, where she can "earn something for" both of them (24). Male economic bankruptcy signifies here as female erotic ruin, and it is "unprotected" poor women who are most vulnerable to the vicissitudes of the (economic and sexual) market. Once again the fashionable seducer's "heartfelt eloquence"—his expressions of romantic individualism and "cunning . . . scenes of happiness and delight" (17)—are tools of gendered class power. And once more working-class female bodies are treated as waste, as refuse. Mary's lover is a murderer as well as a seducer; his utter disregard for life is underscored by the narrative pairing of these two acts. Mary ultimately dies at the hands of an abortionist, to whom she is sent by George in an effort to rid himself of unwanted dependents. The antebellum discourse about poverty provides the social matrix that makes the ubiquitous "seduced and abandoned" stories intelligible. The new contempt for poor women, underwritten by liberal political economy, legitimates their sexual objectification and abandonment, their treatment as social outcasts; male sadism toward economic dependents (the unborn child, the pregnant lover) is given emphatic and horrific narrative expression.

Unlike *Ellen Merton*, which constructs maternalist sentimental literacy as a defense against the male seduction and libertine literature, *Mary Bean* protests the decline of a paternalist social ethos and the ways affective individualism can victimize poor women. Describing the practice among married factory women of changing their names to protect their wages from the grasp of estranged or abusive husbands, one Lowell mill woman, Harriet Robinson, depicted anonymity as liberating for workingwomen;[86] in *Mary Bean* urban anonymity fuels workingwomen's victimization. The "spell" George casts on Mary depends upon secrecy and social isolation; they initially pass surreptitious notes at a dinner party; they meet for the first time in the woods; and Mary's initial objections center on what the "world would think" to find her in company with George. "How can I escape the scorn and derision of my . . . acquaintances," she asks him, and risk the "suspicions of [my] friends?" (17, 18). Traditional forms of love and benevolence are associated with the village peddler, Prosperity Jones, who tells a tale of purchasing gingerbread and cheese in a grocery and, approached in the street by a hungry old woman, sharing his dinner with her; Mary remarks that his story "manifested a benevolent heart" (22). Bereft of such traditions and socially marginalized, Mary, even when pregnant, finds she has limited claims on her lover. A "ruined girl—forsaken of friends," she believes that Hamilton is the "only one" she has "a claim upon, and he, as the cause of her ruin, was bound, in pity and in honor, to protect her from suffering and want" (35). Abandoned, she finds him in Boston and pleads her case; she "threw herself upon his pity and protection" and "moved" his "heart" (34). But his sympathy is short lived; soon thereafter he brings her to the notorious abortionist Dr. Savin, at whose hand she dies. Hamilton then "felt himself relieved of a burden," particularly because "none lived to tell the fearful story" of her seduction and murder (39). In the era of Victorian sexual mores, a woman's fall is utterly shameful, and men like Hamilton rely upon women's internalization of sexual shame to consign them to silence. Mary's deep grief and "melancholy" reflect the material and social losses—losses in benevolence and social care—that fuel and attend this constriction of voice, the poor woman's diminished control over her sexual story. Believing that "to make her conduct known would be sure ruin to her reputation" (26), Mary succumbs in the end to the poverty of sympathy in the liberal-capitalist era. But although she falls silent, the text that bears her name becomes a site for recollecting the mill woman's "fearful story" and mobilizing residual forms of sympathy and care for poor women. The narrative animates the ethic of distributive justice and social rights that, Jennie Collins suggests, is the special preserve of poor and working women; this ethic was at once memorialized within and continues to "haunt" cultural texts such as *Mary Bean*.[87]

The pamphlet novel *Norton: Or, the Lights and Shadows of a Factory Village* (1849), by the pseudonymous Argus, is similarly haunted by factory women's ghosts. The preface describes how textile corporations "drain the surrounding country of its lusty youth, and New England's fair daughters, to weave the web of New England's glory" (3). Labor is infinitely replaceable because "the entire population changes" every six years (4). Like *Ellen Merton*, the novel represents serial seduction as an urban epidemic, as if factory women are mass-produced for the purpose; many in town "make it their almost exclusive business to prey on the girls" (71). Seen through the eyes of Norton, a former card stripper in the mills who returns to Lowell after ten years' absence, the text exposes the erotic camaraderie of the sporting male subculture, localized in oyster cellars, fancy balls, brothels, and model-artist shows. This leisure culture, we learn, largely victimizes workingwomen. Disreputable balls encourage sexual predation on "unsuspecting" operatives, particularly by closing well after the ten o'clock curfew of the boardinghouses; seducers then routinely offer women lodging at public houses. What's more, Lowell's "upper crust—the agents and others" (67), rather than protecting factory women from sexual traffic, are often "joint owners of some of the halls leased for this purpose!" (46). The text foregrounds the illicit, quasi-incestuous sexuality that plagues the factory town, the ubiquitous desires of factory "fathers" for their mill working "daughters."

Throughout the text male control is absolute; even seemingly consensual erotic encounters regularly slide into abduction and rape. The narrative focuses on two seduction stories that occur a decade apart. The first relates the seduction of the factory girl Agnes Moreland by the mill overseer Dick Walton; the second, the seduction of the factory girl Julia Church by the "young libertine" and attorney Alfred Caldwell. Again sexual and labor markets are metaphorically aligned: workingwomen are so much raw material to be shaped to elite men's purposes. Like Lowell employers who feel no responsibility for their workers beyond the wage contract, the seducer Caldwell—vowing to "crush" Julia's "virtuous principle," to "moul'd her ... after my own mind"—hopes to get Julia "under his thumb" (9) but has no plans to "keep her"; indeed he intends to dispose of her "when I get tired of her" (8). The text figures this alignment through the language of mechanization: Norton warns Julia, "[Caldwell] thinks you [and those of your class] a mere automaton, constructed but for the convenience of man's baser passion" (75). The rape of Agnes, now the notorious prostitute "Saucy Meg," is described as follows: her rapist "rifle[d] the casket of its jewels and then thr[e]w it away as an idle thing"; "rob[bing] the girl of her virtue—woman's brightest treasure," he is "not content with becoming her despoiler" but also "swindle[s] her from that which might have been a solace to her" by aborting her child (79). Depicting rape and abortion as robbery, the novel foregrounds the power of wealthy men to appropriate workingwomen's productive and reproductive labor.

Caldwell's actions in particular are guided by a deep skepticism about factory women's virtue and his assumption of their sexual availability and inclination; he refers to mill women as "wench[es]" (8), and his misogyny erupts in expressions of violence. Observing that factory girls foolishly "purchase pianos" to furnish their boardinghouse parlors and aim to become "accomplished," Caldwell views these gestures at self-cultivation as a charade; indeed any professions of "fine and discriminating taste" on the part of factory women, such as delight in nature's scenery, are "assume[d]" to be means to gain intimacy with male suitors, a "cover" for sexual desire (6–8). Caldwell believes wealthy young women who possess cultural capital are the "somebod[ies]" one marries; propertyless factory women, whose seeming refinement is "assumed," not sincere, are "nobod[ies]" made for sexual sport (7). Caldwell's murderous impulses toward factory women are clear: "Never will I marry that accursed daughter of ignorance and low breeding—I'll see her sunk with a millstone about her neck in the canal first!" (76). The text repeatedly evokes the violent impulses of elite men toward poor women legible throughout antebellum popular culture; such violence is the murderous underside of the breadwinner wage, in which men were responsible for dependents, including women, in a culture that valorized masculine economic independency and ritualized contempt for the dependent poor. Particularizing the broader, Malthusian social discourse about the threat of poor women (and their reproductivity) to national prosperity, the text demonstrates that poor women were seen to "unman" respectable masculinity by inciting desire, threatening capital accumulation and career ambition.

Osgood Bradbury's 1844 pamphlet novel, *The Mysteries of Lowell*, details what it represents as the fascinating, dangerous realm of the sexual, foregrounding how sex and power are thoroughly interwoven.[88] Relating the romantic adventures of Augusta Walton and three suitors who compete for her attentions, *Mysteries* is replete with the language of sexual attraction and bodily desire, often cast in the palpably physical idiom of animal magnetism (5): the beautiful heroine's touch gives one suitor "a shock which . . . coursed through his blood with the velocity of light" and "electrified . . . every muscle and nerve" (17); "magneti[zed]" by one suitor, she is more greatly "attract[ed] [by] the glittering prospects [of his rival's] wealth" (15). Devoting significant narrative space to Augusta's point of view, the narrative presents a complex account of working-class female sexuality as it emerges within the field of sexualized power relations. Like the other texts I have considered, *Mysteries* demonstrates how the sexual exploitation conventional in the household master–servant relation could extend to the condition of female industrial servitude;[89] at the same time, more fully than those others, it imaginatively inhabits the working-class female body as subjective terrain, exploring in notable detail its heroine's erotic ambivalence. Like the work of Eugène Sue and American practitioners of urban exposé, *Mysteries* publicizes the excesses, crimes, and hypocrisy of the urban elite: the wealthy Owen Glendower, an evangelical minister and associate owner of the mills, is exposed as a rake, while the wealthy Major Seyton is exposed as the seducer of at least two working-class women. But *Mysteries* is also a narrative of female romantic indecision. Augusta is first drawn to the factory worker Edwin Gilmore, "one of the handsomest, and most pleasing young men in this city"; however, he "was poor, and had nothing but his wages from his employers, and the ambitious Augusta knew this" (8). Midway through the text the young Harvard-educated lawyer Henry Seyton, whose father is a "large owner" in corporation stock (35), arrives at Lowell, and he too is captivated by Augusta's beauty (14). She oscillates among her three suitors—Glendower; the young, wealthy Henry Seyton; and the noble Edwin Gilmore—and between the status of mistress and wife.

Unlike the heroines of factory girl melodramas, conventionally "innocent," unwitting objects of others' machinations, Augusta is exceptionally canny, acutely aware of the prospect of male treachery and the economic value of her own beauty. Steedman describes the agency exercised by working-class women who have "the understanding of [themselves] as object[s] of exchange": "Whilst they do not possess any*thing*, they possess themselves, and may possibly be able to exchange themselves for something else."[90] Augusta aims to capitalize on her body in this way; the obverse of a demure domestic heroine, she exhibits both an acute awareness of her physical assets (she "knew for a dead certainty that she was extremely beautiful, and upon this knowledge . . . were founded her ambitious hopes and high aspirations" [8]) and a thoroughgoing skepticism about male constancy and professions of love. When Edwin proposes, she retorts, "You think you love me sufficiently to warrant an engagement for life; but the heart is deceived and very difficult to be fathomed" (23). Similarly, when Henry claims that he has contemplated their engagement until "my brain is on fire, and my heart is burning with love," she replies coolly, "Wait a few weeks, and the fires on your brain and in your heart will go out," adding, "A young man of your susceptibilities will frequently have such spasms" (31). Finally she responds to Glendower's professions of love by stating that he is likely "self-deceived," for "widowers are more subject to sudden spasms of love than any other class of men" (36). As in Lowell women's journalism, the language of romantic idealization is here a language of class; when college-educated Henry compares Augusta to a painting and statue and admires her "enchanting countenance" in the moonlight (20, 24), she, like her journalistic counterparts, debunks this aesthetic idealization, countering it with a rhetoric of romantic skepticism.[91] Her demystification extends to forms of male power embedded in conventions of romantic love; strikingly the figure of the slave woman is invoked to mark these sexualized power relations. When Henry proposes, addressing her as "my own Augusta," her response is startling: "If I was your property, or your own Augusta, as you say, you could sell me as they do the black females at the south" (31). While seduction narratives typically emphasize elite men's efforts to manipulate and withhold knowledge from poor women and diminish their exercise of reason, the precocious Augusta demonstrates knowledge of "indelicate" subjects (such as the sexual market in slave women) that defy strictures of feminine modesty. She is also self-conscious about the conventions of the seduction narrative itself, playfully accusing Henry, "You city-bred fellows love to play jokes on us poor country girls" (17). Threatened by the perennial womanizer Glendower's melodramatic designs, Augusta is unfazed: she unsettles Glendower by boldly "looking him full in the face as if she would read his very thoughts" and possesses an "intuitive feeling, a sort of instinct . . . by which she searche[d] deep into" male hearts, differentiating "villain[s]" from virtuous men (34–35).

Antisentimental canniness is a quality Augusta shares with other popular fiction heroines (such as *The Hidden Hand*'s Capitola, discussed in chapter 5). Describing the sense of exclusion from dominant myths produced by socio-economic marginality, Steedman notes that such experience can engender "a sharp critical faculty," permitting "sightings of fractures within the [ideological] system we inhabit."[92] It is just such a critical sensibility that informed Lowell women's often sarcastic attacks on the "romance of labor," the moral authority of elites, and the desirability of sentimental femininity. Affirming the value of workingwomen's subaltern perspective, factory women, one Lowell writer asserted, "see things more as they really are, and not through the false medium which misleads the aristocracy."[93] In *Mysteries* Augusta's skepticism toward male authority partly derives from her doubly marginal social position; an "illegitimate child" who "never knew the feelings a daughter exercises towards a father," Augusta bears not the patronymic but the name of her poor but "dearly" loved working-class mother (31). Like the slave woman with whom she is frequently aligned in the text, Augusta is positioned outside the normative frame of patrilineal social relations that produce what Hortense Spillers calls a "*patriarchilized female gender*."[94] In *Mysteries* Lowell women's "sharp critical faculty" is directed especially at romance—in part because the conventions of romantic love (female submission to a benevolent male authority) were ideologically central to the operations of industrial power.

The narrative thus engages in a double move: publicizing the illegitimacy of elite male power and publicizing Augusta's wayward desires. The moral bankruptcy of the corporate "fathers" is sensationally featured; gone entirely are traces of the benevolent (corporate) paternalism celebrated by industrial propagandists and registered in some fictions about mill women. At the same time working-class female desire is itself sensationalized, constructed as the text's principal urban "mystery" (10). The narrator's hyperbolic rhetoric and gallant tone arguably aim to contain the threatening presence of workingwomen's erotic deviancy; this is a narrative in which at least two poor women have borne illegitimate children and have been paid to stay silent about their seducer's identity, and the adult daughter of one of these women seriously considers becoming a wealthy man's mistress to mitigate her poverty. But throughout the narrator insists on the power of the female heart to defy social legibility; the challenge the narrative poses to the patriarchal authority of elite white men is coupled with the evocation of forms of working-class female desire unmoored from patriarchal constraints. The thematization of incest tightens the link between plantation and factory town, further problematizing the authority of Lowell's (corporate) fathers.

The scandal of Augusta's "female heart" is initially signaled by her economic ambition: "Although [Augusta] might have thought as much of love as other females of less ambitious views, yet she was continually looking for richly furnished rooms, and to be mistress of a splendid establishment" (5). The narrator describes Augusta, alternately, as "ambitious as Caesar" (28) and as "ambitious as a queen" (31)—and that ambition disables the resolution of her desire through the usual plot device of marriage. She relishes the public attention her beauty garners, cannily exploiting the mill girl's iconic visibility. She appears in the factory "like a comet when it first makes its appearance in our solar system"; she is the "cynosure of all eyes," the "observed of all observers" (5). Her beauty is on display in the streets as well as in the factory (where men such as Glendower occasionally visit); both these (eroticized) spaces are significant narrative sites in *Mysteries*. The factory is the setting where Augusta first exerts her sexual force over Henry and his father, Major Seyton; while Glendower, initially overtaken when Augusta passes down the street (3–4), derives "spying entertainment" from occasions when she "promenaded by his house" (11). Indeed the street is a crucial setting of courtship and seduction, and Augusta is always an active participant in these eroticized exchanges. In each she exhibits a striking self-consciousness about the male gaze and endeavors to manipulate and potentially profit from male erotic interest; the pleasure of exhibitionism is inseparable from her social and economic ambitions. The narrator describes Augusta's performance in the theatrical space of the factory as follows: "Whenever [Glendower] was present she felt a sort of stimulus which induced her to be as graceful in her motions as she could. She frequently found herself making efforts of this kind, and occasionally her deep blue eyes turned upon him as she was busy about her work. She saw, or thought she saw, that she was deepening the impressions she had made upon him, and, aside from any ambitious objects she had in view, it was pleasing to her to see this work go on in his heart" (9). Her female rivals construe that pleasure as a "shame[ful]" sign of female monstrosity: "To see a young lady who is walking the streets take pains to turn towards a man who is a stranger to her, and smile as she did, does not look very becoming; no strictly modest and unassuming female could think of doing such a thing!" (12). As Susan Buck-Morss writes, if one could identify the female version of flânerie, it would be prostitution: the flâneur "was simply the name of a man who loitered; but all women who loitered risked being seen as whores."[95] As a flâneuse, Augusta risks such definition; certainly she troubles the binary classification of "endangered lady" and "dangerous woman" undergirding the geography of gender in antebellum urban space.[96]

The ambiguity of Augusta's social and sexual location as woman worker peaks when Glendower proposes an illicit connection: "I shall soon be destitute of a housekeeper, and should be glad to have you go and keep my house.... I will give you double the wages you receive in the factory, and then if you are disposed you may become Mrs. Glendower, and be the mistress of the whole establishment" (35). He thus proposes that Augusta (unwittingly) reproduce her mother's narrative: her mother (like Edwin's) was a "fille de chambre in one of the richest and most fashionable families" in Beacon Street, that of Major Seyton, who is Glendower's half-brother, and was seduced shortly after Seyton's wife's death (8). Once again the slavery metaphor is invoked—this time by Augusta's would-be employer—to mark the prospect of an illicit sexual exchange. Glendower states confidingly, "I've no doubt you would enjoy yourself much better than slaving in the factory" (35). Augusta agrees to discuss his proposal with her mother during an imminent visit—a turn of events that occasions the narrative's final resolution.

The arrival of Major Seyton in the final chapters precipitates the final crisis. Sixty-year-old Seyton, a "fine specimen of a gentleman," was "a fair representative of Boston aristocracy. Being a large owner in the corporations at Lowell, and a half brother to Mr. Glendower, he occasionally visited this city.... When he came he always made a point to go through the factories quite as much to see the female operatives as for any other purpose, for he ... had a great penchant for country girls.... He had no particular object in view, only to gratify a natural curiosity [to] look at the girls" (36). In a chapter that might be titled "The Revenge of the Mothers," Augusta's and Edwin's mothers—former "country girls" who had once struck Major Seyton's fancy—come to Lowell to see their children and unmask their identities before Seyton himself. Like other narratives discussed in this chapter, *Mysteries* protests elite men's ability to hide abuses of power and exhibits a commitment to publicizing male crime, but here it is not middle-class moral reformers—or working-class male "protectors" such as Norton—who expose the identity of seducers but workingwomen themselves. Both women had given birth to bastards; both had accepted private payments from the father, though the funds were insufficient to avoid poverty and reproduce their own class position; neither, notably, could avoid sending her child to the mills. While these poor mothers' testimonies might be discredited in antebellum courtrooms, standing together they and their words have impressive authority and force.

The final scenes are a subversive inscription of melodramatic formulae: everyone is revealed to be family, but those relations are marked by illicit, indeed incestuous desire. Glendower's home becomes a courtroom of sorts, a site for publicizing Seyton's past crimes and dramatizing the devastating results of the sins of the fathers. Because Augusta and Edwin have their mothers' surnames, not their father's (30), their true relation is disentangled only through their mothers' testimony in this concluding scene. Caroline Barton first reveals herself as Augusta's mother: she tells Major Seyton, "I am her mother and you are her father" (39). Edwin's mother, Rebecca Marvin, then identifies herself as a former chambermaid in Seyton's house who, "owing to peculiar circumstances, went away with the price of her virtue in your pocket" (40). Edwin, she announces to Seyton, is "your own son" (40). In an Usher-like tableau, "the two mothers rushed toward each other, and, impelled by the strong power of sympathy, fell upon each other. Augusta with streaming eyes and beating heart threw herself upon Edwin, and folded him in her trembling arms, not as a lover but as a sister would embrace a brother." Meanwhile Seyton and Henry "stood silent and trembling witnesses of the scene, almost unconscious of their own individuality" (40). The text gives activist Lowell women's critique of corporate paternalism vivid narrative expression: industrial paternalism is revealed as monstrous, incestuous.[97]

The devastating impact of illicit male power is underscored by the horrific rush of final events: Glendower is poisoned by his jealous housekeeper, Adriana Bertram, and dies before he can repent; Adriana cuts her own throat, becoming "a murderess and a suicide" (40). Elaborating the genealogical confusions and incestuous desires plaguing the factory town, the conclusion draws unmistakable intimacies between factory life and slavery (Adriana's act of poisoning the licentious Glendower evokes well-known slave practices), driving home its argument about the illegitimacy of male corporate power. It is through the sexual(ized) agency of the Lowell mill girl that *Mysteries* publicizes its racialized relations of sex and work, desire and power.

## *Three*. Narrating Female Dependency

THE SENTIMENTAL SEAMSTRESS AND

THE EROTICS OF LABOR REFORM

In Fanny Fern's *Ruth Hall* (1854), the eponymous heroine, an impoverished widow, is cast off by her male relatives after her husband's death and must work as a seamstress to support herself and her two young children. In a scene midway through the novel, Ruth gazes out the window of her boardinghouse at a "large brick tenement" across the street—a "prospect," Fern notes, not designed to inspire "cheerful fancies."[1] In a window scene distinct from the type commonly found in domestic fiction, Ruth observes not the stuff of life—meditated experience to compensate for the deprivations of domestic privacy[2]—but the makings of a cautionary narrative. Although Ruth surveys several poor residents, "emigrants and others," inhabiting the tenement's dingy rooms, the figure that arrests her attention (and commands her sympathy) is a young seamstress, wearily performing her painstaking labor: "There . . . sat a young girl, from dawn till dark, scarcely lifting that pallid face and weary eyes—stitching and thinking, thinking and stitching. God help her!" (90). Underscoring the tragic fatalism of the seamstress's conventional story, Fern makes a point of emphasizing the tenement's proximity to the neighborhood brothel—the unfortunate conclusion, the text implies, of many poor women's tales (91).

*Ruth Hall* both borrowed from and contributed to a growing body of seamstress literature that gained widespread popularity in the 1840s.[3] Highly conventional in characterization and plotting, seamstress literature fashioned an influential but problematic image of antebellum workingwomen. Writers such as Sarah Bagley protested factory women's "feminization," revealing how emerging gender norms undermined workingwomen's efforts at economic democratization; factory women's gendered class critique shaped popular fiction like *The Factory Girl* and *The Mysteries of Lowell*, which create narrative space for registering the complexities of workingwomen's subjectivities, ambition, and agency. Those oppositional class accents are, however, largely suppressed in seamstress fiction. While, as Anne McClintock notes, certain forms of labor were seen to "unsex" women, seamstresses were widely imaged in expressly gendered terms.[4] Although Lowell writers might complain that "[w]omen's weakness, and timidity may be pretty things to sentimentalize upon, but they often prove very inconvenient [and] troublesome realities,"[5] it was just such feminine sentimentalization that was abundantly evident in seamstress literature. A personification of dependency in an era when economic and political dependency was both racialized and gendered, the sentimental seamstress illuminates the way market constraints and disabilities, what Nancy Fraser calls "post-traditional forms of gender subordination" arising from "structural or systemic processes in which the actions of many people are abstractly or impersonally mediated," could converge to produce a cultural "type."[6]

When compared with factory fiction, several things are striking about seamstress stories: first is the singularity of the seamstress figure, the narrative emphasis on a solitary, socially isolated heroine, intensifying the pathos of her story and signaling her independence from the urban milieu. The seamstress is a far cry from the "factory Amazons" described (with equal parts horror and fascination) in the *Pittsburgh Journal*; gone are the collective emphases of factory women's writings and the "excessive" (nondomestic) affectivity with which mill women were associated. These representational differences were, in part, materially shaped; whereas mill women lived and worked side by side in boardinghouses and factories, the typical heroine of seamstress stories performs outwork in the isolation of her home; these working conditions insulated her from the dynamism of urban working-class life. Furthermore, although the emergence of urban out- or piecework was, as fully as mechanized factory labor, a product of the Industrial Revolution, it was also visibly continuous with the (gendered) family economy; mobilizing residual associations of sewing as a female craft, needlework posed less of a challenge to domestic gender norms than did female factory labor. As with domestic service, these associations distanced needlewomen from nineteenth-century conceptions of urban, industrial, and technological change and the progressive temporality of the labor movement.[7] Referencing the female army of laborers, the "mass of cheap human material" that matches the supply of "raw material" in British textile manufacture, Marx observes that the home manufacture of goods, "totally changed [by] modern industry, has long ago reproduced, and even overdone, all of the horrors of the factory system, without participating in any of the elements of social progress it contains."[8]

The distinction between factory women and needlewomen was internal to seamstress literature itself: the protagonists of several narratives (including Charles Burdett's *The Elliott Family*, discussed below) prove their virtue by choosing piecework over factory work, differentiating themselves from the "bad associations" of factory women. Distancing the seamstress from what Jennie Collins depicts as workingwomen's collective "benevolence" and "solidarity," the seamstress's isolation and domestic propriety help make her a "worthy" object of middle-class sympathy. An important figure in the process Stuart Hall terms the "moralization" of the working class during the nineteenth century, the seamstress constituted a "sympathetic" figure for protesting the oppressive conditions of the garment industry—a figure distanced from the laboring collective and threatening practices of labor militancy.[9] Sentimentally rehabilitated, the seamstress also effected a "whitening" of the female worker, rescuing her from industrial "slavery" and (re)situating her within the meliorating fiction of a racialized domesticity.

The racial limits of the seamstress's sentimentalization are evident in *American Slavery as It Is*, where Sarah M. Grimké describes the deplorable plight of one slave seamstress: "A handsome mulatto woman, about 18 or 20 years of age, whose independent spirit could not brook the degradation of slavery," suffered repeated whippings for attempted escapes; consequently, she was

> kept a close prisoner. A heavy iron collar, with three prongs projecting from it, was placed round her neck, and a strong and sound front tooth was extracted, to serve as a mark to describe her, in case of escape. Her sufferings at this time were agonizing; she could lie in no position but on her back, which was sore from scroungings, as I can testify from personal inspection, and her only place of rest was the floor, on a blanket. These outrages were committed in a family where the mistress daily read the scriptures, and assembled her children for family worship. She was ac-

counted, and was really, so far as alms-giving was concerned, a charitable woman, and tender-hearted to the poor; and yet this suffering slave, who was the seamstress of the family was continually in her presence, sitting in her chamber to sew, or engaged in her other household work, with her lacerated and bleeding back, her mutilated mouth, and heavy iron collar without, so far as appeared, exciting any feelings of compassion.

In the same text, Angelina Grimké asserts:

I have known instances where seamstresses were kept in cold entries to work by the stair case lamps for one or two hours, every evening in winter—they could not see without standing up all the time, though the work was often too large and heavy for them to sew upon it in that position without great inconvenience, and yet they were expected to do their work as *well* with their cold fingers, and standing up, as if they had been sitting by a comfortable fire and provided with the necessary light. . . . Seamstresses often sleep in their mistresses' apartments, but with no bedding at all. . . . This is a *great* hardship to [their families]. . . . Every natural and social feeling and affection are violated with indifference; slaves are treated as though they did not possess them.[10]

While in *The Seamstress* the forced (and temporary) separation from her son of the impoverished seamstress Mrs. Gaston generates the narrator's outrage, the familial ties and bodies of slave seamstresses, the Grimkés make clear, are systematically violated. Yet Sarah Grimké avers that the "suffering slave[s]," even among those deemed "charitable" and "tender-hearted to the poor," fail to "excit[e] any feelings of compassion." The shocking contrast between the brutalized, tortured slave seamstresses described by the Grimkés—images conspicuously absent from seamstress fiction—and those examined in this chapter make clear how sentimental constructions of feminine economic "dependency" and their defining erotics (subtended by the family wage) are fundamentally colored by race.

The sentimental seamstress was constructed in three overlapping textual sites: the discourses of poverty, evangelical moral reform, and popular fiction.[11] While most writers in Jacksonian America defended white male economic equality—and had increasing difficulty imagining white men as guiltless victims of capitalism—they regularly depicted white workingwomen as overcome by uncontrollable economic forces. The era's predominant example of the "deserving poor," the sentimental seamstress was a figure whose economic dependency was seen to be dictated by the laws of capital as thoroughly as by the "natural" strictures of femininity.[12] Referred to as "poor helpless females" in the proceedings of the National Trades' Union and denominated "poor and sickly" in the pages of the *Advocate of Moral Reform*, the publishing organ of the New York Female Moral Reform Society, white seamstresses were melodramatically portrayed as beings hemmed in on all sides.[13]

Like the factory girl, the seamstress was the subject of substantial debate about women's roles in the emerging industrial economy. However, unlike mill-workers, seamstresses had few opportunities to engage in acts of literary self-definition: there were no established, prominent venues, such as the *Voice of Industry* or the *Factory Girl's Album*, where needleworkers could articulate their experiences and concerns. No doubt largely because of this, there was surprising homogeneity in depictions of seamstresses: the sentimental seamstress became a conventional type in fiction, poetry, and several discourses of social reform. "Real" seamstresses resisted this literary codification; militant seamstresses—like radical mill women—mobilized languages of radical democracy to repudiate dependency and protest inequities based in gender as well as class.[14] In doing so they could draw on the traditional (indeed mythic) understanding of sewing as female craft and important locus of female creativity and skill; during the Revolution and the War of 1812 women's sewing of garments (like their weaving of homespun) was also a symbol of political independence.[15] While some casti-gated them for impropriety—for example, the *Boston Transcript* characterized a speech by Lavinia Wright, secretary of the United Tailoresses' Society of New York, as containing "clamorous and unfeminine" declarations of woman's rights, which "a wise Providence never destined her to exercise"—labor leaders in the sewing trades, like factory activists, robustly challenged gender strictures: they encouraged female workers to act independently of men, defend their rights, and unmask paternalism as a rationale for discrimination. Sarah Monroe, a leader of the United Tailoresses' Society, urged her sisters, "Let us trust no longer to the generosity of our employers; seeing that they are men in whose heads or hearts the thought of doing justice to a fellow being never seems to enter." She contin-ues, "It needs no small share of courage for us, who have been used to impositions and oppression [since] our youth . . . to come before the public in defense of our rights; but, my friends, if it is unfashionable for the men to bear oppression in silence, why should it not also become unfashionable with the women. Or do they deem us more able to endure hardship than they themselves?"[16] Fashioning an activist identity for female needleworkers and demanding access to new social and economic opportunities, Monroe points to the increasing public presence of workingmen as a model for workingwomen, dismissing as mere "fashion" gender conventions that would stifle female public speech.

Echoing activists like Monroe, some writers linked sewing with a subversive female independence and agency. For example, in her revisionist inscription of the sentimental seamstress and her characteristic garret habitation, Harriet Jacobs's Linda Brent, imprisoned in her grandmother's attic, sews clothing for her children's Christmas presents. Her "loophole of retreat" enables the reappropriation of captive labor to serve her own, not her master's, family and inverts the paternalist myth of slavery by foregrounding the productive and reproductive agency of black female labor and the centrality of needlework to "proletarian womanhood";[17] later, after she joins her daughter in New York, it is Linda, not Ellen's mistress, who supplies the girl with clothing, just as it had been Linda's grandmother who provides her family's food and clothing in the South. This depiction of clothing as bearer of the value of African American labor (and means of economic justice) is highlighted in the story of the abused slave Luke, who steals money from his cruel master by putting it in the pocket of the old man's trousers when he dies (193); he asks for the trousers as a gift—the conventional fate of cast-off clothing and a gesture intended to enact status hierarchies—and gets the cash.

There were various ways female needlework could be scripted. While seamstress narratives centered on the male ready-made or slop trade, female needleworkers were employed in skilled trades such as bookmaking and dressmaking. As Wendy Gamber notes, millinery throughout the nineteenth century was a lucrative trade and a route to female independence. Anglo- and African American women could make careers as dressmakers; the narrative of Elizabeth Keckley, Mary Lincoln's modiste, records one African American woman's success in this endeavor. International developments, covered in the U.S. press, presented other possibilities. In France, with a tradition of militancy among needleworkers and where seamstresses participated actively in the events of 1848, feminists and socialists countered images of victimization by emphasizing needleworkers' productivity and significant contribution to the "wealth of nations." Stressing that "innocence" equates to dangerous ignorance, a French needleworker at a working-class congress in 1859 protested, "A woman who has been sheltered from the social world is completely unaware of the total transformation of commercial relations in our time. . . . It is imperative to bring women into social life so that they can hold their own as producers."[18] In Russian author Nikolai Chernyshevsky's novel *What Is to Be Done?* (1863), the individualized structure of the seamstress tale is repudiated; workers form a seamstress union; in their boardinghouse, as in the sewing shop, duties are shared according to ability. Such writers grasped the centrality of women's labor in the garment trade to the development of global capitalism and identified the making cheap of that labor as a social process, not biological inevitability.

PUNCH, OR THE LONDON CHARIVARI.—JULY 4, 1863.

THE HAUNTED LADY, OR "THE GHOST" IN THE LOOKING-GLASS.

Madame La Modiste. "WE WOULD NOT HAVE DISAPPOINTED YOUR LADYSHIP, AT ANY SACRIFICE, AND THE ROBE IS FINISHED à MERVEILLE."

*Fig 3.1.* John Tenniel, "The Haunted Lady, or 'The Ghost' in the Looking Glass," *Punch,* July 4, 1863. The seamstress haunts the female consumer of the garments she sews; the pale, spectral seamstress is a threatening figure, the bearer of moral retribution as well as class vengeance.

In Anglo American texts the association of sewing work with a threatening agency is conveyed in the trope of the disease-bearing garment (usually tuberculosis or smallpox) featured in fictional narratives such as Charles Kingsley's *Alton Locke.* In Camilla Toulmin's "The Shawl Buyer" (1843), about the moral dilemma of a seamstress who has sold a smallpox-infected shawl to a genteel customer, one needlewoman seethes with class hatred: "Let them sicken, and die. . . . Don't they grind us down to what we are?" Like stories of slave women poisoning their mistresses, such narratives envision expressions of class violence within the gendered relations of "homework."[19] Midcentury visual images gothicize this power: in one classic example the seamstress haunts the female consumer of the garments she sews; the pale, spectral seamstress is a threatening figure, the bearer of moral retribution as well as class vengeance. But most popular narratives insulate the seamstress from threatening agency; seamstress stories portrayed an eroticized image of what was increasingly perceived to be an inherently *feminine* condition of economic dependency and embedded that image within a highly conventional narrative structure. The seamstress was thus typified within literary and political discourse as the sort of emblem of endurance activist needlewomen repudiated; represented as incapable of change, she was textually marked as a primary victim of the "free market" and urban life.[20]

Inscribed in a host of popular fictions, including William English's *Gertrude Howard* (1843), Timothy Shay (T. S.) Arthur's *The Seamstress* (1843), Charles Burdett's *The Elliott Family* (1845), Mary Denison's *Edna Etheril, the Boston Seamstress* (1847), and George Lippard's "Jesus and the Poor" (1848), the sentimental seamstress's characteristic plot was one of relentless, devastating decline, epitomizing how, in the words of one feminist contributor to the *Lily*, "working 'wom[e]n's sphere extends downward instead of upward.'"[21] For example, Arthur describes the seamstress Mrs. Gaston as "struggling with failing and unequal strength against the tide that was slowly bearing her down the stream."[22] The seamstress's diminished economic agency was produced by a confluence of discourses; for example, the conventional downward path of the seamstress borrows some sense of inevitability from the plight of the fallen woman, a figure with which she was regularly linked in reform literature.[23] But the seamstress's economic helplessness was emphatically signaled by her privileged place in the discourse of poverty, evident in Mathew Carey's foundational texts of the 1820s and 1830s and firmly established in works that proliferated during the early 1840s in what amounts to an American version of the English Poor Law debates.[24] A key historical effect of those debates, Mary Poovey demonstrates, was the differentiation of pauperism from poverty: pauperism was increasingly specified as a moral and physical designation, while poverty was considered by many a structural part of the national economy and essential to capitalist production.[25] Through the seamstress pauperism was decisively feminized: her economic vulnerability and need for support were deemed inherent aspects of her moral and physical being, inseparable from her "natural" and irremediable gender dependency.

As depicted by writers from Carey forward, the seamstress was the primary victim of market laws, exemplifying the category Carey designates the "deserving poor." Her prominence partly reflected the centrality of needlework within the charity system: sewing was perfunctory female labor performed in almshouses (and prisons) or by poor women at home and was promoted by the network of Dorcas societies; it was also a skill taught to poor girls in charity schools, where the fruits of that labor were sold for fundraising purposes. (Problematically the minimal prices paid by charity efforts pressured the rates paid all women, while the widespread promotion of sewing skills, by increasing the pool of laborers, further drove down the market value of needlework.)[26] A being "ground down to the earth by [her] employers," the "ill-fated" seamstress is, for Carey, a worthy object of charity: some "from principle . . . refuse assistance to the man who can obtain the means of supplying all his wants by his daily labour. But can they withhold relief from her who comes in her desolation and weakness—woman, who, by the law of her being, IS EXCLUDED FROM PATHS IN WHICH COARSE MAN MAY MAKE A LIVELIHOOD?" Grounding the gender division of labor in "the law of [woman's] being"—natural(ized) strictures of gender, defined as weakness and refinement—Carey ascribes to femininity the seamstress's inevitable economic dependency and claim to public assistance.[27] Even Walter Channing, who theorizes poverty as a "social condition," defines women workers, most notably seamstresses, "under . . . constant pressure of comparatively light work," as most vulnerable to pauperism. Referring to the "amount of time demanded of women who live by daily work, and to the very small compensation they receive for it," Channing writes, "They . . . can do no more than supply the daily returning want, and this only while remaining strength enables them to continue their long, and exhausting toil. When sickness comes, then comes that which to industry is more terrible than all pain. . . . Pauperism is here in the train of contingencies which cannot be controlled, and it often comes in its saddest forms."[28] As the victim of a "train of contingencies" she is helpless to alter, the seamstress becomes the locus of economic determinism, thus distancing a sense of economic helplessness and lack of control from men. Channing suggests how paternalism was being refashioned in these writings in accord with antebellum gender norms; the basis of the seamstress's irresistible claim to support is precisely her femininity, especially her feminine weakness and delicacy—a construction that at once eroticizes dependency and anchors poverty's social claims in the inherent appeal of the appropriately "feminine" woman.[29] Feminizing dependency, writers such as Channing also helped to *privatize* that economic condition, insulating the persistence of poverty and economic inequity from the prospect of systematic or structural economic reform.[30]

NARRATIVIZING FEMININE DEPENDENCY

The seamstress's downward path distinguishes her from the male protagonists of much nineteenth-century urban fiction as well as those memorably enterprising eighteenth-century heroines such as Daniel Defoe's Moll Flanders and Roxana. Defoe's female protagonists exemplify economic ambition: ably navigating the market as independent female entrepreneurs, they readily break contracts (including marriage contracts) when they do not serve their independent interests, easily sacrifice children, envision feminine "virtue" as an inconvenience, rise and fall (repeatedly) in their fortunes, capitalize on economic exigencies by resourcefully turning circumstances to their own account, and, overall, confront the world with optimistic expectations. Thus can Moll Flanders state gamely midway through her tumultuous story, "Though I was a woman without a fortune, I expected something or other might happen in my way that might mend my circumstances, as had been the case before."[31]

Such economic resourcefulness is abundantly evident in nineteenth-century urban literature. In *Signs Taken for Wonders*, Franco Moretti argues that intensified opportunities for mobility—spatial and economic—afforded by the modern city transform the discrete cityscape into a "network of developing social relationships—and hence as a prop to narrative temporality." Because the "meaning of the city . . . [only] manifests itself through a temporal trajectory," the city became the privileged object of narrative; nineteenth-century fiction generated a new rhetoric of temporality, culminating in the "suspense plot of the novel," which captured the dynamic nature of urban experience. For Moretti the unpredictability of urban life—especially its economic and social contingencies—favors the adaptability of urban subjects, their ability to capitalize on what is provisionally available, to translate urban stimuli into "'chances' to be seized":

> City life . . . arms itself against catastrophe by adopting ever more pliant and provisional attitudes. . . . In tragedy everything conspires concertedly in only one direction. In [urban fiction,] . . . the high number of variables inherent to the systems of the city and the novel brings about the conclusion through a continuous and highly unpredictable series of ups and downs. In this way, suspense and surprise encourage city dwellers to believe that only rarely is "everything lost." . . . The novel, and the city dweller's entire "education" do not hinge on the shock image of potential impact—but rather the know-how necessary to avoid it, on competence in "alternative paths" of every kind, and on the ability to latch on immediately to the possibilities that these very often disclose.[32]

Moretti's description of the improvisational facility unleashed and rewarded by the urban context—qualities perhaps most apparent in American literature in the realist fiction of Howells, James, and Dreiser—is a far cry from the character (and usual narrative trajectory) of the sentimental seamstress, whose story follows the contours of tragedy more closely than urban fiction. While Dreiser would later assign his working-class protagonist Carrie Meeber, positioned on the threshold of urban life, essentially two choices—to "become better" or "become worse"—in antebellum seamstress stories the heroine's trajectory is inevitably downward.[33] Not "pliant" and self-transforming but fixed and unwavering, the sentimental seamstress is ascribed a tragic fatalism that borrows from a theological sense of feminine fallenness and determinism, and her characterization suggests that the exemplary urban subject described by Moretti is markedly masculine. Rather than capitalizing on urban opportunities, the seamstress is immobilized by them; hers is a decidedly antimodern, or premodern, sensibility and subjectivity. In an important sense the seamstress's economic ineptitude, her tendency toward self-effacement and passivity rather than self-promotion and entrepreneurial agency, signifies her virtue and especially her *modesty*, called by Addison and Steele "the only Recommendation" in women but "the greatest Obstacle to [men] both in Love and Business."[34] As Ruth Bernard Yeazell observes, "The gendering of modesty . . . follows from the separation of spheres—a division of labor that will increasingly free men for the aggressions of the marketplace by assigning certain 'beautiful' but inconvenient virtues to the safekeeping of women."[35] In seamstress narratives the virtuous seamstress shuns public attention and the competitiveness of market negotiation; her veiled figure characteristically shrinks in a dark corner of the tailor shop. In this way the modest seamstress's economic decline is envisioned as both a sign and a product of her virtue, while she is defined against the typical modern urban subject described by Moretti. Hers is a proto-naturalist narrative: she is the subject of a determinism at once economic and moral/psychological. Wharton's sentimental seamstress Lily Bart, whose delicacy about economic matters, as fully as the unforgiving economic environment she inhabits, ensures her economic victimization, might be seen to embody the culmination of this antebellum narrative tradition.

These gendered associations are engaged with shrewd insight by Fanny Fern, who writes in one newspaper sketch, "There are few people who speak approbatively of a woman who has a smart business talent or capability. No matter how isolated or destitute her condition, the majority would consider it more 'feminine' would she unobtrusively gather up her thimble, and, retiring into some out-of-the-way place, gradually scoop out her coffin with it, than to develop that smart turn for business which would lift her at once out of her troubles, and which, in a man so situated, would be applauded as exceedingly praiseworthy."[36] Importantly for Fern the figure who best embodies the condition of feminine destitution is the seamstress, "unobtrusively" retiring to domestic privacy ("some out-of-the-way place"), who "scoop[s] out her coffin" with her thimble. Implying that this figure is the product of popular prejudice rather than feminine nature, Fern attributes the "majority['s]" appetite for narratives of feminine economic decline rather than success to deeply problematic cultural assumptions about gender. The economic subjectivity of Fern's seamstress is defined by loss and diminishment rather than expansion or growth—a diminishment written on her very body.[37]

As I have suggested, the seamstress's downward path was patterned after that of the fallen woman—an association that served simultaneously to evoke and allay the suspicion of working-class female "immodesty" and active (sexual or economic) desire. Always shadowing seamstress narratives is the possibility of women's active, calculating self-commodification—the kind of female entrepreneurial ambition Fern alludes to, exercised in both the labor and the sexual market. By sentimentalizing the seamstress and emphasizing her dependency, helplessness, and "feminine" submission, crafters of the seamstress image assuaged pressing cultural anxieties about working-class female agency—especially women workers' "immodesty" and the prospect of their sexual-economic independence. Sentimentality is an important tactic in these narratives' reformations of working-class female desire.


THE TRANSATLANTIC CLASS POLITICS OF SYMPATHY

The literary type of the sentimental seamstress, like the factory girl, had a transatlantic genesis. By far the most famous literary production about seamstresses is "The Song of the Shirt" by the English author Thomas Hood, published in *Punch* in 1843.[38] Hood introduces the seamstress, the singer of the "Song," as follows:

> With fingers weary and worn,
> With eyelids heavy and red,
> A Woman sat, in unwomanly rags,
> Plying her needle and thread—
> Stitch! stitch! stitch!
> In poverty, hunger, and dirt,
> And still with a voice of dolorous pitch
> She sang the "Song of the Shirt!" (ll. 1–8)

Using the popular ballad meter but placing the stresses to emphasize the monotony and militaristic rigor of the seamstress's task, Hood relies upon contemporary ideals of womanhood to generate outrage at the unwomanly nature of the seamstress's plight. He depicts the trials of the seamstress's killing labors in the poem's middle stanzas:

Work—work—work!
Till the brain begins to swim;
Work—work—work!
Till the eyes are heavy and dim!
Seam, and gusset, and band,
Band, and gusset, and seam,
Till over the buttons I fall asleep
And sew them on in a dream!
O! Men, with Sisters dear!
O! Men, with Mothers and Wives!
It is not linen you're wearing out!
But human creatures' lives!
Stitch—stitch—stitch
In poverty, hunger, and dirt;
Sewing at once, with a double thread,
A Shroud as well as a Shirt. . . .
Work—work—work!
My labor never flags;
And what are its wages? A bed of straw,
A crust of bread—and rags. (ll. 17–32, 41–51)

Throughout the "Song" the poet emphasizes the searing irony that the seamstress who spends her life sewing garments can afford to dress in nothing better than "unwomanly rags." The diminishment of life that attends this ceaseless drudgery is powerfully conveyed: living in abject poverty, with insufficient food to support her body, the seamstress's very subjectivity is threatened by her work—the monotonous labors even overtake her dreams. By highlighting the suffering worker, Hood reveals the true nature of commodities: fabric as the very stuff of life and the shirt as a shroud. The poem concludes with the plea, "Would that its tone could reach the rich! / She sang this 'Song of the Shirt!'" Reinforcing his message of social paternalism, Hood appeals not to women as consumers but to men: "Oh, Men, with Sisters dear! / Oh, Men, with Mothers and Wives! / It is not linen you're wearing out, / But human creatures' lives!"[39]

Hood's poem spawned a host of literary imitators; it also helped create a "new iconographic vocabulary" of the seamstress in Victorian painting. As T. J. Edelstein notes, painting devoted to "social themes" was a trend that emerged in the late 1830s, and "by far the most popular of . . . social themes in Victorian painting was the seamstress." These works, beginning with Richard Redgrave's *The Sempstress* (exhibited at the Royal Academy in 1844), employ a recurring "symbolic vocabulary" that stresses the seamstress's identity "as a figure exploited by Victorian society." Indebted to Hood, Redgrave established the elements of this visual vocabulary with his compositional choices: the seamstress is solitary; the room is illuminated by a single candle or the dawn light; she is surrounded by a few meager possessions—a spindly plant, a broken bowl, a bed, table, and chair, and an empty fireplace that "acquire meaning by [their] constant repetition" in the era's painting. Traditional artistic associations enriched this imagery. Images of saints in Italian Renaissance paintings—sweet, pious women turning their eyes to heaven—were one such reference: the seamstress, with her pale, illuminated face and upturned gaze, is thus identified as a martyr to modern urban society. Further "the seated female figure recalls not only piety but melancholy, Albrecht Durer's version of this theme being the most important example."[40] The doleful expression of Redgrave's needlewoman alludes to this psychological state; other painters depict her with her head in her hands, the standard visual symbol. Additional compositional elements include a cup of tea (seamstresses were widely shown to need the stimulation of tea to complete their labor); the view of a church steeple or the placement of a clock, referencing the passage of time and ceaseless rhythms of work; medicine bottles, signaling her illness and perhaps imminent death; and often a single flower to mark the contrast between country and city and as a symbol for the seamstress herself. This visual vocabulary shaped and was shaped by literary representations of the seamstress, while melodramatic plays such as Mark Lemon's *The Seamstress* (1844) popularized the type as well. Victorian paintings, plays, and narratives about the seamstress thus fashioned a figure that exemplified and could generate popular sentiment about industrial victimization that resonated on both sides of the Atlantic.

The suffering seamstress was adapted to the American context by a variety of writers, while the visual iconography influenced a host of cultural representations. For example, in Southworth's *The Hidden Hand* (discussed in chapter 5), the seamstress Marah Rocke, frequently seen gazing out the window and lost in dejection, clearly embodies the seamstress's characteristic melancholy and meekness, while Mrs. Gaston in Arthur's *The Seamstress* is characterized through several of the details Edelstein enumerates. Most important in shaping the figure in antebellum America were the writings of middle-class moral reformers, who translated the suffering and poverty of needlewomen depicted by Mathew Carey into a distinctly moral register. Moral reformers gave wide circulation to the seamstress's narrative of decline, while interpreting that downfall in particular ways. Countering the possible moral taint of poverty by crafting the poor seamstress as childlike and "innocent," moral reformers assimilated economic exploitation and victimization to sexual appetites and practices (e.g., male lust and aggression and female "passionlessness") that were increasingly naturalized during this period, while, in circular fashion, locating the remedy for such exploitation in gender itself.

## NEEDLEWORK AND MORAL REFORM:
### THE SEAMSTRESS IN THE *ADVOCATE*

Carey's "A Plea for the Poor" (1832) appeals to philanthropic women to minister to the needs of their struggling sisters; reforming the "horrible oppression" under which seamstresses "groan, cannot be hoped for, unless ladies will come forward with decision, and use their influence to rescue their sex from the prostrate situation in which those unfortunate women are placed."[41] Female moral reformers heard Carey's challenge, and the seamstress was decisively taken up in the literature of moral reform, most influentially by the New York Female Moral Reform Society, founded in 1834 to rehabilitate prostitutes and expose the social effects of the sexual double standard. Through its publishing organ, the *Advocate*, one of the nation's most widely read evangelical papers, the Society circulated countless narratives of seduction and the devastating plight of "fallen" women. Melodramatically splitting villains and victims, these narratives opposed lascivious, sexually aggressive American men and their "innocent and unsuspecting" female victims.[42] One writer captured the *Advocate*'s standard argument, explaining that "the treachery of man" is "one of the principal causes, which furnishes the victims of licentiousness. Few, very few . . . have sought their wretched calling."[43] In particular the Society drew well-publicized connections between women's economic situation—the low wages earned in traditional female occupations by seamstresses, domestics, and washerwomen—and prostitution and was an early critic of New York's garment industry. The *Advocate* absorbed the seamstress's story into its melodramatic sexual script: moral reformers' rhetoric of sexual antagonism—a violent, predatory masculine sexuality subject to reform by virtuous women (especially mothers) versus an innocent, sexually vulnerable femininity—became an important analytic through which poor women's exploitation was interpreted.[44] Notably, moral reformers' rhetorics tended to diminish class differences within gender groups so that poor tailors could appear as economically accountable as wealthy capitalists (indeed often more so) for seamstresses' oppression. Moral reformers' blindness to these matters is evident in the fact that they generally envisioned the greatest sexual dangers in jobs that offered working women the greatest opportunity for financial gain, while envisioning domestic service as the most useful, safest employment for women; indeed they routinely placed prostitutes "rescued" from brothels in Christian homes as servants.[45]

The seamstress exemplified the worst abuses of female labor in a range of moral reformers' writings. Using adjectives such as *poor, sickly, unprotected, hapless,* and *desponding* to characterize needlewomen, writers in the *Advocate* emphasized the "wrongs and oppressions" of garment workers, highlighting their subjection to overwhelming economic forces.[46] An 1836 article titled "Tailoresses and Seamstresses" describes "10,000 females, in this city, dependent upon their needles for their support. . . . [A] valuable, worthy, and indispensable class of the community . . . laboring under a cruel and iron handed oppression . . . [they are] driven by the hand of a merciless oppression into the cellars and garrets of old, worn out, leaky . . . tenements, for which they have to pay an exorbitant rent, and there compelled to toil, from 16–20 hours a day, to gain a bare subsistence."[47] While needleworkers are acknowledged as "indispensable" members of the community, their productivity cannot be leveraged into power: they are passive objects, "driven" and "compelled," by an "iron handed oppression." The connection between sewing and prostitution became a topos of this literature. Assimilating the seamstress's trials to an existing account of female sexual victimization, the *Advocate* declared in 1844, "Especially in cities there are multitudes of the young who . . . are thrown on their own resources and obliged to earn a subsistence . . . or become prey to the tempter. . . . Shame on . . . men who, by oppressing the hireling in her wages, drive the young and unfriended to dens of shame, while they fill their coffers with the avails of unrequited toil."[48] Again the passive construction of the grammar characterizes poor women as compelled by forces beyond their control; prostitution is driven by male desire, defined, alternately, as economic and sexual; men are "tempters" and seducers, and they oppress female "hireling[s]" to increase their profits. The sexual vulnerability of the seamstress and the connection between fallenness and women's wage employment was featured in popular lore; it was a cultural commonplace that young country girls were regularly trapped into prostitution by recruiters who cloaked their intentions with the promise of training and work in millinery and other sewing trades. The *Advocate* reported that many "house[s] of infamy" were connected with millinery establishments, partly to conceal the true character of the houses from the young women and from the public.[49]

Moral reformers emphatically constructed the industrial labor market as a realm of gender struggle. At the same time they assigned key roles to pious, middle-class women in battling male power. As the author of "Tailoresses and Seamstresses" makes clear, the "hand of merciless oppression" can be stayed only by the "protect[ing]" arm of middle-class women. Delineated as privileged objects of sympathy, the suffering seamstress helped legitimate what the *Advocate* called the magnitude of "woman's mission" and the growing sphere of middle-class women's social influence.[50] Gone are the democratic accents of militant needlewomen's rhetoric: the only female agency legible in these accounts is that of the evangelical reformer or rescuer. Crucially the status of sexual fallenness and the seamstress's seemingly inevitable downward path borrow from the same cultural logic. In each case poor women are helpless and abject, and bear the burden of narrative determinism.

## READING SEAMSTRESS NARRATIVES

Antebellum novels about seamstresses regularly reproduce the gendered analytic popularized by moral reformers. Two examples are Arthur's *The Seamstress: A Tale of the Times* and Burdett's *The Elliott Family; or, the Trials of New-York Seamstresses*. Both are recognizably melodramatic, featuring innocent young female workers fallen from economic security by a husband's or father's death and forced into wage labor. Like many workingmen, Arthur emphasizes the restoration of the family and a regenerated patriarchal authority as the basis of social order, while the evangelical Burdett foregrounds middle-class women's philanthropic role and the power of female influence in protesting and reforming illicit male power. In the anonymous serial novella "Stray Leaves from a Seamstress's Journal" (1853–54), published in the feminist journal *Una*, an emphasis on needlewomen's agency and self-determination—their (collective) identity as workers—contests their sentimentalization, challenging their inscription as the "feminine" and feminized poor.

Certain conventional features of seamstress narratives merit attention. As the iconography surrounding Hood's poem suggests, the seamstress frequently takes on the status of a secular saint; the fictional recounting of her sufferings suggests a comparison with saints' lives, especially the hagiography of long-abused female martyrs such as Katherine and Margaret. (In "The Sisterhood of the Green Veil," George Lippard makes explicit this comparison between the economic suffering of needlewomen and the trials of the spiritual ascetic.) Epitomizing what Bruce Dorsey calls the "spiritualization of poverty," this association imbues seamstress narratives with spiritual drama; these narratives make palpable her seemingly endless trials in signs of affliction on her body (the characteristic stoop, the body diminished by perpetual hunger, etc.), which themselves evidence her unremitting virtue and spiritual/psychological constancy. The seamstress, as Burdett notes, clings to virtue (*The Elliott Family*, 160–61)—that is, clings to chastity and the "feminine" virtues of modesty, piety, meekness; her heroism is that, refusing to adapt to urban contingencies, she exhibits the psychological attributes of domestic womanhood in the marketplace—a performance that is severely disabling and aligns her with the logic of self-sacrifice.

That martyrdom is also evident in Arthur's pamphlet novel, a melodramatic rendition of the plight of seamstresses and their vulnerability to male capital in the eroticized terms supplied by moral reformers.[51] Foregrounding gender, the narrative makes tailors the primary villains—though, as historians note, with the rise of the ready-made trade, male apprentices experienced tremendous degradation of labor and wages while even master tailors and proprietors were under great pressure to cut expenses to survive.[52] Although one master states, "We had better put the screws on to our . . . journeymen at once" (*The Seamstress*, 27), no such characters are portrayed in *The Seamstress*. Arthur deploys the language of class drawn from radical workingmen's and -women's discourses; he assails monopoly and excessive competition, twinned subjects in antebellum labor discourses; and in protesting seamstress's wages he draws upon the traditional plebian rhetoric of just price (26). In addition the text uses the language of dreaming (e.g., 37, 48) to figure social fantasies and forms of wish fulfillment coded in its inscriptions of narrative desire. But Arthur overwhelms the text's oppositional class accents by representing the abuses of capitalism through the trope of gender: gender supplants class as the axis of analysis, and a reformed (domestic) paternalism is envisioned as the solution to the problem of female labor.

*The Seamstress* interweaves two different narratives, each featuring an economically distressed woman driven to needlework. Both women's stories figure urban anonymity, interpreted as dangerous to women, through tropes of disguised or mistaken identity, and in both the restoration of identity and financial security is effected melodramatically through the salvific medium of familial recognition. In Arthur's text the seamstress's characteristic plot of decline is particularly attached to the widow Mrs. Gaston, partly because the narrative details the daily grind of her existence and her ceaseless efforts to support herself and her three small children. Mrs. Gaston is characterized in motifs popularized by Hood's poem: friendless and alone in Boston, living with her children in a sparsely furnished tenement, she is emotionally depleted and physically exhausted by her endless labors. She sews by candlelight through the night to complete her daily quota of coarse shirts and jackets, while attending to her sick and undernourished children. When she visits the tailor's shop to request her pay or seek additional work, "half frightened" and speaking "in a deprecating tone" (9, 5), she is rudely treated or ignored; "meek," "submissive," and "despond[ent]" (5, 7), she is clearly positioned as a suppliant, the scene of labor partly scripted as a charity exchange. Her downward plot is temporarily stayed by the kind interventions of the benevolent Dr. R— and is ultimately halted by her reunion with an attractive young woman, a kind of surrogate daughter, whom she and her husband had helped raise. That young woman, Eugenia Ballantine, is her narrative counterpart, known through most of the text as the seamstress Lizzy Glenn. Lizzy's poverty is repeatedly figured as sexual endangerment; here, as in the rhetoric of moral reformers, the seamstress's story of economic decline and helplessness is explicitly sexualized. Witnessing an attempted assault on Lizzy—when she is evidently "misrecognized" as a streetwalker—a former acquaintance tellingly muses, "Can it be that she is some one we have known, who has fallen so low?" (16).

The opposition of predatory (male) villain and innocent, "unprotected" (female) victim is evident in the opening scene, where Lizzy, seeking work in a Boston clothing store, is sexually harassed by a "rough-looking" male attendant behind the counter while the shop's owner, Mr. Berlaps, is occupied at his desk. Arthur melodramatically delineates his characters' moral qualities in a rapid sketch: the young woman is imploring, feeling, and dependent, the men cold and impervious, quick to turn her evident desperation to their economic and sexual advantage. Though the "trembling" young woman speaks in a "timid" but "earnest" voice, both men treat her with contempt: the owner responds in a voice at once "gruff" and "sneering," while the clerk Michael meets Lizzy's imploring look with a "rude, and too familiar gaze" (*The Seamstress*, 3–4). The narrator glosses the scene: "The appearance of this young applicant for work, would have appealed instantly to the sympathies of any one but a regular slop-shop man, who looked only to his own profits, and cared not a fig whose heart-drops cemented the stones of his building" (4).

In mapping this space Arthur explicitly pairs paternalist failure and the unshielded condition of (feminine) dependents. While the owner's disinterest in her situation (and inadequate supervision of his clerk) is ultimately, Arthur suggests, responsible for what transpires, what truly threatens is the suspension of heterosocial rules of politeness in commercial spaces, and the bold familiarity of the subordinate male. While Lowell workingwomen had envisioned different strategies for responding to the mundane reality of harassment and the sexual "familiarity" of dandies and clerks (strategies that might include the unladylike speech of a Bagley or the playful subversiveness of the coquettish young shopper in the *Factory Girl's Album*), Arthur accents the seamstress's wounded delicacy: confronted by Michael, the traditionally misogynist "bachelor libertin[e]" of journeymen's culture, the seamstress is utterly defenseless.[53] Although this is a scene of labor exchange, there is no negotiation or even inquiry into wages;

there is only feminine subordination, submission, and silence. The fear of the "dangerous independence" of urban outworkers—that they labored outside the social controls of the village and the discipline of the factory—is entirely absent.[54] Arthur does briefly acknowledge some of the ways pieceworkers might profit from the freedom of urban anonymity and its destabilization of identities. Michael, demanding to know Lizzy's name and place of residence, complains, "I've been tricked in my time out of more than a little by your newcomers" (*The Seamstress*, 3), and he references needleworkers' "grab game," in which outworkers, instead of sewing the garments, exchange the cloth for money in a pawnshop, telling Lizzy, "I'm not sure that you'll ever bring it back again" (5, 3). However, the text contains such oppositional class accents by foregrounding the seamstress's "feminine" dependency and helplessness. Activist Lowell women understood that delicacy could disable women in the labor market, inhibiting them from advocating for their interests or standing up to abusive or unscrupulous employers. While activist mill women endeavored to write different rules for heterosocial commerce based on mutual equality, Arthur domesticates the seamstress, envisioning the labor market in needlework as, properly, an extension of the (middle-class) home, governed by a paternalist masculinity and a chivalric, respectful deference to women.

Following Lizzy Glenn's introduction and departure, the scene unfolds with the arrival of a "middle-aged woman . . . with a large bundle" (*The Seamstress*, 5). Mrs. Gaston brings six pairs of pants for payment; when Berlaps reminds her that he expected seven, Mrs. Gaston replies with "submissive" demeanor and in a "deprecating tone" that nursing a sick child has slowed her labors: "I wanted some money [so] I have brought them in" (5). Like Lizzy, she is clearly cast as a supplicant, but her pathetic story elicits not sympathy but a heartless rebuke. "Confound the children! . . . They're always getting sick, or something else," Berlaps complains and roughly examines the garments: "Botched to death! I can't give you work unless it is done better. . . . It is always a sick child, or some other excuse" (5). (Michael later complains that Mrs. Gaston's jackets are "murdered outright, and ought to be hung up with a basin under them to catch the blood" (18)—a gothic reminder of what Olive Schreiner would call the needle dipped "deep in the blood" of the seamstress and the uncanny haunting of the oppressed laborer featured in seamstress iconography, though here trivialized in a shop man's joke.)[55] Mrs. Gaston waits for her week's wages a full five minutes, hands deferentially "folded across each other," until Berlaps dismisses her by saying, "I never pay until the whole job is done" (5). Thoroughly dispirited by Berlaps's "angry response," Mrs. Gaston, slowly exiting the shop, "lingered along, evidently undecided how to act, for several minutes" (5).

Though, like many sentimental authors, Arthur shows that market logic dehumanizes, he maintains a gender division of sympathy in the marketplace. He appeals to the maternal sympathies central to the writings of moral reformers; arguably acknowledging the working-class female community, described by Stansell, in which tenement neighborhoods constituted "a female form of association and mutual aid,"[56] he also gestures toward the working-class female solidarity described by Jennie Collins, though he negates its power. After leaving Berlaps's establishment, Mrs. Gaston enters a small grocery run by a female proprietor, allegorically named Mrs. Grubb. Again in a "supplicating voice," Mrs. Gaston asks Mrs. Grubb to extend her credit, though she has promised for weeks to pay the dollar she owes. Mrs. Gaston delivers her "urgent petition" for "a few potatoes and some salt fish," explaining that Mr. Berlaps has refused payment and that her children "have had nothing to eat since yesterday" (*The Seamstress*, 6). Mrs. Grubb had "a woman's heart, where lingered a few maternal sympathies. These were quick to prompt her to duty" (6); she weighs out the items and silently hands them to Mrs. Gaston. After Mrs. Gaston leaves the shop, Mrs. Grubb protests the inequities of the system in a voice imbued with moral authority:

> It's too bad! There's that Berlaps, who grinds the poor seamstresses who work for him to death, and makes them one half of their time beggars at our stores for something for their children to eat. He is building two houses in Roxbury at this very moment; and out of what—out of the money of which he has robbed these poor women. Fifteen cents for a pair of trowsers with pockets in them! Ten cents for shirts and drawers . . . ! Is there any wonder they are starving, and he growing rich? Curse him, and all like him!—I could see them hung! (6)

"Curs[ing]" the capitalists, Mrs. Grubb speaks in the authoritative voice of the moral economy. Her menacing speech enacts violence verbally while threatening bodily harm; specifying hanging, it evokes the anti-aristocratic lynchings of the French Revolution and the anti-aristocratic burnings in effigy of the antebellum mob. But Arthur invokes these rebellious energies to contain them. Unlike the French seamstresses who threatened violent revolt, she does not share these feelings with others (e.g., Mrs. Gaston); her wishes are confined to the page and culminate only in frustration: "The woman set her teeth, and clenched her fist in momentary, but impotent rage" (6).

Feminine sympathy, and the efforts of women like Mrs. Grubb, who "have a little feeling left," possess little social efficacy in Arthur's text. As her daughter's illness worsens and requires more attention, Mrs. Gaston's work proceeds more slowly, so that she can barely feed her family. She is paid less and less, exemplifying Marx's analysis of the highly competitive garment industry in the industrial age, when increased profits came not from technical improvement but from driving down labor costs. Although Adam Smith had argued that in a free market, wages would not drop below the rate needed to secure labor's reproduction, that law does not hold true for seamstresses: in Arthur's text wages are seemingly driven lower and lower without resistance. This is in part, Arthur suggests, because of the existence of an endless supply of needleworkers, a labor pool artificially maintained because the constraints of gender keep women out of other employment. However, in *The Seamstress* the downward pull of seamstresses' wages seems more directly attributable to an essentialized feminine weakness. "Poor, heart-oppressed" Mrs. Gaston exhibits a terrible self-consciousness of the inevitability of her downward path, resulting in a kind of psychological immobility: the "poor, heart-crushed" seamstress develops "a state of almost complete paralization of mind" (18, 17). The sense of impending doom is driven home in the illness, diagnosed as scarlet fever, of the young Ella; each symptom "indicated a speedy, fatal termination" (14).

It is the timely intervention and sympathetic interest of Dr. R— that reverses Mrs. Gaston's fortunes, facilitating Arthur's narrative solution of a refashioned paternalism as the corrective to female (economic and sexual) "fallenness." The narrative appearance of Dr. R— allows Arthur to masculinize moral reformers' gendered class strategy of the home visit; a "standard practice" between 1830 and 1860, the home visit allowed reformers to scrutinize poor residents' needs as well as "habits and dispositions."[57] Perceiving Mrs. Gaston's poverty and feminine virtue, Dr. R— appeals to a "few benevolent friends" for money to bury Ella and provide some relief for Mrs. Gaston (*The Seamstress*, 15). A sympathetic male observer, Dr. R— performs a corrective to the unsympathetic gaze of the exploitative shop men. Learning that Mrs. Gaston is paid only seven cents to sew shirts ("Shameful!" [20]), he wishes to help and advises her to put out her ten-year-old son, Harry, "to a trade" (20). (Mrs. Gaston here affirms her domestic "virtue": she has thus far refused—unlike most working-class mothers—to permit her children to work.) Though the thought of her "fair-haired, sweet-faced, delicate boy" as a laborer "made her sick" (10–11), she relents: "It is a hard fate. But I feel that I have only one way before me—that of submission" (20–21). Both mother and son must learn this lesson of "submission" to a stern "necessity"; in their characters Arthur remedies the economic vulnerability of the weak through recuperation of a sympathetic, benevolent paternal power.

The subplot of Henry's apprenticeship allows Arthur to further portray the degraded patriarchal system of the family economy under pressure of wage labor while exploring the links between women and children as similarly "dependent" beings. Mrs. Gaston's concern that her son will be "but considered as a servant" is entirely justified: David Roediger writes, "The . . . status of apprentices was sometimes little distinguishable from indenture by the 1840s and was . . . increasingly an Irish preserve."[58] The story of Henry's apprenticeship, scripted as a slave narrative in which he is literally and figuratively "blackened," enacts the racial instability of working-class subjects I addressed in the introduction. Arthur depicts a great change in Harry's appearance such as "would have made him unfamiliar even to his mother's eye": his clothes are encrusted with "dirt and grease," and "his skin was begrimed until it was many shades darker"; his shoes "were so far gone that his stockings protruded in several places," so that his feet become frostbitten (*The Seamstress*, 29–31). Harry's condition gradually worsens until his narrative threatens to resemble the seamstress's downward trajectory: "every day, the sense of weakness that so often oppressed him, became more paralyzing to his feelings," so that "he felt weaker and more helpless than ever" (35). Crucially a chance encounter with Dr. R— secures Harry some new shoes and eventually returns him to his mother's care. The narrative's very discomfort with Henry's (temporary) "servitude," embodied as servility (a "cowed look, and a shrinking gait," making him "repulsive" and insulating him from even "a particle of sympathy"), and Arthur's insistence on restoring him to his proper demeanor of "innocent confidence" (29) underscore the narrative's stake in gender: the "deformity" (47) of (white) masculine dependency throws into relief the very normativity of (white) feminine dependency.

*The Seamstress* effects the melodramatic restoration of social identities in a rapid sequence of concluding scenes. After spying Lizzy Glenn in Berlaps's shop, Mrs. Gaston visits her boardinghouse. She learns that Lizzy is actually Eugenia, in Boston caring for her invalid father in the hope that he will regain his memory and become capable of reclaiming his fortune. Eugenia's recognition by Mrs. Gaston, who had been a "mother" to the girl years earlier, initiates the narrative structure through which social identities are recuperated and urban anonymity gives way to a revitalized kinship. Reunited with Eugenia (whom she had believed dead at sea), Mrs. Gaston proposes that the pair, who had lived together years before, combine their earnings and form a household in Boston (37).[59]

Eugenia tells Mrs. Gaston her tale, a complicated story of a disastrous voyage involving a fire, two shipwrecks, and life as castaways on a desert island for eighteen months, experiences that nearly killed her and transformed her father into a "white headed, imbecile old man" (*The Seamstress*, 41). Eugenia herself is much altered "from suffering and privation," and her "countenance [is] marred" (42). Consequently their former New Orleans associates, having long believed the Ballantines dead, view the pair as imposters. Unrecognized, impoverished, and in despair, Eugenia makes no effort to contact her former lover, Mr. Perkins. Taking an "assumed name" (42), she moves to Boston, places her father in an asylum, and determines to live by her needle. As she tells Mrs. Gaston in a statement that underscores Arthur's faith in paternalist responsibility and prerogative, "I turned all my thoughts toward the restoration of my father to mental health, believing that . . . he, as a man, could re-assume his own place and his true position" (42).

The narrative concludes with the restoration of kinship through paternal intervention. Harry, rescued by the good doctor from the clutches of Mrs. Sharp, is restored to his family; Mr. Ballantine regains his reason and endeavors "to prove his identity and claim his property" (48). Perkins and Eugenia are reunited and marry, and Mrs. Gaston and her children take their place as part of the household. The narrative concludes with a final tableau in which the father embraces both Eugenia and Perkins, and the patriarchal family is melodramatically recuperated: "My dear children! The long night has at last broken, and the blessed sun has thrown his first bright beams upon us" (*The Seamstress*, 48).

### *THE ELLIOTT FAMILY* AND THE RHETORIC OF MORAL REFORM

In Burdett's *The Elliott Family* the evangelical imaginary of needlework is acutely evident: the novel presents the promotion of "public sympathy" as the special responsibility of middle-class women.[60] In his preface Burdett asserts that his task "properly belong[s] to the female writers" and explains that he initially approached it "with diffidence, for I felt that it was out of my proper sphere" (v). Bringing the "wrongs and oppressions" of seamstresses "before the public," Burdett hopes that "the condition of some thousands of female operatives in this city may be ameliorated . . . if public sympathy is excited in their behalf," inciting "the ladies of New York" to "step forward, with their usual promptness and energy" (vi–vii). A far darker text than Arthur's, Burdett's novel is contradictory in its portrayal of female sympathy. While featuring the benevolent action of a female moral reformer, Burdett depicts female sympathy as an inadequate social remedy; the moral reformer fails to "ameliorate" the plight of the text's suffering seamstresses, all three of whom are dead by the novel's end. It is as if the seamstresses' helplessness overwhelms both author and text, unsettling the very prospect of sympathetic reform.

The novel opens with the death of Mr. Elliott, immediately linking paternal loss and female misery: "Mrs. Elliott was a widow; Clara and Laura Elliott were fatherless; and oh! how much do those two words reveal of misery, of agony, of wretchedness!" (*The Elliott Family*, 10–11). The scene sets the tone of the novel as a whole; the repeated deathbed scenes mark and measure the unrelenting decline of the Elliott family. Burdett's narrative is pointedly set among the "respectable" working classes: an "industrious, . . . temperate" tailor, Mr. Elliott "married, almost as soon as he was out of his [apprenticeship]," and trained his daughters to work in the sewing trades: "Clara had learned the trade of a dressmaker, and Laura had . . . often worked at tailors' work for her father" (15). Though Mr. Elliott prospers sufficiently to invest in a home, upon his death his wife is forced to sell it. Accustomed to the practices of the family economy, the three women believe that "with their needles, they could earn a comfortable subsistence" (15). However, they are soon disabused of this belief as they become acquainted with the exploitative practices of the needle trades.

In the second chapter Burdett introduces the wealthy Simmons family, principal agents of those exploitative practices. The Simmonses employ the Elliott women to sew for them, and the narrative repeatedly contrasts the two families in order to connect rich and poor and expose the injustice of the class divide. Like Arthur, Burdett suggests that the promotion of knowledge among the wealthy, publicizing the exploitation and suffering of female workers, is the key to social reform. But Burdett complicates the psychology of exploitation: the problem is not only the segregation of rich and poor endemic to modern urban arrangements or producers' utilitarian faith in the benign calculus of market laws; it is also psychological repression—the willful forgetting of the past—that routinely attends the experience of social mobility in America and is structured into the American dream. Mr. Simmons was an orphan of obscure background who started out "as an errand boy in a lawyer's office"; after losing a promising position because of "displeasing" conduct, he "wander[s]" homeless "for several weeks, almost in a state of starvation," before being "picked up by a poor but charitable tailor, who taught him his trade" (*The Elliott Family*, 20). His future wife, Ellen (the daughter of a shoemaker and fruit vendor), begins her life as a seamstress. After they marry "Simmons opened a [tailor] shop for himself" and eventually enters "the wholesale clothing business," while his wife, "whose parents by this time had died, having cut all her old associates, had set up for a fine lady," teaching her daughters "the necessity of forgetting . . . by-gone times, and treating with contempt" those "poorer than themselves" (21–22). Here the psychological injuries of class result not in sympathy but sadism; disavowal of their own economic deprivation and social marginalization drives the Simmonses' treatment of the Elliott women. The "original owner" of the Elliott home, Simmons repurchases it, never considering "the widow and her orphan daughters ... reduced from comparative comfort to a bare subsistence, through his instrumentality" (23). Laura is employed as a dressmaker for the Simmons daughters while Clara works for his ready-made shop. It is the contemptuous, socially aspiring Ellen Simmons and her selfish daughters who come under the most severe authorial criticism (and are the object of its most pointed satire) for this class "forgetting." (It is especially noteworthy that Ellen was once herself a "pretty seamstress" [21].) Wealthy women are especially indicted for the absence of social sympathy: working to construct a sympathetic understanding between female consumers and workers, Burdett repeatedly ties the narcissism and "love of display" of fashionable women to their insensibility to the situation of those who labor to make their garments (41). While Laura owns, "I did expect more sympathy from our own sex" (38), the narrator demonstrates that wealthy women all too often subordinate sympathy for female laborers to consumer desire for attractive possessions.

Foregrounding the "female trade" of millinery—Clara is a dressmaker—serves Burdett's emphasis on the special moral responsibility of middle-class women in reforming the garment trade. Arthur's focus on the male ready-made trade enabled him to highlight the male-female axis of exploitation: women are employed by men to make garments men wear; part of the sexual impropriety of the trade, Arthur implies, is that it directs wifely labors (preparing intimate garments such as pants and shirts) to men outside the family. Burdett foregrounds women's role as both employers and consumers; he raises the possibility of consumer activism to expand the prospects of reform. In another crossover between abolition and "free" labor reform, Burdett draws upon the ideas and rhetorical strategies of the abolitionist "free produce movement," which emphasized the moral responsibility of the consumer for the abomination of slavery; in the words of one adherent, the plantation owner, overseer, and slave trader are "so many AGENTS, employed by and for the CONSUMER in extracting and transferring the products of the unrequited toil, of the poor down trodden suffering slave." Like creators of gothic seamstress images, free producers overlaid, through metonymy, seemingly neutral slave-made products with graphic images of suffering, thus "giv[ing] consumers the tools to take the imaginative leap, to ... defetishize commodities through visualization."[61] Burdett experimented with different narrative strategies for defetishizing commodities and forging affective links between producers and consumers; for example, he wrote a commodity "life history" in the autobiographical voice of a straw hat, *Chances and Changes; or Life as It Is. Illustrated in the History of a Straw Hat* (1845), in which the hat, ensconced in a comfortable residence in New York, recollects the sufferings of French hat trimmers and the death by suicide of the Frenchwoman who made him—a narrative act that, for one thing, extends the class hopelessness and abjection of the American seamstress to French millinery workers.[62]

Burdett further expands the scope of his critique by contextualizing the Elliott women's story in the general plight of antebellum needlewomen. Depicting Clara as a dressmaker and then an employee in Simmons's shop and Laura as a seamstress who sews shirts at home, Burdett represents the range of sewing women's experiences under industrialization, documenting the exploitative practices in factory work, dressmaking, and piecework. The women outworkers are universally miserable; the women who wait in Simmons's warehouse have "pale and anxious countenances" and project "a general appearance of melancholy" (*The Elliott Family*, 36). Like Mrs. Gaston, Laura gives way to feelings of despondency: "I see nothing but a life of gloomy wretchedness. . . . Here we must remain—ever confined—ever at work—denied all social intercourse—forbidden even the necessary enjoyment and relaxation of exercise—shut out from the world, with nothing to look for in the future but a life of dreary toil, or a death in the Alms-House" (49). Articulating the heart of Arthur's reformist vision in *The Seamstress*, Laura voices an evangelical faith in the power of print to transform social feeling: "I wonder . . . if the employers know how hard we *do* work? I almost feel that if they did, they would do something for us" (*The Elliott Family*, 49).

Laura's sister Clara, at least initially after her father's death, expresses the self-confidence, optimism in her "favorable prospects," and even flashes of the militancy that we saw in factory girls' writings. Working as a private dressmaker for the Simmons women, Clara rebels against the ceaseless work, poor wages, and her employers' "haughtiness and heartlessness" and frequent reluctance to pay (*The Elliott Family*, 51). Echoing the voices of militant seamstresses, she sarcastically rails against Mr. Simmons's hypocritical assurance that he pays seamstresses well, and voices the threat of (moral) retribution: "I wonder what his daughters would say, if they should ever come down to making shirts at ten cents, pantaloons at two shillings and sixpence, and vests at the same exorbitant price? Such a thing may happen" (51). Seamstresses, Clara complains, are "compelled to subsist" on a mere two or three shillings a day, a "miserable pittance," while performing "the most unceasing drudgery" (52). Like her sister, Clara believes that current practices are facilitated by employers' ignorance and their social distance from their workers, but she also holds seamstresses themselves accountable, because they "do not complain" (52–53). Challenging seamstresses' passivity, Clara initially asserts that workingwomen's public voice is the remedy for the invisible suffering of female labor. However, her faith in the seamstress's social efficacy and public voice—and in her economic prospects—quickly fades; in Burdett's hands milliners are driven into poverty by the same forces that grind down needleworkers in the ready-made trade. In a few short weeks Clara has failed as a dressmaker and is driven into the slop trade.

The collective plight of needlewomen is further suggested in the interpolated tale of the Elliotts' neighbor Louisa Edwards, whose testimonial is a cautionary narrative and a means for Burdett to publicize the "impositions practiced on" needlewomen by unscrupulous employers (*The Elliott Family*, 56). She is a cap maker, a "branch of [female] manufacture extensively carried on in this city" (vii). Louisa tells the Elliotts that hers "is an every-day story," not an exceptional one (55). Orphaned at fourteen, she has experienced the range of shop owners' "shameful deceptions" (66): some promise to train prospective workers in trades such as cap making and then turn them away when their unpaid training period ends; others give out piecework and then complain of the quality of the sewing to escape payment (57–64); one particularly reprehensible individual closes and moves his shop when payday arrives (65–66). Like Clara, Louisa represents the absence of Christian sympathy as the ground of employers' unscrupulous practices. She blames the heartlessness of wealthy women: "lady employers" through their "very heedlessness . . . will find a hundred modes of putting" workingwomen off (75, 83). Some even convert charity into exploitation; Louisa relates the story of one poor seamstress "asked to make up for nothing, some garments for the poor," which the rich employer had agreed to prepare for "some charitable society" (72). Although her stories point to the collective plight of needlewomen, Louisa herself insists upon her virtuous singularity; while she has witnessed gross frauds against seamstresses, she does not publicize them, and she refuses to work in a shop to relieve the "cheerless . . . monotony" of her labors, averring, "I would rather work [at home] alone, than . . . work among thirty or forty girls, whom one knows not, and perhaps [should not] know" (70).

Reiterating the "black despair" Louisa voices (*The Elliott Family*, 70), the Elliott women's stories replicate the narrative structure of the seamstress's inevitable decline, the stereotype of seamstresses as helpless victims. The first to fall is Mrs. Elliott: while sitting at her work by the window, she suddenly "uttered a deep groan, and fell from her chair to the floor, in a state of insensibility" (88). The consulting physician confirms that she has suffered a "paralytic stroke" (89) and will not recover. The girls are bereft; unable to work during the four weeks of their mother's illness, they are forced to sell their few remaining personal articles at a pawnbroker's. Their absence from their jobs subjects them to "cruel suspicions" ("the poor are almost always objects of" such sentiments [93]) rather than sympathy; one sister, Laura, is blackballed by her employer.

At this point Eva Bellamy, a young "warm-hearted philanthropist, and . . . a member of the Christian church" (*The Elliott Family*, 96), enters the text, embodying the prospect of reform. Eva's "heart was filled with tender sympathy for the sufferings and oppression of her sex, and although her own means were comparatively limited, she found and embraced more opportunities of doing good . . . than thousands" with greater "pecuniary ability" (96). Observing Laura's difficulties in the shop, Eva advises her and promises to "endeavor to procure work" for the girl (101). Called by Laura an "angel" (99), Eva is also an agent of publication, reiterating the Elliott women's narratives of suffering and petitions for help: "With the most persevering energy, [Eva] went about among her friends, narrating the sad circumstances in which they were placed, and receiving . . . such contributions as enabled her to pay their board weekly" (129). However, Eva can do little more than forestall the inevitable. In debt for back rent because of their mother's illness, Laura and Clara are "turn[ed] . . . out of doors" by their "brutal landlord" (106). "Utterly ignorant" of their legal rights (107), the girls submit to the confiscation of their furniture and prepare to leave their apartment. It is once again a woman—in this case, Mrs. Stewart, who takes over their rooms—who intervenes, inviting the homeless sisters to stay with her.

Representing the sympathetic (female) reformer, Eva is also an instrument of class discipline. For example, while Clara initially expresses faith in the (collective) agency of needleworkers, voicing hope in her "prospects" (*The Elliott Family*, 26) and "joyful anticipations of the future" (40), Eva's intervention "spiritualizes" the narrative trajectory: Clara must learn not self-trust and self-confidence but "hope, trust and confidence . . . placed in, the Great Disposer of events" (41); the prospect of "advancing" equates to "ascend[ing] to God" (154, 135). Eva is initially moved by Clara's plight when she sees her reject the sexual advances of the clerk in Simmons's shop; it is Clara's sexual "innocence" and virtue (subscription to middle-class sexual norms) that elicits Eva's sympathy. Later, when Clara, turned away without explanation by Simmons because she had requested prompt payment of her wages (85–86), declares, "I have a mind to be independent for once, and give Mr. Simmons a little of my mind," Eva tells her that such an action would be "in very bad taste" (100). With Eva we see the disciplinary efficacy of middle-class women's sympathy—its delimitation to the "worthy poor" and its power to *make* needlewomen dependent.[63] For Clara faith in the reforming agency of middle-class sympathy entails submission to (working-class female) powerlessness; she tells her sister, "If the wealthy only knew one half the sufferings of those who toil to make them rich, and had any hearts, do you suppose they could not amend our condition? *They are the only ones who can do it*" (52, emphasis added).

Throughout his text Burdett continues to contrast the Simmonses and the Elliotts, to juxtapose rich and poor. Mr. Simmons loses his fortune, and, making their class humiliation complete, he and his family are turned out of doors while vacationing at a hot springs. Simmons's daughters immediately turn against one another. This divisiveness is the direct result of the repression of class sympathy: "among the earliest lessons impressed upon their minds," Burdett pointedly reminds us, "was a perfect and unmitigated contempt for poverty" (*The Elliott Family*, 120). The Simmons family story drives home Burdett's didactic message, that the heartless practices of shop owners generate misery for rich and poor alike.

Following her mother's death, Laura's narrative continues the tale of the Elliott women's decline. Stricken with illness, Laura is confined to her bed for four weeks; "day by day Clara and Eva watched her fading into her early grave, their hearts aching with grief, as they felt they could do nothing for her" (*The Elliott Family*, 129). After Laura's death, Clara's tenement burns to the ground and "all trace of her was lost" to Eva (130); the reader follows Clara as she is forced to work for lower and lower wages and her body wears out from the strain, growing so weak she must sew propped up in bed (133). Finally, unable to find any work, she is reduced to begging from door to door "to keep . . . from starvation"; the overcrowded almshouse cannot provide the "smallest relief" (150). The narrative concludes with Eva visiting Clara on her deathbed (159).

The text's final passages return us to the melodramatic idiom of male predation and female victimization, explicitly interweaving the languages of fallenness and economic decline. While women such as the Elliotts and Louisa Edwards cling to "principles of virtue, religion, and morality" through "all their trials," other workingwomen, "see[ing] only a life of toil, suffering, oppression, cruelty and wrong . . . and preferring even a death of shame when it shall come, to such a life, throw themselves into the vortex" (*The Elliott Family*, 160–61). In Burdett's novel descent into the vortex seems to be needlewomen's inescapable fate; narratives of decline proliferate, and plots of sexual victimization and economic exploitation converge in what seems a deterministic inevitability.

### DESENTIMENTALIZING THE SEAMSTRESS

Both the feminization of dependency embodied by the sentimental seamstress and the authority of middle-class reformers to define that figure were challenged in a remarkable literary revision of the seamstress image, the anonymous "Stray Leaves from a Seamstress."[64] Written in first person, "Stray Leaves" presents the seamstress not as a suffering object but as a resisting subject and contests female economic dependency: the narrator, Lucy Vernon, at the outset vows "never to be dependent on those who would make me feel they grudged me my bread." "Stray Leaves" starts as a familiar narrative of downward mobility: Lucy's father has suddenly died, making her the primary breadwinner for her invalid mother and two young sisters. She asks, "How is it, that with all my toil, we grow every day poorer?" While at one point Lucy fears that her life will "waste away in gloomy loneliness," "Stray Leaves" rewrites the seamstress's characteristic destiny, recounting Lucy's ability to triumph over her circumstances: the story ends with Lucy an independent and contented "old maid" possessing "a small competence, the fruit of [her] own industry," with which she has "purchased a little cottage" in the country."[65] To "gain independence and conquer 'circumstance, that unspiritual God,'" she resists feelings of "tender dependence" toward her former beloved, a Dr. L, and stoically dedicates herself to her "duty." Possessing a "fierce pride and unbending spirit," she declares her resolution at the outset: "I am strong, full of life and vigor. . . . I must not make my own theories a failure, for I have said that woman was equal to any emergency, that she had worlds of latent strength to be developed at the right time." While activist workingwomen were often pejoratively depicted as de-sexed and unfeminine, Lucy proudly embraces what society would deem her masculine traits, stating, "God . . . planted in my very soul all the desperate earnestness of man, with the unchanging, patient constancy . . . of a woman."[66]

That "desperate earnestness" is strikingly manifest in the text; using the format of a journal, "Stray Leaves" presents with surprising intensity and force a bold and independent working-class feminist voice. (Indeed, in its confessional intensity and its record of psychological conflict it is surprisingly modern, closer to *Notes from the Underground* than nineteenth-century women's fiction or popular melodrama.) Envisioning her journal as an intimate "friend" and "sole confident [sic] of my thoughts, my aspirations and desires," the narrator records the daily struggles and pains of poverty and endless work as well as her intellectual and often sharply conflicted emotional responses to those experiences. At times expressing resignation that, as a "child of the people," she is "made for [labor]," she more often records her outrage at class inequity and the callous disregard of her middle-class, mostly female employers; resentment at the wounding slights she regularly experiences from employers, landlords, and shopkeepers; and gratitude for the generosity of other workingwomen ("Poor seamstresses have . . . hearts that are easily touched with the griefs of others").

While she expresses romantic desire and initially pines for the loss of a suitor whose proposals she had rejected but for whom she now bears a "long buried" passion, the "aspirations and desires" she voices are mainly for radical political and economic change: her writing is infused with revolutionary fervor and "haunt[ed]" by "the grand idea . . . of cooperative industry." In a telling reference to French seamstresses, she imagines seamstresses not as passive victims but as agents of violent revolt: "Are women to be born for this, to toil, shrivel, die and rot? Is there never to be an avenue opened for their powers? . . . My very soul is roused with indignation. The women of France once rose in rebellion. Their cry was 'bread for our babes'; will the women of our country ever utter this cry as they gather in crowds from attics, cellars, by lanes, and dark dens of filth and squalor? Alas! Yes, if no change comes for the better, they too will thirst for the purple cup of revolution." And instead of melancholy figures pining in solitary, nun-like domestic retreat, she imagines seamstresses living and working together in cooperation; writing of her domestic partnership with another seamstress, Maria L., she muses, "If two can thus combine their interests for economy, why not more? Why could not a dozen join their slender means, and make shirts and caps, or any other articles demanded in the market, and have the profits? . . . The ants and the bees alone could understand me. I wonder if I was not once a bee." At one point imagining a young bride as a lamb "decked . . . for a sacrifice," the narrator constructs for herself an alternative plot to the standard melodramatic one of decline and (paternal) rescue. Indeed the absence of a romantic plot both serves to register the multiple privations and losses seamstresses experience and enables the narrator to dedicate herself liberally and publicly to "the good of humanity."[67]

Throughout the text the narrator voices outrage at middle-class women's inability to imagine in a complex way the experiences of workingwomen or psychologically surmount the boundaries of class; in interactions with female clients, she characteristically utters "some biting [and] . . . wholesome truth" to "startle" them into "momentary feeling." Her critique of middle-class women's "narrow bigotry" extends from her female employers to feminists such as Margaret Fuller (whose idealism creates "a veil . . . between her and the rude, practical, every-day working world. She may . . . call herself a laborer, but this brings her only into distant relationship with us") and especially to moral reformers like those discussed earlier in this chapter. During a visit to Mrs. Broadson to collect on a long-outstanding bill, she rejects the woman's effort to pay her in cast-off clothing and demands interest on the amount due; embodying the retributory violence she presages above, the narrator states, "My feelings of scorn, contempt, and burning indignation, for the woman held me silent for a moment; I felt as though I could annihilate her with one breath." Attending the "rigidly moral" Mrs. L., who spies her watch and questions "whether a virtuous girl could get articles of that kind," the narrator decries religious women's sexual suspicion of workingwomen and shrewdly suggests that middle-class women's "charitable" preoccupation with their "fallen" working-class sisters entails a projection of their own repressed sexual longings. Vowing that "she should have no power over me," the narrator declares, "I might . . . tell you how I came in possession of this watch . . . but I scorn to enter upon a self defence when there is only a coarse and cruel suspicion against me. You madam, are a sensualist, you have a nature low enough to prostitute yourself for gold, or you would never suspect one of your own sex of unworthy acts." As with Mrs. Broadson, she here envisions herself as an instrument of class vengeance: "Woman, I have been tempted; the tempter still trails along my path; I know the weakness that comes from hunger and weariness; Beware, lest at the last, the blood of my soul be found in your skirts that you deem so pure and spotless."[68] The image of the bloody skirt evokes the idea, discussed above, of cheap garments bearing not only moral contamination but the threat of deadly diseases (here the suggestion is tuberculosis); defetishizing the commodity, the seamstress employs the language of prophetic warning to invoke both the threat of mortality and the prospect of spiritual judgment ("Beware, lest at the last . . .").

But it is especially when two moral reformers visit the narrator and Maria L. at home, bearing tracts and questioning the seamstresses' moral and spiritual practices, that the benevolence of middle-class women is most severely undercut. The women interrogate the seamstresses, expressing the usual preoccupations of moral reformers—Do they attend church? Are they taking the necessary precautions to avoid temptation and preserve their virtue?—and the narrator's responses are recorded in illuminating detail. When the women express shock at the narrator's admission that she does not attend church, she enlightens them on the causes of her (and other workingwomen's) absence: she cannot afford a seat, and the free seats provided for the poor in the galleries "have few of the comforts with which the seats for the rich are furnished"; she has no appropriate clothing; she has no time ("I worship perpetually, if labor is worship"). The reformers seem alarmed at her nondeferential, indeed, defiant stance and endeavor to bolster their authority with a spiritual threat: "It seemed evident . . . that I was in the 'gaul of bitterness and bonds of iniquity'; that I hated the blessed Savior, and I would make my bed in hell at the last." Attempting to persuade the narrator to mend her ways and value spiritual over material concerns, one reformer reproves her, "You are most of the time engaged in such—vanity . . .

as this [dress], and more in earnest about it, than about your precious, undying soul." In response the narrator reaffirms her commitment to the material realm: "Stretch out your hands, *extend your sympathies to their bodies*, and then you may point them to the Infinite Father's love, more successfully. . . . Go to the boardinghouse, at the end of this court. Look at that miserable, haggard crowd, there struggling . . . and then demand of society relief, not a pittance doled out as charity, but demand for them homes, where through attractive industry, they may be made useful, healthy and happy."[69] Demanding not charity and spiritual uplift for individuals but justice effected through collective political action, the narrator contests the authority of moral reformers to understand or publicly define the seamstress's identity, experiences, or needs. Focusing on the material exigencies of seamstresses' lives, she aims to challenge reformers' socially distanced portrait of needlewomen and to refashion and re-form middle-class women's sympathies.

Writing in the New York *Tribune*, Horace Greeley affirmed that "the worst features" of needlework "are its hopelessness and its constant tendency from bad to worse. . . . Small as are the earnings of . . . seamstresses, they constantly tend to diminish."[70] A decade later Catharine Beecher and Harriet Beecher Stowe wrote in *The American Woman's Home* that American readers continued to be "harrowed with tales of the sufferings of distressed needle-women."[71] "Stray Leaves" unravels the popular image of the sentimental seamstress and her conventional downward plot. In particular its narrator—like the text as a whole—reverses relations of discursive authority established by middle-class reformers and other crafters of the seamstress image, wresting control, if only temporarily, of the seamstress's story. By the end of her encounter with the moral reformers, the narrator notes, "In my vehement earnestness . . . I was standing before them, the preacher . . . of the three."[72] In doing so, and in imagining a reformation of middle-class women's benevolence and solidarity, she aims to open the seamstress to history and to the prospect of feminist activism and social transformation the *Una* endeavored to promote.

### THE SEAMSTRESS'S DECLINE AND
### THE HARLOT'S PROGRESS

As noted earlier, the sentimental seamstress's downward path was patterned after that of the fallen woman, an association that served simultaneously to evoke and allay the suspicion of working-class female "immodesty" and active sexual (or economic) desire. Always shadowing seamstress narratives is the prospect of female entrepreneurial "ambition" exercised in the labor and sexual markets.

Such desires are abundantly evident in narratives of the female adventuress, an adaptation of the eighteenth-century popular narrative of the trickster-harlot and a staple of the sensational press. These narratives echoed the complexities of workingwomen's own testimonies of their sexual experience, testimonies recorded in legal records, in the records of houses of refuge and asylum, in claims before bastardy courts, and gathered by reformers and social scientists such as Charles Loring Brace and William Sanger. In Sanger's massive *History of Prostitution* (1858), more than half of the women reported their motivation for prostitution as "inclination"—a possibility Sanger was at a loss to explain. Sensational narratives about prostitutes drew upon such materials, complicating the seamstress's downward path. Charles Smith invokes and unsettles the sentimental seamstress's conventional narrative of economic and sexual victimization in his popular 1847 narrative about the notorious abortionist Madame Restell: "Some girls, and by far the most elegant and beautiful, from the moment their life of prostitution commences, go down a regularly inclined plane, to destruction and death. Commencing as fashionable kept mistresses, they go next to the most luxurious houses: there getting bad habits, they go to those of a lower class, until with drink and disease, they go to the lowest brothels, the hospital, and the potter's field." However, Smith observes, "on the other hand, there are an abundance of cases, where the course is precisely opposite. Commencing with the vilest debasement, I have seen girls rise gradually, through every grade, and finally marry well, and live respected and happy." While "there are all intermediate conditions and destinies," he admits

> that, as a general rule, prostitutes, in from five to seven years, become utterly disgusted with a life of promiscuous prostitution, and take any means that offers to escape from it. Some induce their lovers, to whom they have become attached, to keep them, and the greater portion of them are finally married. Others induce rich men, who take a fancy, to set them up in some kind of business—such as millinery or confectionary. Others are carried off to the South and West, by men who take a liking to them; others resort to various means of obtaining a livelihood; but, in one way or another, more than two-thirds of all our prostitutes manage to escape from this mode of existence.[73]

Whereas moral reformers writing in the *Advocate* codified a trajectory in which seamstresses driven by poverty inevitably become prostitutes, Smith envisions the "precise opposite" of this narrative structure, imagining that some former prostitutes become needleworkers (here, milliners) after they weary of "the trade."

Osgood Bradbury, author of the sensational *Mysteries of Lowell* (discussed in chapter 2), unsettled the (sentimental) seamstress's characteristic innocence in order to proliferate her possible plots. In Bradbury's pamphlet novel *Emily, the Beautiful Seamstress; or the Danger of the First Step* (1853), the seamstress is not powerless and naïve but capable and canny. The beautiful Emily capitalizes on her time on the street going to and from work, observing men's behavior and learning to read their faces, thus engendering a skepticism about their hearts. The poor, objects of middle-class distrust in the era of liberal political economy, learn to adopt that stance as well; they counter the new class antagonism not by an appeal for sympathy but by learning to fight back. In Bradbury's text the narrative of seduction is shunted off from Emily (who marries a wealthy bachelor) to another poor girl, Mary, who not only exposes—and thus seeks revenge upon—her married seducer but manipulates a charity scene to her advantage: when her seducer (hoping to entrap Mary into a house of prostitution) sends a corrupt associate to pose as a priest and offer to escort the girl to a charitable institution for unwed mothers, she recognizes the priest as an imposter, pockets the cash, and disappears before she is captured. Once again Bradbury highlights poor women's agency, intelligence, and power in recognizing the reality of sexualized class warfare and using their wits to manipulate men.

The sexual canniness and self-possession in Smith's and Bradbury's texts are abundantly evident in J. H. Ingraham's *Frank Rivers, or, the Dangers of the Town* (1843).[74] *Frank Rivers* describes how a young orphan from rural New England named Ellen Jewett became the central figure in one of the most publicized sex-and-violence scandals of the antebellum period. As Patricia Cline Cohen explains in her comprehensive study of the real Jewett murder (the victim's actual name was Helen), competing accounts circulated about the murders in the popular press, foregrounding class tensions and crystallizing class emotions. Ingraham's version is particularly interesting for the way it both evokes and contravenes codes of feminine fallenness and economic abjection epitomized by seamstress texts.[75] The text's complex depiction of working-class female subjectivity is once again enabled by its generic alignment with sensationalism rather than the psychological and moral norms of sentimentalism.

The narrative presents a conflicted account of Ellen's agency, depicting her alternately as a seduced victim—a fallen woman—and a willful female adventuress. Ingraham's reconstruction of the narrative elements of the Helen Jewett scandal heightens the story's class accents: the "young, beautiful" Ellen is a "maid of all work" at the rural cottage of an elderly maiden aunt, a woman "relentless in her tyranny" over her niece (8, 4), and Ingraham underscores the wealth, privilege, and ambition of those who corrupt her. In conventional melodramatic terms the narrative presents Hart Granger, a wealthy college student, as an aristocratic rake who employs every tool at his disposal to conquer the affections and person of his victim (9). Granger seduces Ellen with the discourse of paternalism itself: "In trusting to my honor and generosity, you have nothing to apprehend. From this moment I am your friend and protector" (8). At the same time he poses as a democrat, asserting that station is insignificant in love and suggesting that gender refashions structures of class deference and obligation. While Granger insists that "beauty . . . is it itself wealth, rank, aristocracy!" and declares that a "man must bow to [beauty], whenever he beholds it; whether in the palace or in the peasant's hut!," Ellen is skeptical, believing, rightly it turns out, that "your station in society is far above mine and unhappiness can only come of our further intimacy" (3, 7).

Citing melodramatic clichés of the innocent, passive maid and the experienced, conniving seducer, Ingraham also dismantles melodramatic formulae. For example, while clearly condemning Granger's deception and betrayal of Ellen, the narrative splits responsibility for Ellen's fall: "Finding she firmly resisted every temptation he laid for her fall, he deliberately studied to corrupt her mind with the most subtle and specious reasonings. . . . She all the while was fully aware of her danger, but shut her eyes to the precipice upon which she was walking. The society and conversation of the student, had a fascination for her she could not resist, and night after night she . . . listen[ed] with charmed and willing ear, and wildly throbbing passion-heaving bosom to his dangerous and seductive words" (9). While Granger "deliberately studie[s]" to corrupt Ellen, she is "fully aware" of the danger but voluntarily "shut[s] her eyes" (and willingly "open[s] her ears") to it; the passage is replete with images of Ellen's sexual longing. Shifting from this scene of interpersonal struggle, Ingraham frames Ellen's story around an interior conflict involving her awakening if conflicted sexual desire, a struggle between conscience (the feeling that she was "doing wrong") and her "*secret* desire" to continue seeing her suitor (4). The narrative is driven forward at least partly by Ellen's desire; for example, there is a clear sense that she is partly seduced by "the homage . . . to beauty and grace" (4) Granger pays her, granting her a social significance that counters her class invisibility as a rural servant. Dedicating significant narrative space to registering and exploring working-class female desire, Ingraham records Ellen's transformation from a "timid, hesitating, blushing . . . girl of eighteen" to one with "all the spirit and power and independence of a beautiful woman of the world" (10).

Ellen's transformation from melodramatic victim to sensationalistic "female adventuress" is enabled by the urban matrix of New York; soon after her seduction in Granger's college residence, the couple depart for the city, "where Granger hired a suite of elegantly furnished rooms, and occupied them with her. He sent to her fashionable dress-makers and milliners, to adorn her person, and loaded her with jewelry. He took her to places of amusement, and triumphed in the admiration her peerless beauty created. She . . . entered with life and high excitement into the novel scenes around, in which her guilty lover had placed her" (9). Ellen's "ruin" is not followed, as in most seduction narratives, by her inevitable pregnancy and consequent penitence but by her transformation into a worldly, self-possessed—and public—woman.

In the city Ellen learns the power of her beauty, its economic and social value. Abandoned by Granger after three months, she alternates for a time between feminine melancholy ("He was her only dependence. . . . For him she had sacrificed herself, and deserted by him life would be despair" [10]) and haughty pride. Upon receiving a letter in which Granger reveals that he will comply with his father's deathbed request and enter the clergy and in which he promises to pay Ellen 500 pounds a year for her support, she strolls down Broadway, finding in the city streets a diversion from her "painful meditations" (11). Unlike Poe's Man of the Crowd, however, it is not anonymity but conspicuousness Ellen seeks, made possible by her erotically unfettered status. Ellen "triumphed as she felt herself the object of universal admiration. Broadway at the hour she walked, presented the appearance of a magnificent promenade, thronged with richly dressed persons of both sexes. The men of fashion seemed to be lounging up and down, only to gaze upon the beautiful women, and the beautiful women seemed to appear there in full dress, only to be admired. But none of them attracted attention so much as the elegant and charming Ellen. . . . 'Who could she be?'" (11). Seemingly unconscious of admiration, Ellen feels it intensely: "It was a season of secret and deep triumph to her: and in her heart entered the thought, 'if Granger deserts me, I need not his protection. Within the hour I have learned the power I possess over my own destiny'" (11). The narrator observes, "This was a bold thought for one so young and so lately innocent, but a characteristic one for her independent mind" (11). Fallenness is here rewritten as "independence," engendering in Ellen a commercial understanding of the value of her beauty and sexual allure. Rather than viewing men as potential "protectors" or retreating to an "innocence" that might appeal to the sympathy of moral reformers, Ellen confronts men as potential antagonists in a sexual marketplace, each striving for the better bargain. Having learned from Granger to apply economic rationality to the sphere of erotic relations, she affirms the ambition disavowed in domestic literature and seamstress stories. In a sense her fall frees her to wrest control of her own plot.

It also enables a fleshing out of her subjectivity. Shortly after the promenade on Broadway the narrator ascribes to his protagonist interior monologues: "Have I not had a triumph today! Have I not received homage! . . . Granger in bringing me to New York, has opened to me a new world! it is life to live here! *what is beauty buried in the country!* here it is power, wealth and rank! why should I tremble at the prospect of Granger's deserting me!" (14, emphasis added). Vowing that she will not "hesitate to act if the time for action should come," Ellen nearly becomes a melodramatic villainess; indeed on one occasion Ingraham depicts her fall as turning an "angel" into a "demon" and transforming his heroine into the very personification of vice (16). But overall the narrative exhibits real sympathy for Ellen's determination and analyses, and she voices throughout the text a justified anger and rage (as well as compelling critiques of the sexual double standard). Ingraham especially records how Ellen's newfound sense of self-possession generates feelings of autonomy: "There was a proud feeling of independence in being her own mistress" (16).

Ellen, the narrator states, is an "extraordinary young girl, who day by day [is] developing some new and startling feature of her character" (15); certainly she is multiplying for herself a diversity of erotic plots. For example, once she realizes that Granger will not marry her, she seduces another young man, Frank Rivers; according to the narrator, "*She* was the seducer, *not* he; yet such had been her artfulness, so finished had been the seeming artlessness of her character, so confiding, so trustful, that he seemed and felt himself to be the guiltiest of the guilty pair" (22). When Rivers, believing he has ruined an innocent girl, proposes marriage, Ellen confesses that she has been seduced by Granger and so cannot accept (23). Rivers, whose limited sense of honor doesn't extend to pressing his case, observes, in evident relief, "how generous and noble she has been" (23) in her refusal to deceive him. But, the narrator confides, "there was . . . a deeper motive for [Ellen's] generous decision. . . . It was a secret relish for the life of adventure upon which Granger's desertion had thrown her. She knew the power of her beauty, and she felt a reluctance all at once!" (23). (Later she declares to a friend, "Don't talk to me of gentlemen! I have tried their generosity till I have no faith in any one of them. I will be free, and live as I choose" [28].) Her "secret relish" is born in the urban crowd; as in Moretti's analysis, the city is the site for the discursive elaboration and potential realization of Ellen's desire.

Ellen's "career of adventure" is necessarily checkered: Ingraham's evident fascination with what he terms his heroine's "ambition" (25) is constrained by the dictates of narrative closure. The historical Helen Jewett was, after all, the victim of murder and indisputably suffered for her transgressions. However, Ingraham's conclusion is ambiguous: the adventuress is clearly punished, while her plot of female revenge is in many ways spectacularly successful. Giving voice to forms of "inclination" and entrepreneurial ambition disavowed in most seamstress stories, popular sensational texts such as Ingraham's counter the seamstress's sentimental abjection, affording their working-class female characters a surprising range of possible plots.

## *Four.* Harriet Wilson's *Our Nig* and the Labor of Race

We are continually harrowed with tales of the sufferings of distressed needle-women . . . and yet women will encounter all these chances of ruin and starvation rather than make up their minds to permanent domestic service. Now, what is the matter with domestic service? —CATHARINE BEECHER AND HARRIET BEECHER STOWE, *The American Woman's Home*

Published on the brink of the Civil War, Harriet Wilson's *Our Nig* and E. D. E. N. Southworth's *The Hidden Hand* first appeared in print in 1859. Both novels are Bildungsromane of sorts, fictional records of working-class girlhood as it pressures the contours of working-class womanhood; both too highlight imbrications of class and race in the watershed years of the 1850s. Historians often argue that, during that decade, consciousness of the country's racial divide overshadowed consciousness of class inequities in popular culture and political discourse; some claim that the united northern struggle against the South silenced class dissent, generating sectional (and, later, nationalist) sentiment and pride. However, in these women's texts of the 1850s class consciousness was not supplanted by race, but refracted through it: racial signifiers could figure class resentments, aspirations, and desires. Illuminating what Shane White calls the "fluidity of racial categories" in antebellum working-class communities, these texts foreground interdeterminations of race and class in the antebellum United States.[1]

Telling stories of laboring girls and women, including poor single mothers—thus profoundly unsettling middle-class gender norms—these texts engage what were increasingly hypostatized binary distinctions between South and North, slave and free, black laborer and white. By 1860, William R. Taylor writes, "most Americans had come to look upon their society and culture as divided between a North and a South, a democratic, commercial civilization and an aristocratic, agrarian one," a view best captured in William Henry Seward's "Irrepressible Conflict" speech of 1858.[2] It is in the context of an increasingly hegemonic northern "free labor" ideology that Wilson takes pains to depict servitude as not only a sectional but a national problem; as the title page forthrightly states, by locating her tale "in a two-story white house, North," she aims to show "that slavery's shadows fall even there." Replacing northern free labor with black and white servitude and framing the narrative of a mixed-race daughter with that of her (precariously) white working-class mother, Frado's miscegenated tale registers oft-unspoken racial complexities of antebellum working-class life. For her part Southworth presents in *The Hidden Hand* a picaresque narrative that, in propelling her heroine across national space, maps the topography of class—convergences and divergences of racialized class positions. Both texts make it clear that northern "free labor" is fiction rather than fact, and insist upon the emphatically racialized and gendered character of (northern and southern) "servitude." And in centering their narratives on girls and women and opening up a discursive space for representing working-class female subjectivities and lives, both texts focus on the *home* as a site of class "sympathy" as well as (racialized) class conflict.

Assessing the implications of what Trudier Harris terms the "blackening" of domestic service for antebellum constructions of class, I read *Our Nig* as a kind of narrative response to the question Beecher and Stowe pose in my epigraph: "What is the matter with domestic service?"[3] Wilson's novel registers the racialized class politics of domestic labor during a period when the economic value of such work was increasingly negated and rendered invisible (through the process Boydston calls "pastoralization"); recording the projection of domestic labor and embodiment onto black women, *Our Nig* registers an ambivalent identification with the black female laboring body as the site and sign of white women's own economic erasure.[4] But if Wilson's text emphasizes how white women enact their racialized class ambitions on the backs of black women, both the narrator and Wilson's heroine Frado disrupt that (albeit ambivalent) desire for domestic domination. In particular, in *Our Nig* white women's class authority is contested by what Wilson calls the "kitchen version"—the primacy of the black, female, working-class voice.[5] Turning to *The Hidden Hand* in chapter 5,

I examine how that novel's pervasive use of racial signifiers makes visible subaltern class identifications. While in a few instances the trope of blackness is incorporated within the polarized moral idiom of melodrama, with its Manichaean binaries of good and evil, it more frequently designates the racialization of class, marking the way popular sympathies could be figured through racialized heroines and heroes; thus, for example, it is their shared "blackness" that unites the street urchin–cum-heiress Capitola Le Noir and the heroic, manly bandit Black Donald. Drawing on feminist abolitionist accounts of slavery as a "patriarchal institution," Southworth's novel, like *Our Nig*, features a feminine, subaltern perspective on the so-called differences between the southern and northern systems of production and reproduction, labor and sex, focusing especially on the family as the site of paternal authority and female economic and sexual domination.

These continuities North and South were dramatically registered in an 1855 novel by Martha W. Tyler, *A Book without a Title: Or, Thrilling Events in the Life of Mira Dana*. The protagonist's bold independence is traced to rural hoydenism: known by family and neighbors as a "romp" called "Dick," Mira would labor "boy-like" in the fields and "act her own pleasure, not theirs."[6] Thus nursing a taste for "liberty" (23), Mira leaves the family farm at sixteen to work in the Lowell factories to help finance her brother's education. Immediately objecting to the overcrowding and surveillance of workers in boardinghouses and factories, she fiercely resists the exploitation and industrial discipline of factory life, defying both the mill owners and a paternalistic social order that would define her labor as familial service and assimilate it to her brother's ambition. In protest over forms of Lowell "slavery," especially mill owners' efforts to drive down wages, Mira leads a factory girls' walkout that is partly successful; particularly notable is her refusal to defer to sympathetic male reformers, "Esq.'s and Rev.'s" (25) who support the strike but attempt to dominate the women's "*indignation* meeting" (23). After a brief marriage to a sea captain who respects her for her independence, she marries a southern planter and moves south, where plantation life drives home the equation not only of wife and slave, but of wife and wage slave. These parallels are explicitly rendered: Mira's "tyrann[ical]" (141) husband Herbert Tyrrell physically abuses his wife as he does his slaves; he avowedly marries to acquire a domestic servant who will "wait upon him," viewing a wife as property, a "necessary piece of furniture" that should "never murmur or complain" (87) (pointedly, he is most abusive when Mira is physically incapacitated); and he aims to profit from her labor, seizing personal property Mira "earned ... when a factory girl" (148).[7] In addition, Mira's brother Warner, a scoundrel who absconds with the family's wealth and for whom "love of money conquered brotherly affection," counsels Mira during the Lowell strike to go "quietly back to . . . work" (38), just as he later advises her to return to the abusive Tyrrell in a stance of proper wifely submission. Tyler underscores Mira's identity as a worker in these overlapping domains: Mira's experience as a factory worker fuels her repudiation of marital servitude and submission and continues to shape her identity throughout the novel. Like the factory women described by the English workingman James Dawson Burn in *Three Years among the Working Classes*, discussed in the introduction, Mira learns at Lowell to question the legitimacy of husbands' authority to "boss" their wives. She avows that "*she* was a *life-worker*, not an idle toy, to be tossed about by every hand that cared to grasp hers" (17).

Mapping connections between male-dominated factory, male-dominated northern home, and male-dominated southern plantation, *A Book without a Title* implies that women's experience of the home *was* their experience of wage slavery, and that plantation, factory, and home were all "patriarchal institutions," related (though not identical) sites of female subjection and exploitation. Elaborating these links, the novel illuminates poor women's "precarious whiteness," exploring possibilities of interracial solidarity and sympathy.[8] In this and the following chapters I analyze the fraught possibilities and consequences of these regional, racial, and gender symmetries and explore their psychological effects. While in *Our Nig* the mistress Mrs. B., seeking to escape the experience of domestic enslavement—degrading submission to patriarchal authority and the regime of unappreciated, endless domestic work—projects both subordination and enforced labor onto the mixed-race child Frado, taking recourse in an ideology of white supremacy, in Southworth's novel signifiers of blackness mediate labor and domestic conflicts and map shifting links among domesticity, enslavement, and free (female) labor. My final chapter, on narratives of Mexicana domestic workers in the California missions, extends this analysis, examining how the racialization of domestic "service" is reworked within cultural formations of racialized class and labor on the western "frontier."

In an early piece published in the *Lowell Offering* the future unionist Sarah Bagley narrates the making of the factory girl as a female version of Franklinean self-fashioning. While some Lowell women's texts nostalgically present the rural landscape as a harmonious setting of familial closeness and natural beauty against which the discipline, artifice, and moral corruption of factory life is negatively measured, in "Tales of Factory Life, No. 1" the female worker's migration to Lowell is cast as a progress narrative. Employed as a domestic in the household of one "Mrs. J.," Bagley recalls strenuous labor, physical and verbal abuse, and inadequate food as reasons she disliked the position. But it is especially the antidemocratic condescension and flaunting of status distinctions by the family's female members that precipitate her decision to leave. It is when Mrs. J. calls Sarah a "poor little beggar" and her daughter belittles Sarah for being "meanly clad" and ignorant of "French and Music," that "the proud spirit of Sarah could endure such treatment no longer. She determined to leave, and that night made preparation to depart." Mrs. J. attempts to cure Sarah of "Lowell fever" with the rebuke "If you are mean enough in your own opinion, to be a factory girl, I may as well despair of thinking to make any thing of you," but this only intensifies Sarah's resolve.[9] Recalling Ben Franklin's account of the repudiation of his own familial servitude, the story depicts its penniless heroine, possessing only a small bundle, making her way to Lowell, where she seeks opportunities, financial rewards, and an independence and respect denied her by the "J's." If Mrs. J. views domestic service paternalistically, as a call to "make [some]thing" of the young woman employed in her household—a view common among antebellum mistresses—Sarah views urban factory work as a chance to make something of herself.[10]

Set in western Massachusetts and New Hampshire, in close proximity to the mills and the rural areas from which most mill women were drawn, Wilson's *Our Nig* is in part about the domestic worker who fills the places abandoned by young women such as Bagley in search of greener pastures. In *Our Nig* Frado assumes the position formerly occupied by a stream of white domestics—most recently an Irish girl named Bridget—who enact their independence from servitude by claiming the right to terminate employment at will; indeed, Mrs. Bellmont's strenuous effort to control Frado's labor should be read as a reaction against the mobility of labor and what E. P. Thompson describes as the "newly-won psychology of the free laborer."[11] The binary of domestic service/factory work subtends many Lowell women's texts; for example, the choice between domestic service and factory work was narrativized in sketches and stories in Lowell periodicals as well as in pamphlet novels such as *The Factory Girl* and (more complexly) *The Mysteries of Lowell*. Notably, both Bagley and Frado emphasize that the misery of domestic servitude is due to an expressly *gendered* struggle for power within the household: class differences as well as forms of supervision and control are enacted in explicitly gendered terms.

Bagley's and Frado's construction of domestic work as self-negating—one feminist called it "self-denying toil"[12]—reflects domestic labor's devaluation and cultural and political denigration. Servants, although the most numerous type of laborer in the nineteenth century, have typically been excluded from definitions of the working class (not to mention the history of labor organizing).[13] As Carolyn Steedman notes, the general absence of domestic servants from historical scholarship on class can be traced back to Adam Smith's dismissal of domestic labor as "non-work" or "anti-work," Marx's incorporation of Smith, and the fact that social historians of class continue to depend on these theories to tell their stories about labor and class relations. For Smith, servants' labors, which do not "fix . . . or realise" themselves in any "vendible commodity," "perish in the very instant of their performance, and seldom leave any trace or value behind them" that can be exchanged afterward; the fact that antebellum domestic labor was meant to be unseen, that a servant's standard task was to wipe away marks rather than leave a trace, itself contributes to the servant's invisibility in the history of class.[14] Nonetheless, as Thompson notes, it is in "servant-master relations of dependency, in which personal contacts are frequent and personal injustices are [regularly] suffered," that class feelings are often "most violent and most personal."[15] Those class feelings are painfully apparent in *Our Nig* and are central to the drama of the story. What we see in *Our Nig* is the import of the antebellum home for the production and reproduction of racialized class identities as well as an often invisible site of capitalist exploitation.

As Bagley and Wilson suggest, the antebellum construction of factory work as "free labor" shaped and was shaped by a symbolic reconfiguration of domestic labor, one thoroughly structured by the racialized status relations of southern slavery. In tracing the shifting significance of the term *servant* in the developing language of "free" white labor during the first half of the nineteenth century, David Roediger argues that the "free" white repudiation of "servitude" was effected through its association with ideologies of race and the labor relations of slavery. U.S. citizens, observed the American lawyer John Bristed in 1818, "confound[ed]" the term *servant* with *slave*, a confounding authorized by Noah Webster's blurred distinction between their usage in his 1828 dictionary of American English. The repudiation of the designation *servant* in favor of *help* or *hand* was thus not simply, Roediger notes, an index of workers' republican militancy; it was a symbolic means of "becoming *white workers*."[16] White women's flight from domestic service in the antebellum period is an established, well-documented historical fact; numerous historians, from W. E. B. Du Bois to David Katzman, have examined the racialization of domestic service, how black girls and women came to be "a permanent service caste in nineteenth- and twentieth-century America"—a direct carryover from slavery.[17] What Trudier Harris terms the "blackening" of service is a window onto as well as product of cultural constructions of gendered and racialized labor.[18]

Bagley's repudiation of servitude in pursuit of "free labor" bears out Roediger's claim that the negative example of chattel slavery, here identified with the signifier *servant*, was a means through which workers could conceptualize and indeed experience their labor as "free." While Bagley would write and lecture eloquently on the constraint, coercion, and the injustices of "free labor," in this early account she could represent factory work as a liberating alternative to the customary bondage of the household. However, due to the gendered nature of domestic "servitude" and the increasing association of household work with women in the antebellum United States, the feminine repudiation of servitude would have different effects for white female workers than for the white working-men Roediger studies; in addition the intimate setting in which domestic labor takes place can both intensify and further complicate class feelings. *Our Nig* suggests that the new racialization of domestic servitude must be understood in relation to constructions of white working womanhood as well as the emerging, domestic femininity associated with the Victorian formation of separate spheres. The racialization of servitude could fuel interracial class solidarity as well as complicate white workingwomen's class identification, even while it could undermine middle-class women's recognition that they performed any economically valuable work at all.

The racialization of northern servitude and its uneven effects are astutely registered by the antebellum orator and essayist Maria W. Stewart. In "Religion and the Pure Principles of Morality," Stewart asks, "How long shall the fair daughters of Africa be compelled to bury their minds and talents beneath a load of iron pots and kettles? . . . How long shall a mean set of men flatter us with their smiles, and enrich themselves with our hard earnings; their wives' fingers sparkling with rings, and they themselves laughing at our folly?" Similarly in her 1832 "Lecture Delivered at the Franklin Hall," Stewart observes, "Such is the powerful force of prejudice. Let our girls possess whatever amiable qualities of soul they may; let their characters be fair and spotless as innocence itself; let their natural taste and ingenuity be what they may; it is impossible for scarce an individual of them to rise above the condition of servants." Stewart's use of anaphora ("how long") underscores the reiterative power of prejudice to produce service as the near inevitable destination of black women's lives. For Stewart domestic labor as racial destiny is a form of compulsion and negation of self that obliterates black female individuality (black women "bury" rather than express themselves in their work); more specifically it is a species of submergence within the realm of the body. Palpably registering the weight of the material world, Stewart suggests that the implements of domestic labor—"pots and kettles"—are instruments of oppression that bear down on women, threatening spiritual and mental faculties, God-like "minds and talents" and "qualities of soul"; at the same time the eroticization of servitude—the familiar link between domestic service and seduction—strengthens the "powerful force" of the servant's confinement to the body. Opposing spatial images of class "elevation" and mobility (the prospect of "ris[ing] above the condition of servants") to images of emphatic embodiment, Stewart invokes the binary opposition of mind and body, central to antebellum constructions of class, to register the effects of this domestic division of labor: black women, unjustly imprisoned within the realm of the body, are denied vitalizing opportunities of mental and spiritual culture. "I have learnt, by bitter experience, that continual hard labor deadens the energies of the soul, and benumbs the faculties of the mind; the ideas become confined, the mind barren, and like the scorching sands of Arabia, produces nothing; or like the uncultivated soil, brings forth thorns and thistles." Defining domestic work as a racialized instance of the class divide between mental and physical labor, Stewart records that labor's place in a system of capitalist exploitation: mean men "enrich themselves with our hard earnings," converting a portion of that appropriated wealth into "sparkling . . . rings" to adorn their wives' fingers.[19]

As the implied opposition between laboring black hands, compelled to wield "iron pots and kettles," and leisured white bejeweled hands suggests, Stewart correlates domestic class differences not only to a mind–body divide but to racialized, classed versions of gendered embodiment. In her "Lecture Delivered at the Franklin Hall," she continues, "O, ye fairer sisters, whose hands are never soiled, whose nerves and muscles are never strained, go learn by experience! Had we had the opportunity that you have had, to improve our moral and mental faculties, what would have hindered our intellects from being as bright, and our manner from being as dignified as yours? Had it been our lot to have been nursed in the lap of affluence and ease, and to have basked beneath the smiles and sunshine of fortune, would we not have naturally supposed that we were never made to toil? And why are not our forms as delicate, and our constitutions as slender, as yours? Is not the workmanship as curious and complete?" (48). Explicitly addressing white women ("fairer sisters") who possess privileges of wealth and "ease" and "have naturally supposed that [they] were never made to toil," Stewart invokes the period's racialized construction of feminine leisure and female labor to deconstruct it. The black female body, she suggests, exemplifies female strength and emphatic physicality, while the white female body, "slender," "delicate," and clean (with hands that are not "soiled"), signifies leisure and class privilege (a "dignified" "manner"). Specifically invoking feminine delicacy as a product of socialization and "experience," not nature, Stewart undermines its power to naturalize—by anchoring in the body—white women's domestic class position.

As Stewart makes clear, the servant was the counterimage of the new domestic femininity. In *Imperial Leather*, Anne McClintock reviews the now standard account of the emergence of the middle-class "domestic woman" as leisured feminine ideal: "At some point during the eighteenth century, the story goes, the spindle and loom were pried from her fingers and all the 'bustling labor' of the previous century—the candle and soap-making, the tailoring, millinery, straw-weaving, lace making, carding and wool-sorting, flax-beating, dairy and poultry work—were removed piecemeal to the manufactories. . . . Robbed of her productive labor [by the mid-nineteenth century], the middle-class woman became fitted, we are told, only for an ornamental place in society." However, apart from the tiny, truly elite group of women, "idleness was less a regime of inertia imposed on wilting middle-class wives and daughters than a laborious and time-consuming *character role* performed by women who wanted membership in the 'respectable' class." "For most women [of the middling classes] whose husbands or fathers could not afford enough servants for genuine idleness, domestic work," which entailed "the cleaning and management of large, inefficiently constructed houses," "had to be accompanied by the historically unprecedented labor of rendering invisible every sign of that work." Thus for most middle-class women "idleness was less the absence of work than a conspicuous labor of leisure." This "laborious mimicry of idleness" and its attendant "spectacle of leisure" gained the woman and her family "prestige," while contributing to the erasure and devaluation of women's domestic work.[20]

In the United States numerous treatises on domesticity contributed to the dissemination of this "character role" by emphasizing the spiritual rather than the physical or material aspects of women's domestic responsibilities; in the antebellum "cult of domesticity" the ideal domestic activity was seen as nurture—what women did out of love for their family and as their civic and moral responsibility, an activity that was not to be valued in economic terms or seen as labor. Here is one of many possible examples, from Mrs. A. J. Graves's *Woman in America*: "Woman . . . was placed in this world to fill a station embracing far higher duties than those of a mere domestic laborer. She has been endowed with intellectual faculties and moral influence, which were designed to be cultivated, not only for her own advancement . . . but to fit her to be the educator of her children, and the improver of her husband."[21] The historian Elizabeth Blackmar has discussed these developments in the context of the urban North:

> Women engaged in the coarse work of hauling water and firewood,
> throwing out waste and garbage, and washing clothes over open fires

were exposed to abusive insults in a culture of republican simplicity which imagined female virtue to consist of modest, clean, and "naturally" deferential decorum and attire. For an independent citizen to require a mother, wife, daughter, or sister to do heavy and exposed domestic labor associated with slavery . . . was to place her outside his own class. . . . The presence of servants, then, was essential to maintaining the new values of domestic respectability, which were defined in opposition to the "promiscuous" and dependent conditions of female wage labor.[22]

Christine Stansell notes that in the antebellum period the "cult of domesticity and its attendant notions of the 'womanly' became forms of labor discipline"; Wilson's text forcefully inscribes the forms of racial servitude that subtend—materially and symbolically—the white feminine ideal of (middle-class, domestic) leisure.[23]

Those forms of racialized servitude were directly shadowed by the social relations of slavery, embedded in the very heart of the white family.[24] In the South, Jacqueline Jones observes,

just as southern white men scorned manual labor as the proper sphere of slaves, so their wives strove, often unsuccessfully, to lead a life of leisure within their own homes. Those duties necessary to maintain the health, comfort, and daily welfare of white slaveholders were considered less women's work than black women's and black children's work. Slave mistresses supervised the whole operation, but . . . the sheer magnitude [of labor involved in keeping all slaves and whites fed and clothed] meant that black women had to supply the elbow grease. . . . The privileged status . . . of [slave] mistresses rested squarely on the backs of their female slaves.

While most slave women were commandeered for fieldwork during the day, white mistresses "discovered in black children," especially girls, an "acceptable alternative source" of domestic, household labor.[25] The antebellum racialization of domestic service—the new definition of those "duties necessary to maintain the health, comfort, and daily welfare of white [families]" as "less women's work than black women's and black [girls'] work"—thus marked the extension of southern categories of labor and status to the northern, industrializing landscape. During this period domestic service increasingly became the occupation of black women as well as ambiguously racialized European (especially Irish) immigrant women.[26] Northern white women's desire for domestic servants was prominently politicized in 1850s debates about free labor, and the lines Wilson draws are clear; whereas Jessie Fremont, wife of the Republican presidential candidate John Fremont, famously declared during the 1856 campaign that she would rather "do my own work and be my own servant" than that "California should be a Slave State,"[27] Wilson's Mrs. B. is intent upon reproducing slavery in the free state of New Hampshire. The intimacy of domestic work produced a highly charged, potentially antagonistic relation between white women and "their" domestic servants, quite evident in Wilson's text. In particular Mrs. B. and her "favorite," her daughter Mary, anxiously endeavor to enforce race and class discipline and police racial and class boundaries in the household in ways that reveal both those boundaries' very fragility and the intensity of the Bellmont women's (psychic and material) investment in the figure they freely term "our Nig."[28] In Wilson's text domesticity and domestic labor are sites where racialized class relations are both ritually performed and materially produced.[29]

## RACE AND LABOR IN *OUR NIG*

Depicting Frado's "oppression" (*Our Nig*, 127) as a young black female servant, Wilson examines the poverty and economic marginalization of African Americans in the free North. She was not alone in doing so. According to Leslie Harris, by the 1850s a "new activism among blacks, independent of white abolitionists [emerged] to address the problems of racism, under- and unemployment, and poverty in the black community." Wilson would surely have agreed with the short-lived American League of Colored Laborers' 1850 pronouncement: "One very great evil now suffered by the free colored people of the United States, is the want of money."[30] P. Gabrielle Foreman writes, "In the 1840s and 50s, larger numbers of free blacks in the North became more vocally critical of white abolitionists' almost myopic focus on Southern slavery, one that seemed to blind them to the glaringly harsh economic and political conditions that free and fugitive blacks faced within their midst."[31] Wilson's novel contributes to this African American discourse of class, illuminating what the historian James Horton calls the usually invisible "interior of free black life in the shadowy world of the antebellum North."[32]

This attention to class required a new political as well as literary language. In her preface Wilson refers to her narrative as a literary "experiment" that she hopes will "aid me in maintaining myself and child without extinguishing this feeble life." The experimental aspects of her text, a text Foreman describes as a "sophisticated hybrid of autobiography and prose fiction," are linked to a destabilizing of social categories, especially classifications of class and race; aesthetic and social "boundary crossings" are conjoined.[33] In his groundbreaking introduction to *Our Nig*, Henry Louis Gates Jr. outlines how Wilson both fuses and revises two different narrative forms, the slave narrative and the sentimental novel, to narrate Frado's coming of age. In addition, by opening the novel with what amounts to an attenuated seduction narrative—the story of Mag's seduction and abandonment by a wealthy suitor, her denigration as a "fallen woman" and struggle to survive at the margins of society, and her subsequent marriage to the "kind-hearted African" Jim (9)—Wilson also incorporates, and conspicuously positions Frado's story alongside, a popular (white) working-class narrative form. Andrea Williams has recently argued that "genre hybridization" is one of the "literary innovations" postbellum African American authors employ to "represent class distinctions" in the African American community; in *Our Nig* genre hybridization similarly marks the literary effort to "theorize class," in particular by desegregating literary space.[34] Like Sojourner Truth's narrative, Wilson's text at once "instructs [readers] in nineteenth century working-class realities" and acutely reveals the "overlap[ping]" experiences and cultures of white and black workers in the antebellum North, during a period of abolition and racial uncertainty, especially in northern cities.[35]

By introducing her protagonist Frado as the mixed-race daughter of the white needlewoman Mag Smith and Jim, a free black laborer, Wilson immediately calls attention to these cultural and social convergences. Mag's narrative reveals both the possibility of interracial class solidarity and workingwomen's precarious whiteness (since poverty, drudgery, or interracial intimacy could compromise what Martha Hodes calls the "ideal immaculacy of white womanhood"), while testifying to the desperate efforts of many poor white women and men to cling to the psychic and social "wages of whiteness." (To illustrate her nuanced argument about the ways "sinking class standing [could push a woman] to the margins of female dignity," Hodes describes a life narrative that intriguingly combines aspects of Frado's and Mag's stories. Born in Massachusetts in 1831, an Anglo American workingwoman named Eunice Connelly works as a mill girl, housecleaner, and washerwoman and [like Frado] fashions hats out of palm; eventually she marries a mixed-race man from the West Indies.)[36] Both Frado's and Mag's intertwined stories envision the plight of the impoverished single mother, whether the sexually "compromised" or fallen woman (in Mag's version) or the abandoned wife (in Frado's); in both, the trials of the female "dependent" who becomes the sole breadwinner are made powerfully visible. Wilson's use of Mag's story is complex. Certainly there are numerous echoes between the framing maternal text and Frado's coming of age. Like Frado, Mag is "early deprived of parental guardianship" and grows up "unprotected, uncherished, uncared for" (*Our Nig*, 5); also like Frado, Mag is written as a class victim, subject to the exploitative, appropriative desires of the wealthy—in Mag's case, a seducer who "garner[s]" her virtue as a "trophy" and cruelly sacrifices her to his economic ambitions (6). Mag's economically induced mobility anticipates her daughter's own wanderings in search of work at the end of the text, while Mag's decision to "give [her] children away" to a white family while she seeks work (16) prefigures Frado's far more reluctant determination to leave her babe "in charge of a Mrs. Capon" until she can "recruit her health, and gain an easier livelihood for herself and child" (129).[37] Importantly, Mag early learns, like Frado, that the "great bond of [social] union" (6)—what the narrator sarcastically terms "the great brotherhood of man" (7)—is thoroughly corrupted by prejudices of class and race. The limited "sympathy" of white middle-class reformers comes under particular attack: Mag's "fall" leads to her social exile and subjection to the uncharitable, "'holier-than-thou'" attitude of "professed reformers" (7); Wilson similarly attests to the "arrogance" Frado faces as a black "stranger" among hypocritical abolitionists: "Watched by kidnappers, maltreated by professed abolitionists, who didn't want slaves at the South, nor niggers in their own houses, North. Faugh! to lodge one; to eat with one; to admit one through the front door; to sit next one; awful!" (129). While Mag is initially rendered an outcast due to her sexual liaison with a wealthy seducer, that position is sealed through racial transgression—specifically her decision to marry Jim, the only individual who "notice[s]" her and offers assistance while all of Singleton, in Mag's words, "wants to see me punished, and . . . could tell when I've been punished long enough" (9–10). Upon her marriage to Jim, Mag is "expelled from companionship with white people"; her narrative of decline and fall from sexual respectability is produced by a dialectic of race and class (15). (The narrator glosses the marriage with biting sarcasm, "Poor Mag. She has sundered another bond which held her to her fellows. She has descended another step down the ladder of infamy" [13].)

The novel's opening suggests that Wilson is struggling to find a language to represent Mag's story, one adequate to its complexities as well as her own conflicted authorial feelings about it. Addressing the "gentle reader" (8), Wilson immediately writes Mag as a sexual victim, and the text begins in the sentimental, melodramatic idiom conventionalized by publications such as the *Advocate*: "Lonely Mag Smith! See her as she walks with downcast eyes and heavy heart. . . . Early deprived of parental guardianship . . . she was left to guide her tiny boat over life's surges alone and inexperienced" (5). Mag's sexual fall is coupled with her economic decline; driven into social exile by a "sneering world" (7), she lives on the boundaries of the community in an abandoned "hovel" (8) and performs outwork for two years. Gradually unable to "sustain herself" due to immigrant competition, her circumstances so reduced that she is "above no drudgery" (8),

Mag nears starvation because potential employers "seem as afraid to come here as if they expected to get some awful disease" (9). However, Wilson's lonely needleworker is quickly differentiated from the sentimental seamstresses discussed in chapter 3; dialogizing this narrative of fallenness, Wilson accents Mag's desire and class ambition (e.g., 10) as well as her unfeminine, nonnormative emotions. Even Mag's apparently deferential stance captured in the opening ("Removed from the village, she was seldom seen except . . . with downcast visage, returning her work to her employer" [8]) reflects less the becoming modesty of a needleworker who "cling[s] to virtue" than an abused woman's repressed rage.[38] "The world seemed full of hateful deceivers and crushing arrogance" (6), and Mag is "morose and revengeful"; her penitence tempered by class resentment and judgment of her supposed "superiors," she meets their censure not with "patient endurance" but with a defiant determination "to ask no favors of familiar faces; to die neglected and forgotten before she would be dependent on any" (7, 8). This refusal to sentimentalize the poor woman's subjectivity and story similarly marks Wilson's characterization of Mag's daughter, Frado, whose "wild[ness]" (18) and independence enables her to survive years of her employers' abuse, and for whom class and racial deference is qualified by a sense of her "rights" as a worker and a recipient of relief.

For Mag marriage to Jim is clearly racializing; indeed, as Foreman notes, Wilson's real mother, albeit born white, was designated African American in her obituary.[39] While Mag is partly constructed as a locus of cross-racial class solidarity and "sympathy," she is also portrayed as dehumanized by whiteness, her flickering class sympathies qualified by an investment in white privilege. Mag serves as a vehicle through which Wilson can show how racialized power relations—in Frado's family of origin and later in the Bellmont home—fractures what Wilson calls "the human family" (137). As with Mrs. Bellmont, race structures Mag's class identification and aspirations: if Mag's class ambition propels her desire for her seducer, a wealthy (white) man whose "ravishing" (6) voice, falsely promising marriage, "whispered of . . . ease and plenty" and an "elevation before unaspired to" (5), her class descent equates to a fall into "blackness"; her maternal ambivalence toward her mixed-race children is fueled by a hatred of (her own) racialization. After Jim dies, Mag's racist view of her children as "black devils" clearly informs her willingness to "give the children away" and accompany her new lover, Seth, to leave Singleton to "get work in some other place" (16). While Mag does exhibit maternal concern—expressing reservations about Mrs. Bellmont's severity as a mistress and rationalizing her decision to "relieve [her]self" of Frado with the belief that "severe restraint" will be necessary discipline for the willful child (17, 20)—she, unlike Frado later on, permanently abandons her child and evidently makes no subsequent effort to be reunited with her "pretty mulatt[o]" daughter (14). Mag's "insensibility" (21) on the day of her departure from her daughter seems to prefigure the coldness and cruelty of Frado's white mistress, while the animal imagery with which Mag is increasingly associated (e.g., she "snarl[s]" and "growl[s]" rather than speaks [16–17]) is also linked to the inhumane Mrs. Bellmont. In addition to performing reversals common to slave narratives (it is whites, not blacks, who behave like animals), Wilson's rhetoric identifies Mag and Mrs. Bellmont as similarly cold, unfeeling white mothers, challenging a mainstay of white women's moral authority and widening the social distance between the white mother and her mixed-race daughter. For Mag's leave-taking as much as her terminology ("black devils") relegates Frado to one side of the racial divide her very existence calls into question; consigning her daughter to a life of (racialized) bondage, Mag abandons Frado on the doorstep of the wealthy Bellmont family, where she endures thirteen years of indentured servitude. More generally Frado's racialized class subjection is in a dialectical relationship to antebellum (re)definitions of white working-class womanhood: Mrs. B.'s hostility toward Frado and her enforcement of Frado's racial servitude are at least partly a consequence of a new sense of power or agency among white workingwomen, so that Mrs. B., as Mag complains, "can't keep a girl in the house over a week" (18).[40] Abandoned by Mag, the Bellmonts immediately appropriate Frado as "our Nig," an appellation that enables her positioning as a domestic laborer and a sign of the Bellmonts' racialized class elevation (25–26). Frado's "place" in the class and racial hierarchy is quickly staked out: given a tiny attic that Mrs. Bellmont insists is "good enough for a nigger" (26). Frado is warned that should she outgrow those quarters "she'll outgrow the house" (28).

That place is consolidated by Frado's subsequent treatment at the hands of the Bellmont women. When Frado arrives, the family is uncertain "what should be done with her" (25), an uncertainty met with Mrs. B.'s insistence that Frado will "be of some use." As Mag had warned, Mrs. B. "can't keep a girl in the house over a week"; she muses upon Frado's arrival, "If *I could make her do my work* in a few years, I would keep her. I have so much trouble with girls I hire, I am almost persuaded if I have one to train up in my way from a child, I shall be able to keep them awhile" (26, emphasis added). Six-year-old Frado will, it is decided, take the position of Bridget, the Irish servant who had quit the "very day" before Frado's arrival (28). It is crucial to note that, due to the gendered definition of domestic labor, Mrs. B. and her daughter Mary from the outset view Frado as a laborer in ways the Bellmont men clearly do not. (Thus even the relatively benign Aunt Abby states with regret when James expresses his desire to remove

Frado from her abusive situation, "I don't know what your mother would do without her; still, I wish she was away" [76].) The Bellmont women's experience of domestic "servitude" is clearly projected onto Frado, while the proximity of her black body makes the household's relations of power and labor uncomfortably apparent.[41] A feminine, domestic version of the structure of racial "ambivalence," of "love and theft," that Eric Lott identifies in antebellum white workingmen's culture, this structure of racial feeling is complexly inscribed in Wilson's novel and is responded to in various ways by Frado. And it is the racial instability of the antebellum decades in the "free" North, a period of abolition and racial uncertainty, that leads Mrs. Bellmont to enforce Frado's racial "servitude" and performatively reiterate racial boundaries so insistently and violently. Over the course of the novel Mrs. B. and Mary insistently displace the demands of the body, and the forms of physical labor in the household, onto Frado: Frado's labor is crucial both symbolically and materially, for it underwrites the feminine "leisure" that was becoming a requisite sign of genteel "respectability" among the middle class.[42] Frado's presence as a household worker in particular frees the Bellmont *daughters* from the demands of physical labor to pursue educational and other opportunities; as Boydston notes, in the antebellum period domestic servants increasingly engaged in tasks traditionally performed by female kin—a fact that makes Mary, the household member closest in age to Frado and "not many shades darker" (39) than the servant, a particularly charged locus of Mrs. B.'s (racialized) class feelings.[43]

*Our Nig* thus traces the violent assertion of domestic whiteness and Frado's ongoing disruption of it. The mixed-race child of a miscegenous union, Frado is both the locus of social indeterminacy and the object of insistent, often violent efforts to (re)affirm the domestic boundaries of gender, race, and class.[44] "Placing" Frado under the domestic supervision of white mistresses in the Bellmont home, Wilson documents the process through which a young, mixed-race girl is made into a black (female) domestic worker. And indeed Mrs. Bellmont attempts to undergird her own whiteness by installing Frado in the household as a slave, upholding her race and class privilege by inscribing Frado within the bounds of the slave narrative. Such a gesture amounts to resegregation of both domestic and literary space. Although Mary strenuously objects to Frado's placement in the household ("I don't want a nigger 'round *me*" [26]), her mother seems confident that the spatialized hierarchies of the domestic environment can contain the racial "contamination" Mary fears: the narrator observes, "Mrs. Bellmont felt that [Frado's] time and person belonged solely to her. She was *under her* in every sense of the word" (41, emphasis added). Mrs. B. embodies class privilege (what Bourdieu terms the class "habitus") in an array of domestic practices, practices frequently noted by critics. Frado is told to eat standing up, "by the kitchen table, and must not be over ten minutes about it," while the family eat their morning meal in the dining room; Frado eats "a bowl of skimmed milk, with brown bread crusts," while they breakfast on more substantial and savory fare (29). Clothing too differentiates them, which is especially significant in public spaces; when Frado is permitted to attend school for three months of the year, she must appear "with scanty clothing and bared feet," such sartorial markings serving, in Mary's words, to "lowe[r] Nig where, according to her views, she belonged" (31). Transforming the mixed-race Frado into an object of labor requires blackening her, both symbolically and literally: blackness becomes the means by which servitude is written on the body. At the beginning of her stay with the Bellmonts, "at home, no matter how powerful the heat when sent to rake hay or guard the grazing herd, [Frado] was never permitted to shield her skin from the sun. . . . Mrs. Bellmont was determined the sun should have full power to darken the shade which nature had first bestowed upon her as best befitting" (39). The novel in fact demonstrates, with Bourdieu, how class power is embodied and performed in the corporeal or "bodily hexis," defined by Bourdieu as "the political mythology realized, *em-bodied*, turned into a permanent disposition, a durable way of standing, speaking, walking, and thereby of *feeling* and *thinking*," as well as the role of middle-class women in controlling the signifiers of class.[45] Other racial codes complicate Frado's construction as a laboring body; for example, the Bellmont men, especially Jack and James, perceive Frado in highly sexualized terms from the moment she arrives.[46] But the interpellative force of the Bellmont women's efforts to materialize Frado's racial servitude is driven home by the fact that, fantasizing liberation from Mrs. B.'s bondage, Frado dreams only of becoming a domestic servant for James or Jack (e.g., 63, 70).

The main social practice differentiating whites from blacks in the Bellmont household is the "discipline" of labor itself. When Frado arrives at the Bellmont house, she is only six years old but is expected to perform multiple tasks on the farm, including feeding poultry and livestock, driving cows to pasture, washing dishes, collecting wood for the fireplace, and running "hither and thither from room to room": "It was a new discipline to the child. . . . The same routine followed day after day, with slight variation; adding a little more work, and spicing the toil with 'words that burn,' and frequent blows to the head" (29–30). Within a year "her labors were multiplied; she was quite indispensable, although but seven years old" (30). As more time passes, she assumes "additional burdens": "She must now *milk* the cows, she had then only to drive. Flocks of sheep had been added to the farm, which daily claimed a portion of her time" (52–53);

she is also apparently installed as cook (66). Here, as in slavery, the gender division of labor is not adhered to, further differentiating "domestic woman" from (black) laborer. "In the absence of the men," the narrator explains, "[Frado] must harness the horse for Mary and her mother to ride, go to mill, in short, do the work of a boy" (53). Such passages present a surprisingly frank, straightforward accounting of the exigencies of farm labor: in particular Wilson contests the romanticized accounts of farm life and labor central to the pastoral ideal—since Jefferson, a centerpiece of national ideology.[47]

Mrs. Bellmont enforces labor discipline with "words that burn, and frequent blows to the head," applied with a "rawhide, always at hand in the kitchen" (30), while Mary, angered that Frado is winning friends at school by her liveliness and "merriment" (32), resolves to "use physical force 'to subdue her,' to 'keep her down'" (33). The Bellmont women's use of corporal punishment partly expresses what I have identified as the text's feminization of class struggle: their sadism is inseparable from their economic ambition (evidenced in Mrs. B.'s promise to "beat the money out of [Frado], if I can't get her worth any other way" [90]). The aim of both the endless regimen of labor and the use of physical force is to enact a reduction of the subject to the body—the "bur[ial]" of self within the bodily realm that Stewart protested. And indeed the Bellmont women refuse to acknowledge that Frado is other than body, insistently denying that she has a soul and intellect—a very subjectivity—worthy of attention and care. For example, Mrs. Bellmont "did not feel responsible for [Frado's] spiritual culture, and hardly believed she had a soul" (86); "Mrs. Bellmont . . . did not trouble herself about the future destiny of her servant. If she did what she desired for *her* benefit, it was all the responsibility she acknowledged" (87). She tells Frado it would "do no good for her to attempt prayer; prayer was for whites, not for blacks. If she minded her mistress, and did what she commanded, it was all that was required of her" (94). Mrs. B. sees that the girl's school and church attendance undermines racial hierarchies that are as entrenched in the North as in the South. As she complains to her husband, "I found her reading the Bible to-day, just as though she expected to turn pious nigger, and preach to white folks. . . . Why, according to you and James, we should very soon have her in the parlor, as smart as our own girls" (88–89). Mrs. Bellmont's concern is that universalizing access to education and religion will blur the social boundaries of class (always racialized) within the household; it would contest the symbolic, as well as the material, relations of class. Objecting heatedly to Frado's churchgoing, Mrs. Bellmont reminds her husband, "Don't you know that every night she will want to go toting off to meeting? and Sundays too? and you know we have a great deal of company Sundays, and she can't be spared," and she asks,

"Who ever thought of having a nigger go [to church], except to drive others there?" (89). Frado herself describes evening church meetings as a "pleasant release from labor" (69), while Mrs. B. perceives full well the link between Frado's burgeoning spirituality and her economic independence; as she warns Mr. B., "If you should go on [encouraging Frado's church attendance], it would not be six months before she would be leaving me, and that won't do" (89–90).

One can certainly see Mrs. Bellmont's racial phobia as a defensive response to the racial ambiguities of Mag's story. Indeed the desperate efforts of the Bellmont women to police Frado's place suggests a fear of racial contamination and the haunting presence of Mag's precarious whiteness. But it is easy to miss how Mrs. B.'s performance of domestic authority is meant to mask the ambiguities of her own class position; in *Our Nig* racial phobia and class ambition are explicitly and fundamentally intertwined. It is precisely because Mrs. Bellmont, as the matron of a rural homestead whose husband "had not in his family arrangements departed from the example of his father" (22), is quite plainly and unambiguously a worker, that she is at such pains to disavow that identification in the era of hegemonic domesticity and its pastoralization or invisibilization of domestic work. Mrs. B. clearly attempts to project her own identity as a laboring woman onto Frado; as she muses upon Frado's arrival, "If *I could make her do my work* in a few years, I would keep her." Mrs. Bellmont's class ambition, emphasized throughout the novel, is especially evident in negotiations surrounding her children's marriages. While the definition of Frado as a laborer and an instrument of economic and status advancement is in part a vehicle for symbolically and performatively differentiating white from black, middle-class domestic manager from servant, within the household Mrs. B. is also concerned with the reproduction of class; she thus views her children as a means to consolidate her social status. Son James marries Susan, "a Baltimorean lady of wealthy parentage, an indispensable requisite, his mother had always taught him" (55). Mrs. Bellmont next "command[s]" daughter Jane to accept the proposal of their neighbor Henry Reed; Mrs. Bellmont "had counted the acres which were to be transmitted to an only son; she knew there was silver in the purse; she would not have Jane too sentimental" (56). She relents only when her husband intervenes to defend Jane's preference. But Mrs. B.'s ambition for her children's upward mobility is made most clear when Jack marries in the west. Jenny is "an orphan whose home was with a relative, gentle, loving, the true mate of kind, generous Jack" (111). When his mother learns that Jenny "hadn't . . . any property" (111), she complains, "What do you want to bring such a poor being into the family for?" (112) and counsels him to abandon her. When Jack sends for Jenny instead, Mrs. B. extends "a cold welcome to her new daughter, eyeing her dress with closest scrutiny. Poverty was to her a disgrace, and she could not associate with any thus dishonored" (112). She goes so far as to circulate a sexual narrative about Jenny's "illegal intimacy" with another man to justify Jack's "desert[ion]" of his wife and child and relieve him "of his burden" (112–13). Mrs. B. thus produces her own seduction narrative, not in order to gesture toward forms of class "kinship," as in Wilson's framing of Frado's mother's story, but as a form of policing that enforces social and cultural boundaries of class.

While the Bellmont women struggle to assert control over Nig and situate her within slave-like relations of ownership, this inscription, I have suggested, is by no means uncontested. In particular, white female (and domestic) discursive authority is unsettled by what Wilson terms the "kitchen version"—the primacy of the black, female, working-class voice (71). What is striking about the text's account of this resistance is the sheer resourcefulness of its heroine; if Frado's experience of class exploitation and subordination is raced and gendered, her resistances are similarly multivalent, and she makes complex, creative use of materials at her disposal to resist "servitude" and promote her own physical and psychological survival. Her biracialism fuels that resourcefulness and improvisational facility. News of the existence of an abolitionist movement, coming at a crucial point in the story, counters her sense of isolation and the feeling that she is valued only for her work (75); in multiple ways, I have suggested, she seizes upon the language of rights, democratic entitlement, and the dignity of labor associated with activist working men and women—the language of "free labor"—to challenge Mrs. B.'s "ownership" and imagine another destiny for herself.[48] Frado's resistance is partly envisioned as sheer power of endurance: noting that all the Bellmont children—as well as her oft-absent husband—leave Mrs. Bellmont's house as quickly as they are able, the narrator states, "There seemed no one capable of enduring the oppressions of the house but [Frado]" (109). But what Xiomara Santamarina terms the literal and figurative "emancipation" of Frado's labor is principally effected through Wilson's account of Frado's subjective autonomy despite Mrs. B.'s repeated efforts to destroy the girl's independent sense of self. In important ways *Our Nig* uses the conventions of the female Bildungsroman to counter the sense of (racial) servitude that the Bellmont women attempt to engender and enforce.

Although scholars often detail the aspects of Frado's story that resemble enslavement—and, indeed, Mrs. Bellmont uses beatings and other forms of racial terror to instill in the girl a sense of herself as powerless and permanently enslaved—what is startlingly apparent is Frado's refusal, even while a child, to submit to this view of herself. Challenging Mrs. B.'s attempted assertion of "total control" over "her" laborer, Wilson—exploiting the racial instabilities of her text—conspicuously imbues her mixed-race heroine with the "newly-won psychology of the free laborer." From the start, Wilson employs the language of free labor to envision Frado's position in the household. Lying in bed on the night of her arrival, Frado "revolv[es] in her little mind whether she would remain or not until her mother's return. She was of wilful, determined nature, a stranger to fear, and would not hesitate to wander away should she decide to" (28). After the second day Frado "found some attractions about the place" and feels "more willing to remain" (29). Despite Mrs. B.'s and Mary's unrelenting efforts at control, Frado's rebellion against their authority is sustained and striking, especially when viewed alongside the behavior of children in slave narratives, where such "antics" as Frado's largely (for a host of reasons) do not appear. It is partly the presence of sympathetic family members who "protect" her, but also arguably the laws and the broader social norms in New Hampshire—and additionally her mixed-race status—that counter the feelings of abject disempowerment and dependency Mrs. B. hopes to instill. I would suggest that the sense of (class) freedom arising from being free-born, the child of a white working-class mother and a free black father, informs Frado's subjectivity, enabling her to find "hope" even in the misery of her childhood. The product of an interracial family, she is also well positioned to claim kinship and its entitlements in the Bellmont household. Mrs. Bellmont's performance of slavery in the North is a sham, and Frado knows it; she knows enough of New England village norms to recognize that the Bellmonts owe her something for her service—and at the end of the text she aims to enforce those obligations. The presence of white workers on the farm, mostly male, who encourage and applaud her antics—and the trace of Bridget, the white Irish maid who abandons the family because of Mrs. B.'s treatment—all create some sense of class community and help foster the hope of escape. (Here the racialization of the Irish—usually seen to facilitate white workers' ambivalent identification with the black "servant"—might be seen to engender a liberatory affiliation in the other direction.) Once she is eighteen Frado *does* determine to leave the Bellmonts, despite their efforts to retain her, just as Bridget had earlier. In his 1845 *Narrative*, Frederick Douglass similarly registers a productive identification with Irish servants, whose limited indentures instill in him a hope of escape; Frado's maternal inheritance—the "contamination" of Mag's precarious whiteness—has a surprising, liberatory meaning.[49]

Frado directs her working-class critique, in particular, at Mrs. B.'s performance of gentility as embodiment and anchor of her class authority. In *Three Years among the Working Classes*, Burn complains that because everyone in America rose from humble beginnings—in the absence of gentle blood and a hereditary aristocracy, there are no "ladies and gentlemen"—female servants have little "respect" for their domestic employers.[50] Those class feelings were arguably chiefly directed at mistresses, who were principally tasked with supervising servants and were centrally involved with performing the family's class position (through manners, dress, management of cultural capital) in the household. This class-based skepticism of domestic masters and mistresses as a "sham aristocracy" is evident in a number of African American texts from this period; it informs, for example, Frank Webb's satiric depiction of Mrs. Thomas in *The Garies and Their Friends* and his evident delight (arguably tinged with misogyny) in unmasking her class pretentions.[51] And this working-class skepticism is fundamental to Frado's sustained attack on Mrs. B.'s class authority as well as her efforts to destabilize the material enactments of class in a series of highly theatrical scenes we might consider racialized class "counterperformances."[52] The performative nature of (racialized) class identities and their potentially destabilizing effects are several times cited in *Our Nig*: Frado's husband, to whom she is briefly married near the novel's end and who performs "illiterate harangues" (128) to garner abolitionist support, is one example; in another, at the end of the text Mrs. Hoggs, who temporarily harbors the ailing Frado in exchange for "gold and silver" (122), doubts the truth of her disability (and the authenticity of her poverty narrative) and reports her "to the physicians and town officers" as an "imposter" (123).[53] Indeed, attention to the performative dimension of class opens up a space for destabilizing class identities—a space that Frado exploits. She not only disrupts and ironizes Mrs. B.'s performances of sentimental, genteel whiteness; like slave narrators exposing the hypocrisy of "Christian" slave masters, she portrays the elite as sham aristocrats. But she also, as I suggested earlier, refuses to perform the part of a deferential, obedient servant in the domestic theater of class, at times by performing a comic part that seems drawn from minstrelsy's playbook. There is a spectacular, theatrical quality to Frado's acts of domestic insubordination; usually they are performed for others—notably, as in minstrelsy, an appreciative audience of laboring (white) men, including Mrs. B.'s hardworking younger son, Jack (who himself marries a poor woman). Overall, Wilson foregrounds these performances in order to destabilize—de-essentialize—racialized class identities and contest performed class hierarchies. Refusing to embody the racial role scripted for her by Mrs. B. in the family's domestic drama, Frado performs racialized class resistance and subversion.

Centered in the "kitchen version," the discursive performance of the novel itself—a semi-autobiographical text anchored in Wilson's own experience—is a primary enactment of this resistance and autonomy. This is especially important since we see how Mrs. B.'s class performances involve an attempt to wield and control language as a means of what Bourdieu terms "symbolic power." Identified with Frado's perspective, the narrative, for one thing, demystifies the prestige of leisure and white, middle-class authority Mrs. Bellmont banks on: seizing the power to expose the unflattering conditions of the Bellmonts' private life, Wilson proves true the old adage that "No man is a hero to his valet." The home as a "theater for the staging of a family's social position" and the role of middle-class women's domestic performances in anchoring her family's class authority are subjected to Frado's subversive reimagination.[54] Repeatedly characterizing Mrs. B. as "ugly" and hateful, the narrator takes pleasure in exposing the domestic turmoil in the household and Mrs. B.'s disrespectful, cold treatment by her husband and sons. For instance, while showing that Mrs. B.'s "fast flowing tears" leave no impression on her family (47), Wilson documents in several scenes that Frado is the object of near universal solicitude and sympathy among male members of the household (e.g., 36, 88, 24) as well as the invalid Aunt Abby, who bestows on the girl whatever "expressions of sympathy" (37) she can. Exposing the mundane, humiliating workings of the Bellmont household, Wilson thus subversively appropriates for her heroine the power of domestic supervision properly lodged in the "mistress" while claiming for Frado the moral (class) authority of sentimental womanhood, installing her as the central object of what Armstrong terms "domestic desire."[55]

The "expectation of obedient silence" was a conventional feature of domestic servitude; to stabilize the relations of racial servitude described earlier, the Bellmont women aim to make Frado into an object (not subject) of discourse, a bearer of the meanings they wish to impose upon her.[56] Silencing Frado is a key aspect of her punishment: on one occasion Mrs. B. and Mary beat her while "propping her mouth open with a piece of wood" so that she is unable to speak or cry out (35); on another a towel is "stuffed [into] the mouth of the sufferer," "muffl[ing]" her words and cries (82–83). Such treatment is intended to "cure [Frado] of tale-bearing" (93). Most strikingly, Mrs. Bellmont threatens that if Frado "ever exposed her to James [the son most sympathetic to Frado's plight], she would 'cut her tongue out'" (72). Frado's symbolic "liberation" within the household, like Douglass's, is marked by the unqualified assertion of her independent voice. When Mrs. B. threatens to beat her for not gathering wood quickly enough: "'Stop!' shouted Frado, 'strike me, and I'll never work a mite more for you'; and throwing down what she had gathered, stood like one who feels the stirring of free and independent thoughts" (105). Where Mrs. B. threatens violence to increase Frado's performance as laborer, Frado responds with what amounts to the threat of a strike: the withdrawal of her labor altogether. Frado's verbal performance of autonomy stops Mrs. B. in her tracks: "By this unexpected demonstration, her mistress, in amazement, dropped her weapon, desisting from her purpose of chastisement. Frado walked towards the house, her mistress following with the wood she herself was sent after," and "th[e] affair never met with an 'after clap,' like many others" (105). Demonstrating her "power to ward off assaults" and thus contest Mrs. B.'s authority, "the victory at the wood-pile" (108) provokes Frado's "free and independent thoughts" (105), strengthening her resolve to "assert her rights when they were trampled on" (108). Seizing language enables Frado to defy the relations of domestic status—the role of submissive, silent (black) servant who follows commands and of authoritative (white) mistress who delivers and enforces them—that Mrs. B. desperately tries to enforce.

The novel thus can be seen as an enactment, as well as a record, of racialized class counterperformances. Frado's unrelenting, spirited challenge to the Bellmont women's racialized class authority is asserted most effectively through her playfulness and efforts to ironize their attempts at control. (Irony is of course a strategy employed by Wilson herself, most obviously in her appropriation of the racist epithet assigned Frado by the Bellmonts for her novel's title.)[57] Frado's attempts to disrupt class hierarchy involve destabilizing the performative nature of class—and again, her mixed-race status, her proximity to Mag's precarious whiteness, infuses these efforts with a spirit of racial play. Frado's humorous attempts to carnivalize white women's domestic authority expose the fragility of that authority, especially the Bellmont women's (material and psychic) dependence on her to ratify it. In his analysis of everyday forms of workplace resistance, Robin D. G. Kelley argues that few historians have examined "the ways in which unorganized working people resisted the conditions of work, tried to control the pace and amount of work, and carved out a modicum of dignity at the workplace." Among workers who "face considerable barriers to traditional trade union organization," black domestic workers are especially notable for devising "a whole array of creative strategies, including slowdowns, theft or 'pan-toting' (bringing home leftovers and other foodstuffs), leaving work early, or quitting, in order to control the pace of work, increase wages, compensate for underpayment, reduce hours, and seize more personal autonomy." Kelley notes that such practices as "pan-toting" are often authorized by accepted popular traditions of social justice and communal responsibility, what Thompson has called the "moral economy." According to Kelley, available evidence suggests that domestic workers adopt such "sabotage techniques" more creatively and more frequently than traditional workers.[58]

Certainly Frado manages to, in Kelley's words, "jettison the mask of deference" and practice workplace and class "sabotage" throughout Wilson's text.[59]

The "willful, determined nature" first glimpsed in the novel's early chapters is given fuller expression when Frado is permitted to attend school. Mary initially relishes the racist comments of the other children because she sees "a fair prospect of lowering Nig where, according to her views, she belonged" (31); however, to Mary's dismay, Frado quickly becomes a favorite among her schoolmates through her cleverness and wit. When her classmates tease her for her old, worn clothes, "Nig's retorts were so mirthful, and their satisfaction so evident in attributing the selection [of clothing] to 'Old Granny Bellmont,' that it was not painful to Nig. . . . Her jollity was not to be quenched by whipping or scolding" (37–38). Exploiting the inherent subversiveness of the comic mode and its affinity with the "low," Frado here uses her wit to redirect her classmates' racial and class disparagement and turn it against her mistress, derisively nicknamed "Old Granny Bellmont."[60] She performs mischievous pranks, such as filling the teacher's desk drawer with cigar smoke to produce the appearance of a fire, and is "a source of great merriment to the scholars" (37). The white schoolchildren are her allies in subverting classroom discipline: "They enjoyed her antics so fully that any of them would suffer wrongfully to keep open the avenues of mirth. She would venture far beyond propriety, thus shielded and countenanced" (38). In foregrounding such merriment Wilson might seem to reinforce comic, minstrel stereotypes of African Americans performing antics for whites' pleasure. But Wilson seems to use such scenes to underscore that the novel's racial conflict is fundamentally domestic and, especially, to illustrate that Frado's intellectual independence (James calls it her "self-reliance" [69]) and spirit of resistance are unquenched by "whipping or scolding," surviving years of the Bellmont women's abuse. Through comic improvisations, Frado persistently challenges relations of authority and forms of social discipline at school and at home. Indeed, though her labors intensify throughout the book, "one spark of playfulness could remain amid such constant toil; but her natural temperament was in a high degree mirthful, and the encouragement she received [from the Bellmont men] constantly nurtured the inclination" (53). That "spark of playfulness," alive in the disciplinary sites of school and home/workplace, is fundamentally a spirit of class resistance.

"In Mrs. Bellmont's presence [Frado] was under restraint; but in the kitchen, and among her schoolmates, the pent up fires burst forth" (38). However, as we have already seen, on several occasions Frado does actively challenge Mrs. Bellmont's authority. For example, she responds to Mrs. Bellmont's orders and threats with backchat and "sass"; she foils several of Mrs. B.'s schemes (such as her effort to separate Jack from his beloved but poor wife) by exploiting her privileged access, as servant, to her mistress's domestic secrets; she escapes, maroon-like, to a nearby swamp after a particularly severe beating; to stave off abuse she at times appeals to her allies in the household (especially James and Aunt Abby), though threatened with death for doing so (65); and when she can tolerate the abuse no longer, she contemplates the familiar slave practice of poisoning her mistress (108).[61] But Frado's comic imagination is vividly evident in one indelible incident: when Mrs. B. orders Frado to eat from her own used dinner plate, Frado calls her dog to "wash it, which he did to the best of his ability," before she begins eating (71). This performance, more than any other in the novel, is infused with the spirit of subversion seen in African American vernacular performance traditions such as Pinkster, with its "burlesque and complexly satirical displays of mock underclass enfranchisement."[62] Brilliantly following Mrs. B.'s order but improvising on it, Frado challenges her mistress's domestic authority. In addition to signifying the racist equation of blacks with animals, Frado here asserts Mrs. B.'s *inferiority* to rather than elevation above animals, thus spectacularly subverting domestic hierarchies of "high" and "low," spirit and body. Asserting Mrs. B.'s proximity to the realm of animals, the body, and physical "defilement," Frado aggressively undermines the system of racial and class signification (of feminine refinement and disembodiment) upon which Mrs. B.'s domestic authority rests.

Mrs. B. is a subject of normative class discourses, and her performances of domestic womanhood are discursive as well as bodily; for example, her professions of piety, physical weakness and delicacy, her performance of bereavement at James's death—all are citations of the sentimental mode. Further unsettling Mrs. B.'s sham performance of sentimental femininity as the basis of her class authority, Wilson pointedly locates true sympathy not with domestic womanhood but with the working class, especially working-class women. *Our Nig's* final form of genre-mixing appropriates the moral authority of the sentimental mode for the black working-class female subject. Like such working-class activists as Jennie Collins, who records the everyday acts of generosity of poor and working-class people whose benevolence and kindness, unlike that of the middle class, is not "noised about" and is "never heard of by the world," and who describes the kitchen as an incubator of sympathy, Wilson identifies the ethical locus of true "union" and sympathy (defined against the specious "bond[s]" of the middle class) with the traditional values and communal sensibilities of blacks and poor whites. From the "colored brethren" described in the preface as "a faithful band of supporters and defenders" to the impoverished Mrs. Moore, who takes Frado in when sick, and the "plain, poor, simple woman" who instructs her in bonnet making (124), Wilson envisions the humble poor as those who "open [their] door[s] and [their] heart[s]" (124) and recognize Frado's membership in what one appendix to the text terms "the human family" (137). (For many, including the previously wealthy Mrs. Moore, the experience of poverty "unlock[s one's] heart to sympathies" unknown by the rich [123].) Indeed the novel itself should be read as an effort to mobilize such an imagined community of care and sustenance (129) and to position the homeless Frado and her child securely within it; the narrator pointedly instructs her readers at the end of the text, "Enough has been unrolled to demand your sympathy and aid" (130). By the text's conclusion this expanded sense of family and sympathy opens out to encompass the "charities of the public" (124), including and especially Frado's "colored brethren" and those who "call themselves friends of our dark-skinned brethren," the novel's abolitionist audience (140). Situating her own story as (nominally) free black in intimate proximity to accounts of "legal bondmen," Frado hopes to activate the "charities of the public" to address inequities of both class *and* race.

## *Five*. Hidden Hands

### E. D. E. N. SOUTHWORTH AND
### WORKING-CLASS PERFORMANCE

This chapter further problematizes our understanding of the "feminine fifties" by taking up the work of the immensely popular author E. D. E. N. Southworth. Southworth's most widely read novel, *The Hidden Hand*, first serialized in the *National Era* and the New York *Ledger* in 1859, was perhaps the best-selling novel of the century; it was dramatized in at least forty versions between 1859 and 1883.[1] Like *Our Nig*, *The Hidden Hand* foregrounds the racialization of class in the 1850s; also like Wilson's novel, Southworth's focuses on the operations of social class within the home, figuring the struggle to domesticate its young heroine as a form of class power. And again like Wilson, Southworth features the performative nature of class, particularly the ways embodied performance undergirds and potentially unsettles racialized class identities and class power. Like Wilson's Frado, Southworth's heroine Capitola Le Noir (familiarly known as Cap Black) is a performer whose comic antics upend racialized relations of class authority and become a vehicle for resistance and subversion. But Southworth's capacious novel not only unmasks the sham performances of the elite; it also brings to life an array of lower-class performance modes, both stage and vernacular. Examining what one scholar calls the "porous boundaries" between print and performance cultures in the antebellum era, I consider popular performance—a crucial site of workingwomen's culture—as it shapes and is shaped by Southworth's novel.[2] Addressing a number of performance genres but centering especially on melodrama, I argue that Southworth employs the inherent subversiveness of the comic mode to challenge what Stuart Hall calls the "moralisation" of the working classes and to destabilize generic expectations and norms; in particular she attacks the conventional depiction of working-class women as sexual and economic victims ritualized on the melodramatic stage and reiterated, for example, in seamstress literature.[3]

Southworth's highly episodic writing is an especially rich source for engaging the intersection between popular performance and literary text. Contemporary critics frequently pointed to the "dramatic power" of her writing as the "secret of her popularity."[4] Assessing the "dramatic qualities" of *The Hidden Hand*, Ken Egan notes that, like Melville, Southworth was "deeply influenced by Shakespeare," but whereas Melville was inspired by Shakespeare's "printed language," Southworth was influenced especially by the stage dramas (a staple of the popular theater in the antebellum era), especially the structure of double plotting, the alternation of serious and comic materials, and the characterization of Shakespeare's mature comic heroines.[5] *The Hidden Hand*, which borrows many chapter epigraphs from Shakespeare, follows two distinct but related plotlines: the high or serious plot focused on Clara, and the low or comic plot focused on Capitola.[6] Egan further notes that "many of Capitola's speeches read like set pieces for antebellum popular theater."[7] Given the "dramatic power" of Southworth's work, it is not surprising that many of her novels were made into plays; *The Hidden Hand* was only the most frequently and widely staged. Like *Uncle Tom's Cabin*, which was also first serialized in the *National Era*, several companies specialized in Southworth's play, including Whiteley's Original Hidden Hand Company, which advertised it as "The Greatest Sensational Drama Ever Written." Southworth attended at least one performance of a staged adaptation of her work in the late 1850s, evidently applauding the effort. In a speech reported in the New York *Herald* she expressed approval of the dramatic adaptation of *Bride of an Evening*, directed by Henry Watkins, at a benefit performance in her honor at Barnum's Museum in 1858. Notably, Watkins would go on to direct and act in *The Hidden Hand* at New York's Fellows Opera House in February 1860, playing the part of the novel's comic black servant Wool to great acclaim; in 1859 the House was managed by George Christy as a venue for his Minstrels, defining the House in those years as a venue for lower-class, mixed-race amusements.[8] As

*Fig 5.1.* Poster for Whiteley's Original Hidden Hand Company, 1884. Theatrical Poster Collection, Library of Congress.

a professional writer attuned to the popular marketplace, Southworth quite possibly composed the novel's "picturesque scenes" and telling incidents with their potential dramatization in mind. Resituating *The Hidden Hand* within these performance contexts freshly illuminates the novel's popular appeal as well as Southworth's characterization of her "miscegenated" heroine. It can help us see how what Shane White identifies as forms of racial transgression and liminality in the antebellum theater and what W. T. Lhamon calls the "transmission of [lower-class] interracial affiliations" in or by antebellum vernacular performance leave a clear imprint on Southworth's novel.[9]

In important ways *The Hidden Hand* exemplifies the "interpenetration" of dramatic performance and fiction in this era.[10] I focus here on particular instances of this interpenetration: Southworth's novel invokes several ante-bellum, popular, working-class performance modes, especially melodrama, blackface minstrelsy, courtroom drama, and the rogue drama of criminality. Even the text's oft-discussed self-reflexivity, its cagey, self-conscious mockery of the genres and modes it borrows from (particularly sentimentality and melo-drama), seems to signify what Isabel Lehuu calls the "alliance between drama and print"; self-aware theatricality—expressed, for example, in prologues and epilogues and at times in actors' humorous asides to the audience—was a staple of the American theater in the era before what Lawrence Levine calls the "sacral-ization of culture" had begun to shape disciplined spectatorship and naturalistic representation.[11] In addition many of the novel's most memorable scenes, and those most frequently enacted in stage performances of the novel, are set in what we might call working-class vernacular performance sites, including the urban street, the courtroom, the prison, the gallows, even the ministerial "home visit." Settings in which a variety of working-class oral narratives are performed, these become entry points through which vernacular performances and what Ngũgĩ wa Thiong'o calls "orature" make their way into the text. I have found it helpful to view *The Hidden Hand* as an "archive" of this performance "reper-toire," a textual record of embodied enactments of class.[12] Staging this interplay of text and popular performance, the text invokes the bodily performances of class and allows us to glimpse how the "ghosted performances" of the "low"—including gestures of interracial affiliation that proliferate beneath the "institu-tional racism of modern culture"[13]—are recollected within the written archive.

Such performances are germane to Southworth's aesthetic. Describing South-worth's lonely, neglected childhood in the home of her mother and stepfather after her beloved father's death, Joanne Dobson writes that Southworth's "active imagination" was "nourished" both by voracious reading and "by long talks with the family's black servants, whose ghost stories, legends, and tales of the family's wealthy past absorbed her attention."[14] The miscegenated, lower-class origins of her art—a domesticated version of the exchanges recollected in minstrelsy—were figured in her novel *Vivia*. (Notably, there, as in Southworth's biography, do-mestic service signifies the site of this miscegenation, suggesting a new way we might conceptualize the "domestic" as a significant presence in antebellum wom-en's culture.) Writing of the artistic education of the painter Theodora Shelley, Southworth describes the crucial influence of the old black servant Pharaoh, who was "as full of family history, romance, fable, song and story, as any old minstrel retainer of the olden times—and never had he found a listener so attentive, in-terested, and admiring as Theodora. He was her circulating library, her theatre, her academy of music, her gallery of pictures, and her voyage round the world, all in one—and she was his intelligent audience, his appreciating public, admiring posterity, and embodied fame!"[15] This characterization of the female artist as the "embodied fame" of the black servant's voice captures the dynamic I am after here, and is a striking condensation of Southworth's social(ized) aesthetic. (In describing Theodora's receptivity to the black male servant's voice, the passage also implicates the female artist in a scandalously miscegenous act of cultural reproduction.) In *The Hidden Hand*, Cap is similarly positioned as the audience of the black servant's stories—specifically the gossip of Wool and her personal servant Pitapat—stories that spark Cap's dramatic imagination and at times spur her into action, realizing their "embodied fame" in the novel's dramatic episodes. Drawing literary inspiration from the lower-class oral performances of (black and white) servants, Southworth calls attention to the cultural interchanges between low and high, black and white that *Our Nig*'s Mrs. B. attempts to guard against. Like Wilson, Southworth portrays the fluidity of racial and class boundaries and situates that fluidity in the domestic sphere, the very heart of women's culture. But whereas Wilson stresses the moral authority of the "kitchen version," Southworth emphasizes the sensational appeal of the servants' stories. The contaminating presence of servants' "orature" and literacy practices—what Jean Fernandez calls servants' "ill/literacy"—were widespread topics of moral reformers' concern; especially given servants' role in the care of children, those practices generated real cultural anxiety. As Fernandez notes, "Low culture, imported into the household through improprieties of reading and [storytelling] on the part of its menials, possessed insidious powers of cultural contamination."[16] Rejecting in this instance, as in others, the piety of moral reformers, Southworth embraces "ill/literacy" as the inspiration of her popular aesthetic. Writing of the "profound bond of empathy" Southworth felt with her readers, in part born of the poverty she experienced after her father's death and later her husband's abandonment, Dobson calls her a "popular writer in the most accurate sense of the word": "Not only did her work find continual favor with an enormous popular audience, but she herself wrote from the vantage point of the people, always bearing in mind the presence of her audience and their desires and preferences."[17] Grounding her writing in the performances of the "low" is a central expression of this "bond of empathy," defining in key ways Southworth's literary aesthetic.

CLASS, GENDER, AND THE POLITICS OF MELODRAMA

Serialized in the *National Era* and the New York *Ledger*, *The Hidden Hand* is an example of the "cheap fiction" discussed in chapter 2. As discussed in that chapter, scholars have traced changes in book publication in the 1830s and 1840s that gave rise to the emergence of mass literature, focusing on the newspaper revolution in the 1830s and the rise of the penny press, developments fueled by the invention of the steam-powered press and new forms of cheap distribution via rail, newsstands, and dry goods stores. This revolution in print enabled an explosion of popular narratives, including dime and pamphlet novels, as well as story papers such as the New York *Ledger*; established in 1855 by Robert Bonner, the *Ledger* quickly became the nation's most widely read weekly.[18] (Edward Everett spoke of the *Ledger* as "the first attempt in this country, on a large scale" to reach what Dickens called "the unknown public.")[19] The fiction published in pamphlet novels and story papers like the *Ledger*, Michael Denning explains, was a "body [of literature] quite separate from the genteel fiction of the Victorian middle classes, the novels reviewed and serialized in the major periodicals: *Century*, *Scribner's*, *Harper's*, and the *Atlantic*," both in its class accents and in its audience. According to Denning, "The bulk of the audience of dime novels were workers—craftworkers, factory operatives, domestic servants, and domestic workers"; he argues further that the "bulk of workers' reading" was popular fiction. While acknowledging, with Christopher Looby, *The Hidden Hand*'s mass audience, I follow Denning in foregrounding these often elided working-class readers and examining the working-class accents of Southworth's novel—accents amplified when we situate the text within popular performance cultures.[20]

Like many popular texts of the time, *The Hidden Hand* is based on a newspaper report, which Southworth described as "a short paragraph in which it was stated that a little nine-year-old girl dressed in boy's clothing, and selling newspapers, had been arrested. She was homeless and friendless and was sent to some asylum in Westchester County."[21] The novel's serial format facilitated a kind of dialogue between author and reader and gave audience demand an evolving, visible place within the narrative. Scholars have linked serial fiction and its particular temporality with an open-ended sense of politics (including sexual and class politics);[22] Southworth's receptivity to her readers' feedback and wishes imbues her text with the improvisational facility and transformative power of performance, enacting the potentiality of the serial form as perpetually open to revision. Explicitly acknowledging her audience's desires, Southworth begins a chapter late in the text as follows: "How glad I am to get back to my little Cap; for I know very well, reader . . . that you have been grumbling for two weeks for the want of Cap."[23] Indeed it is to her audience's response—"grumbling" as well as applause—that Capitola's very narrative ascendancy can be attributed: as Cap "came to life" and enchanted her audience, Southworth appears to have adjusted authorial expectations for the story; in particular she dropped Gabriel

Le Noir's plot to murder Cap, displacing the threat of his persecutory violence onto more dispensable characters (especially Clara Day and Traverse Rocke). "I have always tried to please the multitude and satisfy the cultured," Southworth wrote in a letter to her editor.[24] In Bonner she found a skilled collaborator; upon his retirement in 1887, the editor of the *New York Times* wrote, "Nobody has approached [Bonner] in knowledge of what the American people liked to read."[25] A brilliant entrepreneur, Bonner did not hesitate to exercise his editorial discretion by "cut[ting] down" installments to intensify narrative pacing and maintain readerly "interest," and he regularly passed on to his authors criticisms received from readers.[26] Such partnerships ensured Southworth's popularity: early in her career she signed a long-term contract with Theophilus B. Peterson, at midcentury "the foremost publisher of sensational fiction and cheap reprints"; in 1857 she completed a lucrative deal with the *Ledger* for exclusive serial publication of her novels. Southworth's fame extended for many decades: Peterson brought out an edition of her collected works in forty-two volumes in 1877, and several of her novels remained in print through 1930, making her, in the words of one historian, "one of the most popular women writers in American publishing history."[27]

Attesting to this popularity, Denning notes that the sensational serial fiction of writers such as Southworth "attracted their wide audience among young working-class women" and sustained their popularity—alongside working-girl novels by Laura Jean Libbey and others—during the final decades of the century.[28] Anecdotal evidence appears to confirm the truth of Denning's claim. It is telling, for instance, that Willa Cather in a disparaging review would (wrongly) recollect that Southworth wrote variations of one plot over and over, "adventures [of] self-sacrificing chambermaids and noble, though affectionate factory girls."[29] An 1851 review of Southworth's *Shannondale*, discussed in chapter 2, characterizes the text as containing countless "inanities" published "to the delight of milliner girls and the terror of editors."[30] It appears that Southworth's novels remained popular among workingwomen into the twentieth century. A letter from a young, working-class female reader published in the Women's Trade Union League's journal, *Life and Labor*, responded to unionists' prescription of "serious" reading for workingwomen: "I am a girl of fifteen years of age and I have already read a good many books which you don't like: most of them are by Mrs. Bertha M. Clay, Georgie Sheldon, Mrs. Southworth, etc. I like instructive books quite well, but I think them a little dry, but as you say I ought to read them, I will try my best to do so."[31] Signaling the importance of dime novel reading in working-girl culture at the turn of the century, Dorothy Richardson relates a telling experience during her brief stint at factory work.

When she revealed that she had never read a dime novel romance, her female coworkers expressed their surprise in the very idiom of popular melodrama: one exclaimed in mock disbelief, "Oh, mama! Carry me out and let me die!"; another clutched her throat, crying, "Water! Water! . . . I'm going to faint!"[32] In addition to expressing the same "self-reflexive irony" exhibited in Southworth's novel (see below), such accounts, as Nan Enstad claims, suggest not only the currency of sensational fiction within workingwomen's culture; they also indicate that reading popular fiction was an "important . . . part of the process of *becoming* a working woman." In other words, dime novels, "as valued objects, played a role in [workingwomen's] subjectivity formation."[33]

Addressed to a popular audience, *The Hidden Hand* presents a sustained revoicing of antebellum languages of class; as demonstrated below, Southworth's heroine serves as a vehicle for recording the political demands and aspirations of working-class women. The novel incorporates, for example, workingwomen's demand for economic equity and the democratic expansion to female workers of what one character calls "human rights" (326); assertions of female autonomy and independence; pointed critiques of paternal authority and the myth of male protection (differently embodied in class relations, chattel slavery, and domesticity); claims of poor women's "right" to forms of relief and public care (a sense of entitlement that quite distressed antebellum writers on the problem of poverty); and especially analyses of what Southworth depicts as a class-based (predominantly male) obsession with, and desire to control, working-class women's sexuality. Feminizing its class critique, the text on at least one occasion gives working-class women explicit presence in the narrative as readers. Alone in Warfield's residence midway through the text, Capitola, the white domestic Mrs. Condiment, and the black servant Pitapat—a notably interracial collective—exhibit what the narrator calls a "natural" female taste for ghost stories and "stories of terror" (191); in a self-reflexive characterization of her own audience (Southworth published several volumes of ghost stories, and *The Hidden Hand* incorporates gothic and sensational elements), lower-class female characters are marked as privileged consumers of popular fictional fare.[34] But the novel's self-consciousness about interpretive codes centers on its heroine: Cap is a "text" that various characters attempt to "read," and she (like Southworth) hopes they find the "page . . . entertaining" (388). As the comic heroine and locus of the text's abundant carnivalesque energies, Capitola disrupts aesthetic expectations as fully as she defies social norms and, in so doing, calls attention to the artifice of both.[35]

By the 1850s, as Christine Stansell has shown, a "true womanhood" for the working class, clothed in meekness and fragility, was widely promoted in popular journalism and literature.[36] Cap decisively departs from this tradition. By birth a wealthy southerner, Capitola is raised by a black nurse and laundress in the slums of New York City and spends her early adolescence living on the streets disguised as a newsboy.[37] The New York chapters reveal what White calls the "fluidity of racial categories" and interracial relationships common especially in poor urban neighborhoods in the North; like Wilson's Frado, Cap is raised by a foster mother in a biracial domesticity, an upbringing that defines her precarious whiteness. Through complexities of plotting and characterization—Cap's cross-dressing is a recurring motif—Southworth unsettles antebellum gender and racial norms, registering class longings and identifications that are expressly politicized. (Indeed, Southworth makes what Engels termed the "struggle for the breeches" in the working-class family intensely visible in this novel.)[38] Although the melodramatic plot of seduction appears repeatedly in *The Hidden Hand*, Southworth refuses to characterize her heroine as a passive victim of male sexual license: in a working-class feminist revoicing of melodramatic codes, the novel emphasizes Cap's agency in manipulating forms of familial power and heterosexual exchange. Southworth presents a powerful critique of patriarchal authority, including what she envisions as its bourgeois institutionalization: the sentimental enshrinement of domesticity as the site of feminine fulfillment. "Rescued" by the wealthy Major Warfield from what he terms the "want, toil, fear, and all the evils of destitute orphanage," Cap finds herself "bored to death" and chafes under her benefactor's presumptive paternalism (51, 173). Refusing to relinquish the physical, psychological, and economic freedoms, as well as the public life and identity, she experienced as a wage earner in the urban North—that is, refusing to become a dependent and "feminine" woman—Cap draws upon her early experiences to resist what she calls domestic "slavery," converting those experiences into a democratic language of rights attuned to the historical inequities of gender (187).[39] Referencing what Linda Williams describes as the insistent racialization of American melodrama, the novel emphasizes how popular sympathies in the 1850s were refracted through race and how racial signifiers could make visible lower-class identifications.[40] Offering a heroine who embodies a remarkable class, racial, and regional fusion of New York street kid and (symbolically miscegenated) southern heiress, *The Hidden Hand*'s popular accents and critique of patriarchal power are figured through both gender and race.

The "eccentri[c]" (296) Cap's general transgressiveness establishes her kinship with the rebellious and adventurous female "Amazons"—cross-dressing pirate captains and western heroines who tame horses, fend off hostile Indians, and dispense with villains—that populated popular and dime novels by the

1850s.[41] But it is Cap's complex relationship to melodrama and the figure of the melodramatic heroine that Southworth most insistently features. The text is replete with theatrical tropes (e.g., Cap is frequently imaged as an actress) and contains multiple references to melodramatic conventions. In his study of American stage melodrama, David Grimsted identifies the type of the "lively girl," a character of humble social position, regularly appearing in low-comedy subplots, who characteristically mocked stage conventions; in Capitola, Southworth elevates this figure to the central narrative role usually assigned to the virtuous (and passive) melodramatic heroine.[42] She thus installs Cap as a figure through which to comment on, and revise, generic conventions.

Southworth's novel takes special aim at melodrama because of its wide cultural (including working-class) appeal and particularly disabling gender scripts. *The Hidden Hand* consistently invokes the "melodramatic mode," reproducing some of its key features: a Manichaean conflict between good and evil, salvation and damnation; the personification of moral absolutes in stock characters, including the virtuous young woman, the noble hero who rescues the heroine, and the satanic villain (whose villainy is often disguised by his elite standing); the elaboration of conventional narratives of familial dispersal and reunion; an emphasis on the revelation and exposure of hidden actions and moral character (what Peter Brooks terms melodrama's "moral occult"); a rhetorical style characterized by expressions of highly charged emotion through hyperbolic utterances and grandiose gestures; and a tendency to convey vivid emotional effects in pictorial tableaux.[43] Grimsted identifies a formulaic "melodramatic structure" reproduced in mid-nineteenth-century American plays; the structure was so consistent that "one competent dramatist's plays were scarcely distinguishable from another's . . . in character, structure, and sentiment." Most melodramas present an unprotected, virtuous female (the heroine is almost always motherless, while her father is usually absent or incompetent) pursued with diabolical subterfuge and occasional violence by the villain. Often a votary of fashion and almost always foreign-tainted, the villain is wholly committed to what one dramatist called "shattering virtue's temple" and satisfying his lust. While the heroine is regularly described in the imagery of divinity (e.g., "heavenly maid," "chaste-eyed angel"), the villain is cast in the language of satanic deception, a characterological opposition elaborated through a gendered plot. The villain actively plans and enacts his foul designs, and the heroine is defined by extreme vulnerability and passivity; in a gesture of self-nomination characteristic of melodrama, one heroine sighs, "I can only wait patiently for the storm to burst on my head and trust to heaven for deliverance." Mediating between these two positions is a third: the villain is defeated and the young woman rescued from sexual infamy by the actions of the virtuous, manly hero. Like the heroine, he is an idealized character: courageous, faithful, virtuous, chaste, and often rural born. Grimsted observes, "The hero proved his goodness, as the villain his evil, primarily by his attitude toward 'defenseless woman' . . . that sex that *nature formed us to defend*."[44] In *The Hidden Hand* there are two distinct erotic triangles of the sort Grimsted outlines, but the emphasis on female passivity and vulnerability and heroic male "protection" of women's chastity are entirely absent. There are no plebian, rescuing male heroes to counter aristocratic villainy: lower-class men are weak and ineffectual (e.g., Traverse Rocke) or off-stage during moments of narrative crisis (e.g., Herbert Greyson), while the chivalric ideal, abandoned by men, is embodied by Cap alone. Like the melodramas Grimsted discusses, Southworth's text foregrounds female sexuality as a primarily narrative problematic, a point to which I will return.[45] But in *The Hidden Hand* forms of male authority and the binary model of gender—of male agency and knowledge and female passivity, modesty, and "innocence"—characteristic of melodrama are fundamentally called into question, subjected to a destabilizing and self-reflexive irony.

To an extraordinary degree *The Hidden Hand* comments on and even mocks melodramatic forms, revealing how familiar melodramatic codes were to antebellum readers of popular fiction while encouraging in those readers a distanced, critical stance. Unlike the audience depicted in Stephen Crane's *Maggie, a Girl of the Streets*, in which working-class onlookers are absorbed in the domestic melodrama before them and "los[e themselves] in sympathy" for the suffering victims, Southworth addresses a readership capable of an ironic, critical distance from cultural texts; like Lowell women who aimed to demystify industrial propaganda, Southworth encouraged in readers a thoroughgoing skepticism toward cultural representations.[46] Cap herself models this practice of critical reading; she loves "old legends well enough to enjoy them," but she "was not sufficiently credulous to believe" them (79). It is arguably its irreverent, playfully ironic tone—a far cry from the elevated moral tone of sentimentalism—that most clearly (and subversively) marks the text's departure from sentimental "woman's fiction"; Sarah Josepha Hale, the editor of *Godey's*, that influential purveyor of the properly feminine and sentimental, censured Southworth for writing with a "freedom of expression that almost borders on impiety," and charges of Southworth's "vulgarity" led to a campaign by the American Library Association later in the century to destroy all of her books.[47] Rather than mobilizing conventions of sympathetic belief, *The Hidden Hand* repeatedly and mockingly calls attention to the fictiveness of cultural codes in order to interrogate and disarm them, promoting a critical distance that owed something to the "metatheatricality" of antebellum stage performance. Like the heroine of *Mysteries of Lowell*, discussed in chapter 2, the orphaned, homeless Cap—raised outside patriarchal domesticity, by a black woman—doesn't quite "believe" in male power; in Carolyn Steedman's memorable phrase, the "iron of patriarchy" didn't "enter into [her] soul."[48] In *The Hidden Hand*, this demystification of male power is directed especially at the popular, melodramatic vocabulary of gender.

Throughout the text, characters reiterate melodramatic clichés such as "your money or your life" (ironized by enclosure in scare quotes) during dramatic situations, and measure their own emotional reactions against those seen featured on the stage (19). For example, when one character's estranged nephew is abruptly restored to him, he wittily states, "I am not sentimental, nor romantic, nor melo-dramatic, nor anything of that sort. I don't know how to strike an attitude and exclaim—'Come to my bosom, sole remaining offspring of a dear, departed sister,' or any of the like stage-playing" (55). "Strik[ing] an attitude" is something Capitola, especially, is practiced at: she frequently comments on melodramatic stage conventions and her performances are pointedly directed at defusing everyday forms of male power. Employed to comic effect, Cap's role-playing is often a blatant form of gender pedagogy; her improvisational efforts to lead men on instruct by forcing their recognition of sexist, prejudicial views. Her performances also bespeak a commitment to publicity: public scenes such as the wedding ceremony, in which Cap poses as Clara Day to prevent the latter's forced marriage, and another where she stages a duel with Craven Le Noir spectacularly contest feminine privatization. Capitola's male guardian wishes to draw the curtain on her performances—"I am not so proud of your masquerading as to publish it," he tells her (53)—aiming to affirm the modesty and maidenly "innocence" her behavior belies. Transgressing bounds of class and gender propriety—what one character terms her "hoydenism" (366) is repeatedly invoked—Capitola defies, and enables Southworth to comment on, hegemonic versions of femininity. Warfield announces, "Cap isn't *sentimental*!" (175), and the narrator asserts that Cap "abhor[s] sentiment" (123); Cap herself affirms the performative nature of sentimental femininity, claiming a facility to "do the sentimental up brown" (312). Comparing the "monotony of her life at Hurricane Hall" with her former existence as a "Bowery boy" (213, 173), Cap exclaims, "I'm bored to death! . . . Nothing ever happens here! The silence deafens me! the *plenty* takes away my appetite! the *safety* makes me low!" (173, emphasis added). For Cap class and gender "privileges" of domestication—including paternalist assurances of material "plenty" and physical "safety"—are reinterpreted as captivity and loss, threatening the obliteration of her public self. She complains to Warfield, "Just decomposing above ground for want of having my blood stirred, and I wish I was back in the Bowery! Something was always happening *there*! One day a fire, the next day a fight, another day a fire and a fight together . . . every day something glorious to stir one's blood!" (173). Richard Brodhead characterizes sentimental texts as offering middle-class, female readers vicarious "experience" to compensate for the privations of domesticity; Cap presents the blood-stirring realm of the urban street—and what was popularly termed "street literature"—as the more appealing locus of (working)women's culture.[49]

Foregrounding Cap's performances, Southworth destabilizes conventions of melodramatic artifice and forms of patriarchal authority to which those conventions have historically been attached.[50] Infused with a revolutionary fervor that Southworth stresses is Cap's maternal legacy—her mother was "the daughter of . . . French patriot[s]" who "perished on the scaffold in the sacred cause of liberty" (177)—Cap counters paternal presumption with republican ideals, claiming the egalitarianism of Painite radicalism and adopting its political rhetoric to women's domestic situation. (Described as a "Napoleon in petticoats" [306] and tellingly compared to the "fear[less]" Chevalier Bayard [351], Cap's French and revolutionary origins contribute significantly to her characterization.)[51] One scene in particular establishes Cap as the textual locus of working-class female desire. Early in the text Warfield attempts to "check" her "wild and dangerous freedom of action"; Capitola responds that "liberty is too precious a thing to be exchanged for food and clothing, and that rather than live in bondage, she would throw herself upon the protection of the court" (180–81), echoing revolutionary slogans with such assertions as "Cowardice is worse than death" (193). Warfield insists upon her compliance and respect for his masculine (class) authority; when she refuses and his efforts at emotional coercion fail, he threatens physical force (187)—with disastrous results. With "glittering eyes" that "flashed like stilettoes" and in a "deep and measured voice that scarcely seemed to belong to a denizen of earth" (188), Cap declares, "In all the sorrows, shames and sufferings of my destitute childhood, no one ever dishonored my person with a blow," coupling this moral appeal with an unnerving threat of retributive violence:

> "If ever you should have the misfortune to forget your manhood so far as to strike me—" she paused, drew her breath hard between her set teeth, grew a shade whiter, while her dark eyes dilated until a white ring flamed around the iris.
> "Oh, you perilous witch, what then?" cried [Major Warfield], in dismay.

"Why then," said Capitola speaking in a low, deep, and measured tone, and keeping her gaze fixed upon his astonished face, "the—first—time—I—should—find—you—asleep—I—would—take—a—razor—and—"

"Cut my throat! I feel you would you terrible termagent [*sic*]!" shuddered [Major Warfield].

"*Shave your beard off smick, smack, smoove!*" said Cap, bounding off and laughing merrily as she ran out of the room. (188)

While Cap's warning, punctuated by a kiss (188), may seem to us playful teasing (though it is notable that Southworth's description lingers over her terrifyingly inhuman appearance), the threat she articulates was in fact a commonly expressed fantasy in nineteenth-century literature of lower-class violence and rebellion. In *The Servant's Hand*, Bruce Robbins identifies the motif of the highly charged shaving scene in nineteenth-century depictions of domestic servants; in a range of texts, from the Waterloo sequence of Thackeray's *Vanity Fair* to Melville's *Benito Cereno*, "the shaver and the executioner are [imaginatively] conflated," and the shaving scene serves to figure both a threatening intimacy between the classes and the violent prospect of lower-class revolt.[52] In Southworth's account it is Warfield who makes explicit the shaver's mortal threat, which Cap defuses with comic merriment. Her class position in the household is ambiguous and unstable: while possessing many household privileges as her guardian's ward, she also dutifully performs tasks of domestic service, identifies with the household's female servants (she regularly defends Mrs. Condiment against Warfield's accusations and wrath), and on at least one occasion "perform[s] most of the duties of Major Warfield's valet" (380). As at once the "master's" trusted "daughter" and lower-class domestic servant, Cap embodies in this scene the threatening possibility of gender and class revolt.

Capitola repeatedly challenges Warfield's paternal authority, displacing traditional forms of domestic deference and the customary dependencies of the household with a republican idiom of natural rights. Indeed at the center of Southworth's revisionist melodrama is a southern patriarch whose power is severely compromised, and who appears primarily as a foil for Cap's acts of defiance. Cap's apparent status as orphan is not sentimentalized; instead she says, "The same fate that made me *desolate* made me *free*! a freedom that I would not exchange for any gilded slavery" (187). Cap, Warfield reluctantly learns, is "not used to being ordered about" and doesn't "know how to submit" (187). She refuses to "sell [her] free will" for material benefit: reminding Warfield that his presents are but "free gift[s]," she unsettles the material basis of his domestic authority (187). Taking special aim at the myth of chivalry, Cap contests paternal authority in its multiple incarnations in the North and the South, for as the reference to "gilded slavery" makes clear, class relations in *The Hidden Hand* are always shadowed by race and racial slavery.

## THE HIDDEN HAND OF FEMALE LABOR: STAGING WORKINGWOMEN'S CLASS CRITIQUE

Featuring the domestic conflict of a wealthy, slaveholding "plantation" (78) owner (considered by his servants a "despotic old master" [189]) and the "little savage" (350) who becomes his ward, the text at once domesticates and racializes class conflict. Unlike Frado at the hands of the Bellmont women, Cap is treated by Warfield as kin: he symbolically adopts (if he cannot legally adopt) the "savage" working-class child as part of the family; domestication is envisioned here as elsewhere as an instrument of class (as well as racial and national) assimilation. However, Cap resists these efforts; in *The Hidden Hand* and in *Our Nig* home is the site not of the dissemination of middle-class influence but of race-mixing and gendered and racialized class conflict. Certainly Cap's newfound privilege makes visible norms of class experience and "culture," localized in the domestic sphere. But the familiar narrative of the domestic trials (and resocialization) of a presumed orphan—the central plot of antebellum women's fiction—appears with an emphasis on domestic comedy. Southworth's mocking, irreverent tone undermines the moral seriousness and "resacralization of experience" associated with melodrama.[53] In particular, in her treatment of Warfield, she employs comedy, including elements from farce, to subvert melodrama's affirmation of paternal authority; Warfield's status as domestic patriarch is regularly unsettled by comic deflation. But if *The Hidden Hand* tempers melodramatic emotionalism with mocking humor in its portrait of Warfield, it elaborates the melodramatic trope of recognition in the central plot devoted to unraveling the mystery of Capitola's identity and the cause of her mother's disappearance sixteen years before the novel opens. That disappearance is revealed to be the work of a "usurping villain" (178), Gabriel Le Noir, the younger son of a prosperous southern family, who has murdered his elder brother Eugene and held Eugene's pregnant wife hostage (she is ultimately discovered in an insane asylum) to claim the family's property. (Born during her mother's captivity, the infant Capitola—along with the black midwife Nancy, who attends at the birth—are sold by Le Noir into slavery.) A principal thrust of Southworth's text is thus to reveal the hidden corruption of so-called respectable elite men, exposing them as scoundrels and criminals. But Southworth directs her class analysis at the gender prerogatives of even "benevolent" patriarchs like Warfield; casting

Warfield and Gabriel Le Noir as "mortal enem[ies]" (178), Southworth also expressly identifies the two in various ways. What Eve Kosofsky Sedgwick calls the doubling of male identification and desire characteristic of the gothic plot of persecution and revenge is quite evident in Southworth's novel.[54]

Southworth's critique of paternal power is legible in the opening pages, which introduce Warfield:

> In character Major Warfield was arrogant, domineering and violent—equally loved and feared by his faithful old family servants at home—disliked and dreaded by his neighbors and acquaintances abroad, who, partly from his house and partly from his character, fixed upon the appropriate Nickname of Old Hurricane.
>
> There was, however, other ground [*sic*] of dislike besides that of his arrogant mind, violent temper and domineering habits. Old Hurricane was said to be an old bachelor, yet rumor whispered that there was in some obscure part of the world, hidden away from human sight, a deserted wife and child, poor, forlorn, and heartbroken. It was further whispered that the elder brother of Ira Warfield had mysteriously disappeared, and not without suspicion of foul play on the part of the only person in the world who had a strong interest in his "taking off." However these things might be, it was known for a certainty that Old Hurricane had an only sister, widowed, sick and poor, who with her son dragged on a wretched life of ill-requited toil, severe privation, and painful infirmity, in a distant city, unaided, unsought and uncared for by her cruel brother. (8)

Melodrama here is the idiom of gossip and communal reproach; the irascible Warfield—nicknamed "Old Hurricane"—is the central villain in two domestic melodramas, one involving a poor "deserted wife" and the other a poor and infirm sister. (Both women, we come to learn, are seamstresses—as chapter 3 documents, a type of melodramatic victimhood in both middle-class reform and workingmen's literature.) Like the self-indulgent bachelors regularly lampooned in workingwomen's journalism (see chapter 1), Warfield violates the gendered obligations of the patriarchal social ethic, refusing to "aid" and "care for" domestic dependents. But communal suspicion doesn't end there, veering instead into gothic: it is "further whispered" that he may be responsible for the death of his older brother, whose mysterious disappearance enabled Warfield's inheritance of the family estate. This threatening suggestion is quickly dropped and never again mentioned, but it forges at the outset a link between Warfield and Le Noir, who—it turns out—has indeed killed his older brother, Eugene (Cap's father), for reasons of inheritance. Strengthening this connection, Hurricane Hall, we discover, originally belonged to Le Noir (73); it and Le Noir's estate, the Hidden House, are twin parts of an "old divided manor" (82).

Such ambiguities in Warfield's character point to the thinly veiled violence of even "benevolent" men. However, Warfield is no stereotypical melodramatic villain: diffusing Old Hurricane's threat with humor and undercutting melodrama with comedy, Southworth depicts the "despotic old tyrant" as something of a buffoon, his violent temper rendered less threatening by his advanced age. Alternately loved and feared by those who know him best, Warfield is far less sinister than the implacable Le Noir, far more capable of (moral) reformation—and narrative development—as a character. On several occasions Capitola "hold[s] up the glass" to Warfield, imitating his "furious temper" and unpleasant behavior to illustrate its damaging effect on the household (128, 127); in this active upbraiding she embodies a determinedly antisentimental version of "female influence." Warfield's growth also ushers from reconciliation with the long-suffering Marah Rocke, the "deserted wife" of communal rumor whom he unjustly accused of adultery years before. (His suspicions were manipulated by Marah's would-be seducer, Le Noir.) This emphasis on Warfield's transformation accents female agency and complicates the temporality and politics of conventional melodrama, which nostalgically gestures toward the restitution of an earlier patriarchal "golden age."[55] In particular, Warfield must be cured of his misogyny, especially his distrust of lower-class women's sexuality and his desire to police and control them. Indeed, he seems as obsessed with policing Cap's sexuality as he had been with his wife's: he had domiciled Marah—"put" his "hidden treasure" in "a pastoral log cabin"—just as he endeavors to confine Cap, imaged in identically proprietary terms (85), to Hurricane Hall.

The ambiguous character of the "capricious old master" is evident in the novel's opening incident. On that stormy night we find Warfield, a "self-indulgent old Sybarite," luxuriating in the "bodily comfort" (9) of his bedroom, relieved to be free of the "annoy[ing]" social responsibilities of such public servants as doctors and ministers, who "never can feel sure, even in the worst of weathers, of a good night's rest" (11). Jennie Collins described wealthy men who routinely "turn a deaf ear" to supplicants' "touching" stories as a way to mark the limits of sympathy in the liberal-capitalist era; Southworth's Warfield is ambiguously identified with such a disposition. When a visitor does ring at the house, Warfield's contradictory directive to the black servant, Wool—"Do you think that I am going to turn a deaf ear to a stranger that comes to my house for shelter on such a night as this? . . . Mind, I am not to be disturbed" (11)—marks both the limits of his sympathy and the appropriative identification with the bodies of his servants (envisioned here as a prosthetic listening ear); it also defines the (black) servant, the repository of the "simple stor[ies]" recounted in Collins's "kitchen encounters," as the locus of narrative authority. When the visitor, the local minister, insists upon seeing Warfield himself, stating that his business is "a matter o' life and death" (12)—the imminent death of an old woman in the community—Warfield reluctantly receives him, but only from the comfort of his bed. Emphasizing Warfield's willful immobility, the narrator again takes pains to mark the appropriative expansiveness of Warfield's "I" and the forms of often invisible (racialized and gendered) labor incorporated within it; for example, assuring the minister, "Anything in reason, I'll do!," he directs Wool, "Look in my breeches pocket and take out my purse and hand it! And then go and wake Mrs. Condiment, and ask her to fill a large basket full of everything a poor old dying woman might want, and you shall carry it!" (13). The pastor's insistence that "humanity... would prompt" Warfield to come to the dying woman's aid has no effect; only the reminder that, as a newly appointed justice of the peace, Warfield's "*official* duty" mandates that he hear the "dying deposition" (13–14) convinces him to go (though not before swearing he will "throw up [his] commission to-morrow" [14]). As in the stories of his abandoned wife and sister, Warfield's sensitivity to female suffering seems decidedly blunted; unmoved by the melodramatic urgency of the deathbed scene, the "great sensualist" (15) subordinates compassion to love of ease. When he meets the dying woman, the description is similarly equivocal: Warfield is a man "who in the actual presence of suffering, was not utterly without pity" (16).

In the first of several such scenes in *The Hidden Hand*, Warfield is positioned as audience and witness to a poor woman's oral performance. Here the testimony belongs to Nancy Grewell, a free black nurse recently returned from the North, who thirteen years earlier was kidnapped, forced to deliver a baby (Capitola, we will learn), and then "stole[n]" (25) and illegally sold with the child into slavery; escaping to New York and "toil[ing] and struggl[ing]—for—ten—long—years," she has finally saved enough money to return home and "expose the evil deeds of them villains [*sic*]" (27). Her own racial identity and the captive labor she performs, the pregnant woman's black crepe disguise, the fate to which Nancy and the child are consigned—all explicitly racialize this sequence of events: emphasizing secret plots and the illicit appropriation of property, Nancy's tale gives what Joseph Roach calls the "mortgage melodrama" clear racial meaning.[56] Uncertain of her disguised captor's identity, Nancy suspects Gabriel Le Noir; an inscribed ring given to her by the child's mother confirms this suspicion to Warfield. Other physical signs, such as Cap's birthmark, "the perfect image of a crimson hand, about half an inch in length," which appears "in the middle of her left palm," ultimately facilitate exposure of Le Noir's villainy and enable the mystery of Cap's identity to be melodramatically resolved (28).[57] Based on the nurse's testimony, Warfield—pleased that his old enemy Le Noir has "fallen into [his] power" and resolved to "have the wicked punished and the innocent protected" (29)—proceeds to New York to retrieve the girl.

Warfield's paternalistic expectations, fostered by the slave system, immediately clash with the democratic accents of the New York streets, an important setting for working-class vernacular performance. Warfield is "offended" by cabmen and porters who solicit business directly rather than wait deferentially for customers to "spea[k] first"; "the crowd, the noise, the hurry and confusion at the wharf almost drove this irascible old gentleman mad!" (31). Despairing at cabmen's insolence, Warfield is approached by "a very ragged lad some thirteen years of age" (33), who offers assistance; the lad, we come to learn, is Capitola in disguise, the first of several "breeches performances" in the novel.[58] Asking about the location of Rag Alley, where Nancy Grewell had directed Warfield to search for Capitola, the newsboy replies, "'Taint called Rag Alley now, though! It's called Hifalutin Terrace! Them *tenements* you talk of were pulled down more'n a year ago, and these houses put up in their place" (35). The conversation progresses:

> "What changes! And what became of the poor tenants?" asked Old Hurricane, gazing in dismay at the inroads of improvements.
> "The tenants?—poor wretches! How do I know? Carted away, blown away, thrown away—with the other rubbish." (35)

Referencing the dynamic of urban renewal in antebellum New York, generated by what Elizabeth Blackmar has described as the growing commodification of housing (a process linked to the city's first housing crisis),[59] the conversation desentimentalizes home, marking housing as an issue in working-class politics—one over which women often took leadership.[60] The dynamic between Cap as "Bowery boy" and Warfield as southern patriarch localizes Southworth's critique of class relations both North and South. The democratic convictions, the righteous, defiant pride and self-respect, and the overall manner of the Bowery boy constitute an integral part of Capitola's characterization, animating her class rebellions even when she occupies southern terrain.

For one thing, the newsboy immediately revises the paternal relationship: Warfield is shown to need guidance and protection when he gives Cap a ridiculously high tip, proving he will be easy prey for confidence men and might "fling way every cent . . . before his friends can catch him!" (37). This incident also conveys Cap's sense of honor ("Honor bright!" is a favorite expression) and justice, including her sense of a fair price or wage for the labor performed—convictions that energize her critiques of abuse and exploitation throughout the novel and help establish her voice as the locus of moral authority. Further, while Cap is described by Warfield in conventional melodramatic terms, as helpless and defenseless—"but a bit of a poor, friendless, motherless, fatherless *child*, lost and wandering in your great Babylon" (39)—she proves this a laughable construction, for she is a resourceful, determined young woman capable of defending and taking care of both Warfield *and* herself.

While Warfield demands silence and deference from his presumed subordinates, the newsboy, like the cabmen and porters, employs a working-class rhetoric of democracy, equality, and mutual respect. Though he expects to incorporate Capitola paternalistically as a familial dependent, she herself invokes the law as an instrument of justice and natural rights. Having been discovered as a girl masquerading in boy's clothing the morning after Warfield's arrival, Capitola testifies before the Recorder's Court in the first of several courtroom scenes in the novel. She relates the sequence of events that led to her arrest as an "unprotected" street urchin: "Granny" Grewell leaves her with the kindly Simmons family, and when they relocate in search of work and the tenement is destroyed, Capitola is prevented from pursuing a livelihood. She states under oath:

> I was trying to get jobs every hour in the day. I'd have done *any*thing honest. I went around to all the houses Granny [Grewell] knew, but they didn't want a girl [domestic servant]. Some of the good-natured landlords said, if I was a *boy* now, they could keep me opening oysters, but as I was a *girl*, they had no work for me. I even went to the offices to get papers to sell, but they told me that crying papers was not proper work for a girl. I even went down to the ferry-boats and watched for the passengers coming ashore, and ran and offered to carry their carpet-bags or portmanteaus; but some growled at me, and others laughed at me, and one old gentleman asked me if I thought *he* was a North American Indian, to strut up Broadway with a female behind him carrying his pack. (43–44)

Cap's "proper" location as a white female worker is discursively defined in negative terms: she should not be an oyster shucker, a newspaper cryer, or a porter; such a gender division of labor, the "old gentleman" implies, is the product and sign of "civilized" societies. Such gender and racial norms of "civility" and paternal protection both privatize women and make their self-support unseemly, a matter of bad taste. Echoing the critiques of contemporary working-women, Cap stresses the unfairness of the situation: "And so, sir, while all the ragged boys I knew could get little jobs to earn bread, I, because I was a girl, was not allowed to carry a gentleman's parcel, or black his boots, or shovel the snow off a shopkeeper's pavement, or put in coal, or do *anything* that *I* could do just as well as *they*. And so because I was a girl, there seemed to be nothing but starvation or beggary before me" (44). In the economic universe Capitola describes, the privilege of feminine protection equates to economic abjection. Finally, beset by "*want . . . and . . . danger*" (41, 47) from her poverty and homelessness, she resolves to "turn [in]to a boy" (41, 47): "I thought to myself *if I were only a boy*, I might carry packages, and shovel in coal, and do lots of jobs by day, and sleep without terror by night!" (46). After exchanging her clothing at a pawn shop for a boy's suit and selling her "black ringlets" for a penny, Capitola for a year "was happy and prosperous! I found plenty to do! I carried carpet-bags, held horses, put in coal, cleaned sidewalks, blacked gentlemen's boots, and did everything an honest lad could turn his hand to!" (46–47). This account of cross-dressing as survival strategy was echoed by other working-class women; for example, as noted in the introduction, Lucy Ann Lobdell in *The Female Hunter* attributes her decision to adopt "male attire" to the pitiful female wage of "a dollar per week," standard compensation for toiling "from morning till night" as domestic servant or seamstress (42). In her novel Southworth denaturalizes the gender division of labor and defends "hoydenism" as survival strategy.

As with Nancy Grewell's confession, Warfield is positioned as a witness and, to some degree, a sympathetic listener; identified as "the chorus of this drama" (44), he registers its emotional impact (though again ironizing paternal benevolence, the narrator notes that he can't hear very well [43–48]). Indeed listening to poor women's testimony is central to Warfield's moral education in the novel, and, by extension, Southworth's readers' as well. Warfield determines to "claim" Capitola as his "ward" (48) and thus "rescue" her from the disciplinary regime of the House of Refuge, one of the many evangelical institutions dedicated to uplifting and reforming the poor.[61] While Hurricane Hall appears to be an alternative site of class and gender discipline, it proves less effective than the intensive technologies of antebellum asylums, and Capitola defies all efforts at reformation and domestication. In particular the gender confusions that usher from the scene in the Recorder's Court (signaled by Warfield's nervous oscillation between "he" and "she" in reference to Capitola) animate her characterization throughout the text. Warfield's first gesture is to "restore" Capitola to her "proper dress" (50) in order to publicly mark her feminine identity. But while Capitola is "transfigured" (50) by her new appearance and experiences her feminine rags-to-riches story ("to find herself blest with wealth, leisure, and safety, under the care of a rich, good, and kind father!") as a "fairy tale" (51), her gender transformation remains incomplete. Her performance as a Bowery boy continues to inform her character throughout the text, supplying a persistent language of democratic aspiration. Not only does she defy domestic confinement, but through her presence "adventure" invades the heart of Hurricane Hall; for example, she claims as her sleeping quarters a remote bedroom, reachable only through a "labyrinth of passages," with a trap door covering a mysterious subterranean pit (75–76). This gothic interior and its "horrible mystery" troubles Cap's domestic captivity, fueling her declared determination that she "*will* be a hero" (77).

Courtroom scenes, such as the one at the Recorder's Court, play an important role in *The Hidden Hand.*[62] Challenging the moral authority of the wealthy (e.g., 443, 423), such scenes depict the courtroom as a site where men such as Gabriel Le Noir, a gentleman with the "most prepossessing exterior as well as . . . most irreproachable reputation" (415), are exposed as vicious and corrupt. Interestingly the spectators at the Recorder's Court, observing Warfield's intense involvement in the proceedings, infer that Capitola is his "unlawful child"; the "crowd" (49) frame their interpretation in the language of sensational exposé. Gauging "the great interest he took in her fate" (51), Capitola herself assumes that Warfield is her father, and the truth of her parentage is not revealed to her until the novel's end. For his part Warfield endeavors to limit the publicity of the courtroom scene, countering Cap's sensational appearance and economic testimonial by invoking gendered norms of private womanhood; he appeals to reporters to "drop [the] case" as a matter of "delicacy" (49), a plea that further convinces the crowd of his "scandal[ous]" paternity (50). Warfield determines to withhold from Capitola the truth of her ancestry so that he can investigate Le Noir's crime in an unobstructed way (a decision that repeatedly places his unwitting ward in great danger). This tactic of course backfires: Capitola resists Warfield's positioning of her as an innocent and passive melodramatic victim and refuses to be defined as the object of male plots. However, the struggle over privatization and control of knowledge—including publication of poor women's stories—is explicitly marked as the terrain of gender and class.

Cap's economic critique, here suppressed, resurfaces in the narrator's account of life in the South. Using a tactic of slave narratives, Southworth unsettles Warfield's paternal authority by emphasizing his dependency on the labor of others. The predominantly female labor of the household is especially evident during Christmas week, a holiday for slaves; when Warfield benevolently proclaims that the slaves "wait on us fifty-one weeks in the year, and it's hard if we can't wait on ourselves the fifty-second," the narrator sarcastically counters, "*He* did nothing for himself or others, and Mrs. Condiment and Capitola had a hot time of it in serving him. Mrs. Condiment had to do all the cooking and housework.

And Cap had to perform most of the duties of Major Warfield's valet. And that was the way in which Old Hurricane waited on *himself*" (380). Further unsettling paternal manhood, Cap—not Warfield—successfully defends the household on several occasions, while he treats her with class condescension and abuse rather than generosity, insulting his ward with such names as "'beggar, foundling, brat, vagabond and vagrant'" and "'New York trash'" and turning her dependency into a badge of shame (361, 466). Warfield similarly maligns other household members, including the faithful Mrs. Condiment (257).

Despite his "terrible tantrums" (125), intimidation, and abuse, Cap refuses to defer to Warfield's authority, defying and at times explicitly mocking his paternal presumptiveness throughout the novel. Although hers is ostensibly a narrative of upward class mobility, she does not forget her working-class past; it shapes her aspirations and animates her character. Nights are spent lost in "vivid dream[s] of the alleys, cellars, and gutters, rag-pickers, newsboys, and beggars of New York" (108), dreams so real that life at Hurricane Hall seems a "lunatic's fancy" (109). Endeavoring to domesticate and "feminize" Cap, Warfield attempts to undermine her self-respect by depicting her impoverished past as something contemptible: when she rides alone he upbraids her, "How *dare* you disobey me? *You*, the creature of my bounty! *you*, the miserable little vagrant that I picked up in the alleys of New York, and tried to make a young lady of. . . . How dare *you*, you little beggar, disobey your benefactor!" (121). But Cap refuses to concede to and therefore legitimate Warfield's gender and class power; she takes the moral high ground, declining to speak to him for days and then calmly instructing him on the injustice of his actions (123). When he attempts affectionate reconciliation, Cap, who "abhorred sentiment," is ever more defiant: "I won't be treated with both kicks and half-pennies by the same person. . . . I'm not a cur to be fed with roast-beef and beaten with a stick! nor . . . a Turk's slave to be caressed and oppressed as her master likes!" Declaring, "Such abuse as you heaped upon me, I never heard—no, not even in Rag Alley," Cap vows to return there for "very little more," for "freedom and peace are even sweeter than wealth and honors" (123–24). Should Warfield attempt to prevent her from authoring her own slave narrative and heading north, she threatens to have him "before the nearest magistrate, to show by what right you detained me! . . . I wasn't brought up in New York for nothing!" (124). Cap again invokes the language of rights against the customary authority of the (white) father, measuring the "privilege" of paternal care against forms of physical freedom, economic independence, and personal dignity. Here as elsewhere active recollection of the democratic education of the New York streets mitigates Cap's domestic enclosure at Hurricane Hall.

Capitola's experiences as a young urban vagrant illuminate the class politics of female sexuality, especially how, in antebellum America, workingwomen's sexuality was a primary site of class discipline.[63] In her representations of Cap's urban adventures, Southworth capitalizes and comments on the intense, midcentury fascination with urban street children, a fascination that extends from the substantial antebellum literature of newsboys and "street arabs" to Hawthorne's portrait of the shabbily dressed but "sturdy little urchin" who is the first patron of Hepzibah's cent-shop. Analyzing Henry Mayhew's story of the little watercress girl, Steedman observes that it is possible to "see the nineteenth century peopled by middle-age men who, propelled by the compulsions of scientific inquiry, demanded stories from young women and girls; and then expressed their dissatisfaction with the form of the narratives they obtained."[64] (What reformers perceived as the uncanny otherness of working-class children often motivated these social investigations; for middle-class male writers these girls embodied contradictory qualities and were at once workers and children, women and girls—a doubleness that defines Cap's character.)[65] The writings of American urban reformers in the 1850s on the problem of street children would seem to support Steedman's claim; reformers such as Samuel B. Halliday and Charles Loring Brace went about collecting the stories of young girls and boys whom they sought out in the streets and impoverished neighborhoods; such stories were also told orally in venues such as vagrancy courts and were generally the required token of admission to asylums for the poor.[66] Because working-class girls' "degeneracy" was principally represented by their sexuality, sexual confession was the principal object of these stories.[67] Several times in *The Hidden Hand* Southworth visits (and ironizes) this scene of cross-class narrative transmission as a site of sexual regulation, highlighting its performative nature and problematizing the "truth" it reveals. Well versed in reformers' cultural expectations, she suggests, working-class girls learned how to tell the right story to get the desired response and could capably play to and manipulate their listener's expectations and cultural assumptions.

In the scene at the Recorder's Court, Cap attests to male sexual violence and abuse directed at "unprotected" poor women and girls in antebellum cities, even while she resists the melodramatic construction that would deprive such women of sexual or economic agency. This exchange follows her account of being forced to live on the street and sleep outdoors after her tenement is demolished:

"That was a dreadful exposure for a young girl," said the Recorder.

A burning blush flamed up over the young creature's cheek, as she answered:

"Yes, sir, that was the worst of all; that finally drove me to putting on boy's clothes."

"Let us hear all about it."

"Oh, sir—I can't—I—how can I? Well, being always exposed, sleeping out-doors, I was often in danger from bad boys and bad men," said Capitola, and dropping her head upon her breast, and covering her crimson cheeks with her hands, for the first time she burst into tears and sobbed aloud.

"Come, come, my little man!—my good little *woman*, I mean—don't take it so to heart! You couldn't help it!" said Old Hurricane, with rain-drops glittering even in his own stormy eyes.

Capitola looked up with her whole countenance flashing with spirit, and exclaimed, "Oh! but I took care of myself, sir! I did, indeed, your Honor! You mustn't, either you or the old gentleman, dare to think but what I did."

"Oh, of course, of course!" said a bystander, laughing. (45)

Cap, we have already seen, is a skilled actress; Warfield has just noted that "the language used . . . during her examination was much superior" to the street slang of her newsboy identity (41), and so it isn't clear if her tearful protestations of virtue are adapted to her audience's expectations and the class circumstances of her interrogation. Most female inmates of reformatory institutions such as Houses of Refuge (where Cap is nearly sent) committed what were known as public order offenses, such as crimes against chastity or decency, a category of offense that "emerged within a sexual ideology of female purity" in the antebellum period.[68] For Cap, who was, as she later owns, "brought up among the detective policemen" (307), playing the virtuous maid might thus seem the best safeguard against imprisonment. But what stands out are the class and gender politics of this scene, in which working-class female sexuality is the coin of narrative transmission.[69] Both Warfield and the bystander assume that Cap has fallen, while the Recorder betrays his prurient interest in Cap's sexual confession by his eager prompting ("Let us hear all about it"). For the laughing bystander the idea of a poor girl's sexual virtue is an implausible joke, whereas Warfield melodramatically pictures Cap as a sexual victim, assuring her that she "couldn't help it." As evident in the scene with the minister, discussed below, Cap is well versed in the narrative conventions surrounding workingwomen's sexuality and capably manipulates them. Here she repudiates such melodramatic positioning, strenuously and somewhat defiantly asserting that she "took care of [her]self."

For Cap, it would appear, Warfield's sympathy is as objectionable as the bystander's ridicule; indeed, according to Estelle Freedman, as concerns with "public order offenses" were taken up by middle-class reformers, sexual "fall-enness" served as justification for "benevolent," and disciplinary, middle-class intervention.[70] While, as Stansell notes, sexual experience outside marriage, including casual prostitution, was quite common among working-class women in the late eighteenth and early nineteenth century, this complex sexual culture (and the economic realities that informed it) was depicted in highly conventional, melodramatic terms by middle-class reformers as well as an increasingly conservative workingmen's movement, which endorsed a breadwinner's wage that would install workingmen as workingwomen's "natural" protectors.[71] Given this context, Cap would find it intensely problematic to testify to complex sexual power relations within working-class communities (including the reality of rape and sexual abuse) because these concerns were taken up in ways deeply disempowering for poor women.

Possessing the "*innocence* of youth, but not its *simplicity*" (51), Cap is sufficiently familiar with the class politics of sexuality to assume that Warfield is her father. Although that turns out not to be true, the charge of seduction has some merit. As an army officer stationed in the West, Warfield had secretly married the poor sixteen-year-old orphan Marah Rocke—he keeps their marriage a secret because he fears the "ridicule of [his] brother officers" (85) for their cross-class union—and then abandons her when it appears that she has been unfaithful, disowning her and her unborn child and forbidding them "ever to take his name," a situation that nearly reiterates the nature of seduction as it afflicted working-class communities (98).[72] Cap both recognizes and upbraids Warfield for his sexual irresponsibility; when he finally confesses his marital history, melodramatically placing blame on the "diabolical villain [who] made me believe that my poor little wife wasn't good," Cap pointedly reflects, "I knew you'd lay it on somebody else. Men always do that!" (471–72). Cap's "exposure" on the New York streets enables her to speak directly to issues of sexuality and contest the imposed silences of feminine modesty. For example, she mocks the assumptions of racially defined sexual danger as a vehicle to police women and blacks in the South: addressing her guardian when he returns from riding alone (something Warfield has repeatedly forbidden her to do), Cap asks, "*Didn't* you know the jeopardy in which you placed yourself by riding out alone at this hour? Suppose three or four great runaway negresses had sprung out of the bushes and—and—and—" (128). In the main, however, sexual discourse is a markedly male realm in the text (e.g., 85), from which women, due to their presumed "delicacy" and modesty, are insistently excluded.

Additional textual scenes focus on female sexuality, revealing the ways (classed and racialized) discourses of sexual virtue leverage male power over women, individually and collectively. Writing of the late eighteenth century, Stansell observes that, although rape and prostitution "directly concerned" workingwomen, "men guarded the public discourse of sexuality"; while women did influentially contribute to antebellum sexual discourses (e.g., in abolitionism and moral reform), they gained a hearing by writing or speaking from the position of middle-class (domestic) women whose virtue was unquestioned and by affirming, melodramatically, poor women's sexual victimization (often appealing to the emergent ideology of "passionlessness" to counter older notions of women's uncontrolled carnality), positions Cap resolutely refuses.[73] Late in the novel Craven Le Noir "basely slander[s]" Cap's character with sexual innuendo, asserting, "[The] pretty little huntress of Hurricane Hall—that niece, or ward, or mysterious daughter of Old Hurricane . . . is a girl of very free and easy manners, I understand!—a Diana in nothing but her love of the chase" (361–62). Like other working-class women who violate domestic expectations, Cap is subject to misogynist (mis)interpretation and male sexual objectification.[74] Craven's actions are framed melodramatically: his secret, "diabolical" plan was to "take advantage of his acquaintance and casual meetings with Capitola" to "malign her character," thus making it "unlikely that any honest man would ever risk his honor by taking her to wife" and clearing his path to sexual conquest (359). But Cap refuses to succumb to melodramatic positioning: without "father or brother to protect [her] from affront," and with her "uncle" Warfield an "invalid veteran," she declares herself "under the novel necessity of fighting [her] own battles" (370). Thus when a relative reveals that she has been spoken of "lightly" by someone at a men's club but states that it would not be "proper" to repeat what was said (363), the novel invokes the barroom talk of antebellum "sporting men" while refashioning the gender relations that discourse produces.[75] Her relatives beg her to ignore these insulting intimations; however, Cap insists "upon knowing the whole length and breadth of [Craven's] baseness and malignity, that [she] may know how to judge and punish him" (363). When these relatives refuse to challenge Craven in a duel, insisting, "Duelling is obsolete. . . . Chivalry is out of date. The knights-errant are all dead" (364–66), Cap revives the southern code of honor on her own behalf: she writes a note to challenge her defamer, "demand[s] from him 'the satisfaction of a gentleman'" (367), and "renounce[s] all acquaintance" with her cousins for their cowardice, all the while uttering oaths that they find "profane and unwomanly" (365). The duel, a staged event in which Capitola shoots Craven in the face with "powder and dried peas" so that he—through "weak nerves, cowardice, and credulity"—believes he is dying and issues a public apology, supplies the revenge she seeks, subjecting her slanderer to "public ridicule" and reversing the (gendered) relations of humiliation and control his discourse had originally established (375–76). This scene, in which male chivalry is subversively reimagined as feminist vigilante justice, includes Cap's most pointed critique of contemporary manhood:

> "The MEN are all dead! if any ever really lived!" cried Cap, in a fury. "Heaven knows I am inclined to believe them to have been a fabulous race like that of the mastadon [sic] or the centaur! *I* certainly never saw a creature that deserved the name of man! The very first of your race was the meanest fellow that ever was heard of! eat the stolen apple, and when found out, laid one half of the blame on his wife, and the other on his maker—'The WOMAN whom THOU gavest me' did so and so! pah! I don't wonder the Lord took a dislike to the race and sent a flood to sweep them all off the face of the earth!" (366)

In this incident female sexuality seems wholly a currency in and of male discourse: a woman's only available defense, her relatives insist, is domestic invisibility. Again dramatically repudiating the role of melodramatic victim, Cap uncouples "innocence" from passivity and silence, claiming the power to manipulate the terms of sexual discourse to her own ends.

The friendship of Capitola and Clara Day, developed at the center of the text, further recasts melodrama's sexual politics. In arguably the text's most conventionally melodramatic sequence (involving an innocent maid, an evil villain, and a forced marriage), the prospect of victimization that haunts Cap is at once staged and exorcized through a figure who serves as a double or surrogate; the sequence also foregrounds the homoerotic possibilities of antebellum workingwomen's culture, possibilities latent in Cap's characterization throughout Southworth's novel. Clara is a young heiress who, when her father dies, comes under Gabriel Le Noir's nefarious influence. Le Noir has been appointed her guardian, and he decides that she shall marry his own son Craven, not her fiancé, Traverse (who receives her father's deathbed blessing). Held hostage in the Hidden House until she will consent to the union, Clara is steadfastly committed to Traverse, eliciting the full measure of Le Noir's villainy:

> "There are evils, to escape which . . . a woman would go down upon her bended knees to be made the wife of such a man!"

Clara's gentle eyes flashed with indignation!

"Infamous!" she cried. "You slander all womanhood in my person!"

"The evils to which I allude are—comprised in—a life of dishonor!" hissed Le Noir, through his set teeth. . . . "It is time we understood each other! You are in my power, and *I intend to coerce you to my will!*"

These words, accompanied as they were by a look that left no doubt upon her mind that he would carry out his purpose to any extremity, so appalled the maiden's soul that she stood like one suddenly struck with catalepsy. (302–3)

With the emotionally heightened language and expressive gesture characteristic of theatrical melodrama, the two play their parts in terms Southworth's readers would instantly recognize. Clara elsewhere appears a helpless "lamb" and Le Noir a predatory "wolf" (234), while the latter's identification with Satan is figured in this passage by his snake-like hissing. The mortal wound of female fallenness, its self-destroying aspect, rendering a woman prostrate before an inexorable male power, is emblematized by Clara's cataleptic insensibility and immobilized body.

However, as the narrator points out, in plotting his domestic melodrama Le Noir had not "calculated upon Capitola" (301). She decides to visit the Hidden House, for "with its mysterious traditions, its gloomy surroundings and its haunted reputation" it possessed a "powerful attraction for one of Cap's adventurous spirit" (269). Cap's appearance on the scene allows Southworth to revisit the genre of female gothic (the legendary resident ghost turns out to be Capitola's mother, held captive by Le Noir for seventeen years) and, again, the chivalric ideal of the Old South. Advancing on Hidden House, Cap declares, "One would think this were the enchanted forest containing the castle of the sleeping beauty, and I was the knight destined to deliver her!" (270). Armed with fearlessness, common sense, and mocking humor, she refuses to succumb to the terrors of the place and commands entrance by claiming a traditional "right to shelter" of wayfaring travelers, defiantly asserting, in true newsboy fashion, "Every storm-beaten traveler has a right to shelter under the first roof that offers, and none but a curmudgeon would think of calling it a *favor*!" (277). Her rhetoric is successful: she gains entrance and is introduced to Clara. While they are the "same size," permitting Capitola to wear Clara's "lilac silk," their faces make visible distinctions of both class and gender: Clara's expression is "pure, grave and gentle" while Cap's is "bright, frank, [and] honest" (282). When, during a subsequent visit, Clara reveals Le Noir's plot, the young women's identification as doubles of sorts—and the differences between them—are given dramatic form.

Southworth sets up a classic instance of the mortgage melodrama so that her "damsel-errant" can perform it otherwise. In particular she gender-bends melodramatic conventions, designating Capitola the virtuous, noble hero who defends the fair maiden against the villain's evil designs. According to Sally Mitchell, the chief difference between middle-class fictional plots and those of cheap serials is the "overwhelming physical nature of the action"; the performance of physical feats in *The Hidden Hand* could validate workingwomen's physical strength and labor while extending heroic narrative forms usually reserved for male characters to its lower-class heroine.[76] Stating that she "wasn't brought up among the detective policemen for nothing," Capitola crafts a "plan [for Clara's] escape" (306–7) and engineers an exchange of identities: disguised as her rescuer, Clara will ride off to safety while Cap will take Clara's place at the enforced wedding the following day. In addition to donning her riding habit, Clara must learn to perform Capitola's defiant physical style, learned on the New York streets: "Draw up your figure, throw back your head; walk with a little springy sway and swagger, as if you didn't care a damson for anybody. . . . Be calm, be cool, be firm. . . . If you go doing the sentimental you won't look like me a bit, and that will spoil all" (307–8). As at once Bowery boy and "gallant" rescuing knight, Cap earns Clara's deep admiration: "O may the Lord in Heaven bless and preserve and reward you, my brave, my noble, my heroic Capitola!" (308). For her part Capitola "do[es] the sentimental up brown" in imitation of Clara, a performance that mainly involves sobbing and speaking "as if her heart would break" (312–13). Disguised by a "thick veil" (313) and sentimental demeanor, Capitola is taken by Le Noir to a remote Roman Catholic chapel, where she finds a "score" of "hard-working farm laborers" who, the narrator pointedly notes, "have no time to come in the day, and who are . . . here to offer their evening prayers" (314). Believing "her final safety" is "ensured" by the presence of this audience, Capitola "abandon[s] herself to the spirit of frolic that possessed her, and anticipat[es] with the keenest relish the denouement of her strange adventure" (315). At the moment of the exchange of vows she disrupts the show: "throwing aside her veil," she announces before her shocked audience, "No! not if he were the last man and I the last woman on the face of the earth, and the human race were to become extinct, and the angel Gabriel came down from above to ask it of me as a personal favor" (315). Capitola replaces the marriage ceremony with a scene of her own, declaring the meaning of her revisionist melodrama: "It means the game's up, the play's over, villainy is about to be hanged, and virtue about to be rewarded, and the curtain is going to drop, and the principal performer—that's I—is going to be called out amid the applause of the audience!" (316). Less playfully she tells the Le Noirs, "It means that you have been outwitted by a girl; it means that your proposed victim has fled, and is by this time in safety" (316). Claiming the "protection" of the "good people" who witness the mock wedding, Capitola transforms the church into a public tribunal, testifying to the Le Noirs' plot and her role in disrupting it while the "baffled villains'" attempts to escape are "effectually prevented by the people," who act as agents of justice (316–18). Witnesses to Cap's exposé of aristocratic villainy, the "people" are identified as the privileged locus of ethical (and aesthetic) judgment—a self-referentiality that, once again, allows Southworth to make visible the class sympathies of her text.

The exchange of identities between privileged, domesticated Clara and born-poor, streetwise Capitola permits Southworth to highlight the working-class accents of Capitola's characterization. Imitating Capitola's swaggering gait and defiant attitude transforms Clara, who subsequently voices a female working-class republicanism reminiscent of the discourse of Lowell women unionists.[77] Safely back at home with Marah Rocke, Clara proposes that they "work for [their] living together": "You can sew the seams and do the plain hemming, and I can work the button-holes and stitch the bosoms, collars and wrist-bands. And 'if the worst comes to the worst,' we can hang out our little shingle before the cottage gate, inscribed with, 'Mrs. Rocke and Daughter, Shirt Makers. *Orders executed with neatness and dispatch*'" (325–26). Like the radical French seamstresses who worked to collectivize needlework in 1848, Clara proposes, "We'd drive a thriving business, mamma, I assure you" (326). When Marah protests, "I trust in Heaven that it will never come to that with you, my dear" (326), Clara counters the "privileges" of feminine leisure with a democratic rhetoric of universal rights: "Why should I not taste of toil and care as well as others a thousand times better than myself? Why should I not work as well as you and Traverse, mamma? I stand upon the broad platform of human rights, and I say I have just as good a right to work as others" (326). This republican discourse of "human rights" and free labor is correctly attributed to Capitola's influence. "I think, dear Clara, that you must have contracted some of your eccentric little friend Capitola's ways, from putting on her habit," Marah observes, while Clara attests that hers are effusions of a "free bird . . . escaped" from imprisonment (326).

The contrast between Clara and Cap allows Southworth to explore class differences in gendered subjectivity. Cap's affect (or lack thereof) is striking; resistant to suffering, she refuses to perform sentimental femininity.[78] *The Hidden Hand*'s two melodramatic heroines, Marah Rocke and Clara Day, are exemplary sufferers; while the "refined" and "delicate" Clara (440), an "angel-girl," endeavors, not unlike Ellen in *The Wide, Wide World*, to "school [her] heart to submission" (255), Marah is a sentimental seamstress, that long-suffering melodramatic type, starving to death—not because of the poor pay of needlewomen but because of a broken heart. Cap, who lacks Clara's "sensitive perceptions [and] fine intuitions," repudiates sentimental "subjection" alongside forms of female powerlessness and dependency associated with melodrama (354). Thus we learn, for example, that when her childhood friend Herbert Greyson (who at the novel's end becomes her husband) leaves to fight in the Mexican-American War, Cap "cried every day of the first week . . . every alternate day of the second; twice in the third; once in the fourth; not at all in the fifth, and the sixth week she was quite herself again . . . ready for any mischief or deviltry that might turn up" (350).

The repudiation of "feminine" sentiment is inseparable from Cap's defiance of gender norms: highlighting the cross-gender aspects of the former newsboy's identity in episodes with Clara, Southworth depicts Cap in masculine, indeed phallic terms, stating that she possesses "a brave, hard, firm nature" (354). The rituals of heterosexual romance are especially ironized by Cap as stagecraft: when Craven Le Noir proposes to Cap late in the text, she exclaims, "Well I declare! . . . This is what is called a declaration of love and a proposal for marriage is it?—It is downright sentimental, I suppose, if I had only the sense to appreciate it! It is as good as a play! pity it is lost upon me!" When Craven complains, "Cruel girl! how you mock me!," Capitola replies, "No I don't! I'm in solemn earnest! I say it is first rate! do it again! I like it!" (356). In Cap's relationship with Clara the transgressive sexuality and sororal sympathy associated with antebellum workingwomen surfaces as an overt homoeroticism. The relationship is infused with homoerotic desire; for example, Cap avows, "I don't know how any one could live in the same house with Clara and not be in love with her" (352). Assimilating that desire to a heterosexual, romantic telos is arguably a primary demand of the plot; the novel ends with multiple marriages, including between Capitola and Herbert Greyson. But that relationship, while idealized, is undercut by its narrative marginality: Cap's attraction to and relationship with the charismatic bandit Black Donald is given far more narrative space than her bond with Herbert, established before the novel begins and undergoing no real narrative development. The plot with Clara both problematizes heterosexual narrative codes and reworks melodramatic formulae to make dramatically visible the text's homoerotic impulses.

One final scene provides Southworth's most explicit commentary on the politics of melodramatic interpretation. Stansell writes, "Working class children by the 1850s were . . . a powerful symbol of urban disorder. In particular, unruly daughters would create reverberations within a propertied class preoccupied with maintenance of female chastity and within a working class concerned with the decline of masculine authority."[79] Once he claims Cap as his ward, Warfield's sympathetic construction of her urban exposure (expressed at the Recorder's Court) gives way to a vigorous defense of her chastity. His patriarchal anxieties about his ward's sexual status—and the class parameters of feminine "virtue"— are evident in his exchange with the local minister back at Hurricane Hall: relating Capitola's history, Warfield heatedly assures the minister that she "has passed unscathed through the terrible ordeal of destitution, poverty and exposure!... She is as innocent as the most daintily sheltered young heiress in the country!... I'd cut off the tongue and ears of any man that said otherwise" (174). That "innocence" becomes the subject of a meeting between the minister and Cap herself, arranged by Warfield, who seeks the minister's counsel on "how to manage the capricious little witch" (180). Recognizing at once that she "shall be lectured by the good parson" (182), Cap resolves to foil his efforts of moral interpretation in a brilliantly parodic performance of what Robin Bernstein terms "racial innocence" (I would call it "racialized class innocence").[80] Exhibiting "the decorum of a young nun," Capitola performs the part of a seduced woman and sadly leads the minister through a "confession" of sexual indiscretions, gratifying her "respectable" male interlocutor's evident desire for sexual narrative and disrupting the melodramatic formula that would cast her as an innocent maid in need of male protection (182). Skillfully employing double entendre, she invites the minister to find the meanings he both seeks and fears. Confiding, "I have been very indiscreet, and I am very miserable!" (183), she builds narrative suspense through heightened rhetoric: "I'm going to inform you, sir! and, oh, I hope you will take pity on me and tell me what to do; for though I dread to speak, I can't keep it on my conscience any longer, it is such a heavy weight on my breast!" (184). Positioning the minister as privileged confessor (and appealing to his "pity") while reminding him pointedly that she "had no mother," Cap relates how she first met Alfred Blenheim "walking in the woods" and has since met him countless times, confessing that he is now "hid in the closet in my room": "I hope you will forgive me, sir! But—but he was so handsome I couldn't help liking him!" (184–85). When the pastor exclaims with "deepest horror," "Wretched girl! better you'd never been born than ever so to have received a man!" (185), Cap turns the tables on her listener; in doing so she deflates the minister's catastrophic view of premarital sex and aligns the sexual corruption of the alleged seducer with the minister's illicit assumptions. Revealing that Alfred Blenheim is a "poodle that strayed away from some of the neighbor's houses," Capitola takes exception with what she represents as the minister's depraved taste for sexual scandal. "MAN?—I'd like to know what you mean by *that*, Mr. Goodwin!... *I*!—*I* give private interviews to a man! Take care what you say, Mr. Goodwin! I won't be insulted! no not even by you!" (185). The distressed minister has no advice for Warfield other than to "thrash that girl *as if she were a bad boy*—for she richly deserves it!" (185, emphasis added). Addressing the frequency of stories of seduction and betrayal in extant testimonials of antebellum prostitutes (most were interviewed by moral reformers), historians have suggested that these women often framed their sexual experience melodramatically because they knew that was what their interviewers expected: it conformed to middle-class ideologies of passive, "passionless" women and would readily garner sympathy from their listeners.[81] Brilliantly ironizing this conventional scene of melodramatic narrative transmission, Cap denaturalizes the class and gender stereotypes activated within it.

## CAP, BLACK DONALD, AND MELODRAMATIC PLOTS

Southworth's characterization of her heroine enacts the racialization of class discussed in chapter 4, installing "precarious whiteness" as a defining feature of Cap's character; it also upends melodrama's conventional racial semiotic, the clichéd association of black with villainy and evil, white with goodness and virtue, which define what Brooks calls melodrama's "polarized" moral categories. Strikingly, in Southworth's novel, in the "high" or serious plot, this moral polarization is intact (e.g., Gabriel Le Noir is unmistakably a melodramatic villain), while in the "low," comic plot it is unsettled and complicated. As we shall see, Southworth's "low" racial(ized) characters—especially Cap and Black Donald—exhibit lower-class affinities and exemplify a kind of plebian heroism.[82] Indeed the text's racialized class sympathies are complexly elaborated through the depiction of Black Donald. Cap is drawn to Donald; he is in some ways her equal, similarly characterized by democratic sensibilities, courage, resourcefulness, and honor, as well as a commitment to what Southworth calls "fair play" (e.g., 259). They are cast as doubles, underscoring the working-class accents of both characters. And they themselves recognize this affinity; for example, affirming, "Our fates are evidently connected," Black Donald tells Cap, "You stick to me like a wife to her husband!" (210, 157). Named by local reputation for his "black soul, black deeds, and . . . for his jet black hair and beard," Donald, like Cap, is expressly racialized (156). He is known as an "outlaw" and "chief of a band of ruthless desperadoes that infest these mountain roads, robbing mail coaches, stealing negroes, breaking into houses, and committing every sort of depredation"—including, according to Mrs. Condiment, the "darker crime" of rape (111). His narrative role seems assured when, after being introduced as a notorious "villain" (156), he is approached by Gabriel Le Noir, who, learning of Cap's return, offers ten thousand dollars for her murder; Donald is thus installed as the heroine's mortal enemy. But his murderous pursuit of Cap is quickly transformed when he meets the girl and is "captivated" by her rebellious spirit; though he continues to pursue her, it is with the secret purpose of preserving her life and marrying her (161).[83] Cap is similarly attracted to Donald, who seems to her the solitary example of heroic manhood. First intrigued by the legends surrounding him (she announces to Mrs. Condiment, "If Black Donald were . . . as honest as he is brave, I should quite *adore* him!" [156]), she responds to his physical presence by "gaz[ing] . . . in admiration and curiosity" (157). Like Cap, who is both street urchin and southern heiress, Donald is both outlaw and "natural" nobleman. While several in his band are "repulsive-looking" (142), their moral viciousness melodramatically inscribed on their faces,

> Black Donald . . . might have been a giant walked out of the age of fable into the middle of the nineteenth century. From his stature alone he might have been chosen leader of [his] band of desperadoes. He stood six feet eight inches in his boots, and was stout and muscular in proportion. He had a well-formed, stately head, fine aquiline features, dark complexion, strong, steady, dark eyes, and an abundance of long, curling black hair and beard that would have driven to despair a Broadway beau, broken the heart of a Washington belle, or made his own fortune in any city of America as a French count or a German baron! He had decidedly "the air noble and distinguished." (143)

Donald's is one in a line of what the theater scholar Peter Reed calls lower-class "rogue performances," "appealing representations of charismatic criminality" that includes Macheath in Gay's *Beggar's Opera*, gallows speeches (often published in pamphlets and broadsides), and criminal testimonies in the *Police Gazette*.[84] His muscular physique and brawny physicality might be seen to cite the performances of heroic masculinity by the famed actor (and working-class hero) Edwin Forrest, even as the style itself gestures toward the masculine (slave and "free") laboring body.

While he seems to legitimate his career with a Hobbesian idiom of unbridled self-interest (e.g., 148), Black Donald's "noble" bearing and natural charm qualify his status as villain and identify him with the heroic figure of the "social bandit," whose lower-class, popular aspects have been analyzed by Eric Hobsbawm.[85] Donald is in many ways an instrument of (racialized) class vengeance: his "lawless" depredations (with the help of his dark-skinned "comrades" [150]) on the property of southern aristocrats such as Warfield register the illegitimacy of ownership in the slaveholding South and enact a form of vigilante justice, redressing the legalized thievery of slavery and expressing a (racialized) class vendetta. Furthermore Donald, like Cap, is an agent of class critique, explicitly questioning the authority of elite white men; his dialogue with Gabriel Le Noir (whom he ironically addresses, in Cap's Bowery boy idiom, as "Your Honor") is punctuated by what the narrator terms "impudent slander" (150). Associating bravery and "work" with "poor" men and cowardice and inactivity with the rich, he significantly figures his banditry as a "business" and the relation between himself and his "employer" as a wage relation, asserting, "My pals are too poor to hire their work done; but then they are brave enough to do it themselves," while his own "lawless" behavior and Hobbesian views are a reaction to what he understands to be thoroughgoing economic and political corruption (149, 150). Just as radical workingmen presented emphatic masculinity as class insignia (positioned against the effeminacy of aristocrats and middle-class professionals),[86] Donald's heroic masculinity, bravery, and physical prowess identify him as a locus of working-class virtue. Reproducing, with Le Noir, the structure of the wage relation (Donald is body to Le Noir's depraved mind), Donald—whom we learn at the end of the novel is a thief but has refused to commit violent crimes—is represented as a kind of class hero.

However, if identification with Donald complicates Cap's "breeches" role and further elaborates her democratic aspirations, by the end there is no question about the identity of the novel's true "hero." Although the working-class accents of Donald's character are plainly legible, his class heroism—like that of many workingmen—is qualified by a fundamental misogyny, which is at times expressed as violence. There are no women in his band except for Granny Raven, "the daughter of the last proprietor of the inn" where the men gather, whose tongue has been cut out to ensure her silence (140, 212); Donald is an alleged rapist, and his men are easily convinced to abduct Cap so that Donald can "do as [he] please[s] with her" (164). The identification between Donald and Cap evolves into an epic antagonism, and Cap emerges the clear victor. Giving herself courage during their final, frightening encounter, she steadies herself, "Think of Jael and Sisera! Think of Judith and Holofernes! And the devil and Doctor Faust, if necessary, and don't you blench!" (384–85). It is in her encounters with the dashing bandit that Cap's dramatic powers are most strenuously tested and, at last, triumphantly affirmed, in part because Donald is her match at role-playing. Like Capitola, he is a master of disguise: according to Warfield, Black Donald "does not *disguise* he *transforms* himself" (256). Disguised as a peddler he attains unobstructed access to Hurricane Hall although Warfield relentlessly seeks his capture; disguised as the itinerant preacher Father Gray he is Warfield's honored guest at a camp meeting, sharing the family's table and even his host's bed; disguised as a "negro," he lurks in the woods around Hurricane Hall, hoping to encounter Capitola (209). In the beginning of the novel Cap exclaims that she "would like the glory of capturing Black Donald" (111), and in the end she accomplishes just that. While Warfield is repeatedly humiliated by Donald's encroachments onto his domestic territory, Capitola successfully pursues and finally captures him and his men, largely through her own dramatic powers. She bravely pursues Black Donald when others refuse to follow him (157); she arranges to trap three of his men who invade her bedroom in the hopes of kidnapping her; and finally she manages to capture the outlaw himself.

Cap's finest performance takes place during Christmas week, when "all the house servants and farm-laborers from Hurricane Hall went off in a body to a banjo break-down" so that "Major Warfield, Mrs. Condiment and Capitola were the only living beings left in the old house" (380). Late one night, while Warfield walks in the garden, Black Donald slips inside the house, disguising himself in Warfield's clothing to make his way to Capitola's remote bedroom; when she retires he locks them inside and reveals his intention to carry her off. Recognizing that the traditional "feminine" means of escape will not avail her ("The loudest scream . . . would never reach the distant chamber[s] of Major Warfield, or . . . Mrs. Condiment"), Cap perceives that she is "entirely in the power of Black Donald" (384). She addresses herself in a soliloquy: "If you don't look sharp your hour is come! Nothing on earth will save you, Cap, but your own wits! . . . Now Cap, my little man, be a woman! . . . All stratagems are fair in love and war—especially in war, and most especially in such a war as this is likely to be—a contest in close quarters for dear life!" (384–85). The narrator again stresses her improvisational facility: "All this passed through her mind in one moment, and in the next her plan was formed" (385). Playing it "cool" and "undaunted," Cap recasts their bedroom encounter in the polite terms of a parlor visit: "Well, upon my word, I think a gentleman might let a lady know when he means to pay her a domiciliary visit at midnight!" (385). When this fails to deter Donald, Cap tries the role of romantic heroine: addressing him as "my hero," she reminds him that, during their first encounter, she had declared to everyone's shock that she "*liked* Black Donald" and claims she has endeavored to capture him in the hopes he would "carry me off": "I was tired of hum-drum life, and I wanted to see adventures" (386–87). Here Cap attempts to defuse Black Donald's plot, in which she is the melodramatic victim—he calls her a "caged starling" (388)—through her own self-construction as a desiring, sexually knowing woman; when Donald observes, "I am afraid you are not good," she responds, "Yes I am—before folks!" (387). The scene shifts to an intimate domestic encounter: refusing to kiss Donald until he has eaten and washed, Cap coolly makes him a "nightcap" of eggnog. He attempts to unmask her scene-making, vowing, "I know your tricks, and all your acting has no other effect on me than to make me admire your wonderful coolness and courage; so, my dear, stop puzzling your little head with schemes to baffle me" (388). However, it is Donald, not Cap, who is "uncanny" (387): Cap has managed the blocking of this scene to place him directly over the trap door, so that while he believes she is "in [his] power! at [his] mercy" (390), in reality he is in hers. Offering Donald "five minutes' grace," Capitola transforms the scene into a gallows scene and, in a sermon worthy of Jonathan Edwards, preaches the imminent need for penitence: "Death might come with sudden, overwhelming power and hurl you to destruction. What a terrible thing for this magnificent frame of yours, this glorious handiwork of the creator, to be hurled to swift destruction, and for the soul that animates it to be cast into hell!" (391–92). She implores Donald to see that "there is really something great and good *in yourself* that might yet be used for the good of man, and the glory of God" (390). When despite her entreaties he remains intent on carrying her off, Cap releases the trap door, and Donald's dramatic fall stands in for her own impending one. While Cap is afterward described as a "sacrificial priestess" (395), it is the man, not the maiden, who is sacrificed; Cap is positioned in this scene as both judge and executioner, and the scene's obvious apocalyptic overtones (Donald is hurled into the abyss) confer on Cap god-like stature. She thus devises the ultimate punishment (divine retribution) for those who would destroy poor virgins; strategically invoking, then decisively revising, the formula of the seduction narrative, Southworth presents a kind of working-class female revenge fantasy. Cap's authority is underscored in the concluding sequence: Donald, miraculously, lives; when he is (unjustly) sentenced to death on "circumstantial evidence" and a "bad reputation"—though his "hands are free from blood-guiltiness" (465–66)—Cap, feeling responsible for his fate and bound by the spirit of "fair play," determines to set him free. Although she admittedly can't "change clothes with him as I did with Clara," she resolves to "save his life . . . by one means or another" (468). Learning that he "had pretended to consent to her death only for the purpose of saving her life" (477), she smuggles him the means to escape, even giving him her pony to "quit the country" (483). Cap is here the instrument of Donald's liberation and redemption: imploring him, "Use well the life I . . . give you, else I shall be chargeable with every future sin you commit," she transforms him from convicted felon into, in his own words, a "Reformed Robber" (480, 484). Crucially, however, she "reforms" him through female heroism, not domestic desire.

In his creative genius as an escape artist, Donald evokes the drama of what Peter Linebaugh terms "excarceration"—resistance to and even escape from punitive authority "played out in escapes, flights, desertions, migrations and refusals."[87] But in this final instance, captured by Cap, his genius fails him. In their final encounter the "poor banned and blighted outlaw," "doubly ironed" and chained to the wall, is "very pale and haggard from long imprisonment and great anxiety" (479). It is Cap who now harnesses the power of "excarceration": first capturing and then liberating Donald from prison, she enacts her own "rogue performance." Challenging the judge's ruling by appealing to a "higher law," as did abolitionists in the 1850s, she adapts her performance to the aims of (racialized class) justice. Through her virtuoso performances, Cap not only foils Donald's plot to abduct her but also wins his admiration and respect. If the "ideology of the gang," as Denning describes it, posits the potential of the low to enact independent forms of socialization, Southworth's final chapters qualify the masculinism (and the misogyny) of Donald's organization, even envisioning new roles for women. In his final meeting with his gang after escaping from prison, Donald acknowledges, "No one on earth could have helped me but the one who really freed me—Capitola" (482), while his men listen in "wonder" and "astonishment" (483). When one gang member asks if this means his captain has "got her at last" (483), Donald now repudiates any longing for "possession" (e.g., 211). Imbuing Cap with the "excarceral" potential of performance and its liberatory, transformative potency, *The Hidden Hand* adopts performance to working-class feminist ends.

## *Six*. Writing Mexicana Workers

RACE, LABOR, AND THE WESTERN "FRONTIER"

This chapter extends my analysis of the dialectic of race and class in the mid-nineteenth century, situating it within the frame of U.S. empire building and territorial expansion. Specifically I trace how the "blackening" of women's household labor, discussed in chapter 4, shaped by the sectional conflict over slavery, is reworked within cultural formations of class and labor on the western "frontier." As Tomás Almaguer demonstrates, the racial complexity of nineteenth-century California—its mix of Native Americans, elite Californios, and more recent Latino, chiefly Mexican immigrants; immigrants from China and Japan; and, especially with annexation, an influx of Euro-Americans—produced distinct dynamics of class-based racialization. In particular, racialized images of African Americans as "servants" and "unfree laborers" were in complex ways "displaced" onto other racial groups.[1] I focus on the Californio *testimonios*, first-person narratives by Mexicanos/as living in Mexican California during annexation to the United States that were collected by Hubert Howe Bancroft in the 1870s. Of the nearly one hundred *testimonios*, twelve are by women; especially revealing for this study are narratives by Apolinaria Lorenzana and Eulalia Pérez, domestic workers in the missions, who shed critical light on relations of gender and labor in Alta California. I consider Mexicanas' *testimonios* in the context of major economic and social transformations in California, which shaped the forms of Mexican workingwomen's exploitation, agency, and self-expression. Like autobiographical narratives by African American laboring women, such as Sojourner Truth and Elizabeth Keckley, that register the "symbolically powerful yet highly contested nature of black women's self-supporting labor during the antebellum period," these narratives by Lorenzana and Pérez affirm Mexican women's "often-disparaged labor as socially and culturally valuable," constituting an important "archive" of Mexican (American) "working womanhood."[2]

I set the stage for this discussion by turning briefly to the novels of María Amparo Ruiz de Burton, especially *Who Would Have Thought It?* (1872), a historical romance set during and after the Civil War. Recollecting a past "efface[d]" by annexationist discourses,[3] the novel illuminates the history of class in annexed western territories, depicting contested legacies of racialized servitude and class power. In particular, revealing what Rosaura Sánchez and Beatrice Pita term the "ambivalence" of Californianas' class position as both elite propertied women and the propertyless dispossessed, the text highlights what we have come to recognize as the "mercurial nature of race" in this era—and especially poor women's precarious whiteness.[4] Introduced into the white Norvals' New England household, the "dark-skin[ned]" Mexican girl Lola is assigned the racial position "black" by Mrs. Norval, who sends her to the kitchen, while her "benevolent" husband claims that "her position in [the] family will be that of an adopted child." Bringing Lola "home"—incorporating her within racial categories that anchor the nation—aligns racialized class inscription with imperial appropriation; the treatment of Lola might be seen to figure efforts by Anglos of all classes to restructure the material terrain of California so that Mexican (Americans) were transformed into "a permanent service caste."[5] Turning to the *testimonios*, I examine the Pérez and Lorenzana narratives as sites of racialized class dialogue. Although framed by Bancroft's oral historians in particular ways, the *testimonios*, I argue, should be read as part of a broader effort in nineteenth-century print culture, especially Spanish-language newspapers, to "archive" the oral culture of Mexican Americans, both historical narratives and cultural traditions such as the *décimas* and *corridos*. Print culture here is used as an instrument of cultural memory and reproduction in the face of Anglo erasure.[6] Like Southworth's *The Hidden Hand*, the text becomes an archive of a repertory—here, Mexicana "orature," the oral performances of history by laboring women. Taken together these fictional and autobiographical texts illuminate complex interrelationships between domestic class identities and an international division of labor, shedding critical light on the racialization of class in the antebellum United States.

California was centrally bound up with debates about "free labor" in the 1850s; the politics of land reform, the free soil movement, and later the homestead movement all identified western expansion with labor's emancipation. While the Wilmot Proviso, which would have banned slavery's extension into California and the rest of the Mexican territorial cession, stalled in Congress, California was admitted to the Union as part of the Compromise of 1850 as a free state, and in popular mythology California was the "ultimate free-labor landscape, a place where autonomous, mobile individuals were at perfect liberty to pursue their economic interests and raise their social status."[7] Affirming that ideal, Jessie Fremont, the wife of the Republican presidential candidate John Fremont, memorably declared during the 1856 campaign that she would rather "do my own work and be my own servant" than that "California would be a Slave State."[8] But as the historian Stacey L. Smith has recently argued, "California's free soil was far less solid, its contests over human bondage far more complicated, contentious, and protracted" than its reputation would suggest. Various forms of involuntary "unfree labor"—African American slavery, Native American servitude, sexual trafficking in bound (usually Native or Chinese) women, and species of bound labor that included what contemporaries called Mexican or South American "peonage" and Asian "serfdom"—persisted throughout the state. While geographically distinct from both the slave South and the free North, California was "a theater of the sectional crisis, a place where Americans reworked and remade the boundaries of freedom and slavery in the antebellum era."[9]

This "theater" had a clearly gendered dimension. Expansionist "free labor" rhetorics conspicuously enshrined masculinity and what Amy Greenberg calls "manifest manhood," but the language could be feminized as well. In 1847 newspapers reported that a New England mill girl, Irene Nichols, had married the president of Mexico and that her husband "would not be opposed to the union of Mexico with the United States"—an inscription of what Doris Sommer calls "national romance" that dramatically conjoins female economic mobility and westward expansion.[10] Such efforts to tie the mill girl's fortunes to the expansion of empire were rhetorically and politically significant: justifying territorial expansion as a solution to class conflict and unrest was fundamental to frontier ideology, and as scholars of imperial discourses note, imperialism was often justified at home as a boon to the economically disenfranchised. In the case of the mill girl, however, the link was more specific, for cotton, a major cash crop in the plantation economy of Texas, played a crucial role in the war with Mexico. President John Tyler wrote, "The war with Mexico gave the U.S. a monopoly of the cotton plant and thus secured to us a power of boundless extent in the affairs of the world. . . . The monopoly . . . was the great and important concern. . . . It places all other nations at our feet; an embargo [on cotton exportation during] . . . a single year produced in Europe a greater amount of suffering than a 50-year war."[11] In 1845, the year Tyler left office, newspapers were replete with "declarations about Americans' cotton monopoly and how it could be used against Britain"; now, with Texas annexed, the object was the Pacific Coast, especially California and Oregon. Cotton was thus recognized as an important geopolitical tool. James Gordon Bennett, editor of the *New York Herald*, wrote in 1845, "Not a gun need be fired—not a grain of gunpowder expended—no need of steamers and fleets and armies and munitions of war. The cotton bales will fight the battles of the country that produces them." Indeed, he gleefully noted, Britain was "completely bound and manacled with the cotton cords" of the United States: "The trade of England with this country is probably worth to that power twenty times as much as the whole value of that distant territory would be to it, and the supply of cotton, under the present British manufacturing system, is a lever with which we can successfully control the operations of England."[12] Employing a startling sequence of metaphors (cotton becomes, in turn, a battling army and material implements of slave bondage), such rhetoric highlights the imperial significance of the iconic New England mill girl and suggests how expansionists attempted to tie white workingwomen's fortunes to imperial expansion. The story of Irene Nichols domesticates the unruly mill girl and illuminates how what Greenberg calls white women's "traveling domesticity" could underwrite territorial expansion.[13]

If California was largely written as utopian space for the regeneration of white working-class manhood (and, less prominently, properly domesticated working-class womanhood), this gendered imagery was set in opposition to images of gendered disorder in Mexican California. Numerous Anglo accounts depicted Mexican men as lazy and unproductive, incapable of initiating the economic "improvements" that would justify their title to the territory—representations that, as Rosaura Sánchez argues, "feminized" Californio and Mexican men to distance them from the (political and economic) privileges of Anglo masculinity. Proponents of the Mexican-American War argued that a U.S. invasion and occupation could regenerate Mexico by transforming its people into a nation of workers; according to John O'Sullivan, it would "impart energy and industry gradually to the indolent Mexicans, and give them such a consistency as a people, as would enable them to hold and occupy their territories in perfect independence."[14] Other accounts emphasized the unnatural industriousness of Mexicanas and Californianas, in clear violation of Anglo gender norms; their husbands lounged about while "the women," in the words of one observer, were "by far the more industrious half of the population."[15] Resembling reports of Native American women's drudgery I discussed in the introduction, such accounts imagine a condition of gender disorder and exploitation characteristic of "savage" societies that invited correction by a chivalric Anglo masculinity. As we shall see, in their accounts of themselves as women workers Pérez and Lorenzana countered depictions of racialized "unfree labor" with images of female economic agency, pride, and power. In doing so they made visible what the historian Antonia Castañeda calls the "significant economic power"—including a tradition of female property and inheritance rights rooted in Mexican and Spanish law—exercised by Mexicanas and Californianas, as well as the women's cultural origins in a Mexican society that engaged women in a wide range of productive employments, including (after the lifting of guild restrictions in 1799) skilled trades. Enlisting what Lourdes Torres calls "active memory,"[16] recounting personal and collective pasts suppressed with U.S. annexation, Pérez and Lorenzana bequeath this occluded history of female labor to the future.

If California was being scripted in Anglo accounts as a site of social regeneration and gender order, those constructions were always tenuous: as a "frontier" California was a space of instability, transformation, and potential hybridization. Albert Hurtado notes, "The journey to California [itself] involved crossing environmental, psychological, racial, and cultural orders as well as national boundaries"—a fact true even after the United States had acquired the Mexican cession as a result of the war.[17] Such border crossings readily unsettled the fixity of gender, class, race, or national identity, an instability often countered by the violent affirmation of Anglo whiteness. There is abundant archival evidence of such instability: narratives of cross-dressing (male and female) gold miners (and the mines were, historians note, among the most cosmopolitan places in the nation) and rampant violations of a gender division of labor; dizzying accounts of class transformation in the rapid making and unmaking of fortunes; travel narratives that testify to the numerous marriages between Anglo men and Californio women (the latter were sometimes racialized); records of rampant miscegenation, including accounts of the practices of "Squaw Men" (Anglo men cohabiting with Native women) in the Gold Rush era and the sexual slavery of Native American women, girls, and boys. Eliza W. Farnham, one of the region's female migrants, thus wrote that in California "it is no more extraordinary for a woman to plough, dig and hoe with her hands . . . than for men to do all their household labor for months, never seeing the face nor hearing the voice of [a] woman during that time."[18] In her recent work on the social world of the Gold Rush, Susan Johnson cites a letter by Lucius Fairchild, a future governor of Wisconsin, who wrote to his family about his unusual job waiting tables in a hotel: "Now in the states you would think that a person . . . was broke if you saw him acting the part of *hired Girl* . . . but here it is nothing, for all kinds of men do all kinds of work. . . . I can *bob around the table*, saying 'tea or Coffee Sir' about as fast as most hombres."[19] The transformative nature of the frontier could readily unsettle the supposed fixity of identity in the East. The effects of such instability on the making and unmaking of identities, including racialized class identities, regularly feature in the narratives I discuss here.

"Exit, tramp! Enter gentleman!" — MARÍA AMPARO RUIZ DE BURTON, *The Squatter and the Don*

The author of two novels depicting the conquest, Ruiz de Burton explores how the West, as myth and historical location, unsettles discourses of class forged in the North/South binary of the East. Works of historical fiction, both novels register what scholars describe as the "fluidity of social categories" in pre- and post-1848 California, a period of rapid social change.[20] As I have suggested, going west appears in a host of antebellum novels as the solution to landlessness and factory work, a way to unmake and remake class identity—mainly for white workingmen; as narratives by women homesteaders describe, the "freedom" of-fered to white female migrants was far more ambiguous. (Existing frontier auto-biographies of cross-dressing women, such as the renowned "Mountain Charley" who became a Colorado saloon keeper, reveal that some women successfully at-tempted to claim the "masculine" economic prospects of western migration.)[21] Consolidated in the "free labor" ideology of the Republican Party during the 1850s, migration captured what Almaguer calls the "class aspirations and ra-cial entitlements of white labor," promising Euro-American men "privileged economic mobility" in the western territories.[22] Depicting the West, especially California, as the object of U.S. imperial reach, Ruiz de Burton forces us to see domestic class relations in a global frame, to perceive their inseparability from what Etienne Balibar and Immanuel Wallerstein call "multiple forms of class conflict" in the world economy.[23]

According to Patricia Limerick, "Race relations [in the U.S. Southwest] par-allel the distribution of property, the application of labor and capital to make the property productive, and the allocation of profit. Western history has been an ongoing competition for legitimacy—the right to claim for oneself and . . . one's group the status of legitimate beneficiary of Western resources."[24] This process is allegorized by Ruiz de Burton; in her novels white working-class men and women are simultaneously agents of class dispossession and representatives of the class dispossessed. What she calls the "American shame" (*The Squatter and the Don*, 103), the dispossession of those she denominates "native Californians"—prosperous, landowning Californios represented in *The Squatter and the Don* by the Alamar family—of their land and livelihood is facilitated by the Homestead Act and perpetrated by propertyless working-class squatters mainly from the Northeast. The state plays a crucial role in this process; figuring the inseparability of the international division of labor from domestic class relations, Ruiz de Burton's novels provide a window on the role of the state in the making and remaking of class. The law is here an instrument of "gringo justice": starting with the 1848 Treaty of Guadalupe Hidalgo, Anglo laws (including the Foreign Miner's Act and the Homestead Act) enabled the economic dispossession and political disenfranchisement of displaced Mexicans, facilitating a "process by which Chicanos have become . . . associated with criminality" and, over time, creating Mexicanos and Chicanos as a tractable workforce.[25] As one character in *The Squatter and the Don* attests, it is Anglo laws that "drive [Californios] into squalid hovels, and thence into the penitentiaries or the poor houses" (146). The Californios are "impoverished" and "ruin[ed]" (146) by the combination of illegal squatter activities, corrupt laws, and Anglo political indifference (177), and Ruiz de Burton is principally concerned with documenting the Californios' dispossession, using her novels to give the voiceless a voice. (It should be acknowledged that this construction of white workers as perpetrators of racial theft—for example, in *The Squatter and the Don*, Anglo squatters such as John Gasbang cheat both Indians [e.g., 332] and Californios out of their property—enacts a historical sleight of hand; in particular it erases the class conflict between Californios and the Indios who performed most of the work in the missions and on the ranchos, a relation foregrounded in the *testimonios*.) Ruiz de Burton illuminates the racial ideologies that shape the class conflict between homesteading squatters—landless white settlers in pursuit of their "one hundred and sixty acres"—and Californio landowners; glossing the stereotype of the "sleepy Mexican," she examines how Mexicans are portrayed as "lazy, thriftless, ignorant natives" unfit "to own such lordly tracts of land" (175).[26] These racializing discourses subtend an imperial narrative of national prosperity and economic "progress"; depicting Californios as "a hindrance to the prosperity of the state," such discourses made "despoil[ing] them, to make them beggars," seem "if not absolutely righteous, certainly highly justifiable"

(175). Once again white workers' economic "freedom" entails differentiation from forms of racialized "unfree labor"; the construction of elite Californios as racialized "greasers" facilitates and justifies their economic and political marginalization.[27] This attachment of Mexican Americans, even wealthy landowners, to forms of "unfree labor" is allegorized in the story of Gabriel Alamar, the eldest son of a former landowning don. Driven from his land to the city, Gabriel becomes a "common day laborer" and eventually a poor "hod carrier"—an image of proletarianization in which, Ruiz de Burton contends, "*the entire history of the native Californians of Spanish descent* was epitomized" (344, 349, 352).[28]

As the Homestead Act makes clear, it is domesticity—specifically what Mike Davis calls the "bourgeois utopia" of homeownership—that fuels imperial conquest; as Don Mariano tells the squatters, "'The reason why you have taken up land here is because you want homes'" (*The Squatter and the Don*, 91). In this endeavor white workingwomen's position is, again, shifting and ambiguous. For one thing, as noted earlier, antebellum political discourses of land reform were distinctly masculine; landownership was tied to what Neil Foley terms the ideal of "manliness."[29] Working-class proposals for distribution of public land as the solution to labor exploitation—such as those debated in National Reform newspapers and pamphlets, culminating in the 1862 passage of the Homestead Act—typically promoted a conservative gender script. Proponents of land reform, including George Henry Evans, invoked an image of a harmonious farm family in which "proper" and "natural" gender roles would be restored; men would reclaim their role as household heads, and women and children would no longer have to perform wage work (especially in the factory).[30] As discussed in chapter 1, radical Lowell women responded to workingmen's scathing depiction of female factory work with an antipastoral critique of the agrarian ideal; other working-class women, such as Aurora Phelps, aimed to feminize land reform, decoupling *masculine* from *breadwinner* and endorsing "garden homesteads" for workingwomen.[31] Ruiz de Burton highlights gender conflicts within the homesteading Darrell family: Mrs. Darrell refuses to move onto land illegitimately taken from Californio landowners, though the moral agency of her "sympathy" is rendered "useless" by her squatter husband's patriarchal power (186). Indeed "the squatters did not make any pretense to regard female opinion with any more respect than other men" (89). These silenced women do get their revenge: when her son, the politically ambitious squatter Peter Roper, "a child of the . . . poor people" (333), shows "no respect for the memory of his mother" when making a speech, the "ghost of the poor reviled cook" seems "like . . . Banquo, to frighten off the audience" and dash her son's political hopes (333–34). (Ruiz de Burton similarly compares Mrs. Darrell to "some Banquo spectre" [254] when she appears before a meeting of squatters, terrifying them with eloquence compelled by moral outrage; her husband, haunted by her memory, eventually acknowledges his "wickedness" and instructs his son to make "reparation" [359].) Other white working-class women are more than silent collaborators, such as the "dishonorable" (104) servant Mrs. Hogsden, who, with her husband, appropriates "one hundred and sixty acres" of their master's land when the latter is ill; Mrs. Hogsden "brace[s] up" her faltering husband and "brazenly" steals articles of furniture from the house (332, 333). The class "sympathies" of workingwomen, who are at once politically marginal and potential beneficiaries of male family members' activities, are complicated by their own domestic subordination and by what the narrator calls the patriarchal "monopol[y]" on "money-making . . . politics and . . . many other pursuits" (183).

*The Squatter and the Don* underscores the gendered nature of the squatters' economic rapacity and "hunger" for land. At times that hunger is plainly sexualized; accusing Don Alamar of enticing his son with the Don's beautiful daughter, Darrell construes Mexicanas as sexual property, claiming that Clarence's purchase of the land is driven by his desire to possess Mercedes Alamar. Indeed the portrayal of Californianas in both *The Squatter and the Don* and *Who Would Have Thought It?* is shadowed by the sexual commodification of Indian women in greater Mexico and Anglo California, disavowed by Californianas' unstable "whiteness." Meanwhile disempowered white women's "Banquo-like" haunting evokes the California gothic, defined by the uncanny presence of the racially dispossessed.[32] That haunting renders California uncanny by registering a layering of class pasts, a sedimentation of historical eras inscribed on the landscape in ways that can profoundly destabilize "identities" in the present. Memorialized in "old-fashioned" (*The Squatter and the Don*, 123) Spanish and Californio institutions, architecture, and culture, such haunting disrupts the capitalist temporality of progress—the expectation of "coming prosperity" (122)—and unsettles the class regime in which "every one is for himself" and "money [is] . . . the sole requisite [of] social claims" (316, 351). Indeed, the present is figured as the culmination of what David Montejano calls "a sequence of class orders"[33] from the Spanish period to the Mexican postrevolutionary period to the U.S. period, each with its distinct labor system: the paternalistic mission system of debt peonage; the ranchero period of the Californios when, as in "feudal times in Europe," the "landowners with their servants" were bound together by a set of reciprocal duties and obligations (176). Ruiz de Burton particularly details the paternalist ethic of hospitality, courtesy, and social care embedded in the "superior" rancho culture of the "native Californians"; constructing the dons as an "anachronistic gentry"[34] whose "high culture, talents

[and] accomplishments" legitimize their authority, she unsettles the class power of the Anglos while envisioning the survival of this ethic of benevolence in the capitalist present (351). In *The Squatter and the Don*, Clarence's "noble" (355) rescue of his kin, paying more than market value ("no more than what is right," he tells Doña Josefa [360]) for the Alamar rancho, which is "full of squatters, and without a patent" (360), arguably enacts this social ideology. Whereas squatters are generally "short-sighted" and "unappreciative," Clarence is both a "money-making Yankee" and an "honorable" man (103, 360).

These themes are taken up explicitly in *Who Would Have Thought It?*, a novel published in 1872 but set in the years leading up to and during the Civil War. The novel documents how, in Bruce Robbins's words, domestic class identities and divisions are "blurr[ed]" and "relativized" by imperialism and the "international division of labor."[35] Again, as in *The Squatter and the Don*, the home is the vehicle of class dispossession; the novel shows how the politics of "white egalitarianism" in the mid-nineteenth-century United States depend explicitly on imperial conquest and the economic absorption of imperial "possessions" into the "domestic" space of the nation. California's role as an "antidote to . . . modernity" serves as both an invitation to Anglo conquest and a repository of the racial past.[36]

In *Who Would Have Thought It?*, Lola's arrival in the Norvals' home provokes forms of racial seeing that naturalize her economic subordination while facilitating the upward mobility of the Norval family. Shifting the site of racial dispossession from west to east, from California to Boston and Washington, Ruiz de Burton throws into relief the dependence of the "metropolis" on the colonial "periphery"; Lola's appearance enacts what Edward Said terms the "voyage in," bringing the "international division of labor" into the intimacy of metropolitan space.[37] Her characterization as both servant and heiress contains images of California Mexican(American) women's class identity as bearers of wealth and desired objects of marital alliance and as exploited, proletarianized workers. When Lola arrives with Dr. Norval draped in a "red shawl" (14), she is misrecognized by his wife as a bold-eyed erotic rival (23); when Mrs. Norval "discover[s]" that the figure is female, her eyes "magnified [Lola] into a very tall woman," but she is quickly recast as a "little black girl" (16). "'How black she is!,' uttered Mrs. Norval with a slight shiver of disgust"; when her daughter Mattie observes that the girl's "hand is as white as mine" and takes it between her own, Mrs. Norval fears that Mattie will contract a "contagious disease" (17). All the Norval women refer to Lola as a "specimen," barely distinguishable from the "boxes full of stones" Dr. Norval regularly brings home: "Having exhausted the mineral kingdom, [he] is about to begin with the animal, and this is our first specimen" (16). This scene is a kind of rewriting of the opening chapters of *Our Nig*, though Lola is ten years old and Frado only five; Reverend Hackwell observes that Lola is "rather pretty, only very black" (16), a point disputed by Mrs. Norval, who is chiefly concerned with determining "what position [Lola] is to occupy in my family" (19). As in *Our Nig*, Mrs. Norval dictates that the "horrible little negro girl" (25) will sleep and eat in separate quarters, declaring, "She will learn to work—I'll see to that" (23). Also as in *Our Nig*, the family dog is Lola's chief comfort and best friend (31), and while the mother and sister are her principal enemies, the male members of the household are benefactors and allies. Dr. Norval counters the imperialist gaze that constructs Lola as a racialized servant, asserting that her "position in our family will be that of an adopted child" (19). Lola's identity as the site of (imperial, racial) contest and her ambiguity as both "colored" and "white" is literalized in the middle of the narrative, where she is described by the Norval women as a "spotted mongrel" covered with "Pinto . . . spots" (149, 78), allegedly the product of her Indian captivity, when the chief dyed Lola's and her mother's skin black to prevent their recapture (100). At the same time we are told that there is nothing "whiter" than Lola's neck and shoulders (232).

Lola's characterization ambiguates class as well as race. Mrs. Norval is rightly concerned that Lola will spread an infection: the "contagion" she bears is the unsettling of class. As in *The Squatter and the Don*, in *Who Would Have Thought It?* imperial contact troubles the distinction between "high" and "low"; Lola is both a "lad[y]" (24) and a "servant" with whom the Irish cook and chambermaid refuse to share a bed (30). Her treatment by Dr. Norval as a (racialized) aristocrat will, Mrs. Norval fears, turn class relations topsy-turvy: the Norval women will have to wait on her (19), she imagines, while Lola's arrival transforms Dr. Norval himself from a "gentleman" into a "rough" (79). But quickly, once she learns of Lola's inheritance, Mrs. Norval finds herself willing to "give worlds to keep" the "despised black child": "She would go on her knees to serve her, as her servant, her slave, rather than let her go" (30). When he is at home, Mrs. Norval can do little but consent to her husband's dictate that Lola be treated as an equal; in the Norval household, as in *Our Nig*'s Bellmont home, it is men who rule (19). But when the doctor departs on a research trip, a battle ensues over Lola's person and property; the Norval women use Lola's wealth to enhance their standard of living and social status. Thus rather than causing the family's class decline, as Mrs. Norval initially fears, Lola's wealth fuels their upward mobility. Writing in 1913, the Puerto Rican labor organizer and author Luisa Capetillo described workers as an "eternal mine" from which the bourgeoisie "extract[s] enormous treasures";[38] "robb[ed]" by Mrs. Norval to display her home and person in the "richest style" (81, 231), Lola becomes just such a "mine" for the Norval family. In the debate over war with Mexico, some Americans had imaged the economic and cultural "elevation" of Mexicans as the special mission and obligation of white Americans; Ruiz de Burton inverts this logic: Lola is not a "burden" but a "great acquisition" (25). Reiterating the romantic plots of Anglo men before annexation, when settlers arranged marriages with wealthy Californianas as a vehicle of what Mike Davis calls nonviolent dispossession,[39] Mrs. Norval momentarily "plot[s] matrimony" (27) between her son Julian and the heiress. When Mrs. Norval (with a glancing reference to Mexican social bandits such as Joaquin Murieta) states that Lola is a "good Mexican . . . and knows how to put the dagger to the throat" (180), Julian points out, "We have appropriated the purse not she" (180). And as in *The Squatter and the Don*, Anglo thievery is legitimated by law, centered here on inheritance and the legal instrument of Lola's mother's will; Mrs. Norval and her associates gain possession of the will and determine to keep Lola's wealth out of the hands of those who could enforce it. Once again upward and downward mobility are paired, as Anglo class aspirations are expressly tied to Californios' racial and class disinheritance.

Mrs. Norval's misrecognition of Lola as black assimilates her into the familiar, racialized class economy of the East, in which African Americans' designation as "servants" helped stabilize the definition of Anglo Americans as "free laborers." Echoing historical parallels between southern chattel slavery and "quasi slave labor"—forms of racialized peonage—in New Spain, Lola's "blackening" evokes the ways that native and immigrant Mexicans after 1848, in Jose Limón's words, "endured economic exploitation and racial discrimination in many parts of the country, but especially in Texas and California, conditions akin to those faced by African Americans in the South."[40] Notably, however, Mrs. Norval also (mis)recognizes Lola as an Indian; in fact Lola is alternately seen by Mrs. Norval as "black" and "Indian" (23). The Norvals' oldest daughter, Ruth, similarly wields this racializing gaze: Lola's parents, Ruth immediately assesses, were "Indians or negroes, or both . . . Anyone can see that much of her history" (17). The text here registers hegemonic forms of racial seeing, especially the tendency among American settlers to conflate "Californios, Mexican immigrants, and local Indians" in California, visually enacting forms of class leveling that elite Californios in particular found troubling.[41] The racial(izing) gaze had social efficacy; after 1848 Californios were increasingly pushed into occupations previously "filled by neophytes and other reviled Indian employees."[42] But in tracking the class elisions of the racial gaze, Ruiz de Burton again reveals a kind of historical palimpsest of regimes of labor and servitude within the Americas: in or behind the (dispossessed) Mexican servant we can glimpse the long, violent history of Indian servitude in the New World, extending from the debate between la Casas and Sepúlveda over Indian slavery to the history of Indian servitude in the mission and ranchero systems. It is that expansive social frame that Mrs. Norval, her vision profoundly circumscribed by a chauvinistic provincialism and a hatred of foreigners, refuses to see.

Lola's "history" is, thus, what the text unfolds; she is at once a "romantic . . . heroine" (17) and bearer of the collective, racial past. Late in the narrative she is tellingly misrecognized as the servant Mina, an identification that proves fateful: stung by the Norval women's haughty comments during the misrecognition scene, Mina decides to leave the employ of Ruth Norval and join Lola in Mexico. Mina plays a crucial role in the plot: acting as a liaison, she helps frustrate Hackwell's nefarious plan to abduct Lola and force her to marry him in Cuba, a plot that emphatically situates the economic and sexual exploitation of the servant in an imperial frame. Described as a French "grisette" (234) and bearing what Bruce Robbins terms the "secret pressure" of the servant's hand, Mina serves as Lola's class double and an agent of economic justice (she is also, albeit ironically, briefly aligned with the utopian socialist discourse of "*free love*" [277]), while the "moral economy" she voices has, in this instance, transnational purchase.[43] The novel exploits the instabilities of class to present a scathing critique of U.S. nationalism and the "*fatal* influence" (198) of U.S. national "ideals" exported abroad: those ideals reduce to the pursuit of economic gain, while the nation is a space where corrupt well-connected power wielders like the Cackles (especially Caesar Cackle, who "hate[s] poor people" [288]) prosper while virtuous, patriotic Dr. Norval and his son Julian are shunned as traitors. Julian is the novel's chief object lesson in nationalist "disenchant[ment]" (244); confronting the failure of U.S. national ideals of economic and political independence, he recognizes that "it would take a long time before he should again believe that in America there is not as much despotism as in Europe—'despotism of a worse kind, because we pretend so loudly the contrary. . . . We are hypocrites and imposters'" (244).

Representing these class shifts, Ruiz de Burton again highlights interrelations of gender and class. Indeed both her novels reveal how depictions of Mexicanas and Californianas "derived from and served the ideological interests of the changing political economy in the United States."[44] If *The Squatter and the Don* features the gendered nature of white homesteading—the way, in Foley's words, landowning is tied to an ideal of "manliness"—*Who Would Have Thought It?* presents the exploitation of Mexicanas—Mexican women's sexual commodification and exploitation of their devalued female labor—as a vehicle of Anglo acquisition. It is important to note that the wealth Lola bears is a maternal legacy. The gold and gems that accompany her to the Norval house—gold and gems that Mrs. Norval appropriates to lavishly decorate her home, adorn her daughter, and eventually purchase an "extravagant" house on Fifth Avenue—were bequeathed to her in a will hastily drawn up before her mother's death. The text thus acknowledges the explicitly *gendered* class effects of conquest. According to Lisbeth Haas, while in the Mexican and rancho eras Mexican women could own property, U.S. antimiscegenation laws created racial boundaries around ownership and, in particular, kept land out of Mexican American women's hands; these laws constructed women of color as illicit sexual partners, not legitimate wives.[45] Lola's narrative nearly enacts this pattern; she is abducted by the villain Hackwell, who desires to possess her person and appropriate her fortune. But the portrayal of Mexicanas' victimization is undone by the conclusion, in which Lola marries Julian. While referencing the dominant historical narrative in which Californios' way of life "must sadly fade and pass away" (*The Squatter and the Don*, 177), Ruiz de Burton reenacts the marriage of alliance as a gesture of cultural and biological reproduction that interrupts this hegemonic historical chronology with its paired temporalities of Anglo progress and Mexican loss. In *The Squatter and the Don*, Clarence's millions stabilize the fortunes of the Don's family, rescuing brother Gabriel from wage labor by restoring him to the family farm and re-creating the famed hospitality of the Don; the white settler's son is less the offspring of a "ruffian" father than the true son of the Don, with whom he is tied through secret agreement. The marriage in *Who Would Have Thought It?*, in which Julian joins Lola at her paternal homestead in Mexico, more closely reenacts the marital patterns of pre-1848 California. Julian, "voluntarily exiling himself" (84) from his country after witnessing its betrayal of democratic principles, ends the novel in a state of national disaffiliation, while it is Lola's wealth—her father's landholdings in Mexico and the property she inherits from her mother—that become the economic grounds of the couple's future.

READING THE *TESTIMONIOS*

It is just such class shifts that are evidenced in the *testimonios*. Like Ruiz de Burton's novels, these autobiographical narratives illuminate the "racialization of class" in the antebellum decades—in particular the construction of Californios as nonwhite and their alignment with forms of unfree labor. At the same time the *testimonios* are infused with loss, memorializing the displaced racial and class past of the ranchos and mission system. The *testimonios* reveal the instabilities of gendered and racialized labor in the era of conquest; recollecting, at times in idealized terms, the racial and gender hierarchies of the mission system, they put on display the forms of racialized labor that sustained that system and gave way to the postconquest era, when Mexican Americans were proletarianized and forced to become wage workers.

Looking back to the transitions from the mission system and its subsequent secularization to the rancho system of the Mexican period and the period following U.S. conquest, these narratives record dizzying shifts in status and identity. In the Gold Rush era a migrant named Edmund Booth said California, characterized by a rush of migration and a clash of cultures, was a "world upside down."[46] As suggested earlier, Anglo writers had at times written about the West as just such a transgressive space, of class and race—as well as gender—disorder. In *Life in California* Alfred Robinson describes how a New England man who marries into elite Californio families can "become, in manner and appearance, a complete Californian," and in a series of letters from the California mines published in the *Pioneer Magazine* in 1853–54, the California author Louise Clappe, known in print as "Dame Shirley," presents the West as a space of gender transformation and transgression; for example, she portrays a woman miner known as the Indiana Girl, a "gentle creature" who dresses in the "thickest kind of miner's boots," has "the dainty habit of wiping the dishes on her apron," and can carry "fifty pounds of flour on her back" in five feet of snow: "As is often said, nothing is strange in California. I have known of sacrifices requiring, it would seem, superhuman efforts, made by women in this country, who, at home, were nurtured in the extreme of elegance and delicacy." In Dame Shirley's writing mines were also spaces in which class differences are illegible, if not entirely erased; registering race and class slippages addressed by Ruiz de Burton, Shirley writes that in the gold country "it is very common to hear vulgar Yankees say of the Spaniards" (many of whom are "highly educated gentlemen"), "O, they are half-civilized black men!," and the Spaniards are "unable to distinguish [among Anglos] these nice *shades* of manner" that "effectively separate the gentleman from the clown with *us*."[47] Such writings depict California as a social space in which transformation is normalized and social identities are refashioned and remade.

The *testimonios* bear witness to these shifts as they impact those Ruiz de Burton calls "native Californians." When researching his multivolume *History of California*, Hubert Howe Bancroft employed two oral historians, Enrique Cerruti and Thomas Savage, to conduct interviews with Californios; of the almost one hundred personal narratives collected in the 1870s, just twelve were from women. Genaro M. Padilla notes in his study of women's "autobiographical agency" in the *testimonios* that because Bancroft was chiefly interested in supplementing the "public," political history of California, women's narratives "were considered merely supplemental to men's," and he referred to them only briefly in his published text. The "women's narratives—and the social knowledge they contained—were [thus] remanded [by Bancroft] to the margins of the margin," that is, the margin of already marginalized Californio history. Until 2006, when they were gathered for an English-language collection, few of these narratives had appeared in print, "silenced," Padilla says, in the archives of the Bancroft library. Women such as Lorenzana and Pérez were further marginalized; the narratives of workers in the missions, unlike those of the elite landowning class (as were most of the interviewed women), still more rarely made it into the literary historical record. Their *testimonios* contested the "patriarchal orchestration of history," claiming discursive authority and constructing a female laboring identity in complex and illuminating ways.[48] I am especially interested in how these texts constitute an archive of class memory that situates workingwomen's subjectivities in economic and political history. As Claire Perry notes, erasing the Mexican past was central to the project of annexation: "For Anglo-Americans [in the 1850s and 1860s] who decided to settle in El Dorado, part of their efforts to re-create the communities and institutions they had left behind in the East included erasing all evidence of the Latin way of life." An English journalist in the 1870s described the "effacement" in California of "the Spanish element"—remnants of the mission culture, the rancho system, and the influence of important Mexican American families: "The 'nombres de Espana' only remain; the 'cosas' thereof have entirely vanished."[49] Contesting the stereotypical image of Californianas as a leisured elite and depicting the racialized and gendered forms of labor in the missions, Pérez's and Lorenzana's *testimonios* document the centrality of female labor to the historical making of California. In doing so they intervene in the preservative labor of Bancroft's history making, transforming Californios—called "relics" and "spared pillars of the past" by Richard Henry Dana[50]—from human statuary into active creators of the California landscape.

In early Anglo accounts of California women's labor was a site of ideological contest. Following the script of the "Black Legend," a set of negative stereotypes about the Catholic Spanish that Anglo Americans inherited from their Protestant English forebears, Mexicans, as former inhabitants of the Spanish Empire, were widely depicted as alternately "servile" and "villainous" despots; both images were intended to demonstrate the unsuitability of Mexicans for republican self-government.[51] This stereotype was expressly gendered: numerous texts presented Mexican men as lazy and unproductive. Robinson told his readers that indolence, a "trait of character" inherited from "the Old Spaniards," "still exists among their descendants, and you might as well expect a sloth to leave a tree, that has one inch of bark left upon its trunk, as to expect a Californian to labor, whilst a *real* glistens in his pocket."[52] Although some authors, such as Dana, described California women's excessive "fondness for dress" and aristocratic pretensions, Californianas were generally exempted from this image of the "lazy Mexican." Challenging Ruiz de Burton's characterization of the Californiana through images of dainty feet and "white hand[s]," Anglo observers regularly claimed that women were far more industrious than their male counterparts.[53] Such descriptions aimed to disparage Mexican men as cruel tyrants (in keeping with the Black Legend) and ineffectual rulers.

But California women's industriousness and economic skill are also featured in Californio and Mexican narratives, which routinely depict women riding horses and roping cattle, chopping wood, and "generally doing all kinds of work done by men."[54] Such images reference a complex historical reality. Women in Alta California were accustomed to a kind of economic agency—Haas calls it a "sense of entitlement"—denied Anglo American women during this era. Describing Californianas' tradition of "exercising their property rights," Haas writes, "Spanish and Mexican law gave them the right to control their property and wealth and to litigate on questions related to their person, their families, and their holdings. Daughters had the right to inherit property equally with male siblings; upon marriage, women retained as their own the property they brought into the arrangement. . . . Adult women could conduct their own legal affairs [without their husband's consent]."[55] Antonia Castañeda adds, "Mexican women, particularly elite women, held significant economic power as large property owners in their own right, as conveyors of property to others, and as consumers in a nascent but expanding market."[56] Californianas were pursued as desirable spouses by aspiring Anglo merchants for precisely that reason; marriage enabled the Anglos to acquire land and to settle and trade in Californio society. And these women came from a society in Mexico, Sylvia Arrom demonstrates, that engaged women in a wide range of productive employments: through the lifting of guild restrictions in 1799 and the efforts of liberal labor reformers, women were able to enter the skilled trades and various occupations previously monopolized by men.[57] Encoded within the image of California women as industrious workers were significant forms of female economic agency.

The *testimonios* foreground that agency and the not-so-invisible labor of California workingwomen. Both Pérez and Lorenzana occupy an ambiguous and shifting social position: as workers in the missions, they are distinguished from both mission Indians and elite Californianas. Their narratives illuminate the regime of gendered and racialized labor that sustained the mission system. Haas describes a "spatial, territorial order" that shaped "social identities" in California during the Spanish colonial and Mexican periods and perpetuated the definition of Indians as subject, servile labor. Under the mission system converted Indians (*neofitos*) were a "captive labor force" that sustained the colonial empire; Indian labor was regulated by a spatial framework that included confinement, formal work schedules, and surveillance by the priest. Male and female *neofitos* were trained as artisans to make saddles, boots, and shoes and "worked as spinners of cotton and wool, dyers and weavers of cloth; they cut and sewed clothing; they made soap and adobe bricks; they worked as carpenters, chocolate makers, winemakers, and olive press workers; and they performed rural work in fields and orchards, on the range as vaqueros, shepherds, and shearers, and in other jobs involving crops or livestock." Some *neofitos* "were trained as catechists to translate prayers and religious dogma into native languages; others were the special servants and messengers of the priests."[58] This spatial order largely regulated life in the rural villages as well. When the missions were secularized in the 1830s, heads of native families were to receive land, livestock, and supplies so they could settle in communities or pueblos. However, the mission administrators, most of whom were Californios, appropriated much of the property earmarked for the *neofitos*, leaving them with few options.[59] Haas notes that Mexican documents from the 1836 and 1844 California censuses assigned all the *indios* listed the occupation of *sirviente*, a blanket designation that obscured the multiple skills they practiced on the ranchos.[60] During the Mexican period the large ranchos of the Californio social order similarly depended upon the labor of Indian artisans and servants, while California territorial law dictated that former *neofitos* were required to perform "indispensable common labor" on undistributed mission lands for the "public good." These policies continued in the American period; in the 1850s, in the first session of the California legislature, legislators enacted a vagrancy law requiring that "any Indian able to work and to support himself . . . [and] who shall be found loitering or strolling about, or frequenting public places where liquors are sold, begging or leading an immoral . . . life, shall be . . . arrested on the complaint of any citizen." Cities passed similar ordinances: in Los Angeles Native Americans who were arrested were made to labor on public works; if the city had no projects, prisoners were to be "auctioned off to the highest bidder for private service" and compelled to work for their "employer" until they completed their sentence or paid a fine for their offense. The status of Indian servants was consolidated by public practice. Documents refer to Indians bought and sold at public auction; Indian women in particular were subject to public sale (practices that contextualize Lola's position in Ruiz de Burton's novel).[61]

As Almaguer explains, Indians were the "principal source of cheap labor" during both the Spanish and Mexican periods; however, because of the decimation of their population in the first decades of Anglo conquest, they "were not strategically integrated into the new Anglo economy." As Indians were killed off, this status of the "useful class" in California passed to Mexicans, including dispossessed Californios.[62] Miroslava Chávez-García writes that the "newly-impoverished Californio-Mexicans displaced" Native Americans as laborers in the towns and on the ranchos. Describing the widespread impoverishment of formerly well-to-do Californio landowners as well as midstrata urban residents, Chávez-García notes that by the 1860s dispossessed Californios as well as Mexican immigrants increasingly drifted into manual or domestic jobs in the growing urban and agricultural economy; many "Californio-Mexican women . . . turned to wage labor as domestics," so that by the 1880s domestic service was the primary occupation of California women of Mexican descent.[63] As Mary Romero argues, the legacy of racialized domestic service locked many Mexican American women into immobility; indeed it has been a status and occupation frequently "passed on" from mothers to daughters.[64]

Lorenzana and Pérez attest to this racialized labor system and the precarious mobility the mission system afforded propertyless Mexicanas. Their narratives depict how geographic mobility and migration can remake class. As Castañeda notes, Californios' supposed whiteness itself constituted a negation of their mestizo and poor origin; their grandparents or parents, who were given large land grants, typically "migrated to California from the impoverished classes of Mexico's Northern frontier provinces."[65] Such was the case for Lorenzana and Pérez; the racialized benevolence and class hierarchies of the mission system benefited both, while the labor shortages of the frontier facilitated their mobility. Born in 1793 and left as an infant on the doorstep of the Real Casa de Expósitos (Royal House for Abandoned Children) in Mexico City, Lorenzana, like all of the children who lived in this charity home, was named after the Real Casa's founder, Francisco Antonio Lorenzana y Butron. Identity is thus problematized and visibly inscribed by poverty and class. Lorenzana's deeply engaging *testimonio* describes how, at "barely seven years old," the orphaned girl was sent "by the Government of Mexico," along with "a large number of families and children of both sexes," to "Alta California," as part of a policy to populate the California frontier. When they arrived in Monterey, she states with clear resentment, "The government distributed some of the children, as if they were puppy dogs, to the families there." She was one of the "fortunate children" who stayed with her "mother" (her teacher) in Monterey. Eventually, however, when she is "probably about twelve or thirteen years old," her teacher marries an artilleryman and returns to San Blas in Baja California. Lorenzana attests to the great grief of this separation for both: "I never saw [my teacher] again. Shortly after she arrived in San Blas my mother died, perhaps from a broke heart because she had to leave me behind." Lorenzana is taken to San Diego and, like the other "pupp[ies]," is placed with a family, in her case that of Don Raymundo Carrillo, a soldier at the San Diego presidio. She says, "I lived with his family for many years." Later, "when it was time for [her] to leave"—most likely when she reaches her majority—she "moved to the home of Sergeant Mercado [and his wife, Doña Sal]," where she labored as a domestic worker and seamstress. She soon "became very ill" and was admitted to the mission, a refuge for the sick; when she recovers she returns to Doña Sal's home, but only temporarily, evidently because the recently widowed Doña Sal is experiencing economic hardship herself. Lorenzana's illness is especially devastating because it immobilizes her, taking away her means of livelihood. "I supported myself by working with my hands," she attests, "[but when sick] I could not work. . . . My left hand was so paralyzed that it looked like it was dead. I could not move my hand at all for about two years and eight months. Then over a period of about four months my hand began to recover very slowly." Impoverished, with no kin, in poor physical health, Lorenzana says, "The Fathers wanted to help me, so they took me back to the mission to become a nurse [in the newly built women's hospital]. . . . [Father Sánchez's] reason for giving me that job was an act of charity, because I was still quite ill and could do very little work."[66]

Lorenzana highlights the importance of the mission system's paternal "charity" in sustaining her; she reiterates several times, "Father Sánchez took me in as an act of charity because I could not work" (172). However, she also emphasizes her own economic agency and industriousness as a worker, and clearly takes pride in her numerous competencies and ability to support herself. Being a worker—especially laboring with her hands—was a fundamental part of her self-identity. Although she learned to read and was "taught the catechism" in Mexico, in California she extends her education: "When I was older and already in California, I taught myself how to write," an activity that affirms her manual agency and dexterity. Her account of her acquisition of literacy evokes the ingenuity and resourcefulness of a Frederick Douglass: "Using whatever books I could find, I would copy the letters onto any sort of paper I could obtain, such as empty cigarette papers or a blank piece of paper that somebody had thrown out. That is how I managed to learn enough to make myself understood in writing whenever I needed something" (171). Lorenzana makes it plain that the education of poor girls like herself is no social priority; finding value in refuse (cigarette papers, blank paper), she transforms it into a means of intellectual improvement and casts writing as a tool of self-assertion and agency (it allows her to communicate "whenever I needed something"). Self-taught, she makes economic and social use of her literacy skills by teaching other girls. While living with Doña Sal, she teaches girls how to read and the catechism: "After she became a widow, Doña [Sal] started a school to teach girls how to read, pray, and sew. Since she had a large garden that kept her very busy, I was in charge of the school almost exclusively. Some parents"—including some community leaders—"entrusted their daughters to me specifically and I also taught them" (171). Listing the names of scholars from prominent Californio families, she continues, "Many . . . girls learned how to read and how to sew with me" (172). Lorenzana's labor clearly gains her status within the community. Highlighting her industry and skill as well as her hard-won economic independence, she states, "I [also] supported myself by working with my hands—for example, by sewing. I made meticulously finished embroidered shirts. I also sewed shirts however people wanted them made. I embroidered sashes and vests and decorated the silk garters for the soldiers' and the civilians' suede boots," and she made other decorated garments and materials that "were difficult to work with" (172). Like the seamstresses discussed in chapter 3, Lorenzana here emphasizes the importance of needlework as a site of female creativity, skill, and productive agency. The training she receives in the mission hospital as a nurse serves as validation of her industry and a boost to her economic and self-development.

Much of Lorenzana's narrative—indeed the likely reason her narrative was sought—presents a first-person account of the racialized and gendered labor regime of the mission, outlining the daily schedule and the various jobs performed by *neofitos*: agricultural and ranching tasks (many performed by men); male artisanal labor of "carpenters, blacksmiths, cartwrights, [and] saddle makers" (174); food preparation, cloth production, and sewing (performed by women). She describes how *neofitos* worked for subsistence, for their meals and one set of clothes (coarse shirts and blouses for women, shorts and loincloths for men) and one blanket each year; neophytes who "did not fulfill their obligations or were somehow delinquent" would be punished by imprisonment or whippings (176). She makes it clear that the supervisory positions of *mayordomo* and *llavero* (the keeper of the keys) were always held by *gente de razón*, which kept the racialized power hierarchy of the missions plainly in sight. Lorenzana becomes just such a supervisor: on the California frontier of Spain and later Mexico, Apolinaria la Cuna (Apolinaria the Foundling) becomes "La Beata" (the Pious) and supervisor of a significant workforce of mission Indians. "After I regained the use of my hand, I began to do a lot of work at the mission," she states, including supervising the buying and selling of grain and distribution of rations to soldiers. She is clearly proud of her responsibilities when ships arrive at the port: "I would board the ship with some servants to receive the goods. I always was authorized to take any goods I thought might be useful for the mission, even if they were not written down on the list prepared by the Fathers" (174, 175). She is "authorized" to supervise a wide range of tasks: "I taught the Indian women how to sew. I had them working continuously on the sewing projects for the church or for the Fathers. Everything was done under my direction and care," including washing the church garments and attending to "the sick women in the hospital" (174). However, Lorenzana reveals the precariousness of the racialized distinction between supervisor and worker, tied to the secularization of the missions ("The Indians were somewhat free" [176] in the last years of the mission system) and later the dispossession of the Californios—but also due to her abiding commitment to work. For example, Lorenzana relates, "During the three years that my hand was paralyzed, I could not [sew]. Instead, I took care of the sick in the mission hospital, even though Father Sánchez told me not to do this all by myself. He said I should teach others how to care for the sick and be present to supervise them and make sure they did the job well. But I was always involved in caring for the sick women" (172). Work is such an important part of her self-identity that she returns to the topic in the addendum to her narrative: "I forgot to say that many times each year I would take the sick women and even the sick men from the mission to Agua Calienta, which was in the Sierra de Sante Isabel, twenty-four leagues from the mission. I would stay there with them for two months. I would bathe them and take care of them" (192). That commitment to work is equally evident after secularization; despite shifts in regime, Mexicanas' labor remains a key source of value. Once "the missions were taken away from the Fathers" and "there were no longer any neophytes there," Lorenzana states, "there was nobody at San Diego to do the planting, or for that matter anything else" (180, 176). Affirming, "I worked at the mission for many years, even after it was secularized," she declares herself the former mission's sole worker (180). "I found it very hard to provide Father Oliva with food," she claims, describing trips north to purchase "seeds, corn, chile, and other things" for cooking and planting (180). The shifts in the racial division of labor intensified during the period of U.S. conquest. Notably although her narrative relates how Sérvulo Varelas, the leader of a group of Californios who "unit[ed] to see if they could throw the Americans out of California" (181), assures the Indians that "they and the *gente del país* [Mexicans] were one" (184), many Indians in the region "supported the Americans" (182) and rebelled against their former masters.

With Mexican independence from Spain and the secularization of the missions, neophytes were supposed to receive land grants; in reality, historians have shown, few did. Instead many Californios claimed large grants during this era, establishing the ranchos featured in Ruiz de Burton's fiction. Unlike almost all mission Indians, La Beata was granted land, the Jamacha Valley, formerly part of the Mission San Diego holdings, on which she established a rancho. She describes several incidents of Indian "rebell[ion]" (191) during the era of secularization—including the well-known attack on Rancho Jamu, which belonged to Don Pío Pico, a former governor of California, in which two young girls were abducted—which she frames as retaliatory acts for the violence of Mexican soldiers, who frequently kidnapped and raped Indian women during the Spanish colonial and Mexican periods. It is easy to read these incidents of Indian rebellion (like their rampant horse thefts [189]), as retaliatory acts for the rapacity of Spanish Mexicans, their racially sanctioned appropriation of Indian labor, land, and women.

As Lorenzana's narrative demonstrates, race status during the Spanish and Mexican periods brought clear economic privileges, but the economic value of "whiteness" is internally stratified. Elite Californianas, the daughters of substantial landowners, were sought after as wives during the Mexican period; as a mission worker this was not Lorenzana's situation. "I was not drawn to the state of matrimony," she boldly asserts (191); notably, as a single woman, she could benefit most from entitlements to female economic independence in Mexican law. Her position in the mission secured her a substantial role in the community; a foundling by birth who found in the charity home a surrogate kinship, she represents herself as one whose "family" becomes the entire mission community. She is godmother to "probably more than one hundred children," both *"gente de razón* as well as Indian children," and she "had the satisfaction of being well loved by young and old and rich and poor" (191). Attesting to her role as the chief organizer ("I would organize everything") of the *Pastorela* (traditional shepherds' plays performed at Christmas), she states, "Since I had no daughters of my own, I took care of everybody's daughters" (192). Race privilege translates into economic mobility and security; but as a single woman her claims are vulnerable. This vulnerability intensifies in the American era. In the end she loses her rancho to the Americans, an occurrence so painful she refuses to discuss it. At the time she is interviewed she is once again impoverished, in ill health, and living on the charity of friends. "I imagine that if I went to San Diego, I would be well received. But I live far away and I am blind, and those people are not in a very good position to help me. So here I am, poor, weak, and in failing health. I will manage like this until God calls me to his bosom" (191). As in Ruiz de Burton's fiction, the hard-won "whiteness" and prosperity of Californianas, founded on Indian labor, dissipates before the racist gaze of the Anglos, which could define everyone of Mexican descent as "greasers"; the unstable dictates of race legislate the fate of class.

Eulalia Pérez's *testimonio* similarly registers historically shifting forms of racialized labor on the California "frontier." Interviewed by Thomas Savage in December 1877, Pérez was probably recommended to Bancroft's oral historians because of her renown as the world's oldest woman; publicizing that status, Mrs. Frank Leslie's best-selling book, *California: A Pleasure Trip from Gotham to the Golden Age* (1877) described Pérez as "among the remarkable objects to which the members of the Frank Leslie Transcontinental Excursion had their attentions attracted, while [visiting] California last spring."[67] Pérez's status as "object" was navigated by her family; in an addendum to the *testimonio*, Pérez's daughter Maria describes how her sister "wanted to make some money, so she 'sold' my mother for $5,000 for a period of six weeks, during which time she would be on exhibit in San Francisco at the Woodward Garden and then she would be taken to the [Centennial] exposition in Philadelphia," though Maria intervened before the Centennial and took her mother secretly to Los Angeles.[68] Bancroft's oral history project would seem to both reinscribe and contest Pérez's objectification: the "specimen" claims a voice. Punctuated by details about earthquakes, the arrival of "insurgents," and the "first adobe house" built in the territory (101), Pérez's narrative is a first-person account of her growing, if contested, economic autonomy and authority.

Born at the presidio of Loreto in Baja California to Diego Pérez, who worked in the presidio naval department, and Antonia Rosalía Cota, Pérez arrived in Alta California in 1802 with her husband, Miguel Antonio Guillén, a soldier who was transferred to San Diego; she and her husband had twelve children, seven of whom survived into adulthood. Like Lorenzana, Pérez takes great pride in her ability as a worker; her labor gives her an indispensable, and singular, identity and status. Within the narrative of local history and the *diputación territorial*, Pérez recounts a story of female economic development and self-sufficiency, both within and after her marriage. While living with her husband in San Diego, she works as a midwife; reinforcing her legendary status as the oldest woman in California, she proudly affirms that some "eighty years ago" she attended at the birth of Don Pío Pico, a former acting governor of California (110). So valued is Pérez as a midwife that "the presidio commander would not let me [visit relatives in Los Angeles], because there was no other woman at the presidio who knew how to deliver babies" (100). She is a revered community member: "Everyone in San Diego respected me very much. I was treated with much affection in the homes of the important people. Even though I had my own house, those families would have me stay at their homes all the time" (100).

After living in San Diego for eight years, the Pérez family "went to Mission San Gabriel, where my husband served in the guard" (100). But four years later the family returns to San Diego when Pérez's husband becomes "gravely ill" (100) and subsequently dies. Though her youngest daughter is only four at the time (1819), Pérez becomes her family's chief means of support. The missionary at San Gabriel, Father José Sánchez, "beg[s]" the presidio commander to transport Pérez and her family safely back to San Gabriel; Pérez represents this as a dispute over a desirable worker and community member. Father Sánchez "provided me and my family with a small house where we could live temporarily until I found work" (101); she lived in the house with her five young daughters (her son served as a soldier in the mission escort).

Like Lorenzana, Pérez is employed at the mission, and although she frames this in terms of mission paternalism—"The Fathers wanted to help me because I was a widow supporting a family" (103)—she makes it plain that her skill is responsible for her economic success. Her physical power, stamina, and longevity juxtaposed against her husband's frailty and early death, Pérez casts herself as a prodigious laborer, performing feats both productive and reproductive; for example, she gives birth to one of her nine children directly after an earthquake, when she "was knocked to the ground" in the sacristy: "I was pregnant and could not move, and people stepped on top of me. Soon after, I returned to San Diego and almost immediately gave birth to my daughter María Antonia" (100). She highlights with pride her prolific reproductivity, of crucial economic and political value in settlement efforts.[69] Her prowess as a cook is equally noteworthy. The Fathers "looked for ways to give me work without upsetting the other women" (103); evidently apprised of her culinary skill, the Fathers propose a contest to see who can cook the best dinner. The contestants are Pérez and the "only two [other] women in this whole part of California who really knew how to cook" (102); the judges are the fathers and important military and civic officials, including Governor Pío Pico's brother. Pérez prepares "several soups, a variety of meat dishes, and anything else that came to mind that I knew how to make" (103). The judges praise the meal highly—one claims "he doubted that a person would eat better food at the king's table" (104)—and Pérez is awarded the prize, "a job at the mission" (104); assigned two Indians to supervise, she has "the pleasure of seeing them turn out to be very fine cooks . . . perhaps, the best cooks in this whole part of the county" (104). Because of her success as a cook and teacher, she is eventually made the *llavera* (104). A highly versatile worker, she is also skilled as a tailoress and is in "in charge of cutting and making clothes and other items, from head to toe, for the vaqueros who used saddles" (104). She cuts and arranges the pieces of material, and her "five daughters would do the sewing" (105); when they needed more help the father "would hire women from the pueblo of Los Angeles and pay them" (105). She supervises the production of soap and olive oil and performs some of the labor herself: "I . . . worked in the crushing of olives to make olive oil" (105). She also produces lemonade, chocolate, and other sweets, some of it of export quality: "I made quite a bit of lemonade that was bottled and sent to Spain" (110). She is equally adept as a nurse and healer: when Commander General Victoria is wounded by a lance in 1832, the surgeon "left him in my hands" after treating the wound; "when he left he was practically cured" (109). Strong and agile into old age, she is an excellent dancer—a sign of her physical strength, capability, and endurance, in which she clearly takes pride (113). Her legend as a centenarian is that of a prodigious worker; according to Savage, she is not "feeble or helpless," and can "do some needlework and walk about the house unsupported even by a staff" (99).

Much of Pérez's narrative, like Loranzana's, testifies to the centrality of Indian labor in the mission system. Native girls as young as seven would perform indispensable labor, such as "weaving, unloading items from *carretas* [carts used to transport goods], sewing, or something else"; a girl who escaped would be brought back and punished (generally "locked up for her carelessness"), and if she had a family her mother would be punished "for keeping the girl away" (107). Although Pérez repeatedly affirms the Fathers' benevolence toward the Indians, she leaves room for doubt: "I am not going to talk about what the others did, because I did not live at the mission" (109). She also devotes a paragraph to describing different physical punishments inflicted upon criminals and "delinquent[s]," such as confinement to stocks, being tied to a cannon, and whippings, calling one punishment, *"Ley de Bayona"* (tying prisoners' hands to a shotgun placed behind their knees), "very painful" (109). Most strikingly she attests to the enormous profits secured from Indian labor. She explains, "Around 1830 [the year missions were secularized] we heard people say that money was being taken from the mission on mules and in *carretas*. However, I did not see that. What I do know is that at one time there was a lot of money at the mission stored in boxes, sacks, and *guajes* (an Indian name for some big things that had small openings)" (111). She recalls that one of her daughters discovered the Fathers burying money in the ground in the storehouse (111); she herself catches Father Sánchez and José Chapman "burying a box in the Father's room": "Of course the box contained money" (112). If a link is drawn between Indian and (female) mission workers in the accumulation of this wealth, that link is seemingly severed by racialized practices of distribution: the priest gives Pérez's daughters gifts "because they have worked for it" (111), and Pérez herself, like Lorenzana, is rewarded for her labor: "In addition to supporting me and all my daughters until they married, Father Sánchez gave me two ranchos, that is, land for one rancho and land for an orchard" (112). She even describes the Indians as condoning the Father's "gift": "Father Zalvidea, who spoke their language, asked them if they wanted to give me that land for an orchard and for a rancho, since I had always taken care of them and helped them. He said that those who agreed should raise their hand. All of the Indians raised their hands and said they wanted me to have the land" (112). However, excluded like many Californios from the cash economy in the Anglo era and lacking means to stock and cultivate her land, Pérez in the end loses her property. Dispossessed of her land and reduced at the end of her life—not unlike Indian women sold at auction—to a "remarkable object" in an imperial exhibition, her economic privilege dissolves with the Californios' precarious whiteness.

## *Postscript.* Looking for Antebellum Workingwomen

Memory is all we got. . . . We got to remember everything. . . .
We got to remember to be able to fight. . . . Nobody can be forgotten. . . .
The last thing they take is memory. —MERIDEL LE SUEUR, *The Girl*

The study of working-class literature, including working-class women's literature, inevitably presents the researcher with a problem of archives. This is certainly true in the United States, where the exceptionalist skepticism about class generates uncertainty about the existence of class (as) culture. Although the digitization of many textual sources, including periodicals, has increased accessibility and broadened the textual field, the material relevant to my study has remained difficult to locate. Take, for instance, the genre of working-class autobiography—a popular form of writing for working-class autodidacts and activists. In Britain, facilitated by John Burnett, David Mayall, and David Vincent's exhaustive research and compilation of the three-volume bibliography *The Autobiography of the Working Class* (1984–89), hundreds of working-class autobiographies have been gathered in archives, republished, and digitized, an effort that has fostered the production of a robust critical scholarship. In the United States, however, the collections remain to be assembled, the critical studies remain to be written.[1] The ephemerality of cheap print that constituted the bulk of most poor and working-class people's reading obviously contributes to this problem; such material, considered "trash," was rarely preserved. The final chapters of this book propose ways we might rethink the relationship between working-class literary and performance cultures—a crucial site of working-class cultural production and consumption in this era—to reimagine that ephemerality and the textual limits of working-class expression. Especially because, in Diana Taylor's words, textual archives can "sustain power," shoring up privileged "traditions" and identities, performance has often enabled "vital acts of transfer [for] transmitting social knowledge, memory, and a sense of identity," particularly for oppressed peoples. Chapters 4–6 demonstrate how attending to the rich, productive exchanges between what Taylor calls the "repertoire"—here both vernacular and staged performances of class—and written texts can shift our view of the latter (considered, as in *The Aristocrat and Trade Union Advocate*, discussed in the introduction, as repositories of working-class memory) while expanding in crucial ways our understanding of the working-class "archive."[2]

Even in those rare cases where textual archives are substantial, the gaps are emphatic, the silences pronounced. Due to the preservation of a significant collection of historical and literary materials documenting the "birth" of New England manufactures, the Lowell mill girl has remained a fixture in the national imagination; mill women, whom the labor historian Ardis Cameron calls "phantoms on the industrial landscape," have continued to haunt national memory.[3] One of many historical novels about the Lowell mill girl, Elizabeth Graver's *Unravelling* (1999) explores that spectral presence directly, making class silence and loss dominant motifs. Graver's complex characterization of her protagonist's subjectivity is inscribed in a poetic first-person narration. Aimee (named after an article in the *Ladies Pearl*, a sign of her mother's own thwarted class aspirations and desires) is at the outset defiant and passionate, possessing what her father terms an "animal" fierceness and sensuality, and the narrative is startling in its record of her desire. She is a girl "who might go bad" and the one her mother loves best, the prettiest and quickest at school, a girl who can watch unflinching while chickens and calves are killed and who follows with attentive pleasure the changes in her body. She finds in the protections of New England silence a space for a luxuriant eroticism: "I was alone most often in my thoughts, which the others could not read." Aimee's budding sexuality—"Something was slow-rising in me, putting pressure on my bones, crowding my blood, making me short of breath"—evident in the novel's early chapters leads to an incestuous encounter with her younger brother Jeremiah and then propels her directly to Lowell.[4]

Graver introduces her defiantly acquisitive, desirous heroine through her recollection of Lowell:

It is a fact that I was prettier than most at the factory, pretty as an angel, I was told. When the strangers came through, the factory owners from England looking at how it was done, I was one of the girls who was led to the front looms and asked to demonstrate. When the men from Washington came through, I was one of the girls to carry the banner: "Welcome to the City of Spindles." We wore white muslin dresses with blue sashes that day. We carried parasols edged in green. We marched singing to the factory; "How Doth the Busy Bee." Afterwards they made us give the dresses back.

I wove that, I wanted to say, or if not that one, then one like it. I knotted the knots when the thread broke, and ran from one crashing loom to another, and threaded the two thousand weft threads until my fingers swelled like rising dough.

*Mine*, I wanted to say.

I only looked like an angel. (2–3)

In Lowell the narrative follows what has become a familiar pattern; it is as if Aimee cannot escape the fate of being "just another Operative" in a place assembling "so many girls" who "all looked the same" (143). Aimee has an affair (is "seduced"), gets pregnant, is abandoned by her lover, and bears but is forced to give up twins. But underneath this story is another: Graver's narrative is preoccupied with what cannot be told and, in particular, what fractures the discursive bond between mother and daughter. Lowell, Aimee learns, "was a place of secrets" (148). The incest taboo places the sexual encounter with Jeremiah, as well as the desire Aimee feels for her brother, beyond articulation, so that the act creates a "huge, billowing wilderness" between mother and daughter (47). This unspeakability is intensified not only by the punitive theology of the region, which interprets all fleshly desire as sinful, but also by the strictures imposed by "innocence" on feminine speech, the fact that "touching . . . was not a word a girl was supposed to say" (156). In Graver's aptly titled novel, expressions of acquisitive desire and defiant ownership ("*Mine*, I wanted to say") give way to an inventory of loss: the dress (the labor) that is taken away; the lover that is taken away; the children that are taken from her; the mother that she loses and, only partly, regains. The novel suggests that the very "type" of the mill girl signifies class loss. Hoping to share her experiences with her lover, Aimee resorts to the platitudes of the myth of Lowell: "I could have told him about coming to the mill and not finding Eliza, about my brother dying while I was there and Constance leaving, about starting as a drawing-in girl and how that made all the other girls dislike me. . . . Instead I talked about the money I had saved, the lectures I had gone to, how happy I was to be in a big town like this, so much to see, how much faster I was getting at my work" (184). In *Unravelling* the narrative of urbanization and (individual and collective) industrial "progress" is unsettled by a "grief-filled, clockless time" (177) that Graver marks through modernist techniques of narrative recursivity. "Nothing leaves you," Graver writes; "things just . . . tumble and return" (203).

The primary mark of class unspeakability is the mute orphan girl Plumey. Recalling similar grotesque characters in factory fictions, such as Phelps's *The Silent Partner*, Plumey is a figure for the dislocations and losses experienced by working people, the gaps in the (female) working-class archive. After returning home Aimee lives on the margins of the social world, occupying the "farthest corner" of her family's property, a hunting shack on the edge of a bog (230–31). There she raises chickens and rabbits and takes up with Amos, known in town as the "village cripple" (2), who "was studying to be a preacher before he lost his leg, and with it the love of a woman and all faith in the workings of the Lord" (5). They are joined in their makeshift family by Plumey, who lives in town but feels a kinship with Amos and especially Aimee, who wishes to keep her "as my own" (176). Plumey was brought to New Hampshire from Maine, where her family died in a terrible fire: "When the townspeople searched for traces among the ashes, they thought they found the bones of all the children, but three weeks later a creature crawled into town, its hair matted, its skin the color and dusty hardness of dry clay. The pastor's wife planted it in a tub of steaming water and removed layer after layer to find the girl unbroken in her pale white child's body, but with no voice. What happened? asked the town. . . . But she could not seem to find the words" (31–32). Plumey's "rare moments of speech" are punctuated by "long lists," apparently of advertisements "drawn from the papers" (33–34): "'Healing Lotions,' she chants. . . . 'Excellent Vanilla Anti-dyspeptic Bitters Family Groceries Last Chance Summer Boots Four Cent Reward Chairs and Tables Rooms to Let Periodical Pills New Music Ladies' Slips Misses Ties'" (34). The language of popular periodicals is here little more than a placeholder for class silence. But the alternative, ragtag family on the bog enables a kind of recollection and healing, constituting a community of witness to class pain and loss. Out on the bog Aimee tells her surrogate daughter (264) some of her stories, "bits and pieces of myself" (267); Plumey remembers her own traumatic loss in words as "clear as spring water" (172). The narrative of mother–daughter rupture and partial restitution is a way to frame the silences of history, the gaps within the narrative (including historical narrative), the facts that don't get recorded, the stories that are not passed on. Positioned within the national narrative of industrial "progress," the unraveling of the mill girl's story becomes an accumulation of disarticulated grief.

INTRODUCTION

1 On the discursive masculinization of working-class political rights and agency in the contemporaneous Chartist movement in England, see Scott, *Gender and the Politics of History*, 53–67. She writes, "We cannot understand how concepts of class acquired legitimacy and established political movements, without examining concepts of gender. . . . The link between gender and class . . . [is] every bit as material as the link between productive forces and relations of production" (66).

2 *The Aristocrat and Trades Union Advocate,* iii–iv.

3 Zboray and Zboray, *Voices without Votes*; Kelley, *Learning to Stand and Speak.*

4 According to Gilje and Rock, the emergence of republican motherhood and cult of domesticity marked a "process of redefinition" and a "denial of the more radical gender meanings—including greater political awareness and economic independence—implied in the experience of poorer women who had sacrificed so much during the course of the war" (*Keepers of the Revolution*, 246). I argue that the historical memory of the range of women's economic activities and identities, disavowed by the new ideology of gender, were preserved in cultural texts. Workingwomen's reproductive labors are, in part, cultural and literary labors, facilitating the preservation and transmission of class memory.

5 On the history of this counterknowledge in the revolutionary era, which mobilized plebian women's participation in popular politics "not as republican wives or mothers but as social and economic actors within household, neighborhood, and marketplace," see Smith, "Food Rioters and the American Revolution." The complex interrelationship in antebellum working-class culture between orature and written texts is explored throughout this book.

6 Like many radical workingmen from this period, the poet was largely self-taught; she clearly embraced the working-class movement's republican emphasis on educational equity and the dissemination of knowledge as means of freedom. On the debate about educational reform among radical workingmen, see Wilentz, *Chants Democratic*. On the emphasis on education among British workers, see Vincent, *Bread, Knowledge and Freedom.*

7 On Chartist poetry, see Vicinus, *The Industrial Muse*.

8 Montgomery, *Citizen Worker*, 72.

9 On the conventional appeal to Shakespeare in working-class culture, see Nathans, "'A Course of Learning and Ingenious Studies'"; White, *Stories of Freedom in Black New York*; and Levine's classic *Highbrow/Lowbrow*.

10 "From the Valentine Offering," *Voice of Industry*, February 27, 1846.

11 On dependency as a sign of gender, see Fraser and Gordon, "A Genealogy of 'Dependency.'" In "Contract versus Charity," Fraser and Gordon argue that women's "subsumption in coverture" was not so much a holdover from the feudal era as the "enabling ground" of a gendered version of modern civil citizenship predicated on women's domestic servitude and subordination (55). In the antebellum era *servitude* had a racial as well as a gender legacy; both must be considered in relation to one another.

12 Clark, *The Struggle for the Breeches*.

13 Lobdell, *The Female Hunter of Delaware and Sullivan Counties, N.Y.*, 40–41, emphasis added.

14 On popular fiction of gender transgression, see for example Smith, *Virgin Land*, 112–20. Lobdell is cited as an example of transgender or "passing women" in Katz, *Gay American History*, 214–25.

15 As seen in Taylor, *Eve and the New Jerusalem*, 168.

16 On the emergence of a "moral environmentalism" that imbued the signs of domestic poverty with moral import during this period, see Mort, *Dangerous Sexualities*; for American examples, see Boyer, *Urban Masses and Moral Order in America*.

17 SenGupta, *From Slavery to Poverty*; Federici, *Caliban and the Witch*, 97.

18 Painter, Introduction to *Narrative of Sojourner Truth*, xx.

19 White, *Stories of Freedom in Black New York*, 214. In "The Mercurial Nature and Abiding Power of Race," Martha Hodes similarly notes, "As much as ancestry was most often the legal and social determinant of whiteness in the nineteenth-century United States, a certain porousness nonetheless prevailed in daily life. Ideologies about class and gender came into play, since poverty could intervene to cloud the supposed or ideal immaculacy of white womanhood.... A woman's behavior mattered, too. In New England [a woman's] sinking class standing [could push] her to the margins of white womanhood" (107). Hodes examines in particular the "precarious whiteness" of laboring women, whose "poverty and plebian occupations crowded [them] into circumstances closely resembling... [that of] black women" (94). Hodes traces the life of one Anglo American working-class woman, Eunice Connelly, a life that acutely reveals the "mercurial nature" of race; born in Massachusetts in 1831, Eunice works as a mill girl, housecleaner, and washerwoman and (like Frado in *Our Nig*) fashions hats out of palm; eventually she marries a mixed-race man from the West Indies and migrates to the Cayman Islands.

20 Washington, *Sojourner Truth's America*, 167. On (auto)biography, see Smith, *A Poetics of Women's Autobiography*.

21 Guarneri, *The Utopian Alternative*.

22 Fanuzzi, *Abolition's Public Sphere,* xxxiv; Ellis, *Silent Witnesses.*

23 Rose, "Class Formation and the Quintessential Worker."

24 Rogers, *Women and the People.*

25 Siegel, *The Image of the American City in Popular Literature*, 83, 81, 79.

26 Anderson, *Tainted Souls and Painted Faces.*

27 "A Working Woman's Statement," *Nation*, February 21, 1867.

28 Ross, *Love and Toil.*

29 Gilje and Rock, *Keepers of the Revolution*, 246.

30 Acker, *Class Questions*, 7.

31 Gilmore, "Hawthorne and the Making of the Middle Class," 215.

32 Lott, *Love and Theft*, 64.

33 Steedman, *Landscape for a Good Woman*; Kaplan, "Pandora's Box."

34 Negt and Kluge, *Public Sphere and Experience*. On popular culture as "social horizon of experience" for working-class women, see Hansen, *Babel and Babylon.*

35 Montgomery, *Citizen Worker*, 2.

36 Duggan, *The Twilight of Equality?*, 7.

37 Duggan, *The Twilight of Equality?*, 83–84.

38 Hayden, *Grand Domestic Revolution*; Cobble, *The Other Women's Movement.*

39 For example, Claybaugh, *The Novel of Purpose.*

40 Robinson, *Loom and Spindle*, 98.

41 McGill, *American Literature and the Culture of Reprinting.*

42 On the expansion of popular print culture and a working-class readership during this period, see Denning, *Mechanic Accents*. Drawing from the work of materialist feminist theorists on the relationship between culture and class, I argue that women's class identifications are defined, at least in part, by language or discourse, and that popular literature, especially periodical literature, was an important cultural site for the construction of working-class womanhood.

43 See, for example, Jameson, "Reification and Utopia in Mass Culture," 132.

44 Jameson, *The Political Unconscious*, 85–86, 70.

45 Volosinov, *Marxism and the Philosophy of Language*, 21–23; Jameson, *The Political Unconscious*, 85.

46 Stuart Hall makes a related point: "Transformation is the key to the long and protracted process of the 'moralisation' of the labouring classes, and the 'demoralisation' of the poor, and the 're-education' of the people. Popular culture is neither, in a 'pure' sense, the popular traditions of resistance to these processes; nor is it the forms which are superimposed on and over them. It is the ground on which the transformations are worked" ("Notes on Deconstructing 'the Popular,'" 232, 228).

47 On the legacy of the "moral economy" in America, see Thompson, "The Moral Economy of the English Crowd"; Gutman, *Work, Culture and Society in Industrializing America*, 3–78; Kelley, *Race Rebels.*

48 Hobsbawm, *The Age of Revolution*, 304.

49 Poovey, *Uneven Developments*, 3.

50 Kessler-Harris, "The Just Price, the Free Market, and the Value of Women," 482–83.

51 Boydston, *Home and Work.*

52  Gordon and Fraser, "A Genealogy of 'Dependency'"; Montgomery, *Citizen Worker*.

53  For example, Gilmore, "Hawthorne and the Making of the Middle Class"; Pfister, *The Production of Personal Life*.

54  Hawthorne, *The House of the Seven Gables*, 55, 7, 9, 7.

55  On the role of the law in the production of economic inequities during this period, see Tomlins, *Law, Labor, and Ideology in the Early American Republic*.

56  Michaels, *The Gold Standard and the Logic of Naturalism*, 92.

57  Skidmore, *Rights of Man to Property!*, 4–5, 86.

58  Michaels, *The Gold Standard and the Logic of Naturalism*, 98.

59  Brownson, *Defense of the Article on the Laboring Classes*, 79, 80, 85. Brownson's essays, republished as pamphlets, first appeared in the *Boston Quarterly Review*. For a broader discussion of how utopian socialists aimed to rehabilitate the spirit of love and counter the "fanaticism of the family," see Rancière, *Proletarian Nights*.

60  "Factory Life: Romance and Reality," *Voice of Industry*, December 3, 1847. See my discussion of this text in chapter 1.

61  See, for example, the Factory Tract by "Amelia" entitled "Some of the Beauties of Our Factory System—Otherwise Lowell Slavery." The Tracts were published in 1845 by the Lowell Female Labor Reform Association. The first Tract and excerpts from the second are reprinted in Foner, *The Factory Girls*, 134–36.

62  Stansell, *City of Women*, 129.

63  Burn, *Three Years among the Working-Classes in the United States during the War*. Born in Glasgow, Burn was a weaver and a "physical force" Chartist who moved to London in the early 1850s before leaving for Newark and New York in 1862; after working in a federal munitions factory during the war, he returned to London. Burn's writing is discussed at length in Vincent's *Bread, Knowledge and Freedom*.

64  *Factory Tracts*, in Foner, *The Factory Girls*, 132–33.

65  Sarah Bagley, "The Ten Hour System and Its Advocates," *Voice of Industry*, January 16, 1846.

66  An editorial entitled "Plants and Flowers in the Mills" refers to the "cultivation of Flowers in the Mills," noting, "Several proprietors have displayed commendable liberality in sending floral contributions, in rich variety, to ornament the mills" (*Lowell Offering*, series 1, no. 2 [1840]: 32).

67  Clark, *The Struggle for the Breeches*; Taylor, *Eve and the New Jerusalem*, 193; Stansell, *City of Women*.

68  Bettie, *Women without Class*, 40.

69  Slotkin, *The Fatal Environment*; Nead, *Myths of Sexuality*, 29.

70  Merish, *Sentimental Materialism*.

71  Kessler-Harris, *Out to Work*, 51.

72  Sennett and Cobb, *The Hidden Injuries of Class*. On ways "women can experience the consequences of structural relations [of class and gender] as personal failure," see Acker, "Class, Gender, and Relations of Distribution," 483.

73  Stansell, *City of Women*, 143. For example, John Commerford, a chair maker and president of the New York General Trades Union, described wage earners as "the family of labor" and the "working classes" (143).

74 Acker, "Class, Gender, and Relations of Distribution," 480.

75 Acker, "Class, Gender, and Relations of Distribution," 486.

76 Orleck, *Common Sense and a Little Fire*.

77 Robinson, *Loom and Spindle*, 68, 69, 70, 76.

78 The reference is to the title of the classic feminist essay by Nancy K. Miller.

79 Brace, *The Dangerous Classes of New* York, 119.

80 Collins, *Nature's Aristocracy*, 160.

81 Le Sueur, "Women on the Breadlines," 166.

82 Poovey, "Ideology and *The Mysteries of Udolpho*," 317, 308, 314.

83 Marx, *Capital*, 516.

84 See note 34.

85 On this refracting, see Lott, *Love and Theft*.

86 Lhamon, *Raising Cain*, 216.


### 1 • FACTORY FICTIONS

1 A Maine lawyer turned popular author, Bradbury published chiefly in the Boston paper *Uncle Sam*, one of the first American story papers and the first to present work by predominantly American authors rather than pirated English and European materials. See Noel, *Villains Galore*.

2 Foster, *New York by Gas-Light*, 120.

3 Stallybrass and White, *The Politics and Poetics of Transgression*.

4 Lehuu, *Carnival on the Page*; see also chapter 2.

5 Schiller, *Objectivity and the News*.

6 Anna Jameson, "The Milliners," *Athenaeum*, March 4, 1843, 203.

7 On links in mainstream reports between utopian socialism and (particularly female) sexual disorder, see Barbara Taylor's fine study *Eve and the New Jerusalem*.

8 Pessen, *Most Uncommon Jacksonians*. Robert Dale Owen's widely circulated early birth control tract, *Moral Physiology* (1830), and its reception are discussed in Taylor, *Eve and the New Jerusalem*, 54–55, 215–16.

9 Gray, "The Languages of Factory Reform in Britain," 143.

10 Factory women's precarious whiteness was registered, indeed valorized, by some activist workingwomen, such as the following contributor to the *Factory Girl's Album*: "No matter if our hands are less white than others', or our arms more 'coarse and brawny,'" for "all work is honorable, and in the faithful performance of our work is centered our highest credit" ("The Factory Operative," March 14, 1846).

11 Berman, *All That Is Solid Melts into Air*.

12 Lown, *Women and Industrialization*, 214.

13 Marx, *Capital*, 620–21. As noted, the image of the mill woman was an Anglo American construction. Called by Zlotnick the "prototype of the wage earning woman," the English female factory worker "emerged in the 1830s and 40s as the future face of the workforce" (*Women, Writing, and the Industrial Revolution*, 16–17). While signifying for some the social progress enabled by industrialism, for many contemporaries, especially elite men and workingmen, the mill girl was

a symbol of social disorder, connoting women's distraction from domestic duties while men lost economic status (through the degradation of artisan work, often blamed on female factory labor) and at times even employment.

14 Anderson, *In the Tracks of Historical Materialism*, 90.

15 Cameron, *Radicals of the Worst Sort*, 45. On the role of such spaces in the "identificatory erotics" of female subject formation and on the queer desires they can enable and foster, see Kent, *Making Girls into Women*.

16 Quoted in Moran, *The Belles of New England*, 29.

17 Kessler-Harris, *A Woman's Wage*, 7–8.

18 Smith, *Lectures on Jurisprudence*, 178. Dru Stanley discusses the coupling of familial dependency and free labor in liberal economic theorists' definition of the wage in *From Bondage to Contract*. The image of female carnality persisted in discussions of workingwomen, especially factory women. For example, one Lowell overseer reportedly "thought it a great blessing to the city of Lowell" that factory operatives' hours were increasing in the mid-1840s, since giving them leisure would only "increase their viciousness, immorality, and degradation" (quoted in Murphy, *Ten Hours' Labor*, 166).

19 Hodes, "The Mercurial Nature and Abiding Power of Race."

20 On the ideological construction of women as dependents during this period, see Fraser and Gordon, "A Genealogy of 'Dependency,'" 129.

21 Fuller, *Woman in the Nineteenth Century*, 40. In *A Woman's Wage*, Kessler-Harris writes, "The wage frames gendered messages; it encourages or inhibits certain forms of behavior; it . . . shapes the expectations of men and women and anticipates their struggles over power, [impacting] the relationships of the sexes inside and outside the family" (8). Extending Kessler-Harris's account, it is possible to see how a woman's wage is embedded within (and *carries within itself*) a certain *narrative* structure, a normative feminine developmental narrative or life story, in which female wage work defines a certain phase of female development en route to marriage—a narrative structure central to the genre of American domestic fiction.

22 On the history of Lowell and debates about the factory system, see Kasson, *Civilizing the Machine*; Pessen, *Most Uncommon Jacksonians*.

23 In Kasson, *Civilizing the Machine*, 30.

24 See Boston, *British Chartists in America*; Blewett, *Constant Turmoil*. The Scottish Chartist and temperance lecturer John Cluer was active in the Lowell Ten-Hour Movement and delivered an influential address at the Lowell Lyceum. A transatlantic history of Anglo American discourses of labor and class remains to be written.

25 Wilentz, *Chants Democratic*, 253, 250. See also Lott, *Love and Theft*; Foner, *Women and the American Labor Movement*.

26 Rogers, *Women and the People*, 20.

27 In Foner, *Women and the American Labor Movement*, 40–41.

28 "Report of the Female Labor Reform Association in Lowell," *Voice of Industry*, September 18, 1845. The discourse of female influence, routinely addressed by scholars of antebellum domesticity, must be situated within broader debates about class in the 1830s and 1840s; it was inflected within discourses of class unrest, especially

the Chartist discourse about physical force (which itself had parallels in abolitionism). At times the opposition between moral and physical force was used to
bolster emerging gender norms, but this was not uncontested. While one Chartist
implored Chartist women to use their influence to restrain men from "strong
language," another exhorted Chartist women to employ the same "gentle influence"
that Parisian women used in 1789 to overthrow the feudal system, "for there was
not a single measure of Reform then accomplished, except what was accomplished
by the women" (in Rogers, *Women and the People*, 97).

29 According to Siegel, images of women and children were emphatically used to represent the degradation of the urban labor force in antebellum popular fiction (*The
Image of the American City in Popular Literature*, 79). See also chapters 2 and 3.

30 Quoted in Pessen, *Most Uncommon Jacksonians*, 158.

31 Quoted in Pessen, *Most Uncommon Jacksonians*, 162.

32 Greenberg, *Advocating the Man*.

33 Foner, *Women and the American Labor Movement*, 17.

34 Born in Rhode Island in 1795, the son of a Revolutionary War pensioner, Luther
worked for a time as a carpenter, then, after extensive travels in the West, returned
to New England to devote his full energies to labor reform. During the summer
of 1832 he delivered his *Address* throughout the region; when published it went
through three editions.

35 On Marx's use of sensational imagery, see Cvetkovich, *Mixed Feelings*.

36 On this gendering of nerves and muscles, see Jordanova, *Images of Gender in Science and Medicine between the Eighteenth and Twentieth Centuries*, 58.

37 As Wilentz notes of New York's radical workingmen, women and day laborers
were kept at arm's length by journeymen as dependent persons; many assumed that
women had no clear sense of their rights, let alone the capacity to fight for them.
While in the early 1830s there was more openness among workingmen to include
women and children in a "family of labor," this was followed by a plebian cult of
domesticity—a model, distinct from feminized evangelicalism, based on older notions of the primacy of male authority and duty (*Chants Democratic*, 248–49, 253).

38 On Paine's influence on the "language and culture of [Anglo American] plebian
rationalism," see Epstein, *Radical Expression*, 110–12.

39 Stallybrass and White, *The Politics and Poetics of Transgression*, 80–124; Bourdieu,
*Distinction*, 485–500.

40 "Factory Life—Romance and Reality," *Voice of Industry*, December 3, 1847.

41 Bromell, *By the Sweat of the Brow*, 15–39.

42 Streeby similarly notes that while sentimentalism "emphasizes refinement and
transcendence," sensationalism, which "emphasizes materiality and corporeality,"
should be seen as a "meaningful response to the rise of body-transforming institutions such as the prison and the factory and disciplinary practices aimed at the
body in the nineteenth century" (*American Sensations*, 31, 43).

43 Harvey, *Spaces of Hope*.

44 Warner, "The Mass Public and the Mass Subject."

45 See Buck-Morss, *The Dialectics of Seeing*, 81–82.

46 In Murphy, *Ten Hours' Labor*, 117–19.

47 In Bromell, *By the Sweat of the Brow*, 30.

48 *The Rights of Man*, in Epstein, *Radical Expression*, 111.

49 Lowell women writers similarly endeavor to startle their readers with graphic imagery, thus enlisting them to "awake from the lethargy which has fallen upon them" (Amelia, in *Factory Tract*, no. 1, reprinted in Foner, *The Factory Girls*, 137). See note on *Factory Tracts* below.

50 Armstrong, *Desire and Domestic Fiction*.

51 Jacobs, *Incidents in the Life of a Slave Girl*.

52 The phrase appears in "Factory Life—Romance and Reality." See discussion below.

53 Roach argues that the spectacle of slaves for sale signifies "the abundant availability of all commodities" by the 1850s ("Slave Spectacles and Tragic Octoroons," 174).

54 See Stansell, *City of Women*, on this dynamic among the "Bowery b'hoys" and "gals," expressed in workingmen's anger about elite men's "slumming" and erotic exploits in working-class neighborhoods. See also Gilfoyle, *City of Eros*.

55 Mort, *Dangerous Sexualities*, 48.

56 Armstrong and Tennenhouse, "Gender and the Work of Words," 238. See also Bourdieu, *Distinction*, 207, 190.

57 This "poetics of gender" was central to what Boydston in *Home and Work* terms the "pastoralization" of women's domestic labor during this period, which culturally marked its exclusion in political economy from classification as productive work.

58 Trollope, *The Adventures of Michael Armstrong*, 93.

59 Tonna, *Helen Fleetwood*, 560. The *Factory Girl's Album* assails leisured women's sense of class superiority and their disdain for the laboring "hand": women who hold that "it is a disgrace to labor" and who "behold their pretty, delicate hands, and think and talk of their superiority" (August 29, 1846).

60 Taylor, *Eve and the New Jerusalem*, 201. On the ways working-class and poor women were invoked in nineteenth-century radical and reform discourses to embody labor's degradation and the trauma of poverty, see Rogers, *Women and the People*.

61 Guarneri, *The Utopian Alternative*. The debate was published as a pamphlet: *Association Discussed; or, The Socialism of the Tribune Examined* (New York, 1847).

62 On the "intimate connection" between the wage and marriage contract, see Isenberg, *Sex and Citizenship in Antebellum America*, xv, 170–71. Christopher Tomlins observes in "Subordination, Authority, Law" that because the common law of master and servant continued to shape both capitalist relations in the workplace and gender relations in the household, there was an important (if often unspoken) parallel between women and workers. As Charles Sears wrote in a letter published in the *Una* in 1854, the power of treating workers as servants was used to "appropriate to private use the fruits of labor produced by other hands" (quoted in Isenberg, *Sex and Citizenship in Antebellum America*, 171), a dynamic that operated in both factory and household.

63 Folbre, "Unproductive Housewife," 465.

64 Boydston, *Home and Work*, 9.

65 Continuing a legal challenge to coverture that began with the Married Women's Property Acts and extended to the passage of earning statutes, antebellum feminists challenged what Reva Siegel terms the "doctrine of marital service" that granted husbands a property right to their wife's (paid and unpaid) labor; "Home as Work," 1076. Siegel charts as antecedents to feminist arguments those of utopian socialists (who challenged women's domestic servitude and what Brisbane termed their "pecuniary dependence") and abolitionists. On the impact of the ferment of European radicalism and the revolutions of 1848 on American feminism, see Anderson, *Joyous Greetings*.

66 "The Sex," *Lily* (April 1, 1856). An author in the monthly journal *The Genius of Liberty* notes that the "class of females" who perform household drudgery—paid domestics—are "out of the pale of [male] sympathies, as they are not supposed to be 'gifted with those acute sensibilities' which come within the range of [men's] guardian care and tender compassion" (in Russo and Kramarae, *The Radical Women's Press of the 1850s*, 138).

67 "Dear E.," *Una*, May 2, 1853, 63; Paulina Wright Davis, "Pecuniary Independence of Woman," *Una*, January 1854, 200; Paulina Wright Davis, "Remarks at the Convention," *Una*, September 1853, 137.

68 "My Dear H.," *Lily*, October 1, 1856.

69 "The Every-day Life of Woman," *Lily*, February 1, 1852. Unwilling to "grapple but with one head of the Hydra," writers in the *Una* and *Woman's Advocate* refused the racial bait of an opposition between "white slavery" and chattel slavery. One writer declared, "We feel earnestly for all victims of tyranny whether they be slaves of the cotton lord, or the slaves of the cotton loom. Our compassion is equally excited by the story of the black slave dragging out her weary life in constant terror of her brutal overseer, as by that of the slave of the needle in continual fear of beggary or starvation" (Anne E. McDowell, *Woman's Advocate*, February 16, 1856, as seen in Russo and Kramarae, *The Radical Woman's Press of the 1850s*, 234).

70 "A Convention in the Inner Life," *Una*, June 1, 1853, 71.

71 The *Voice of Industry*, described by Foner as the most widely read and influential labor paper of the 1840s, was originally the organ of the New England workingmen but contained a "Female Department" edited by Sarah Bagley. In early 1846 the paper was purchased by workingwomen and became the official paper of the Lowell Female Labor Reform Association, continuing publication through December 1847. The *Factory Girl's Album, and Operatives' Advocate* (in August 1846 it became *The Factory Girl's Album, and Mechanics Offering*), although published by a man, was edited entirely by "an association of females who are operatives in the factories, and consequently qualified to judge the wants of those whose cause they will advocate" (in Foner, *Women and the American Labor Movement*, 61); it was published through May 1847. On the influence of these journals Foner writes, "The importance of the factory magazines cannot be overemphasized. Workers smuggled them into the mills, and they were read eagerly and passed along" (63). An article in the *Factory Girl's Album* describes how a male overseer regularly confiscates the journal "from some of the girls employed in his room, under the

pretence that he 'didn't allow any reading in his room'" ("A Mean Man," October 10, 1846).

72 *Factory Tracts*, no. 1, in Foner, *The Factory Girls*, 131. The *Factory Tracts* were a series of pamphlets published by the LFLRA in 1845, at the height of the Ten-Hour Movement. The *Tracts* were widely circulated, and excerpts appeared in the *Voice of Industry*.

73 "Sarah Bagley as Editress," *Voice of Industry*, May 15, 1846, emphasis added.

74 Quoted in Guarneri, *The Utopian Alternative*, 293.

75 In Murphy, "Sarah Bagley," 38.

76 Orleck, *Common Sense and a Little Fire*.

77 See especially Laclau and Mouffe, *Hegemony and Socialist Strategy*. On gendered republicanism, see Kelley, *Learning to Stand and Speak*.

78 Johnson, *A Shopkeeper's Millennium*, 137–41.

79 Thompson, *The Poverty of Theory*, 254.

80 Raymond Williams outlines this process in the entry for "Family" in *Keywords*.

81 On the history of workingwomen's activism in the 1840s, and especially the emergence of workingwomen as speakers at workingmen's meetings and as writers in factory publications, see Murphy, *Ten Hours' Labor*, 203; Foner, *Women and the American Labor Movement*. Murphy observes, "To speak rather than to be spoken of constituted a dramatic change in the language of the ten-hour movement" (*Ten Hours' Labor*, 205). On access to periodical literature among marginalized women, see Cane and Alves, *"The Only Efficient Instrument."*

82 *Voice of Industry*, September 4, 1846, in Murphy, *Ten Hours' Labor*, 207.

83 "New England Workingmen's Association," *Voice of Industry*, June 5, 1845; "New England Workingmen's Association," *Voice of Industry*, May 22, 1846; "Extracts of a Letter Received by a Member of the Female Labor Reform Association in Manchester," *Voice of Industry*, May 22, 1846. Laclau and Mouffe's concept of disarticulation is relevant here (*Hegemony and Socialist Strategy*).

84 For an example of factory women's use of millenarian rhetoric to democratic ends and their redefinition of philanthropy beyond anything middle-class evangelicals might imagine, see "Preamble of the Lowell Female Labor Reform Association," published in *Voice of Industry*, February 27, 1846.

85 "Preamble of the Lowell Female Labor Reform Association," *Voice of Industry*, February 27, 1846. On genealogical rhetoric, see Castronovo, *Fathering the Nation*.

86 "Taylor Diary," April 28, 1843, in Foner, *The Factory Girls*, 233; "Article 9th," *Voice of Industry*, February 27, 1846.

87 *Factory Girl's Album*, February 28, 1846; Sarah Bagley, "Aristocracy," February 14, 1846.

88 "Female Labor," *Factory Girl's Album*, April 25, 1846. On opposition to monopoly as a key motif in workingmen's discourse, see Laurie, *Working People of Philadelphia*. This writer rearticulates antimonopoly in gendered terms, against men's monopolization of nearly the entire field of productive work.

89 "Factory Tracts No. 2," *Voice of Industry*, November 14, 1845; "The Rights of Women," *Voice of Industry*, May 8, 1846. This writer appealed to the rationalism of free thought, boldly contending, "If the Christian faith were carried out, it, of all others would the

most subject the female sex to the lowest point of subjection in servile dependence on man," but others infused the rhetoric of human rights with millenarian overtones. Bagley, for instance, referred to the "holy cause of human rights and human equalities" ("Report of Female Labor Reform," *Voice of Industry*, June 12, 1845). On Lowell women's varied use of religious rhetoric, see Murphy, *Ten Hours' Labor*.

90  "There Must Be Something Wrong," *Factory Girl's Album*, February 1, 1847; An Operative, "A Reply to *Spectator*," *Voice of Industry*, January 17, 1847.

91  "Beauties of Factory Life," *Factory Girl's Album*, November 21, 1846; Operative, "A Reply to *Spectator*," *Voice of Industry*, January 17, 1847; Acker, "Class, Gender, and Relations of Distribution."

92  E.g., "To the Female Labor Reform Association in Manchester," *Voice of Industry*, April 24, 1846.

93  Ellen Munroe, "To the Editor of Bee," *Voice of Industry*, March 13, 1846.

94  The letter appeared in the short-lived *Wampanoag and Operatives Journal*, July 9, 1842, published in Fall River (in Foner, *The Factory Girls*, 75–76).

95  Sarah Bagley, "To W.E.B., Correspondent to the *Dundee (Scotland) Warder*," *Voice of Industry*, September 18, 1846.

96  Olivia, "Are the Operatives Well Off?," *Voice of Industry*, September 16, 1845; Sarah Bagley, "The Ten Hour System and Its Advocates (Continued, III)," *Voice of Industry*, February 6, 1846; An Operative, "Factory Tract No. 1: Factory Life as It Is," in Foner, *The Factory Girls*, 132.

97  Amelia, "Some of the Beauties of Our Factory System—Otherwise, Lowell Slavery," in Foner, *The Factory Girls*, 134–38.

98  Sarah Bagley, "Voluntary?," *Voice of Industry*, September 18, 1845.

99  Slotkin, *The Fatal Environment*, 554n16.

100  Dublin, *Women at Work*, 132–44.

101  Ware, *The Industrial Worker*, 74.

102  "Response to article about the Workingmen's Convention in the *Lowell Journal*," *Voice of Industry*, July 3, 1845.

103  Bagley, "The Ten Hour System and Its Advocates, Again," February 6, 1846; Amelia, in *Factory Tract*, no. 1, reprinted in Foner, *The Factory Girls*, 136.

104  See, for example, "Response to article about the Workingmen's Convention in the *Lowell Journal*," *Voice of Industry*, July 3, 1845. According to Roediger, by the mid-1840s the phrase *white slavery* had taken on clear sexual meanings; by the Civil War an association with female prostitution eclipsed the term's earlier connotation of the unjust exploitation of wage labor (*Wages of Whiteness*, 72).

105  "Letter from a Local Factory Girl," *Nashua Gazette*, October 1, 1846, in Foner, *The Factory Girls*, 82–84.

106  Mary, "North and South," *Voice of Industry*, February 13, 1846; letter to the editor, *Voice of Industry*, September 25, 1845; "A Mile of Girls," *Voice of Industry*, December 26, 1845.

107  Martha Hollingworth, "Letter to *Spectator*," *Voice of Industry*, June 18, 1847; see also Munroe, "To the Editor of Bee," and Lynn Pioneer, "Rights of Married Women," *Voice of Industry*, August 14, 1847. On Lowell women's marital patterns (includ-

ing the fact that mill women often married later than other women), see Dublin, *Women at Work*, and introduction to *Farm to Factory*, 1–38.

108 See Cott, "Divorce and the Changing Status of Women in Eighteenth Century Massachusetts," on the contractual, pragmatic character of marriage among laboring classes in the eighteenth century. See also Greenberg, *Advocating the Man*.

109 Margaret Fuller, "Thoughts on Marriage," *Factory Girl's Album*, September 5, 1846.

110 See, for example, "The Bandit," *Factory Girl's Album*, August 15, 1846; "Principle before Patrimony," *Factory Girl's Album*, August 22, 1846.

111 "Female Courtship in Rome," *Factory Girl's Album*, August 22, 1846.

112 Stansell, *City of Women*, 77, 89, 86. On the radical subculture of libertinism and the traditional centrality of male bonding in journeymen's culture, see Clark, *The Struggle for the Breeches*.

113 Clark, *The Struggle for the Breeches*, 196. On antebellum "sporting men," see Gilfoyle, *City of Eros*. Stansell assesses what she terms workingmen's "radical paternalism" in *City of Women* (139).

114 Clark, *The Struggle for the Breeches*; Rogers, *Women and the People*, 82.

115 A "life of single blessedness" was treated in the *Factory Girl's Album* quite differently when applied to women. For example, an article entitled "Old Maids" avers, "Old maids are usually very industrious; and for this reason they are hated by many who were brought up in idleness, and would wish to cast reflections upon the laboring classes," challenging those who would "endeavor to cast a *stigma* upon those who wish to remain absolved from the cares and responsibilities incident to a married life" (October 17, 1846).

116 Throughout the *Factory Girl's Album* tropes of fashion figure market desires not organized by the regulatory institution of the family.

117 On a working-class gay subculture and male homoeroticism, see Stansell, *City of Women*; Lott, *Love and Theft*. On the bachelor as a cultural type, see Sedgwick, *Epistemology of the Closet*.

118 "Bachelorism Unnatural," *Factory Girl's Album*, March 28, 1846; Dow Jr., "Short Patent Sermon," *Factory Girl's Album*, February 14, 1846.

119 On working-class codes of sexuality and courtship practices such as betrothal, and on seduction as transgression and manipulation of those practices, see Stansell, *City of Women*, 76–101.

120 A facetious advertisement in the *Factory Girl's Album* reads as follows: "Wanted Immediately—777 young dandies to form a 'gazing corps,' to be placed at the corners of the various streets, and in the doors of the different churches in this village. Their business will be to stare at respectable people as they pass to and from church, and to make remarks in regard to Ladies' dresses, personal appearances, &c." (August 29, 1846).

121 "Yes, Get Married," *Factory Girl's Album*, March 14, 1846; "I Can't Afford It," *Factory Girl's Album*, May 9, 1846. On the class meanings of the dandy in working-class discourse (focusing on the black dandy), see Lott, *Love and Theft*.

122 "The Credit System," *Factory Girl's Album*, June 20, 1846; Stansell, *City of Women*, 86. On exchanges with tin peddlers as sites of heterosexual antagonism and danger, see "A Chapter on Tin Pedlars," *Factory Girl's Album*, August 22, 1846.

123 Williams, *Marxism and Literature*, 50.

124 Dickens, *American Notes for General Circulation*, 39.

125 Williams, *Marxism and Literature*, 49, 48, 51.

126 Rose, *The Intellectual Life of the British Working Class*.

127 Armstrong, *Desire and Domestic Fiction*, 28; Eagleton, *The Rape of Clarissa*.

128 Harriet Farley, "Editorial," *Lowell Offering*, November 1843, 24; "Editor's Table," *New England Offering*, July 1848, 95.

129 Brodhead, *Cultures of Letters*, 85.

130 Bagley's comment appeared in the *Lowell Express*, August 7, 1845. See Foner, *The Factory Girls*, 58.

131 "Report," *Voice of Industry*, July 10, 1845.

132 Sarah G. Bagley, "Reply to Harriet Farley's Statement in the *Courier*," *Voice of Industry*, July 17, 1845.

133 In Foner, *The Factory Girls*, 63–66.

134 Amelia Sargent, "A Report of an Adjourned Meeting of the Improvement Circle Held in Lowell, Mass. Sept. 16th, 1845," *Voice of Industry*, September 25, 1845.

135 Quoted in Sargent, "A Report of an Adjourned Meeting of the Improvement Circle Held in Lowell, Mass. Sept. 16th, 1845," *Voice of Industry*, September 25, 1845. As Karen Sánchez-Eppler observes in her study of white women's abolitionist literature (*Touching Liberty*, 14–49), and as Bagley keenly understood, feminine delicacy and "politeness" could easily serve as an excuse for political censorship.

136 Bagley's reply, a "Letter to the Editor" also published in the *Lowell Advertiser*, July 26, 1845, appears in Foner, *The Factory Girls*, 66–68.

137 Characterizing antebellum print culture as a carnivalesque realm where "elite and popular accents clash against each other," Lawson discusses an 1844 speech by Gansevoort Melville that highlights the class nature of this linguistic struggle: Melville grants the fact that the Whigs "have the advantage of us plain-spoken democrats in scented hair, diamond rings, and white kid gloves—[roars of laughter,] in the language of compliment and the affectation of manner. . . . If one of these exquisites wished to express the idea contained in the home-spun adage, 'There is the devil to pay and no pitch hot,' he would say, 'There is a pecuniary liability due to the old gentleman, and no bituminous matter, of the proper temperature, wherewith to liquidate the obligation'" (*Walt Whitman and the Class Struggle*, xix, 38).

138 "Report," *Voice of Industry*, July 10, 1845. Bagley's reconstructed erotics are inflected by socialist discourses of the family in the early 1840s, which portrayed the isolated household as the "tomb of love," "the grave of harmony, of genius, and of love['s]" system of "universal, integral, and uniform education" (Brisbane, "On Association and Attractive Industry," 578).

139 "Factory Life—Romance and Reality."

140 "Factory Life—Romance and Reality."

141 Newberry, *Figuring Authorship in Antebellum America*, 41–42; Bromell, *By the Sweat of the Brow*, 34.

142 Juliana, "Written for the Improvement Circle," *Voice of Industry*, June 12, 1846.

1 Melville, "The Paradise of Bachelors and the Tartarus of Maids," 324.

2 Shank, *A Token of My Affections*.

3 "Valentine Offering" was reprinted in *Voice of Industry*, February 20, 1846; selections appear in Foner, *The Factory Girls*, 146–54.

4 "Valentinatory," from "Valentine Offering," in Foner, *The Factory Girls*, 147.

5 Taylor, *Eve and the New Jerusalem*.

6 Letter, *Voice of Industry*, February 20, 1846.

7 Preamble and Constitution of the Lowell Female Labor Reform Association, in *Voice of Industry*, February 27, 1846.

8 Armstrong, *Desire and Domestic Fiction*, 201.

9 Kaplan, "Pandora's Box," 860, 876, 868, 870.

10 Steedman, *Landscape for a Good Woman*; Enstad, *Ladies of Labor, Girls of Adventure*.

11 Peter Brooks identifies ambition as the predominant motor of plot in the nineteenth-century bourgeois novel, the "elaborated and socially defined form" of narrative desire (*Reading for the Plot*, 39). As activist Lowell women complained, female wage earners' ambition was strictly curtailed, and their stories were conventionally told not in plots of upward mobility but in plots of unrelenting economic decline (see chapter 3). The fiction I examine in this chapter illuminates what Cvetkovich terms the "contradictory construction of [feminine] affect" in the nineteenth century as a "source of both social stability and social instability" (*Mixed Feelings*, 6).

12 On popular culture as a "social horizon of experience" for working-class women, see Hansen, *Babel and Babylon*.

13 Armstrong and Tennenhouse, "Gender and the Work of Words," 238.

14 Berlant, *Anatomy of National Fantasy*, especially 1–56.

15 As discussed in chapter 1, traces of those intimacies are legible in Lowell women's writings, but they have often been invisible in histories of New England industrialism; as Ronald Bailey puts it, it often seems as if "cotton jumped off the stalk and [directly] onto people's bodies" ("'Those Valuable People, the Africans,'" 19).

16 "Body discourses" appears in Streeby, *American Sensations*, 31.

17 Denning, *Mechanic Accents*, 10.

18 Zboray, *A Fictive People*.

19 On the working-class readership of cheap and sensational fiction, see Denning, *Mechanic Accents*; Enstad, *Ladies of Labor, Girls of Adventure*; Streeby, *American Sensations*; see also chapter 5. On the consumption of popular literature among working-class and poor readers (including rural readers), see Zboray, *A Fictive People*; Merish, "Story Paper Weeklies."

20 Larcom, *New England Girlhood*, 244; Hale, "American Literature," 534.

21 In Thomsen, "'It Is a Pity It Is No Better,'" 87–88.

22 Charles M. Harvey, "The Dime Novel in American Life," *Atlantic Monthly* 100 (July 1907): 37–38.

23 W. H. Bishop, "Story Paper Literature," *Atlantic Monthly* 44 (September 1879): 384.

24 "Disgraceful Hebdomadals," *Round Table: A Saturday Review of Politics, Finance, Literature, Society*, November 17, 1866, 252.

25 On girls' reading practices and avid consumption of "boys' books" during this era, see Romolov, "Unearthing the Historical Reader."

26 Clark, *The Struggle for the Breeches*; Levy, *Other Women*.

27 Smith, *Virgin Land*, 112–20.

28 For example, when propositioned by her factory boss and would-be seducer, the eponymous heroine of Libbey's *Willful Gaynell* responds by issuing "a staggering blow" that "fell with crushing force upon his insolent handsome face" (5), claiming for herself the pugilistic agency usually attributed in popular texts to virtuous working-class heroes.

29 Denning, *Mechanic Accents*; Mitchell, "Reading Class," 338–39.

30 At times the taste for fancy dress and the taste for cheap fiction were conflated; in an article on "sensation novels" originally published in London's *Quarterly Review* and reprinted in American magazines, Henry Mansel described "works of this class" as "redolent of the manufactory and the shop . . . so many yards of printed stuff, sensation pattern, to be ready at the beginning of the season." The text–textile link—visible in Melville's story and structured by the fact that paper was still made from cloth rags in this period—was put to multiple uses; for instance, in debates about copyright law, writers often analogized literary texts and cloth (or cotton) in making the case that American literary texts were valuable national commodities that merited economic "protection" (Mansel, "Sensation Novels," 436). In *American Literature and the Culture of Reprinting*, McGill contextualizes this link, citing one antebellum critic who expressly describes Hawthorne's writing as domestic manufactures and "commend[s] [Hawthorne] for not having 'imported his literary fabrics, nor made them after patterns, to be found in either obscure or noted foreign warehouses'" (200). In debates about literary nationalism, the Lowell mill girl was often invoked as an important national type who anchored a distinctly American literature; she served as a means of branding American textile goods as well as literary texts.

31 "Notes, News and Chat," *Girls of Today: A Mirror of Romance*, February 19, 1876, 4; Denning, *Mechanic Accents*; Enstad, *Ladies of Labor, Girls of Adventure*.

32 Greer, "'Some of the Stories Are like My Life, I Guess,'" 156.

33 In Thomsen, "'It Is a Pity It Is No Better,'" 87.

34 Lehuu, *Carnival on the Page*, 157.

35 On maternal literacy, see Robbins, *Managing Literacy, Mothering America*.

36 Lehuu, *Carnival on the Page*, 200, 3–4.

37 In Thomsen, "'It Is a Pity It Is No Better,'" 89.

38 In Naranjo-Huebl, "The Road to Perdition," 128–29.

39 See Bernstein, "Dirty Reading," 221.

40 Streeby, *American Sensations*, 27–37.

41 On workingwomen and periodical literature, see Hamilton, *America's Sketchbook*; Cane and Alves, *"The Only Efficient Instrument."*

42 Lehuu, *Carnival on the Page*, 34.

43 Doyle, *Sex Objects*, 59, 51.

44 Stallybrass and White, *The Politics and Poetics of Transgression*.

45  Kester, "'Out of Sight Is Out of Mind,'" 73.

46  Phelps, *The Silent Partner and the Tenth of January*, 16–19.

47  To cite a few examples from the *Voice of Industry*: "An Operative" reports the "misfortune" of a girl "who broke her arm in two places" in a weaving room and who never "received a mill from the Corporation"; another writer describes how workers "wear out existence in merely obtaining the necessaries of their physical being"; yet another documents signs of "physical and mental exhaustion" and illness from overwork (January 8, 1847; February 20, 1846; December 3, 1847).

48  Arguing that capitalism is "precisely about the production of a new kind of laboring body," David Harvey examines how, for Marx, control of the body is central to class struggle: "Marx's primary point of critique of capitalism is that it so frequently violates, disfigures, subdues, maims, and destroys the integrity of the laboring body (even in ways that can be dangerous to the further accumulation of capital). It is, furthermore, in terms of the potentialities and possibilities of that laboring body (its 'species being' as Marx . . . called it in his early work) that the search for an alternative mode of production is initially cast" (*Spaces of Hope*, 108).

49  Libretti, "What a Dirty Way to Get Clean," 176.

50  Bourdieu, *Distinction*.

51  Brooks, *The Melodramatic Imagination*, ix, xi, xii.

52  Newman, *Embodied History*.

53  See, for example, *Brief and Impartial Narrative of the Life of Sarah Maria Cornell* (New York, 1833).

54  Negt and Kluge, *Public Sphere and Experience*. On this bracketing, see Fraser, *Justice Interruptus*.

55  Rancière, *Proletarian Nights*, 124.

56  Baym, *Woman's Fiction*, 26

57  On meanings of the seduction formula in British working-class culture, see Clark, *The Struggle for the Breeches*; Vicinus, "'Helpless and Unbefriended.'"

58  Stansell, *City of Women*; Peiss, *Cheap Amusements*; Haag, *Consent*.

59  Raymond Williams, *The Country and the City*, 102.

60  Harvey, *Spaces of Hope*, 97–116.

61  Vicinus, "'Helpless and Unbefriended,'" 141.

62  Brooks, *The Melodramatic Imagination*, 27.

63  *Anna Archdale, Or, the Lowell Factory Girl and Other Tales*, 2, 7.

64  Gossip, especially the power of sexual accusation and innuendo to (in the narrator's words) "ruin" an operative's "character," was expressly politicized in discourse about Lowell. Assigning to workingwomen themselves the role of "moral police," the Lowell propagandist Henry A. Miles writes that "a girl, *suspected* of immoralities, or serious improprieties of conduct, at once loses caste" among her coworkers and finds herself "everywhere talked about, and pointed at, and shunned." Miles notes with satisfaction, "From this power of opinion, there is no appeal. . . . [It] is one of the most active and effectual safeguards of character" (*Lowell*, 144–45). For their part Lowell women writers protested the power of overseers and the

sexual double standard in the mills, urging their sisters to identify with and defend rather than police or malign accused fellow laborers (e.g., Eisler, *The Lowell Offering*, 98).

65  *The Factory Girl*, title page.

66  Murphy, *Ten Hours' Labor*, 3–4, 8.

67  See the earlier discussion of Lowell women and clothing. Lowell women manipulated dress to contest inclusion within—and indeed the existence of—what Richmond in *Clothing the Poor in Nineteenth Century England* calls a "sartorial underclass" in the nineteenth century.

68  Sarah Bagley, "The Introduction into the Mill, Chapter II," *Voice of Industry*, June 12, 1846; see chapter 1.

69  See, e.g., "Gold Watches," in Eisler, *The Lowell Offering*, 184–87.

70  "Evening before Pay Day," in Eisler, *The Lowell Offering*, 162–72.

71  Enstad, *Ladies of Labor, Girls of Adventure*.

72  The phrase "economic identification" is in Steedman, *Landscape for a Good Woman*, 90.

73  Peiss, *Cheap Amusements*.

74  Enstad, *Ladies of Labor, Girls of Adventure*.

75  On sexualized class violence, see Stansell, *City of Women*; Cohen, *The Murder of Helen Jewett*.

76  Marx, *Economic and Philosophic Manuscripts*, 133.

77  Trattner, *From Poor Law to Welfare State*, 53; Dorsey, *Reforming Men and Women*, 58, 55. On the increased contempt with which the poor were viewed in this period, see Trattner, *From Poor Law to Welfare State*, 52–54.

78  Cody, "The Politics of Illegitimacy in an Age of Reform," 132.

79  *The Jacksonians on the Poor*, 29, 96.

80  Grossberg, *Governing the Hearth*, 216.

81  Lyons, *Sex among the Rabble*.

82  On incest and paternalism, see Leverenz, *Paternalism Incorporated*.

83  Middle-class reformers had similarly critiqued the assumptions of delicacy that stifled women's sexual speech; for example, members of the Female Moral Reform Society observed that they had "been terrified into silence by the cry of 'INDELICACY,'" but they vowed to remain steadfast in their commitment to publicize sexual crimes. "My Dear Sisters," *Advocate* (April 15, 1836), 61. However, as Stansell notes in *City of Women*, while women did influence and contribute to antebellum sexual discourses (e.g., in abolitionism and moral reform), they gained a hearing by writing and speaking as middle-class (domestic) women whose virtue was unquestioned—a possibility that "public" workingwomen were not granted. Popular seduction narratives about factory women explore in a more complex way possibilities and opportunities, as well as liabilities, of a sexualized urban culture.

84  On the gendered import of the "flash press," see Cohen et al., *The Flash Press*.

85  On the association between capital acquisition and unbridled lust, see Folbre, *Greed, Lust and Gender*.

86  Robinson, *Loom and Spindle*, 67.

87 Collins, *Nature's Aristocracy*. According to Fraser and Gordon, the new forms of civil citizenship established in the new republic—especially the enshrinement of private property—were a setback for the evolution in the United States of "social citizenship." Arguing that the very strength of civil citizenship in the United States undercuts social citizenship, Fraser and Gordon note that the new definition of citizenship marginalized traditional, kin-based claims on social resources; reducing kinship to the nuclear family, it established the hegemony of wage labor as a privileged basis of entitlement and construed charity as the other of contract. While "traditional kinship practices" persisted, they "lost public recognition and official political legitimacy" ("Civil Citizenship against Social Citizenship?," 59). I argue here that working-class texts constituted an important site in which these "traditional kinship practices" were legitimated and struggled for recognition. On the ways that social welfare ideals were transmitted and publicized in nineteenth-century cultural texts, see Robbins, *Upward Mobility and the Common Good*.

88 Like many of popular author Joseph Holt Ingraham's novels (including *Frank Rivers; or, The Dangers of the Town* [1843] discussed in chapter 3), *Mysteries* was published by Edward P. Williams of Boston. The publisher of the popular story paper *Uncle Sam*, Williams specialized in "mass audience adventure, crime, and romance thrillers. The cheap format often included double columns, as in the fiction magazines" the firm produced. See Dzwokoski, *American Literary Publishing Houses*, Part II, 493–94.

89 On the "shared genealogy" within the law of domestic relations of master–servant with husband–wife, see Tomlins, "Subordination, Authority, Law," 64.

90 Steedman, *Landscape for a Good Woman*, 68.

91 Significantly, while Henry waxes eloquent on the perfection of Augusta's features, Glendower's housekeeper Adriana asks whether her beautiful ear "is well constructed to drink in a tale of blood" (20)—an instance of the proletarian grotesque that self-reflexively positions the mill girl as a consumer of sensational fiction like *Mysteries* itself.

92 Steedman, *Landscape for a Good Woman*, 72.

93 "Gold Watches," *Lowell Offering*, October 1842.

94 Spillers, "Mama's Baby, Papa's Maybe," 73.

95 Buck-Morss, "The Flaneur, the Sandwichman, and the Whore," 119.

96 Ryan, *Women in Public*, 64, 73, 86.

97 On the extension of the "master-servant dynamic within industrial relations," see Tomlins, "Subordination, Authority, Law."


3 • NARRATING FEMALE DEPENDENCY

1 Parton [Fanny Fern], *Ruth Hall and Other Stories*, 90.

2 Brodhead, *Cultures of Letters*, 65–66.

3 On seamstress literature, see Reynolds, *Beneath the American Renaissance*, 355. On the popularity of seamstress literature in England, see Gallagher, *The Industrial Reformation of English Fiction*, 126–46. For Gallagher seamstress tales exemplify

the "feminization of the image of the working class in [English] industrial fiction" that helped repurpose the ideology of social paternalism contested by Chartists and other radical workingmen (129–30).

4 McClintock, *Imperial Leather*, 116.

5 "On 'Woman's Weakness,'" *Boston Bee*, reprinted in *Voice of Industry*, March 13, 1845, in Foner, *The Factory Girls*, 303.

6 Fraser, *Fortunes of Feminism*, 225. Such "mediated processes of subordination are the lifeblood of [liberal] capitalism" (225).

7 For a history of domestic workers' exclusion from the women's labor movement, see Vapnek, *Breadwinners*.

8 Marx, *Capital*, 516.

9 Hall, "Notes on Deconstructing 'the Popular.'" On the history of militancy in the garment industry, see Foner, *Women and the American Labor Movement*, 1–17.

10 In Weld, *American Slavery as It Is*, 56–57.

11 I borrow "sentimental seamstress" from Stansell, *City of Women*, 110.

12 On antebellum constructions of the "deserving poor," see Stansell, *City of Women*. Analyzing the "production of women workers' marginality" in the nineteenth century, Joan Scott notes that political economy was imbued with moral catego- ries: "Analyses of wages linked gender and economics: the 'natural dependency' of women on men within families explained the differential between male and female wages; the 'natural laws' of supply and demand explained why women would al- ways have to depend on men. One set of 'natural' laws articulated and constructed the other" (*Gender and the Politics of History*, 147–48).

13 The National Trades' Union quotation appears in Sumner, *History of Women in Industry in the United States*, 141. For the *Advocate*, see below.

14 Starting in New York in 1825 seamstresses organized to secure higher wages and formed unions, cooperatives, and associations, including the United Tailoresses' So- ciety in New York (founded 1831), the Female Improvement Society for the City and County of Philadelphia (1835), and the Shirt Sewers' Cooperative Union in New York (1851). Activities sometimes culminated in strikes; between 1825 and 1855 newspapers reported several strikes by seamstresses in Boston, New York, Baltimore, Philadelphia, and other cities. See Foner, *Women and the American Labor Movement*, 1–17.

15 Zakim, *Ready-Made Democracy*.

16 In Foner, *Women and the American Labor Movement*, 5–6.

17 Jacobs, *Incidents in the Life of a Slave Girl*, 118; Richmond, *Clothing the Poor in Nineteenth Century England*.

18 Gamber, *The Female Economy*; Coffin, *The Politics of Women's Work*, 61.

19 Toulmin, "The Shawl Buyer," *The Illuminated Magazine*, vol. 2 (1843–44), 217–21; quotation appears on 217. "Homework" is another commonly used term for various forms of labor, including outwork, in the home. See Boris and Daniels, *Homework*.

20 The very ubiquity of these images, I am suggesting, signals a strong cultural need to make workingwomen dependent. The stakes were high; in the 1840s working- women's dependency was understood as the basis of working-class discipline and class stability.

21 In Isenberg, *Sex and Citizenship in Antebellum America*, 175.

22 Arthur, *The Seamstress*, 10. Arthur's novel was published by a short-lived publisher, R. G. Bedford of Philadelphia. During the early 1840s Bedford specialized in romances and temperance novels and published a few novels by George Lippard and Ned Buntline; see Dzwonkoski, *American Literary Publishing Houses*, Part 1, 50.

23 Anderson discusses the "idea of fallenness as a predelineated narrative" expressing gendered ideas about "attenuated autonomy," agency, and determinism (*Tainted Souls and Painted Faces*, 12, 15).

24 On the emergence of "systematic discussion[s]" of poverty and its sources by the 1820s, see Stansell, *City of Women*, 19, and chapter 2. Montgomery observes that "a rapidly rising tide of urban poverty in the 1810s [a consequence of the War of 1812] and 1820s provoked widespread controversy over the costs and purposes of poor relief," undermining patrician confidence in the effectiveness of traditional forms of urban benevolence ("Wage Labor, Bondage, and Citizenship in Nineteenth-Century America," 20).

25 Poovey, *Making a Social Body*, 11.

26 Sewing was taught as part of the curriculum in "dame schools" as well as common schools that emerged in the 1850s. In 1854 the Boston School Board asserted, "No girl could be considered properly educated who could not sew." *Annual Report of the School Committee of the City of Boston*, 72.

27 Carey, *Miscellaneous Essays*, 285, 281; Mathew Carey, "A Plea for the Poor," reprinted in *The Jacksonians on the Poor*, 1. Carey was criticized by the labor press for demanding charity instead of justice (Sumner, *History of Women in Industry in the United States*, 133).

28 Walter Channing, "An Address on the Prevention of Pauperism," reprinted in *The Jacksonians on the Poor*, 20, 37–38, 39, emphasis added.

29 Nead addresses the constitutive erotics of feminine "dependency" in *Myths of Sexuality*, 29.

30 On the antebellum privatization of economic relief and its insulation from democratic control, see Montgomery, "Wage Labor, Bondage, and Citizenship in Nineteenth-Century America": "Gender profoundly shaped the everyday experience of class in the distribution of public charity" (21).

31 Defoe, *Moll Flanders*, 112.

32 Moretti, *Signs Taken for Wonders*, 112, 109, 117, 118, 123.

33 Dreiser, *Sister Carrie*, 3–4.

34 In Yeazell, *Fictions of Modesty*, 9.

35 Yeazell, *Fictions of Modesty*, 9.

36 Parton [Fanny Fern], "A Bit of Injustice," in *Ruth Hall and Other Stories*, 318.

37 For Brooks economic "ambition" is a "dominant dynamic of plot" in nineteenth-century fiction; Fern's analysis underscores the gendered nature of this scripting of what Brooks calls "narrative desire" (*Reading for the Plot*, 39).

38 Engels drily remarked of "The Song of the Shirt" that it "wrung many compassionate but ineffectual tears from the daughters of the bourgeoisie" (*The Condition of the Working Class in England*, 240n5). As Stansell notes, Hood's widely circulated

poem was a "sentimental sensation on both sides of the Atlantic" in the mid-1840s (*City of Women*, 152).

39  Compare Hood's sentimentalized seamstress with a poem published in the Lynn Transcript called "The Stitching Girls" (1869), in which needleworkers (imaged here as a collective) appear sexually alluring and dangerous:

> The stitching girls, the witching girls.
> The jaunty, dainty, stitching girls
> With Cupid's dart they pierce the heart—
> The pleasing, teasing stitching girls. . . .
> They break your heart and then depart
> The naughty, haughty stitching girls.

These young working women are not merely "naughty" and "witching"; they also wield the dangerously phallic "Cupid's dart" as effortlessly as they do stitching needles. The poem appears in Blewett, *Men, Women, and Work*, 158–59.

40  Edelstein, "They Sang 'The Song of the Shirt,'" 183–84, 188, 192.

41  Mathew Carey, "A Plea for the Poor," reprinted in *The Jacksonians on the Poor*, 49.

42  Waity Z. Brinkerhoff, "Letter from the Nunda F.M.R. Society," *Advocate* 4 (April 1, 1838): 56.

43  As seen in Berg, *The Remembered Gate*, 181–82.

44  On antebellum moral reformers' treatment of the economic exploitation of women workers as an extension of their metaphor of male dominance and female submission, see Hobson, *Uneasy Virtue*.

45  Hobson, *Uneasy Virtue*, 64.

46  *Advocate* 9 (1843): 24; 2 (1836): 17–19; 11 (1845): 109.

47  J. H. M., "Tailoresses and Seamstresses," *Advocate* 2 (December 1, 1836): 171–72.

48  *Advocate* 10 (October 15, 1844): 165.

49  "Mothers in the Country, Beware," *Advocate* 2 (February 8, 1836): 19.

50  "Woman's Mission," *Advocate* 21 (June 15, 1855): 93. See Ginzberg, *Women and the Work of Benevolence*.

51  A prolific member of Poe's literary set in Baltimore, Arthur was a popular antebellum writer, best known for his temperance narrative, *Ten Nights in a Bar-Room*, and sentimental tales published in *Godey's Lady's Book*. On Arthur as a dime novelist and the editor of the popular story paper *Arthur's Home Gazette*, see Denning, *Mechanic Accents*.

52  Stansell, *City of Women*, 109.

53  On journeymen's sexual culture, see Clark, *The Struggle for the Breeches*, 170; Stansell, *City of Women*.

54  Thompson, "Patrician Society, Plebian Culture," 386.

55  Schreiner, *From Man to Man*, 323.

56  Stansell, *City of Women*, 55.

57  Stansell, *City of Women*, 65.

58  Roediger, *Wages of Whiteness*, 146.

59 On sharing of households and domestic resources as a common practice among workingwomen, see Stansell, *City of Women*; Clark, *The Struggle for the Breeches*.

60 On Burdett's publisher, Baker and Scribner, see Dzwonkoski, *American Literary Publishing Houses*, part 2, 412. Stansell notes that the plot of Burdett's novel is derived from charity accounts of virtuous seamstresses (*City of Women*, 248).

61 Glickman, *Buying Power*, 75, 80.

62 On Victorian "it-narratives," see, for example, Freedgood, "What Objects Know." There is a robust critical scholarship about these texts in British studies; American examples have yet to be considered.

63 See Richmond, *Clothing the Poor in Nineteenth Century England*, on sewing as a form of class discipline, of making proper (working-class) women.

64 "Stray Leaves from a Seamstress" was serialized in *Una: A Paper Devoted to the Elevation of Women* from May 2, 1853 through March 1854.

65 The narrative of the seamstress as a "fallen woman" does appear in "Stray Leaves": the narrator relates the story of "Laura L.," whose "long[ing] for rest, for freedom" from labor is exploited by her married seducer, and who, after being abandoned, dies in childbirth. *Una* 1.8 (1853): 117; 1.9 (1853): 132. This narrative structure, however, is dialogized and critiqued by and through the narrator's story.

66 *Una* 1.4 (1853): 68, 69; 2.1 (1854): 195; 1.7 (1853): 100; 2.3 (1854): 228; 1.9 (1853): 133; 1.4 (1853): 69, 68; 2.1 (1854): 195.

67 *Una* 1.4 (1853): 68; 1.10 (1853): 150; 1.9 (1853): 133; 1.7 (1853): 100; 1.4 (1853): 69; 1.8 (1853): 117; 1.12 (1853): 178, 179; 1.9 (1853): 134; 1.10 (1853): 150; 1.12 (1853): 179; 2.3 (1854): 227; 2.12 (1854): 211.

68 *Una* 2.3 (1854): 227; 1.12 (1853): 179; 1.10 (1853): 150; 1.4 (1853): 69; 1.7 (1853): 101; 1.12 (1853): 179, emphasis added; 1.12 (1853): 179.

69 *Una* 1.12 (1853): 179, emphasis added; 1.12 (1853): 179.

70 In Sumner, *History of Women in Industry in the United States*, 136.

71 Beecher and Stowe, *The American Woman's Home*, 322.

72 *Una* 1.12 (1853): 179.

73 Smith, *Madame Restell*, 28–29.

74 Published by Boston's E. P. Williams (on Williams, see chapter 2, n. 88).

75 Cohen, *The Murder of Helen Jewett*.

### 4 • HARRIET WILSON'S *OUR NIG* AND THE LABOR OF RACE

1 White, *Stores of Freedom in Black New York*, 214.

2 Taylor, *Cavalier and Yankee*, xv.

3 Harris, *From Mammies to Militants*, 8.

4 Boydston, *Home and Work*.

5 Wilson, *Our Nig*, 71.

6 Tyler, *A Book without a Title*, 10. My analysis is indebted to Eric Lott's brief discussion of this novel in *Love and Theft*, 198.

7 Tyrrell's sister, who keeps his house after he deserts Mira, "works like a slave" in that capacity (Tyler, *A Book without a Title*, 250). On parallels between house-

hold and labor laws, see Tomlins, *Law, Labor, and Ideology in the Early American Republic*.

8 Slotkin notes in his discussion of this text, "Tyler's book is extraordinary, in that it attacks the Lowell-plantation myth at its root: the myth of female/black dependence" (*The Fatal Environment*, 149).

9 Sarah Bagley, "Tales of Factory Life, No. 1," *Lowell Offering*, 1 (April 1, 1841), 65–68.

10 On the ways antebellum mistresses, "imbued with the evangelizing message of true womanhood," increasingly understood the task of "reforming" their servants "as women" to be part of their charge as domestic employers, see Stansell, *City of Women*, 155–68. Robbins explains that this paternalism was largely defensive: "The observation of servants was only one point of the many-pronged, long-term process of imposing a new discipline on the new industrial work force. . . . The notion that supervision and correction of servants can make 'good subjects' of them belongs . . . to a 'patriarchal vision' that had in fact lapsed but was now suddenly revived. It was revived not because domestic servants had become more unruly or households more complicated to manage but because the rest of the work force had gone out of control" (*The Servant's Hand*, 110).

11 Thompson, "Patrician Society, Plebian Culture," 384.

12 In Russo and Kramarae, *The Radical Women's Press of the 1850s*, 80.

13 Vapnek, *Breadwinners*.

14 Steedman, *Labours Lost*, 41. On this invisibility, see Murray, *Maid as Muse*, which tracks a cultural and linguistic (as well as material and economic) dependency of middle-class women on "their" domestic servants. On the specific embodied performances of Victorian mistresses, see Davidoff, *Worlds Between*.

15 Quoted in Steedman, *Labours Lost*, 8–9.

16 Roediger, *Wages of Whiteness*, 47, 49.

17 Katzman, *Seven Days a Week*, 184; Du Bois, *The Philadelphia Negro*, 136.

18 Harris, *From Mammies to Militants*, 8. Fern's *Ruth Hall* traces the travails of its title character, a middle-class white woman who is suddenly widowed and must dismiss her servants to make ends meet. Ruth's associates are unsupportive of this decision, warning her that she cannot perform all of the household labor herself, for "you are as white as a sheet of paper" (Parton [Fanny Fern], *Ruth Hall and Other Stories*, 65). For an extraordinary account of how the racialization of domestic service and labor could become a source of sexual pleasure and desire for a white domestic, see Stanley, *The Diaries of Hannah Cullwick, Victorian Maidservant*.

19 Stewart, *Maria W. Stewart, America's First Black Woman Political Writer*, 38, 46, 47.

20 McClintock, *Imperial Leather*, 160–62.

21 In Bromell, *By the Sweat of the Brow*, 126.

22 Blackmar, *Manhattan for Rent*, 117.

23 Stansell, *City of Women*, 163.

24 In the antebellum period black children were especially vulnerable to induction into the system of racialized servitude; in the North it was not uncommon for free black women to bind their children into indentured servitude, while many southern states had laws that "all 'free baseborn children of color [were] liable to be bound out as

apprentices'" (Hodes, *White Women, Black Men*, 56). The presumptive binding out of free-born black children in the South approximates Frado's condition in *Our Nig*. The legal basis of her indenture is never articulated, though the Bellmonts as well as Frado herself appear to assume that she is bound to the family until the age of eighteen.

25 Jones, *Labor of Love, Labor of Sorrow*, 21–23.

26 See Dudden, *Serving Women*.

27 In Pierson, *Free Hearts and Free Homes*, 132.

28 In *Love and Theft*, Lott examines the racialized class ambivalence through which antebellum white workingmen's subjectivities were constituted. Here domestic labor enables a feminine version of this dynamic: I argue that the Bellmont women's racial hostility is the sign of a disavowed (unconscious) identification with Frado as embodied domestic laborer. Wilson's novel reveals the dependency of the white domestic woman on the black laboring body—not just materially but for the very production of her subjectivity.

29 In a fine reading of Elizabeth Keckley's *Behind the Scenes*, Santamarina similarly argues that "norms for black female labor . . . conflict with . . . common sense assumptions about . . . the invisibility of the labor that produces the racial and class privilege at the core of white, sentimental subjectivity" and that "symbolic conflict erupts when dominated . . . black labor is literally and figuratively emancipated"— the latter through overt inscription in cultural discourse (*Belabored Professions*, 145). An astute, deeply felt record of this "symbolic conflict" and its psychological entailments, *Our Nig* enacts this literal and figurative "emancipation" in ways I discuss throughout this chapter, documenting Frado's gradual escape from the Bellmont household into economic agency as one who "provide[s] for her own wants" (*Our Nig*, 121) and repeatedly challenging the cultural binaries upon which the capture of black female labor depends.

30 In Foreman, "Recovered Autobiographies and the Marketplace," 133.

31 Foreman, "Recovered Autobiographies and the Marketplace," 133.

32 Horton, *Free People of Color*, 18. Foreman recommends "placing discussions of Wilson's work . . . at the intersections of labor and gender" ("Recovered Autobiographies and the Marketplace," 134), which I endeavor to do here.

33 Foreman, introduction to *Our Nig*, xxiv.

34 Williams, *Dividing Lines*, 3.

35 Painter, Introduction to *Narrative of Sojourner Truth*, xx.

36 Hodes, *The Sea Captain's Wife*, 182.

37 Wilson thus "deliberately and forcefully conflates the economic situations of working-class whites and . . . blacks" (Ernest, "Economies of Identity," 431).

38 Wilson uses the gothic mode to register the class-based violence of domestic power relations as well as "unfeminine," nonnormative emotions. Stern discusses Wilson's use of the gothic in "Excavating Genre in *Our Nig*." In a nuanced psychoanalytic analysis, Stern reads the intense domestic discord in *Our Nig* as evidencing a daughter's psychic ambivalence and rage in the face of maternal abandonment. I read these textual inscriptions as symptoms of racialized class struggle.

39 Foreman, "Recovered Autobiographies and the Marketplace," 127.

40 The text thus makes visible white workingwomen's race privileges in the field of labor, evident both in their policing of racial boundaries at work (e.g., in walkouts in mixed-race workplaces) and in practices of racial "bumping" (displacing women of color in lower-status jobs in periods of high unemployment). See Green, *Race on the Line.*

41 Thus we learn early in the text that, though Mr. Bellmont "was a man who seldom decided controversies at home," his authority over the household, when executed, "admitted of no appeal" (Wilson, *Our Nig*, 30–31). Numerous Victorians expressed the view that wives and servants differed in name only; I am suggesting that Mrs. B.'s words and actions demonstrate both awareness and repudiation of this fact, illuminating how domestic subjectivities are founded on what Stallybrass and White call a "mobile, conflictual fusion of power, fear, and desire" (*The Politics and Poetics of Transgression*, 5).

42 Hobsbawm describes the importance of servants in securing middle-class status: "The safest way of distinguishing oneself from the labourers was to employ labour oneself" (*Industry and Empire*, 85). Writers in the *Factory Girls' Album* describe the "*great* pride" privileged women take in feminine leisure and not knowing "how to perform ordinary domestic duties" (e.g., August 29, 1846). Describing changes in domestic service in northern homes in the decades before the Civil War, Kessler-Harris writes, "The servant suffered from notions of unacceptable wage work which threw up barriers between her and her mistress. Her lot visibly deteriorated as she shouldered the work of an entire household" (*Out to Work*, 55). Wilson pointedly states that Frado performs "all the washing, ironing, baking, and the common et cetera of household duties" when she is just fourteen (*Our Nig*, 63).

43 Boydston notes that during this period the "emerging middle class was . . . withdrawing its daughters" from household work "in favor of education and the development of more refined social skills" (*Home and Work*, 80). *Our Nig*'s Mary Bellmont, who "did not choose to be useful in the kitchen" or the sickroom and spends "over a year" with her brother in Baltimore before dying away from home (79, 106), seems to bear out the truth of Boydston's claim.

44 Examining the culturally destabilizing presence of miscegenation in the antebellum South, Hodes observes that "sanctions against sex between white women and black men helped to ensure the perpetuation of slavery based on race . . . in part to avoid augmenting a class of free people of African ancestry residing in a society based upon racial slavery" (*White Women, Black Men*, 121). This boundary was policed by targeting adult transgressors and mixed-race offspring of miscegenation; many southern states had laws dictating that "all free base-born children of color are liable to be bound out as apprentices," so that the indenture system served as a way to police the lives of free people of African ancestry (56).

45 Bourdieu, *Outline of a Theory of Practice*, 93–94.

46 In what is perhaps an indirect acknowledgment of the illicit sexual relations of slavery, the narrator emphasizes that the Bellmont men regularly inscribe Frado within (sexualized) property relations; as Seth Shipley correctly predicts, Frado, "six years old, and pretty" would "be a prize somewhere" (Wilson, *Our Nig*, 17). As

I noted earlier, Jack's initial response to Frado is "Keep her.... She's real handsome and bright, and not very black, either"; James refers to Frado as the "last acquisition to the family" (42). However, unlike Samuel Richardson's account of a female servant's domestic conflict with another "Mr. B" in *Pamela*, Wilson focuses less on the dynamics of male sexual entitlement and cross-class heterosexual conquest than on a volatile mix of female racial phobia and identificatory desire. Endeavoring to desexualize (and defeminize) Frado, Mrs. B. cuts her "glossy ringlets" (68) so that she looks "anything but an enticing object" (69). Certainly such efforts are intended to perform Mrs. Bellmont's power over, indeed ownership of, Frado's body.

47 Timothy Sweet observes that "farming often required a good deal of wage labor, supplied by landless men and women," once northern slavery was abolished ("American Pastoralism and the Marketplace," 59). In *Our Nig* the Bellmont farm employs several "hired men" (48), who are Frado's (sometime) allies on the farm.

48 Wilson's emphasis on Frado's strong desire for "self-dependence," "steadfast purpose of elevating herself," and abiding "resolution to take care of herself" (*Our Nig*, 127, 130, 124) similarly marks her accession to rhetorics of free labor and independence.

49 Frederick Douglass, *Narrative of the Life of Frederick Douglass*, 46–47.

50 Burn, *Three Years among the Working-Classes in the United States during the War*, 83.

51 See Merish, "Materializing Identification."

52 These performances cite, in complex ways, the unsettling presence of what Brooks calls "the spectacular display of racially indeterminate bodies in transatlantic theatre culture" in the nineteenth century (*Bodies in Dissent*, 22).

53 On the antebellum preoccupation with fraudulent beggars and beggar-imposters, see Fabian, *The Unvarnished Truth*.

54 Langland, *Nobody's Angels*, 9.

55 Armstrong, *Desire and Domestic Fiction*.

56 On silence and servitude, see Robbins, *The Servant's Hand*, 60.

57 See my discussion of irony in chapter 5.

58 Kelley, *Race Rebels*, 17–20. Frado also engages in the subversive tactic of fleeing the Bellmont home, what Hartman calls "stealing away" (*Scenes of Subjection*, 69).

59 Kelley, *Race Rebels*, 23.

60 On women's comedy and the low, see Rowe, *The Unruly Woman*.

61 On Frado's "resistant orality," see Mullen, "Runaway Tongue," 254. On poisoning and arson by black girl servants in the antebellum North, see Stansell, *City of Women*, 274n29.

62 Shane White, quoted in Reed, *Rogue Performances*, 97.

5 • HIDDEN HANDS

1 Subsequently serialized in the *Ledger* in 1868–69 and 1883, the novel first appeared in book form in 1888. On the publication history of Southworth's novel, see Dobson, introduction to *The Hidden Hand*.

2 As historians of the working class note, popular performance and "cheap amusements" —as well as forms of what Ngũgĩ wa Thiong'o calls "orature"—were especially significant cultural forms for lower-class and poor audiences, especially those with no or limited literacy.

3 Hall, "Notes on Deconstructing 'the Popular,'" 232.

4 Review of *The Deserted Wife*, *Peterson Magazine* 18.4 (1850): 175. See also the review of Southworth's *The Discarded Daughter* in *Harper's New Monthly Magazine* 5:29 (October 1852): 713.

5 Egan, *The Riven Home*, 143.

6 Cap is reminiscent of *Twelfth Night's* Viola, while Marah Rocke and Old Hurricane's story recall aspects of *The Winter's Tale*.

7 Egan, *The Riven Home*, 143.

8 Brown, *History of the New York Stage*, 469.

9 Lhamon, *Raising Cain*, 216.

10 Meisel, *Realizations*. In America this interpenetration was broadly disseminated through theatrical publishing (serialized dramas were a staple of the story papers) and the popular practice of reading fictional melodramas aloud (Lehuu, *Carnival on the Page*, 74).

11 Lehuu, *Carnival on the Page*, 74; Levine, *Highbrow/Lowbrow*. On self-reflexivity in the theater, see Reed, *Rogue Performances*, 21.

12 The distinction between archive and repertoire is borrowed from Taylor, *The Archive and the Repertoire*.

13 Lhamon, *Raising Cain*, 217.

14 Dobson, introduction to *The Hidden Hand*, xvi.

15 Southworth, *Vivia*, 182–83.

16 Fernandez, *Victorian Servants, Class, and the Politics of Literacy*, 4.

17 Dobson, introduction to *The Hidden Hand*, xxi.

18 The most popular story papers (such as the *Ledger* and Philadelphia's *Saturday Evening Post*) had a circulation in the hundreds of thousands; aimed at the entire family, they contained a mix of genres to appeal to this wide audience. Noel discusses Bonner's "spectacular" success in *Villains Galore*, 58.

19 In Noel, *Villains Galore*, 56.

20 Denning, *Mechanic Accents*, 12, 27; Looby, "Southworth and Seriality."

21 In Dobson, introduction to *The Hidden Hand*, xxvii.

22 For example, Roof, *Come as You Are*; Langbauer, *Novels of Everyday Life*.

23 Southworth, *The Hidden Hand*, 465.

24 March 1887, in Dobson, introduction to *The Hidden Hand*, xi.

25 In Noel, *Villains Galore*, 56.

26 Noel, *Villains Galore*, 94–95.

27 Tebbel, *Between Covers*, 71, 72. Tebbel writes that "of [Southworth's] fifty or more novels, nearly all sold at least 100,000 copies" (72).

28 Denning, *Mechanic Accents*, 189.

29 Willa Cather, "In Washington," *Nebraska State Journal*, March 3, 1901, 12.

30 In Naranjo-Huebl, "The Road to Perdition," 128–29.

31 In Enstad, *Ladies of Labor, Girls of Adventure*, 58.

32 Dorothy Richardson, *The Long Day*, in Enstad, *Ladies of Labor, Girls of Adventure*, 57.

33 Enstad, *Ladies of Labor, Girls of Adventure*, 57.

34 The novel is remarkably self-conscious about the literary languages and conventions it employs: one character meets the revelation of fortuitous circumstances by exclaiming that he must be "the hero of a fairy tale" (429); another compares her history to the makings of a "modern romance" (449); and Capitola is repeatedly distinguished from heroines of sentimental fictions (see below).

35 On female humor, the Bakhtinian carnivalesque, and the low, see Rowe, *The Unruly Woman*.

36 Stansell, *City of Women*.

37 Southworth's use of the language of the Bowery boy in characterizing Capitola is a complex aspect of her working-class feminist critique; she adopts the liberatory, democratic aspects of this popular figure to challenge both the hegemony of bourgeois class and gender norms and the sexism of Bowery boy culture itself. On the Bowery boy, see Buckley, "To the Opera House," 294–409; Stansell, *City of Women*, 76–102.

38 On ways the wage system "threw into question relationships of male authority and female subservience long taken for granted," see Stansell, *City of Women*, 77.

39 Importantly she is eventually acknowledged as an heiress, inheriting (notably through her *mother*) "a fortune—in land, negroes, coal-mines, iron-foundries, railway shares and bank stock, of half a million of dollars" (149), an outcome that reveals the unsteady mix of racialized class dominance and precarious whiteness that define Cap's characterization. For a reading of nineteenth-century rags-to-riches narratives that highlights their utopian class accents, see Denning, *Mechanic Accents*.

40 Williams, *Playing the Race Card*.

41 Smith, *Virgin Land*, 112–20.

42 Grimsted, *Melodrama Unveiled*, 185. On melodrama as a popular, working-class form, see Vicinus, "'Helpless and Unbefriended'"; McConachie, *Melodramatic Formations*. Singer argues that the sensation scenes of nineteenth- and early twentieth-century melodrama "correlated, even if only loosely, with certain qualities of corporeality, peril, and vulnerability associated with working-class life" (*Melodrama and Modernity*, 53).

43 Brooks, *The Melodramatic Imagination*, 5. As Noel explains, midcentury American serial fiction was a literature of "remarkable coincidence"; "time-worn" melodramatic plot devices, especially "the Grand Reunion theme" involving far-flung relatives miraculously restored to one another, constituted its narrative vocabulary. For Noel "the greatest triumph of the Grand Reunion theme was 'The Hidden Hand'" (*Villains Galore*, 144, 146).

44 Grimsted, *Melodrama Unveiled*, 171, 176, 172, 173, 174, 180–81.

45 Southworth's novel might be considered a feminist variant of what McConachie calls the subgenre of Jacksonian "heroic melodrama," best exemplified by the vehicles for Edwin Forrest (*Melodramatic Formations*, 69). On subversive female roles

in English melodrama, see Duffy, "Heroic Mothers and Militant Lovers"; Reed, *Rogue Performances*.

46 Crane, *Maggie*, 37.

47 Hale is quoted in Hart, *The Popular Book*, 215. On the campaign to ban Southworth's books from public libraries, see Habegger, "A Well Hidden Hand," 200.

48 Steedman, *Landscape for a Good Woman*, 19.

49 Brodhead, *Cultures of Letters*. The novel challenges the "corrective domesticity" increasingly recommended during the 1850s by middle-class reformers obsessed with the "problem" of poor street children (Stansell, *City of Women*, 193–216).

50 Vicinus, "'Helpless and Unbefriended.'"

51 On the popularity of Napoleon in antebellum America (and the "Napoleonic aura" of Edwin Forrest), see McConachie, *Melodramatic Formations*, 85. The comparison to Pierre de Bayard, the legendary French soldier of the fifteenth century, not only evokes "a masculine realm of legend, adventure and heroism" associated, in Southworth's time, with the writings of Walter Scott and Alexandre Dumas (Dobson, introduction to *The Hidden Hand*, xix); it also links Cap to cross-dressing female soldiers common in Anglo American popular balladry since the seventeenth century (Dugaw, *Warrior Women and Popular Balladry*).

52 Robbins, *The Servant's Hand*, 139–44.

53 Brooks, *The Melodramatic Imagination*, 17. Antebellum critics perceived the (gender and class) subversiveness of Southworth's irreverence and her "enthusiasm for depicting character . . . beyond the limits prescribed by correct taste" (Sarah Josepha Hale, quoted in Hart, *The Popular Book*, 215).

54 Sedgwick, *Between Men*, 92.

55 Vicinus, "'Helpless and Unbefriended.'"

56 Roach, *Cities of the Dead*, 181.

57 For the first decade of her life Cap is raised by Nancy (Cap calls her "Granny Grewell"). As a heroic black mother, Nancy contributes centrally to Cap's characterization and endows her with a mixed-race working-class genealogy (not unlike Wilson's Frado). Capitola's own racialized inscription is underscored when Herbert writes her name and birthday on her forearm in India ink (28), an apparent reference to the practice of tattooing slaves.

58 On breeches performances as a staple of the antebellum stage, see Reed, *Rogue Performances*.

59 Blackmar, *Manhattan for Rent*.

60 These initial exchanges between Warfield and Cap allow her to voice some key issues affecting women within working-class communities: in addition to the inadequacies of tenement housing, she refers to the dangers of male sexual abuse (45) and the evils of intemperance (52).

61 Boyer, *Urban Masses and Moral Order in America*, 95. On cultural anxieties about poor children wandering the streets—especially sexual anxieties provoked by young female vagrants—see Boyer; Stansell, *City of Women*, 54, 180–83.

62 On the role of the courtroom and crime reportage in the emergence of popular sensation fiction in the 1830s, see Schiller, *Objectivity and the News*.

63 Stansell, *City of Women*.

64 Steedman, *Landscape for a Good Woman*, 130.

65 On unsettling contradictions in Victorian depictions of working-class girls—the ways they are perceived as both girls and women, workers and children—see Steedman, *Landscape for a Good Woman*; for American examples, see Brace, *The Dangerous Classes of New York*, especially 119–21, 302–3.

66 Halliday, *Lost and Found*, in which the author identifies himself as a "missionary of the managers of the 'American Female Guardian Society and Home for the Friendless'" (3). A philanthropist and the founder of the Children's Aid Society, Brace was the influential author of *The Dangerous Classes of New York* (1872) and the less well-known *Short Sermons for Newsboys* (New York, 1866).

67 On the regulatory framework in which stories of "precocious little girls" were contained, see Foucault, *History of Sexuality*, 47, 46, 40.

68 Freedman, *Their Sisters' Keepers*, 10–11, 22–45.

69 The scene stages how "working class women's [sexual] stories . . . are mediated through middle-class desires to discover sexual ownership" (Bauer, *Sex Expression and American Women Writers*, 1).

70 Freedman, *Their Sisters' Keepers*, 14, 22.

71 Stansell, *City of Women*.

72 On working-class codes of sexuality and courtship practices such as betrothal, and on seduction as transgression and manipulation of those practices, see Stansell, *City of Women*, 76–101.

73 Stansell, *City of Women*, 26. Stansell writes, "Evangelicalism [and its ideal of 'true womanhood'] gave women the spiritual armor . . . to defend their reputations from the slurs women incurred [when entering] men's sexual terrain" (69).

74 On respectability as class discourse, see McConachie, *Melodramatic Formations*.

75 On "sporting men," see chapter 2.

76 Mitchell, *The Fallen Angel*, 151; Enstad, *Ladies of Labor, Girls of Adventure*, 75.

77 See chapter 1.

78 On psychic suffering and maternal melodrama, see Cvetkovich, *Mixed Feelings*.

79 Stansell, *City of Women*, 54.

80 Arguing that "the cult of domesticity demanded performances of sexual innocence within the home," Bernstein defines sexual innocence as follows: "Sexual innocence is not a state of absence (asexuality or presexuality) but is instead a state of deflection: a constantly replenishing obliviousness that causes sexual matters to slide by without sticking" (*Racial Innocence*, 41). Bernstein and others argue that this sexual innocence is explicitly racialized as well as classed; both lower-class and African American women were widely imagined as sexually knowing. Cap's exaggerated, parodic performance of innocence exposes it *as* performance.

81 Hobson, *Uneasy Virtue*.

82 Brooks, *The Melodramatic Imagination*, 4. In its critique of melodramatic formulae, Southworth's novel bears affinities with Dion Boucicault's *The Octoroon*, which opened at New York's Winter Garden Theatre in December 1859. According to Rebhorn, the play "destabilized the melodramatic mode by alienating the audience from the main

plot's melodramatic investments," a destabilization that generated spectatorial pleasure. Boucicault's play "pointed to the way that melodrama's black-and-white mode, which could not tolerate figures who were black and white, had become the common language for the articulation of racial power in America" (*Pioneer Performances*, 117).

83  The identification between Black Donald and Cap is insightfully explored by Dobson, introduction to *The Hidden Hand*, xxxix–xl.

84  Reed, *Rogue Performances*, 31.

85  Hobsbawm, *Bandits*.

86  McConachie, *Melodramatic Formations*.

87  Linebaugh, *The London Hanged*, 23.

### 6  •  WRITING MEXICANA WORKERS

1  Almaguer, *Racial Fault Lines*, 206.

2  Santamarina, *Belabored Professions*, x–xi. On the *testimonios*, see Sánchez, *Telling Identities*; Padilla, *My History, Not Yours*.

3  In Perry, *Pacific Arcadia*, 136.

4  Sánchez and Pita, *Conflicts of Interest*, 18; Hodes, "The Mercurial Nature and Abiding Power of Race."

5  Ruiz de Burton, *Who Would Have Thought It?*, 18–19; Katzman, *Seven Days a Week*, 184.

6  See Melendez, *Spanish-Language Newspapers in New Mexico*. Part of what the historian Emma Pérez calls the "decolonial imaginary," these narratives are an effort to recollect the personal and communal past under conditions of conquest and domination in ways that allow cultural producers to "decolonize a historical imaginary that veils our thoughts, our words, our languages" and claim a history Mexicanos/as and Chicanos/as need to survive (*The Decolonial Imaginary*, 27).

7  Smith, *Freedom's Frontier*, 3.

8  In Pierson, *Free Hearts and Free Homes*, 132.

9  Smith, *Freedom's Frontier*, 2, 80, 50.

10  Several newspaper excerpts are cited in Harriet Farley's fictional version of the story, "Factory Romance," published in the *Lowell Offering* 5 (1845): 253–59.

11  In Lebergott, *The Americans*, 69.

12  James Gordon Bennett, editorial, *New York Herald*, July 10, 1845; James Gordon Bennett, editorial, *New York Herald*, November 14, 1845.

13  Greenberg, *Manifest Manhood and the Antebellum American Empire*, 203.

14  Sánchez, *Telling Identities*, 174; O'Sullivan, "Occupation of Mexico," 388.

15  Sir George Simpson, *An Overland Journey Round the World* (Philadelphia, 1847), 208.

16  Castañeda, "The Political Economy of Nineteenth Century Stereotypes of Californianas," 223; Torres, "Violence, Desire, and Transformative Remembering in Emma Pérez' Gulf Dreams," 237.

17  For example, the fastest way from the East Coast to California was by water and involved crossing through Panama or Nicaragua, a border crossing that could acquaint voyagers with Latin American mestizos/as and require ferrying by

seminude, dark-skinned boatmen, described by Jessie Fremont as "naked, scream-ing, barbarous negroes and Indians." Hurtado, *Intimate Frontiers*, 52–53.

18 Farnham, *California, In-Doors and Out*, 28.

19 In Johnson, *Roaring Camp*, 199. See also Sears, "All That Glitters."

20 Pitti, *The Devil in Silicon Valley*, 16.

21 Guerin, *Mountain Charley*.

22 Almaguer, *Racial Fault Lines*, 104, 13.

23 Balibar and Wallerstein, *Race, Nation, Class*, 124.

24 In Almaguer, *Racial Fault Lines*, 29.

25 Gutiérrez-Jones, *Rethinking the Borderlands*, 1.

26 On interdeterminations of class and race and the ways white racial identity was defined by landownership in nineteenth-century California, see Haas, *Conquests and Historical Identities in California*, 10.

27 On how U.S. conquest reconfigures class relations as well as political identities among Californians of Mexican descent, so that the distinction between *Californio* and *cholo* ceases to signify, see Griswold del Castillo, *The Los Angeles Barrio*, 28.

28 Pitti notes, "While many incoming American settlers prided themselves on their newfound economic success after 1850, no significant Mexican American middle class would develop [in the region] for almost a century" (*The Devil in Silicon Valley*, 40). *The Squatter and the Don*, Ruiz de Burton's narrative of racial dispos-session, is strongly inflected by class and region. For example, depicting the urban, industrial Northeast as the locus of political and economic power that spreads its "blight" over "Southern California, and over the entire Southern States" (372), she sites its narrative of racialized class dispossession and economic "appropri-at[ion]" (103) in San Diego within a transnational geography of an "impoverished," feminized South and a "cold," masculine North. Scholars note Ruiz de Burton's sympathies for the Old South and the parallels between her nostalgic evocation of Spanish California and romanticized portrayals of the plantation system. In *The Squatter and the Don* she locates what C. Vann Woodward calls the "colonial status for the Southern economy" vis-à-vis the Global South (including what Limón terms "Greater Mexico"), highlighting a shared subjection to "northern capitalist domination, a domination always deeply inflected with racism" (Limón, *American Encounters*, 16).

29 Foley, *The White Scourge*, 12.

30 Bronstein, *Land Reform*, 78–84.

31 See Vapnek, *Breadwinners*.

32 At times these motifs combine; in Frank Norris's *The Octopus*, the spirit of a sexu-ally violated Mexicana (raped, Norris suggests, by the Mission's Franciscan father) continues to haunt the California landscape.

33 Montejano, *Anglos and Mexicans in the Making of Texas*, 8.

34 Almaguer, *Racial Fault Lines*, 53.

35 Robbins, *Upward Mobility and the Common Good*, 239; Robbins, *Feeling Global*, 109.

36 Limón, *American Encounters*, 26.

37 In Robbins, *Feeling Global*, 112.

38 Capetillo, *A Nation of Women*, 87. Lola's wealth has allegorical import: Mexico's mineral resources figured prominently in debates about empire.

39 Davis, *City of Quartz*, 106.

40 Limón, *American Encounters*, 10–11, 29.

41 Pitti, *The Devil in Silicon Valley*, 35.

42 Pitti, *The Devil in Silicon Valley*, 40.

43 Robbins, *The Servant's Hand*, 1.

44 Castañeda, "The Political Economy of Nineteenth Century Stereotypes of Californianas," 225.

45 Haas, *Conquests and Historical Identities in California*, 81–82.

46 In Johnson, *Roaring Camp*, 100.

47 Robinson, *Life in California*, 37; Shirley, *The Shirley Letters from California Mines in 1851–52*, 41–42, 74, 256–57.

48 Padilla, *My History, Not Yours*, 111–12.

49 Perry, *Pacific Arcadia*, 136. As postcolonial scholars note, the construction of new national and local narratives and the subordination of indigenous or other previous histories and myths are an important part of the colonization process.

50 In Padilla, *My History, Not Yours*, 120.

51 Weber, *Myth and the History of the Hispanic Southwest*, 160.

52 Robinson, *Life in California*, 142. If Mexicans were "unfit" to "govern the country [Alta California]," in the words of a New England visitor, Thomas Jefferson Farnham, they were also considered incapable of initiating the economic "improvements" that would justify their title to the territory and enable them to "control the destinies of that beautiful country" (in Weber, *Myth and the History of the Hispanic Southwest*, 154).

53 Dana, *Two Years before the Mast*, 127; Sánchez, *Telling Identities*, 199–200.

54 In Sánchez, *Telling Identities*, 194.

55 Haas, *Conquests and Historical Identities in California*, 81–82. "Equal ownership of property between husband and wife [was] one of the mainstays of the Spanish and Mexican family systems" (Griswold del Castillo, *The Los Angeles Barrio*, 69).

56 Castañeda, "The Political Economy of Nineteenth Century Stereotypes of Californianas," 223.

57 Arrom, *The Women of Mexico City*.

58 Haas, *Conquests and Historical Identities in California*, 33, 24–25.

59 Chávez-Garcia, *Negotiating Conquest*, 153. On barrioization, see Haas, *Conquests and Historical Identities in California*, 8.

60 Haas, *Conquests and Historical Identities in California*, 43.

61 Haas, *Conquests and Historical Identities in California*, 36; Chávez-Garcia, *Negotiating Conquest*, 154.

62 Almaguer, *Racial Fault Lines*, 143.

63 Chávez-Garcia, *Negotiating Conquest*, 150, 149, 176. In *The Los Angeles Barrio*, Griswold del Castillo affirms that by 1880 most workingwomen in Los Angeles worked as domestic servants (73).

64 Romero, *Maid in the USA*, 75. According to Pérez, "Domestic service in Latin America has dominated women's occupations since the early twentieth century" ("'She Has Served Others in More Intimate Ways,'" 44).

65 Castañeda, "The Political Economy of Nineteenth Century Stereotypes of Californianas," 224.

66 "Recollections of Doña Apolinaria Lorenzana, 'The Pious Woman,'" in Beebe and Senkewicz, *Testimonios*, 170–72, xv.

67 An excerpt describing the meeting was reprinted in the January 12, 1878, issue of *Frank Leslie's Illustrated Magazine*.

68 Padilla, *My History, Not Yours*, 130–31; "An Old Woman and Her Recollections, dictated by Doña Eulalia Perez," in Beebe and Senkewicz, *Testimonios*, 95–117.

69 On the colonial duty of biological reproduction in Mexican California, see Reyes, *Private Women, Public Lives*, 114.


POSTSCRIPT

1 One major archive is the Burnett Archive of Working-Class Autobiographies, held at Brunell University. In his introduction to the collection of essays *American Autobiography*, Eakin observes that, while British scholars such as Vincent and Regenia Gagnier have "demonstrated the richness of the field of British working-class autobiography," American working-class autobiography "remains largely unexplored." He adds, "It was one of my chief disappointments in preparing this collection that I could not locate anyone—literary critic or labor historian—to tackle this subject" (18). More than two decades later this absence persists, at least for the antebellum era. The one major exception is, of course, African American autobiography, but here the focus of archival and scholarly efforts has been on slavery rather than the experiences of free (working-class) African Americans.

2 Taylor, *The Archive and the Repertoire*, 2–3.

3 Cameron, *Radicals of the Worst Sort*, xiii.

4 Graver, *Unravelling*, 16, 14, 23, 49.

NEWSPAPERS AND PERIODICALS

*Advocate of Moral Reform*
*El Clamor Público*
*Factory Girl's Album, and Operatives' Advocate*
*The Factory Girl's Album, and Mechanics Offering*
*Flag of Our Union*
*Lowell Offering*
*The Lily: A Monthly Journal, Devoted to Temperance and Literature*
*The Una: A Paper Devoted to the Elevation of Women*
*Voice of Industry*


ARCHIVES AND COLLECTIONS

American Antiquarian Society, Worcester, Massachusetts
American Textile History Museum, Lowell, Massachusetts
Bancroft Library, University of California, Berkeley
Center for Lowell History, University of Massachusetts at Lowell
Library of Congress, Washington, D.C.
New York Public Library
Philadelphia Library Company


PRIMARY AND SECONDARY SOURCES

Acker, Joan. "Class, Gender, and Relations of Distribution." *Signs* 13.3 (1988): 473–97.
———. *Class Questions: Feminist Answers*. New York: Rowman and Littlefield, 2006.
Almaguer, Tomás. *Racial Fault Lines: The Historical Origins of White Supremacy in California*. Berkeley: University of California Press, 1994.
Amireh, Amal. *The Factory Girl and the Seamstress: Imagining Gender and Class in Nineteenth Century American Fiction*. New York: Garland, 2000.

Anderson, Amanda. *Tainted Souls and Painted Faces: The Rhetoric of Fallenness in Victorian Culture*. Ithaca: Cornell University Press, 1993.

Anderson, Bonnie S. *Joyous Greetings: The First International Women's Movement, 1830–1860*. New York: Oxford University Press, 2000.

Anderson, Perry. *In the Tracks of Historical Materialism*. Chicago: University of Chicago Press, 1984.

*Anna Archdale, Or, the Lowell Factory Girl and Other Tales*. Boston: Gleason, c. 1850.

*Annual Report of the School Committee of the City of Boston*. Boston: Rockwell and Churchill, 1889.

Argus. *Norton: Or, the Lights and Shadows of a Factory Village*. Lowell, Mass.: Vox Populi, 1849.

*The Aristocrat and Trades Union Advocate: A Colloquial Poem, by a Working Woman of Boston*. Boston: Leonard W. Kimball, 1834.

Armstrong, Nancy. *Desire and Domestic Fiction: A Political History of the Novel*. New York: Oxford University Press, 1987.

Armstrong, Nancy, and Lennard Tennenhouse. "Gender and the Work of Words." *Cultural Critique* 13 (1989): 229–81.

Arrom, Sylvia M. *The Women of Mexico City, 1790–1857*. Stanford: Stanford University Press, 1985.

Arthur, T[imothy] S[hay]. *The Seamstress: A Tale of the Times*. Philadelphia: R. G. Berford, 1843.

Bailey, Ronald. "'Those Valuable People, the Africans.'" In *The Meaning of Slavery in the North*, ed. David Roediger and Martin Blatt. New York: Garland, 1998. 3–31.

Balibar, Etienne, and Immanuel Wallerstein. *Race, Nation, Class: Ambiguous Identities*. New York: Verso, 1991.

Bauer, Dale M. *Sex Expression and American Women Writers, 1860–1940*. Chapel Hill: University of North Carolina Press, 2009.

Baym, Nina. *Woman's Fiction: A Guide to Novels by and about Women in America, 1820–70*. 2nd edition. Urbana: University of Illinois Press, 1993.

Beebe, Rose Marie, and Robert M. Senkewiecz, eds. and trans. *Testimonios: Early California through the Eyes of Women, 1815–1848*. Berkeley: Heyday Books, 2007.

Beecher, Catharine, and Harriet Beecher Stowe. *The American Woman's Home*. New York: J. B. Ford, 1869.

Berg, Barbara J. *The Remembered Gate: Origins of American Feminism. The Woman and the City, 1800–1860*. New York: Oxford University Press, 1978.

Berlant, Lauren. *Anatomy of National Fantasy: Hawthorne, Utopia, and Everyday Life*. Chicago: University of Chicago Press, 1991.

Berman, Marshall. *All That Is Solid Melts into Air: The Experience of Modernity*. New York: Penguin, 1982.

Bernstein, Robin. *Racial Innocence: Performing American Childhood from Slavery to Civil Rights*. New York: New York University Press, 2011.

Bernstein, Susan David. "Dirty Reading: Sensation Fiction, Women, and Primitivism." *Criticism* 36.2 (1994): 213–41.

Bettie, Julie. *Women without Class: Girls, Race, and Identity*. Berkeley: University of California Press, 2003.

Blackmar, Elizabeth. *Manhattan for Rent: Housing and Property Relations in New York City*. Ithaca: Cornell University Press, 1989.

Blewett, Mary H. *Constant Turmoil: The Politics of Industrial Life in Nineteenth-Century New England*. Amherst: University of Massachusetts Press, 2000.

———. *Men, Women, and Work: Class, Gender, and Protest in the New England Shoe Industry, 1790–1910*. Urbana: University of Illinois Press, 1990.

Boris, Eileen, and Cynthia R. Daniels. *Homework: Historical and Contemporary Perspectives on Paid Labor at Home*. Urbana: University of Illinois Press, 1989.

Boston, Ray. *British Chartists in America*. Manchester, England: Manchester University Press, 1971.

Bourdieu, Pierre. *Distinction: A Social Critique of the Judgment of Taste*. Trans. Richard Nice. Cambridge: Harvard University Press, 1984.

———. *Outline of a Theory of Practice*. Trans. Richard Nice. New York: Cambridge University Press, 1977.

Boydston, Jeanne. *Home and Work: Housework, Wages, and the Ideology of Labor in the Early Republic*. New York: Oxford University Press, 1990.

Boyer, Paul. *Urban Masses and Moral Order in America, 1820–1920*. Cambridge: Harvard University Press, 1978.

Brace, Charles Loring. *The Dangerous Classes of New York, and Twenty Years' Work among Them*. New York: Wynkoop and Hallenbeck, 1872.

Bradbury, Osgood. *Emily, the Beautiful Seamstress; or the Danger of the First Step*. Boston: G. H. Williams, 1853.

———. *The Mysteries of Lowell*. Boston: E. P. Williams, 1844.

Brisbane, Albert. "On Association and Attractive Industry." *United States Magazine and Democratic Review* 10 (1842): 560–80.

Brodhead, Richard H. *Cultures of Letters: Scenes of Reading and Writing in Nineteenth-Century America*. Chicago: University of Chicago Press, 1993.

Bromell, Nicholas K. *By the Sweat of the Brow: Literature and Labor in Antebellum America*. Chicago: University of Chicago Press, 1993.

Bronstein, Jamie L. *Land Reform and Working-Class Experience in Britain and the United States*. Stanford: Stanford University Press, 1999.

Brooks, Daphne. *Bodies in Dissent: Spectacular Performances of Race and Freedom, 1850–1910*. Durham: Duke University Press, 2006.

Brooks, Peter. *The Melodramatic Imagination: Balzac, Henry James, Melodrama, and the Mode of Excess*. New Haven: Yale University Press, 1995.

———. *Reading for the Plot: Design and Intention in Narrative*. New York: Vintage, 1985.

Brown, Thomas Allston. *History of the New York Stage: From the First Performance in 1732 to 1901*. New York: Dodd, Mead, 1903.

Brownson, Orestes. *Defense of the Article on the Laboring Classes*. Boston: William H. Greene, 1840.

———. *The Laboring Classes*. New York: Elton's, 1840.

Buck-Morss, Susan. *The Dialectics of Seeing: Walter Benjamin and the Arcades Project.* Cambridge, Mass.: MIT Press, 1989.

———. "The Flaneur, the Sandwichman, and the Whore: The Politics of Loitering." *New German Critique* 39 (1986): 99–140.

Buckley, Peter George. "To the Opera House: Culture and Society in New York City, 1820–1860." PhD dissertation, SUNY Stony Brook, 1984.

Burdett, Charles. *Chances and Changes; or Life as It Is. Illustrated in the History of a Straw Hat.* New York: Appleton, 1845.

———. *The Elliott Family; or, the Trials of New-York Seamstresses.* New York: Baker and Scribner, 1850.

Burn, James. *Three Years among the Working-Classes in the United States during the War.* London: Smith, Elder, 1865.

Burnett, John, David Mayall, and David Vincent. *The Autobiography of the Working Class: An Annotated, Critical Bibliography.* Vol. 1. Brighton, England: Harvester, 1984.

Burnett, John, David Mayall, and David Vincent. *The Autobiography of the Working Class: An Annotated, Critical Bibliography.* Vol. 2. Brighton, England: Harvester, 1987.

Burnett, John, David Mayall, and David Vincent. *The Autobiography of the Working Class: An Annotated, Critical Bibliography.* Vol. 3. Brighton, England: Harvester, 1989.

Cameron, Ardis. *Radicals of the Worst Sort: Laboring Women in Lawrence, Massachusetts, 1860–1912.* Urbana: University of Illinois Press, 1993.

Cane, Aleta Feinsod, and Susan Alves, eds. *"The Only Efficient Instrument": American Woman Writers and the Periodical, 1837–1916.* Iowa City: University of Iowa Press, 2001.

Capetillo, Luisa. *A Nation of Women: An Early Feminist Speaks Out.* Ed. Félix V. Matos Rodríguez. Trans. Alan West-Durán. Houston: Arte Publico, 2004.

Carey, Matthew. *Miscellaneous Essays.* Philadelphia, 1830.

Castañeda, Antonia. "The Political Economy of Nineteenth Century Stereotypes of Californianas." In *Between Borders: Essays on Mexicana/Chicana History*, ed. A. R. Del Castillo. Encino, Calif.: Floricanto Press, 1990. 213–36.

Castronovo, Russ. *Fathering the Nation: American Genealogies of Slavery and Freedom.* Berkeley: University of California Press, 1995.

Chávez-García, Miroslava. *Negotiating Conquest: Gender and Power in California, 1770s to 1880s.* Tucson: University of Arizona Press, 2004.

Clark, Anna. *The Struggle for the Breeches: Gender and the Making of the British Working Class.* Berkeley: University of California Press, 1995.

Claybaugh, Amanda. *The Novel of Purpose: Literature and Social Reform in the Anglo-American World.* Ithaca: Cornell University Press, 2007.

Cobble, Dorothy Sue. *The Other Women's Movement: Workplace Justice and Social Rights in Modern America.* Princeton: Princeton University Press, 2005.

Cody, Lisa. "The Politics of Illegitimacy in an Age of Reform: Women, Reproduction, and Political Economy in England's New Poor Law of 1834." *Journal of Women's History* 11.4 (2000): 131–56.

Coffin, Judith G. *The Politics of Women's Work: The Paris Garment Trades, 1750–1915.* Princeton: Princeton University Press, 1996.

Cohen, Patricia Cline. *The Murder of Helen Jewett.* New York: Vintage Books, 1998.

Cohen, Patricia Cline, Timothy J. Gilfoyle, and Helen Lefkowitz Horowitz, eds. *The Flash Press: Sporting Male Weeklies in 1840s New York*. Chicago: University of Chicago Press, 2008.

Collins, Jennie. *Nature's Aristocracy: A Plea for the Oppressed*. Ed. Judith Ranta. Lincoln: University of Nebraska Press, 2010.

Cook, Sylvia Jenkins. *Working Women, Literary Ladies: The Industrial Revolution and Female Aspiration*. New York: Oxford University Press, 2008.

Cott, Nancy. "Divorce and the Changing Status of Women in Eighteenth Century Massachusetts." *William and Mary Quarterly*, 3rd series, 33 (1976): 586–614.

Crane, Stephen. *Maggie: A Girl of the Streets, and Other Tales of New York*. Ed. Larzer Ziff. New York: Penguin, 2000.

Cvetkovich, Ann. *Mixed Feelings: Feminism, Mass Culture, and Victorian Sensationalism*. New Brunswick: Rutgers University Press, 1992.

Dana, Richard Henry. *Two Years before the Mast*. New York: Penguin, 1981.

Davidoff, Leonore. *Worlds Between: Historical Perspectives on Gender and Class*. New York: Routledge, 1995.

Davis, Mike. *City of Quartz: Excavating the Future of Los Angeles*. New York: Haymarket, 1998.

Defoe, Daniel. *Moll Flanders*. Ed. Juliet Mitchell. New York: Penguin, 1987.

Denning, Michael. "Beggars and Thieves: The Ideology of the Gang." *Literature and History* 8.1 (1982): 41–55.

———. *Mechanic Accents: Dime Novels and Working-Class Culture in America*. London: Verso, 1987.

Dickens, Charles. *American Notes for General Circulation*. Boston: Ticknor and Fields, 1867.

Dobson, Joanne. Introduction to *The Hidden Hand*. Ed. Joanne Dobson. New Brunswick: Rutgers University Press, 1988.

Dorsey, Bruce. *Reforming Men and Women: Gender in the Antebellum City*. Ithaca: Cornell University Press, 2006.

Douglass, Frederick. *Narrative of the Life of Frederick Douglass, an American Slave*. Ed. Ira Dworkin. New York: Penguin, 2014.

Doyle, Jennifer. *Sex Objects: Art and the Dialectics of Desire*. Minneapolis: University of Minnesota Press, 2006.

Dreiser, Theodore. *Sister Carrie*. Introduction by Alfred Kazin. New York: Penguin, 1981.

Dublin, Thomas, ed. *Farm to Factory: Women's Letters, 1830–1860*. New York: Columbia University Press, 1993.

———. *Women at Work: The Transformation of Work and Community in Lowell, Massachusetts, 1826–1860*. New York: Columbia University Press, 1979.

Du Bois, W. E. B. *The Philadelphia Negro*. Millwood, N.Y., 1899.

Dudden, Faye E. *Serving Women: Household Service in Nineteenth-Century America*. Middletown, Conn.: Wesleyan University Press, 1983.

Duffy, Daniel. "Heroic Mothers and Militant Lovers: Representations of Lower-Class Women in Melodramas of the 1830s and 40s." *Nineteenth Century Theatre* 27 (1999): 41–65.

Dugaw, Dianne. *Warrior Women and Popular Balladry, 1650–1850*. New York: Cambridge University Press, 1989.

Duggan, Lisa. *The Twilight of Equality? Neoliberalism, Cultural Politics, and the Attack on Democracy*. Boston: Beacon Press, 2003.

Dzwonkoski, Peter. *American Literary Publishing Houses, 1638–1899*. Parts 1 and 2. Detroit: Gale Research, 1986.

Eagleton, Terry. *The Rape of Clarissa*. Oxford: Blackwell, 1982.

Eakin, Paul John, ed. *American Autobiography: Retrospect and Prospect*. Madison: University of Wisconsin Press, 1991.

Edelstein, T. J. "They Sang 'The Song of the Shirt': The Visual Iconology of the Seamstress." *Victorian Studies* 23.2 (1980): 183–210.

Egan, Ken Jr. *The Riven Home: Narrative Rivalry in the American Renaissance*. Cranbury, N.J.: Associated University Presses, 1997.

Ehrenreich, Barbara. *The Hearts of Men: American Dreams and the Flight from Commitment*. New York: Knopf, 2011.

Eisler, Benita, ed. *The Lowell Offering: Writings by New England Mill Women, 1840–1845*. Philadelphia: Lippincott, 1977.

*Ellen Merton, the Belle of Lowell: Or, the Confessions of the "G.F.K." Club*. Boston: Brainard, 1844.

Ellis, Jacqueline. *Silent Witnesses: Representations of Working-Class Women in the United States*. Bowling Green, Ohio: Popular Press, 1998.

Engels, Frederick. *The Condition of the Working Class in England*. Stanford: Stanford University Press, 1958.

Enstad, Nan. *Ladies of Labor, Girls of Adventure: Working Women, Popular Culture, and Labor Politics at the Turn of the Twentieth Century*. New York: Columbia University Press, 1999.

Epstein, James. *Radical Expression: Political Language, Ritual, and Symbol in England, 1790–1850*. New York: Oxford University Press, 1994.

Ernest, John. "Economies of Identity: Harriet E. Wilson's *Our Nig*." *PMLA* 109.3 (1994): 424–38.

Fabian, Ann. *The Unvarnished Truth: Personal Narratives in Nineteenth-Century America*. Berkeley: University of California Press, 2002.

*The Factory Girl*. By a Friend. Pamphlet. Providence, R.I., 1854.

Fanuzzi, Robert. *Abolition's Public Sphere*. Minneapolis: University of Minnesota Press, 2003.

Farnham, Eliza W. *California, In-Doors and Out*. New York, 1846.

Federici, Silvia. *Caliban and the Witch: Women, the Body, and Primitive Accumulation*. Brooklyn: Autonomedia, 2004.

Fernandez, Jean. *Victorian Servants, Class, and the Politics of Literacy*. New York: Routledge, 2009.

*Flora Montgomerie, the Factory Girl: Tale of the Lowell Factories*. New York, 1856.

Folbre, Nancy. *Greed, Lust and Gender: A History of Economic Ideas*. Oxford: Oxford University Press, 2009.

———. "The Unproductive Housewife: Her Evolution in Nineteenth Century Economic Thought." *Signs* 16 (1991): 463–84.

Foley, Neil. *The White Scourge: Mexicans, Blacks, and Poor Whites in Texas Cotton Culture*. Berkeley: University of California Press, 1997.

Foner, Philip S. *The Factory Girls*. Urbana: University of Illinois Press, 1977.

———. *Women and the American Labor Movement: From the First Trade Unions to the Present*. New York: Free Press, 1979.

Foreman, P. Gabrielle. Introduction to *Our Nig; Or, Sketches from the Life of a Free Black in a Two-Story White House, North*, by Harriet E. Wilson. New York: Penguin, 2011.

———. "Recovered Autobiographies and the Marketplace: *Our Nig*'s Generic Genealogies and Harriet Wilson's Entrepreneurial Enterprise." In *Harriet Wilson's New England: Race, Writing, and Religion*, ed. JerriAnne Boggis, Eva Raimon, and Barbara White. Hanover, N.H.: University Press of New England, 2007. 123–38.

Foster, George G. *New York by Gas-Light and Other Urban Sketches*. Ed. and introduction by Stuart M. Blumin. Berkeley: University of California Press, 1990.

Foucault, Michel. *The History of Sexuality*. Vol. 1: *An Introduction*. Trans. Robert Hurley. New York: Vintage, 1980.

Fraser, Nancy. *Fortunes of Feminism: From State-Managed Capitalism to Neoliberal Crisis*. London: Verso, 2013.

———. *Justice Interruptus: Critical Reflections on the "Postsocial" Condition*. New York: Routledge, 1997.

Fraser, Nancy, and Linda Gordon. "Contract versus Charity: Why Is There No Social Citizenship in the United States?" *Socialist Review* 22.3 (1992): 45–65.

———. "A Genealogy of 'Dependency': Tracing a Keyword of the U. S. Welfare State." In *Justice Interruptus: Critical Reflections on the "Postsocialist" Condition*. New York: Routledge, 1997. 121–49.

Freedgood, Elaine. "What Objects Know." *Journal of Victorian Culture* 15.1 (2010): 83–100.

Freedman, Estelle. *Their Sisters' Keepers: Women's Prison Reform in America, 1830–1930*. Ann Arbor: University of Michigan Press, 1981.

Fuller, Margaret. *Woman in the Nineteenth Century*. New York: Norton, 1970.

Gallagher, Catherine. *The Industrial Reformation of English Fiction*. Chicago: University of Chicago Press, 1985.

Gamber, Wendy. *The Female Economy: The Millinery and Dressmaking Trades, 1860–1930*. Urbana: University of Illinois Press, 1997.

Gilfoyle, Timothy J. *City of Eros: New York City, Prostitution, and the Commercialization of Sex, 1790–1920*. New York: Norton, 1992.

Gilje, Paul, and Howard Rock, eds. *Keepers of the Revolution: New Yorkers at Work in the Early Republic*. Ithaca: Cornell University Press, 1992.

Gilmore, Michael T. "Hawthorne and the Making of the Middle Class." In *Rethinking Class: Literary Studies and Social Formations*, ed. Wai-Chee Dimock and Michael T. Gilmore. New York: Columbia University Press, 1994. 215–38.

Ginzberg, Lori D. *Women and the Work of Benevolence: Morality, Politics, and Class in the Nineteenth Century United States*. New Haven: Yale University Press, 1990.

Glickman, Lawrence B. *Buying Power: A History of Consumer Action in America*. Chicago: University of Chicago Press, 2009.

Graver, Elizabeth. *Unravelling*. New York: Hyperion, 1997.

Gray, Robert. "The Languages of Factory Reform in Britain, 1830–60." In *The Historical Meanings of Work*, ed. Patrick Joyce. New York: Cambridge University Press, 1989. 143–79.

Green, Venus. *Race on the Line: Gender, Labor, and Technology in the Bell System, 1880–1980*. Durham: Duke University Press, 2001.

Greenberg, Amy S. *Manifest Manhood and the Antebellum American Empire*. New York: Cambridge University Press, 2005.

Greenberg, Joshua. *Advocating the Man: Masculinity, Organized Labor, and the Household in New York, 1800–1840*. New York: Columbia University Press, 2006.

Greer, Jane. "'Some of the Stories Are like My Life, I Guess': Working-Class Women Readers and Confessional Magazines." In *Reading Sites: Social Differences and Reader Response*, ed. Patrocinio Schweickart and Elizabeth Flynn. New York: MLA Press, 2004. 135–64.

Grimsted, David. *Melodrama Unveiled: American Theater and Culture, 1800–1850*. Berkeley: University of California Press, 1988.

Griswold del Castillo, Richard. *The Los Angeles Barrio, 1850–1890: A Social History*. Berkeley: University of California Press, 1982.

Grossberg, Michael. *Governing the Hearth: Law and the Family in Nineteenth-Century America*. Chapel Hill: University of North Carolina Press, 1985.

Guarneri, Carl J. *The Utopian Alternative: Fourierism in Nineteenth-Century America*. Ithaca: Cornell University Press, 1991.

Guerin, Elsa Jane. *Mountain Charley; Or the Adventures of Mrs. E. J. Guerin, Who Was Thirteen Years in Male Attire*. Dubuque, Iowa, 1861.

Gutiérrez-Jones, Carl Scott. *Rethinking the Borderlands: Between Chicano Culture and Legal Discourse*. Berkeley: University of California Press, 1995.

Gutman, Herbert G. *Work, Culture and Society in Industrializing America*. New York: Vintage, 1976.

Haag, Pamela. *Consent: Sexual Rights and the Transformation of American Liberalism*. Ithaca: Cornell University Press, 1999.

Haas, Lisbeth. *Conquests and Historical Identities in California, 1769–1936*. Berkeley: University of California Press, 1995.

Habegger, Alfred. "A Well Hidden Hand." *NOVEL: A Forum on Fiction* 14.3 (1981): 197–212.

Hale, Edward Everett. "American Literature." In *The Encyclopedia Americana: A Library of Universal Knowledge*. Vol. 1. New York: Encyclopedia Americana, 1918. 528–36.

Hall, Stuart. "Notes on Deconstructing 'the Popular.'" In *People's History and Socialist Theory*, ed. Raphael Samuel. London: Routledge and Kegan Paul, 1981. 227–39.

Halliday, Samuel B. *Lost and Found; or, Life among the Poor*. New York, 1860.

Hamilton, Kristie. *America's Sketchbook: The Cultural History of a Nineteenth-Century Literary Genre*. Athens: Ohio University Press, 1998.

Hansen, Miriam. *Babel and Babylon*. Chicago: University of Chicago Press, 1991.

Harris, Trudier. *From Mammies to Militants: Domestics in Black American Literature*. Philadelphia: Temple University Press, 1982.

Hart, James D. *The Popular Book: A History of America's Literary Taste*. Berkeley: University of California Press, 1961.

Hartman, Saidiya. *Scenes of Subjection: Terror, Slavery, and Self-Making in Nineteenth-Century America*. New York: Oxford University Press, 1997.

Harvey, David. *Spaces of Hope*. Berkeley: University of California Press, 2000.

Hawthorne, Nathaniel. *The House of the Seven Gables*. Ed. Seymour L. Gross. New York: Norton, 1967.

Hayden, Delores. *Grand Domestic Revolution*. Cambridge, Mass.: MIT Press, 1982.

Hobsbawm, Eric. *The Age of Revolution: Europe 1789–1848*. New York: Vintage, 1996.

———. *Bandits*. New York: Pantheon, 1981.

———. *Industry and Empire: From 1750 to the Present Day*. Harmondsworth, England: Penguin, 1969.

Hobson, Barbara. *Uneasy Virtue: The Politics of Prostitution and the American Reform Tradition*. New York: Basic Books, 1987.

Hodes, Martha. "The Mercurial Nature and Abiding Power of Race." *American Historical Review* 108.1 (2003): 84–118.

———. *The Sea Captain's Wife: A True Story of Love, Race, and War in the Nineteenth Century*. New York: Norton, 2006.

———. *White Women, Black Men: Illicit Sex in the Nineteenth Century South*. New Haven: Yale University Press, 1997.

Horton, James Oliver. *Free People of Color: Inside the African American Community*. Washington, D.C.: Smithsonian Press, 1993.

Hurtado, Albert L. *Intimate Frontiers: Sex, Gender, and Culture in Old California*. Albuquerque: University of New Mexico Press, 1999.

Huyssen, Andreas. "Mass Culture as Woman: Modernism's Other." In *Studies in Entertainment: Critical Approaches to Mass Culture*, ed. Tania Modleski. Bloomington: Indiana University Press, 1986. 188–208.

Ingraham, Joseph Holt. *Frank Rivers, or, the Dangers of the Town*. Boston: E. P. Williams, 1843.

Isenberg, Nancy. *Sex and Citizenship in Antebellum America*. Chapel Hill: University of North Carolina Press, 1999.

*The Jacksonians on the Poor: Collected Pamphlets*. New York: Arno Press, 1971.

Jacobs, Harriet. *Incidents in the Life of a Slave Girl. Written by Herself*. Introduction by Jean Fagan Yellin. Cambridge: Harvard University Press, 1987.

Jameson, Fredric. *The Political Unconscious: Narrative as a Socially Symbolic Act*. Ithaca: Cornell University Press, 1981.

———. "Reification and Utopia in Mass Culture." *Social Text* 1 (1979): 130–48.

Johnson, Paul. *A Shopkeeper's Millennium: Society and Revivals in Rochester, New York, 1815–1837*. New York: Hill and Wang, 1978.

Johnson, Susan Lee. *Roaring Camp: The Social World of the California Gold Rush*. New York: Norton, 2001.

Jones, Gareth Stedman. *Languages of Class: Studies in English Working Class History, 1832–1982*. New York: Cambridge University Press, 1996.

Jones, Jacqueline. *Labor of Love, Labor of Sorrow: Black Women, Work, and the Family, from Slavery to the Present*. New York: Vintage, 1995.

Jordanova, Ludmilla. *Images of Gender in Science and Medicine between the Eighteenth and Twentieth Centuries*. Madison: University of Wisconsin Press, 1989.

Kaplan, Cora. "Pandora's Box: Subjectivity, Class and Sexuality in Socialist Feminist Criticism." In *Sea Changes: Essays in Culture and Feminism*. London: Verso, 1986. 147–76.

Kasson, John F. *Civilizing the Machine: Technology and Republican Values in America, 1776–1900*. New York: Penguin, 1977.

Katz, Jonathan. *Gay American History: Lesbians and Gay Men in the U.S.A.* New York: Harper and Row, 1976.

Katzman, David M. *Seven Days a Week: Women and Domestic Service in Industrializing America*. Urbana: University of Illinois Press, 1981.

Kelley, Mary. *Learning to Stand and Speak: Women, Education, and Public Life in America's Republic*. Chapel Hill: University of North Carolina Press, 2006.

Kelley, Robin D. G. *Race Rebels: Culture, Politics, and the Black Working Class*. New York: Free Press, 1994.

Kent, Kathryn R. *Making Girls into Women: American Women's Writing and the Rise of Lesbian Identity*. Durham: Duke University Press, 2003.

Kessler-Harris, Alice. "The Just Price, the Free Market, and the Value of Women." In *Women, Class, and the Feminist Imagination: A Socialist-Feminist Reader*, ed. Karen V. Hansen and Ilene J. Philipson. Philadelphia: Temple University Press, 1990. 476–90.

———. *Out to Work: A History of Wage Earning in the United States*. New York: Oxford University Press, 1982.

———. *A Woman's Wage: Historical Meanings and Social Consequences*. Lexington: University of Kentucky Press, 1990.

Kester, Grant. "'Out of Sight Is Out of Mind': The Imaginary Space of Postindustrial Culture." *Social Text* 35 (1993): 72–92.

Laclau, Ernesto, and Chantal Mouffe. *Hegemony and Socialist Strategy: Towards a Radical Democratic Politics*. New York: Verso, 1990.

Langbauer, Laurie. *Novels of Everyday Life: The Series in English Fiction, 1850–1930*. Ithaca: Cornell University Press, 1999.

Langland, Elizabeth. *Nobody's Angels: Middle-Class Women and Domestic Ideology in Victorian Culture*. Ithaca: Cornell University Press, 1995.

Larcom, Lucy. *A New England Girlhood*. New York: Houghton Mifflin, 1889.

Laurie, Bruce. *Working People of Philadelphia, 1800–1850*. Philadelphia: Temple University Press, 1980.

Lawson, Andrew. *Walt Whitman and the Class Struggle*. Iowa City: University of Iowa Press, 2006.

Lebergott, Stanley. *The Americans: An Economic Record*. New York: Norton, 1984.

Lehuu, Isabelle. *Carnival on the Page: Popular Print Media in Antebellum America*. Chapel Hill: University of North Carolina Press, 2000.

Le Sueur, Meridel. *The Girl*. Introduction by Linda Ray Pratt. Albuquerque, N.M.: West End Press, 2006.

———. "Women on the Breadlines." In *Harvest Song: Collected Essays and Stories*. Albuquerque, N.M.: West End Press, 1990. 166–71.

Leverenz, David. *Paternalism Incorporated: Fables of American Fatherhood*. Ithaca: Cornell University Press, 2004.

Levine, Lawrence W. *Highbrow/Lowbrow: The Emergence of Cultural Hierarchy in America*. New York: Harvard University Press, 1988.

Levy, Anita. *Other Women: The Writing of Class, Race, and Gender, 1832–1898*. Princeton: Princeton University Press, 1991.

Lhamon, W. T. *Raising Cain: Blackface Performance from Jim Crow to Hip Hop*. Cambridge: Harvard University Press, 1998.

Libbey, Laura Jean. *Willful Gaynell, or, The Little Beauty of the Passaic Cotton Mills*. New York: N. L. Munro, 1890.

Libretti, Tim. "What a Dirty Way to Get Clean: The Grotesque in the Modern American Novel." In *Literature and the Grotesque*, ed. Michael J. Meyer. Atlanta, Ga.: Rodopi, 1995. 171–90.

Limón, José E. *American Encounters: Greater Mexico, the United States, and the Erotics of Culture*. Boston: Beacon, 1999.

Linebaugh, Peter. *The London Hanged: Crime and Civil Society in the Eighteenth Century*. London: Verso, 2003.

Lobdell, Lucy Ann. *The Female Hunter of Delaware and Sullivan Counties, N.Y.* New York, 1855.

Looby, Christopher. "Southworth and Seriality: The Hidden Hand in the New York Ledger." *Nineteenth Century Literature* 59 (2004): 179–211.

Lott, Eric. *Love and Theft: Blackface Minstrelsy and the American Working Class*. New York: Oxford University Press, 1993.

Lown, Judy. *Women and Industrialization: Gender at Work in Nineteenth-Century England*. Minneapolis: University of Minnesota Press, 1990.

Luther, Seth. *Address to the Working-Men of New England on the State of Education and on the Condition of the Producing Classes in Europe and America*. New York, 1833.

Lyons, Clare. *Sex among the Rabble: An Intimate History of Gender and Power in the Age of Revolution. Philadelphia, 1730–1830*. Chapel Hill: University of North Carolina Press, 2006.

Mansel, Henry. "Sensation Novels." *Quarterly Review* 113 (1863): 481–514.

Marx, Karl. *Capital*. Vol. 1. Trans. Ben Fowkes. New York: Vintage, 1977.

———. *Economic and Philosophic Manuscripts of 1844*. Ed. D. J. Struik. New York: International, 1964.

*Mary Bean: The Factory Girl*. Boston: Hotchkiss, 1850.

McClintock, Anne M. *Imperial Leather: Race, Gender, and Sexuality in the Colonial Contest*. New York: Routledge, 1995.

McConachie, Bruce A. *Melodramatic Formations: American Theater and Society, 1820–1870*. Iowa City: University of Iowa Press, 1992.

McGill, Meredith L. *American Literature and the Culture of Reprinting, 1837–1853*. Philadelphia: University of Pennsylvania Press, 2003.

Meisel, Martin. *Realizations: Narrative, Pictorial, and Theatrical Arts in Nineteenth-Century England*. Princeton: Princeton University Press, 1983.

Melendez, A. Gabriel. *Spanish-Language Newspapers in New Mexico, 1834–1958*. Tucson: University of Arizona Press, 2005.

Melville, Herman. "The Paradise of Bachelors and the Tartarus of Maids." In *The Piazza Tales and Other Prose Pieces, 1839–1860*. Chicago: Northwestern University Press, 1987. 316–35.

Merish, Lori. "Materializing Identification: Theorizing Class Identification in Nineteenth-Century Literary Texts." In *Class and the Making of American Literature: Created Unequal*, ed. Andrew Lawson. New York: Routledge, 2014. 94–112.

———. *Sentimental Materialism: Gender, Commodity Culture, and Nineteenth Century American Literature*. Durham: Duke University Press, 2000.

———. "Story Paper Weeklies, 1830–1920." In *U.S. Popular Print Culture, 1860–1920*, ed. Christine Bold. New York: Oxford University Press, 2012. 43–62.

Michaels, Walter Benn. *The Gold Standard and the Logic of Naturalism: American Literature at the Turn of the Century*. Berkeley: University of California Press, 1987.

Miles, Henry A. *Lowell: As It Was, and As It Is*. Lowell, Mass., 1845.

Miller, Nancy K. "Emphasis Added: Plots and Plausibilities in Women's Fiction." *PMLA* 96.1 (1981): 36–48.

Mitchell, Sally. *The Fallen Angel: Chastity, Class, and Women's Reading, 1835–1880*. Bowling Green: Bowling Green University Press, 1981.

———. "Reading Class." *Victorian Literature and Culture* 33.1 (2005): 331–39.

Montejano, David. *Anglos and Mexicans in the Making of Texas*. Austin: University of Texas Press, 2010.

Montgomery, David. *Citizen Worker*. New York: Cambridge University Press, 1993.

———. "Wage Labor, Bondage, and Citizenship in Nineteenth-Century America." *International Labor and Working-Class History* 48 (1995): 6–27.

Moran, William. *The Belles of New England: The Women of the Textile Mills and the Families Whose Wealth They Wove*. New York: Macmillan, 2007.

Moretti, Franco. *Signs Taken for Wonders*. Trans. Susan Fischer et al. New York: Verso, 1997.

Mort, Frank. *Dangerous Sexualities: Medico-Moral Politics in England since 1830*. London: Routledge, 1987.

Mullen, Harryette. "Runaway Tongue: Resistant Orality in *Uncle Tom's Cabin, Our Nig, Incidents in the Life of a Slave Girl*, and *Beloved*." In *The Culture of Sentiment: Race, Gender and Sentimentality in Nineteenth Century America*. New York: Oxford University Press, 1992. 244–64.

Murphy, Teresa Anne. "Sarah Bagley: Laboring for Life." In *The Human Tradition in American Labor History*, ed. Eric Arnesan. Wilmington, Del.: Scholarly Resources, 2004. 31–45.

———. *Ten Hours' Labor: Religion, Reform, and Gender in Early New England*. Ithaca: Cornell University Press, 1992.

Murray, Aífe. *Maid as Muse: How Servants Changed Emily Dickinson's Life and Language*. Durham: University of New Hampshire Press, 2010.

Naranjo-Huebl, Linda. "The Road to Perdition: E. D. E. N. Southworth and the Critics." *American Periodicals* 16.2 (2006): 123–50.

Nathans, Heather S. "'A Course of Learning and Ingenious Studies.'" In *Shakespearean Educations: Power, Citizenship, and Performance*, ed. Coppélia Kahn, Heather S. Nathans, and Mimi Godfrey. Newark: University of Delaware Press, 2011. 54–70.

Nead, Lynda. *Myths of Sexuality: Representations of Women in Victorian Britain*. London: Blackwell, 1988.

Negt, Oskar, and Alexander Kluge. *Public Sphere and Experience: Analysis of the Bourgeois and Proletarian Public Sphere*. Minneapolis: University of Minnesota Press, 1993.

Newberry, Michael. *Figuring Authorship in Antebellum America*. Stanford: Stanford University Press, 1997.

Newman, Simon. *Embodied History: The Lives of the Poor in Early Philadelphia*. Philadelphia: University of Pennsylvania Press, 2000.

Noel, Mary. *Villains Galore: The Heyday of the Popular Story Weekly*. New York: Macmillan, 1954.

Orleck, Annelise. *Common Sense and a Little Fire: Women and Working-Class Politics in the United States, 1900–1965*. Chapel Hill: University of North Carolina Press, 2000.

O'Sullivan, John L. "Occupation of Mexico." *Democratic Review* 21 (1847): 381–90.

Padilla, Genaro. *My History, Not Yours: The Formation of Mexican American Autobiography*. Madison: University of Wisconsin Press, 1993.

Painter, Nell Irvin. Introduction to *Narrative of Sojourner Truth* by Sojourner Truth. Ed. Nell Irvin Painter. New York: Penguin, 1998.

Parton, Sara [Fanny Fern]. *Ruth Hall and Other Stories*. Ed. Joyce W. Warren. New Brunswick: Rutgers University Press, 1990.

Peiss, Kathy. *Cheap Amusements: Working Women and Leisure in Turn-of-the-Century New York*. Philadelphia: Temple University Press, 1986.

Pérez, Emma. *The Decolonial Imaginary: Writing Chicanas into History*. Urbana: Indiana University Press, 1999.

———. "'She Has Served Others in More Intimate Ways': The Domestic Service Reform in Yucatan, 1915–1918." *Las Obreras: Chicana Politics of Work and Family*. Los Angeles: UCLA Chicano Studies Research Center Publications, 2000. 41–64.

Perry, Claire. *Pacific Arcadia: Images of California, 1600–1915*. New York: Oxford University Press, 1999.

Pessen, Edward. *Most Uncommon Jacksonians: Radical Leaders of the Early Labor Movement*. Albany: SUNY Press, 1967.

Pfister, Joel. *The Production of Personal Life: Class, Gender, and the Psychological in Hawthorne's Fiction*. Stanford: Stanford University Press, 1991.

Phelps, Elizabeth Stuart. *The Silent Partner and the Tenth of January*. New York: Feminist Press, 1983.

Pierson, Michael D. *Free Hearts and Free Homes: Gender and American Antislavery Politics*. Chapel Hill: University of North Carolina Press, 2003.

Pitti, Stephen J. *The Devil in Silicon Valley: Northern California, Race, and Mexican Americans*. Princeton: Princeton University Press, 2003.

Poovey, Mary. "Ideology and *The Mysteries of Udolpho*." *Criticism* 21:4 (1979): 307–30.

———. *Making a Social Body: British Cultural Formation, 1830–1864*. Chicago: University of Chicago Press, 1995.

———. *Uneven Developments: The Ideological Work of Gender in Mid-Victorian England*. Chicago: University of Chicago Press, 1988.

Rancière, Jacques. *Proletarian Nights: The Workers' Dream in Nineteenth Century France*. Trans. John Drury. New York: Verso, 2012.

Ranta, Judith A. *Women and Children of the Mills: An Annotated Guide to Nineteenth-Century American Textile Factory Literature*. Westport, Conn.: Greenwood, 1999.

Rebhorn, Matthew. *Pioneer Performances: Staging the Frontier*. New York: Oxford University Press, 2012.

Reed, Peter P. *Rogue Performances: Staging the Underclasses in Early American Theatre Culture*. London: Palgrave Macmillan, 2009.

Reyes, Bárbara O. *Private Women, Public Lives: Gender and the Missions of the Californias*. Austin: University of Texas Press, 2009.

Reynolds, David S. *Beneath the American Renaissance: The Subversive Imagination in the Age of Emerson and Melville*. New York: Knopf, 1988.

Richmond, Vivienne. *Clothing the Poor in Nineteenth Century England*. New York: Cambridge University Press, 2013.

Roach, Joseph. *Cities of the Dead: Circum-Atlantic Performance*. New York: Columbia University Press, 1996.

———. "Slave Spectacles and Tragic Octoroons: A Cultural Genealogy of Antebellum Performance." *Theatre Survey* 33 (1992): 167–87.

Robbins, Bruce. *Feeling Global: Internationalism in Distress*. New York: New York University Press, 1999.

———. *The Servant's Hand: English Fiction from Below*. Durham: Duke University Press, 1986.

———. *Upward Mobility and the Common Good: Toward a Literary History of the Welfare State*. Princeton: Princeton University Press, 2007.

Robbins, Sarah. *Managing Literacy, Mothering America: Women's Narratives on Reading and Writing in the Nineteenth Century*. Pittsburgh: University of Pittsburgh Press, 2004.

Robinson, Alfred. *Life in California: During a Residence of Several Years in That Territory*. New York: Putnam, 1846.

Robinson, Harriet H. *Loom and Spindle; Or, Life among the Early Mill Girls*. Boston, 1898.

Roediger, David R. *Wages of Whiteness: Race and the Making of the American Working Class*. London: Verso, 1991.

Rogers, Helen. *Women and the People: Authority, Authorship and the Radical Tradition in Nineteenth-Century England*. Brookfield, Vt.: Ashgate, 2000.

Romero, Mary. *Maid in the USA*. New York: Routledge, 1992.

Romolov, Nancy Tillman. "Unearthing the Historical Reader, or; Reading Girls' Reading." In *Pioneers, Passionate Ladies, and Private Eyes: Dime Novels, Series Books, and Paperbacks*, ed. Larry E. Sullivan and Lydia Cushman Schurman. New York: Haworth Press, 1996. 87–102.

Roof, Judith. *Come as You Are: Sexuality and Narrative*. New York: Columbia University Press, 1996.

Rose, Jonathan. *The Intellectual Life of the British Working Class*. New Haven: Yale University Press, 2003.

Rose, Sonya O. "Class Formation and the Quintessential Worker." In *Reworking Class*, ed. John Hall. Ithaca: Cornell University Press, 1997. 133–66.

Ross, Dorothy. *Love and Toil: Motherhood in Outcast London, 1870–1918*. New York: Oxford University Press, 1993.

Rowe, Kathleen. *The Unruly Woman: Gender and the Genres of Laughter*. Austin: University of Texas Press, 1995.

Ruiz de Burton, María Amparo. *The Squatter and the Don*. Ed. and introduction by Rosaura Sánchez and Beatrice Pita. Houston: Arte Público, 1997.

———. *Who Would Have Thought It?* Ed. and introduction by Rosaura Sánchez and Beatrice Pita. Houston: Arte Público, 1995.

Russo, Ann, and Cheris Kramarae, eds. *The Radical Women's Press of the 1850s*. New York: Routledge, 1991.

Ryan, Mary P. *Cradle of the Middle Class: The Family in Oneida County, New York, 1790–1830*. New York: Cambridge University Press, 1981.

———. *Women in Public: Between Banners and Ballots, 1825–1880*. Baltimore: Johns Hopkins University Press, 1990.

Sánchez, Rosaura. *Telling Identities: The Californio Testimonios*. Minneapolis: University of Minnesota Press, 1995.

Sánchez, Rosaura, and Beatrice Pita. *Conflicts of Interest: The Letters of María Amparo Ruiz de Burton*. Houston: Arte Público, 2001.

Sánchez-Eppler, Karen. *Touching Liberty: Abolition, Feminism, and the Politics of the Body*. Berkeley: University of California Press, 1993.

Sanger, William. *History of Prostitution*. New York, 1858.

Santamarina, Xiomara. *Belabored Professions: Narratives of African American Working Womanhood*. Chapel Hill: University of North Carolina Press, 2006.

Schiller, Dan. *Objectivity and the News: The Public and the Rise of Commercial Journalism*. Philadelphia: University of Pennsylvania Press, 1981.

Schreiner, Olive. *From Man to Man, or, Perhaps Only*. London: Virago, 1982.

Scott, Joan. *Gender and the Politics of History*. New York: Columbia University Press, 1987.

Sears, C. "All That Glitters: Trans-ing California's Gold Rush Migrations." *GLQ* 14 (2008): 383–402.

Sedgwick, Eve Kosofsky. *Between Men: English Literature and Male Homosocial Desire*. New York: Columbia University Press, 1985.

———. *Epistemology of the Closet*. Berkeley: University of California Press, 1990.

SenGupta, Gunja. *From Slavery to Poverty: The Racial Origins of Welfare in New York, 1840–1918*. New York: New York University Press, 2009.

Sennett, Richard, and Jonathan Cobb. *The Hidden Injuries of Class*. New York: Knopf, 1972.

Shank, Barry. *A Token of My Affections*. New York: Columbia University Press, 2004.

Dame Shirley [Mrs. Louise A. K. S. Clappe]. *The Shirley Letters from California Mines in 1851–52*. San Francisco: Thomas C. Russell, 1922.

Siegel, Adrienne. *The Image of the American City in Popular Literature, 1820–1870*. Port Washington, N.Y.: Kennikat Press, 1981.

Siegel, Reva. "Home as Work: The First Women's Rights Claims Concerning Wives' Household Labor, 1850–1880." *Yale Law Journal* 103 (March): 1073–1217.

Singer, Ben. *Melodrama and Modernity: Early Sensational Cinema and Its Contexts*. New York: Columbia University Press, 2001.

Skidmore, Thomas. *The Rights of Man to Property!* New York, 1829.

Slotkin, Richard. *The Fatal Environment: The Myth of the Frontier in the Age of Industrialization, 1800–1890*. Norman: University of Oklahoma Press, 1998.

Smith, Adam. *Lectures on Jurisprudence*. Ed. R. L. Meek, D. D. Raphael, and P. G. Stein. Oxford: Oxford University Press, 1978.

Smith, Barbara Clark. "Food Rioters and the American Revolution." *William and Mary Quarterly*, 3d Series, 51.1 (1994): 3–38.

Smith, Charles. *Madame Restell: An Account of her Life and Horrible Practices: Together with Prostitution in New-York: Its Extent, Causes, and Effects upon Society*. New York: Charles V. Smith, 1847.

Smith, Henry Nash. *Virgin Land: The American West as Symbol and Myth*. Cambridge: Harvard University Press, 1950.

Smith, Sidonie. *A Poetics of Women's Autobiography: Marginality and the Fictions of Self-Representation*. Bloomington: Indiana University Press, 1987.

Smith, Stacey L. *Freedom's Frontier: California and the Struggle over Unfree Labor, Emancipation and Reconstruction*. Chapel Hill: University of North Carolina Press, 2013.

Sommer, Doris. *Foundational Fictions: The National Romances of Latin America*. Berkeley: University of California Press, 1991.

Southworth, E. D. E. N. *The Hidden Hand*. Ed. Joanne Dobson. New Brunswick: Rutgers University Press, 1988.

———. *Vivia; Or, the Secret of Power*. New York: T. B. Peterson & Brothers, 1875.

Spillers, Hortense. "Mama's Baby, Papa's Maybe: An American Grammar Book." *diacritics* 17 (1987): 65–81.

Stallybrass, Peter, and Allon White. *The Politics and Poetics of Transgression*. Ithaca: Cornell University Press, 1986.

Stanley, Amy Dru. *From Bondage to Contract: Wage Labor, Marriage, and the Market in the Age of Slave Emancipation*. New York: Cambridge University Press, 1998.

Stanley, Liz, ed. *The Diaries of Hannah Cullwick, Victorian Maidservant*. New Brunswick: Rutgers University Press, 1984.

Stansell, Christine. *City of Women: Sex and Class in New York, 1789–1860*. Urbana: University of Illinois Press, 1986.

Steedman, Carolyn. *Labours Lost: Domestic Service and the Making of Modern England*. Cambridge: Cambridge University Press, 2009.

———. *Landscape for a Good Woman: A Story of Two Lives*. New Brunswick: Rutgers University Press, 1987.

Stern, Julia. "Excavating Genre in *Our Nig*." *American Literature* 67 (1995): 439–66.

Stewart, Maria W. *Maria W. Stewart, America's First Black Woman Political Writer: Essays and Speeches*. Ed. Marilyn Richardson. Bloomington: Indiana University Press, 1987.

Streeby, Shelley. *American Sensations: Class, Empire, and the Production of Popular Culture*. Berkeley: University of California Press, 2002.

Sumner, Helen L. *History of Women in Industry in the United States*. New York: Arno Press, 1974.

Sweet, Timothy. "American Pastoralism and the Marketplace: Eighteenth Century Ideologies of Farming." *Early American Literature* 29.1 (1994): 59–80.

Taylor, Barbara. *Eve and the New Jerusalem: Socialism and Feminism in the Nineteenth Century*. Cambridge: Harvard University Press, 1993.

Taylor, Diana. *The Archive and the Repertoire: Performing Cultural Memory in the Americas*. Durham: Duke University Press, 2003.

Taylor, William R. *Cavalier and Yankee: The Old South and American National Character*. New York: George Braziller, 1961.

Tebbel, John. *Between Covers: The Rise and Transformation of Book Publishing in America*. New York: Oxford University Press, 1987.

Thiong'o, Ngũgĩ wa. "Oral Power and Europhone Glory: Orature, Literature, and Stolen Legacies." In *Penpoints, Gunpoints and Dreams*. New York: Oxford University Press, 1998. 103–28.

Thompson, E. P. "The Moral Economy of the English Crowd in the Eighteenth Century." *Past and Present* 50 (1971): 76–136.

Thompson, E. P. "Patrician Society, Plebian Culture." *Journal of Social History* 7.4 (1974): 382–405.

———. *The Poverty of Theory and Other Essays*. New York: Monthly Review Press, 1978.

Thomsen, Dawn Fisk. "'It Is a Pity It Is No Better': The Story Paper and Its Critics in Nineteenth-Century America." In *Scorned Literature: Essays on the History and Criticism of Popular Mass-Produced Fiction in America*, ed. Lydia Cushman Schurman and Deidre Johnson. Westport, Conn.: Greenwood, 2002. 83–96.

Tomlins, Christopher L. *Law, Labor, and Ideology in the Early American Republic*. Cambridge: Cambridge University Press, 1993.

———. "Subordination, Authority, Law: Subjects in Labor History." *International Labor and Working-Class History* 47 (1995): 56–90.

Tonna, Charlotte Elizabeth. *Helen Fleetwood*. Vol. 1 of *The Works of Charlotte Elizabeth*. New York, 1847.

Torres, Lourdes. "Violence, Desire, and Transformative Remembering in Emma Pérez' *Gulf Dreams*." In *Tortilleras: Hispanic and U. S. Latina Lesbian Expression*, ed. Lourdes Torres and Inmaculada Pertusa. Philadelphia: Temple University Press, 2003. 228–39.

Trattner, Walter I. *From Poor Law to Welfare State: A History of Social Welfare in America*. 6th edition. New York: Free Press, 2007.

Trollope, Frances. *The Adventures of Michael Armstrong, the Factory Boy*. 1840. London, 1888.

Truth, Sojourner. *Narrative of Sojourner Truth*. Ed. Nell Irvin Painter. New York: Penguin, 1998.

Tyler, M.[artha] W. *A Book without a Title: Or, Thrilling Events in the Life of Mira Dana*. Boston, 1855.

Vapnek, Lara. *Breadwinners: Working Women and Economic Independence, 1856–1920*. Champaign: University of Illinois Press, 2009.

Vicinus, Martha. "'Helpless and Unbefriended': Nineteenth-Century Domestic Melodrama." *New Literary History* 13 (1971): 127–43.

————. *The Industrial Muse: A Study of Nineteenth-Century British Working-Class Literature*. New York: Barnes and Noble, 1974.

Vincent, David. *Bread, Knowledge and Freedom: A Study of Nineteenth Century Working Class Autobiography*. London: Europa, 1981.

Volosinov, V. N. *Marxism and the Philosophy of Language*. Trans. Ladislav Matejka and I. R. Titunik. Cambridge, Mass.: Harvard University Press, 1986.

Ware, Norman J. *The Industrial Worker, 1840–1860: The Reaction of American Industrial Society to the Advance of the Industrial Revolution*. Gloucester, Mass.: Peter Smith, 1959.

Warner, Michael. "The Mass Public and the Mass Subject." In *Habermas and the Public Sphere*, ed. Craig Calhoun. Cambridge, Mass.: MIT Press, 1992. 377–401.

Washington, Margaret. *Sojourner Truth's America*. Champaign: University of Illinois Press, 2009.

Weber, David J. *Myth and the History of the Hispanic Southwest*. Albuquerque: University of New Mexico Press, 1988.

Weld, Theodore D., ed. *American Slavery as It Is: Testimony of a Thousand Witnesses*. New York, 1839.

White, Shane. *Stories of Freedom in Black New York*. Cambridge: Harvard University Press, 2002.

Wilentz, Sean. *Chants Democratic: New York City and the Rise of the American Working Class, 1788–1860*. New York: Oxford University Press, 1984.

Williams, Andrea. *Dividing Lines: Class Anxiety and Postbellum Black Fiction*. Ann Arbor: University of Michigan Press, 2013.

Williams, Linda. *Playing the Race Card: Melodramas of Black and White from Uncle Tom to O. J. Simpson*. Princeton: Princeton University Press, 2001.

Williams, Raymond. *The Country and the City*. New York: Oxford University Press, 1973.

————. *Keywords: A Vocabulary of Culture and Society*. Revised edition. New York: Oxford University Press, 1985.

————. *Marxism and Literature*. New York: Oxford University Press, 1977.

Wilson, Harriet E. *Our Nig; Or, Sketches in the Life of a Free Black*. Introduction by Henry Louis Gates, Jr. New York: Vintage, 1983.

Yeazell, Ruth Bernard. *Fictions of Modesty: Women and Courtship in the English Novel*. Chicago: University of Chicago Press, 1991.

Zakim, Michael. *Ready-Made Democracy: A History of Men's Dress in the American Republic, 1760–1860*. Chicago: University of Chicago Press, 2003.

Zboray, Ronald. *A Fictive People: Antebellum Economic Development and the American Reading Public*. New York: Oxford University Press, 1993.

Zboray, Ronald, and Mary Saracino Zboray. *Voices without Votes: Women and Politics in Antebellum New England*. Lebanon, N.H.: University Press of New England, 2010.

Zlotnick, Susan. *Women, Writing, and the Industrial Revolution*. Baltimore: Johns Hopkins University Press, 1998.

Acker, Joan, 9, 24, 254n72

Adams, John Quincy, 42

*Advocate of Moral Reform*: on "fallen women," 127–29; on seamstresses as locus of narrative determinism, 117, 127–29, 147, 165

aesthetics: and bourgeois "poetics of gender," 46, 77–78; class specialization of the "literary," 67–68; and distance from the bodily "low," 42, 44–48, 83–86; and ideal of feminine bodily "delicacy," 46–47, 101; and pastoralization of female labor, 15, 154, 171, 258n57; and the "proletarian grotesque," 83–86, 90, 268n91; and sensationalism as counteraesthetic, 30, 33–35, 37, 41–48, 72, 76, 78, 81–86, 97–112, 152; and use of "polished" language, 43, 44–48; and working-class women's critique of the "literary," 66–72. See also Armstrong, Nancy; "beauties of factory life"; Bourdieu, Pierre; Boydston, Jeanne; Luther, Seth; Rancière, Jacques; "romance of labor"; Stallybrass, Peter; White, Allon; Williams, Raymond

Almaguer, Tomás, 219, 224, 237

"ambition": as gendered desire in nineteenth-century fiction, 19, 26, 122–24, 264n11, 270n37; in eighteenth-century female plots, 121–22; obverse of "feminine" modesty and self-denial, 124; and working-class women, 56–58, 76, 88, 90, 107–12, 114, 146–52. See also Brooks, Peter

*American Woman's Home, The* (Beecher and Stowe), 146, 153–54

Anderson, Perry, 36

apprentices, 85; and racialization of servitude, 135; in *Our Nig* (Wilson), 273–74n24, 275n44; in *The Seamstress* (Arthur), 134–35. See also Roediger, David

*Aristocrat and Trades Union Advocate*, 1–4, 9, 10, 12, 29, 248

Armstrong, Nancy: on bourgeois "poetics of gender," 25, 46–47, 77; on domestic desire, 19, 20–22, 25, 175; on the "literary" as apolitical, 67

Arthur, T. S. (Timothy Shay), 120, 129–36, 137, 138, 139, 270n22, 271n51

associationism: and first-wave feminism, 48–51; and reconstruction of the family and familial love, 29, 48–9, 254n59; and working-class women, 7, 11, 29, 35, 52–53, 75. See also Brisbane, Alfred; Brownson, Orestes; Fourier, Charles

autobiography: as working-class genre, 4–7, 12, 31, 78, 163, 174, 220–21, 232–45, 247–48, 284n1. See also

autobiography (*continued*)
  Larcom, Lucy; Lobdell, Lucy Ann;
  Lorenzana, Apolinaria; Pérez, Eulalia;
  Robinson, Harriet; Truth, Sojourner

bachelor: as nineteenth-century cultural
  type, 262n17; and sexual nonnorma-
  tivity, 262n117; and workingwomen's
  social criticism, 64–66, 195
Bagley, Sarah, 21, 22, 47, 52, 54–56, 59, 60,
  68–70, 75, 93, 114, 131, 156–57, 158–59
"beauties of factory life," 21, 71–72, 84.
  *See also* aesthetics
Bancroft, Herbert Howe, 31
Baym, Nina, 86
Beecher, Catherine, 146, 153–54
Benjamin, Walter, 43
Berlant, Lauren, 77
Bernstein, Robin, 212
Blackmar, Elizabeth, 161–62, 198
body: as "accumulation strategy"
  under capitalism, 43, 87, 266n48; in
  antebellum feminism, 49–51; and
  civilizationist ideology, 25, 49–50; and
  female (productive and reproductive)
  labor, 6, 21, 43, 46–48, 71, 76–78, 84,
  154, 159–60, 168–70; and middle-class
  ideal of feminine "delicacy," 46–51, 68,
  101, 121, 160–62, 178–79, 233, 258n59.
  *See also* aesthetics; Bourdieu, Pierre;
  Boydston, Jeanne; sensationalism;
  sexuality
*Book without a Title: Or, Thrilling Events
  in the Life of Mira Dana* (Tyler),
  155–56
Bourdieu, Pierre, 84, 168–69, 175
Boydston, Jeanne, 15, 49, 154, 168, 258n57,
  275n43
Brace, Charles Loring, 27, 147, 203,
  280n66
Bradbury, Osgood: *Emily, the Beautiful
  Seamstress*, 148; *Mysteries of Lowell*,
  33–34, 35, 87, 107–12, 114, 148, 157, 191,
  255n1

Brisbane, Alfred, 48–49, 52, 259n65,
  263n138
Bromell, Nicholas, 42–43
Brooks, Peter, 26, 87–88, 189, 213, 264n11,
  270n37
Brownson, Orestes, 15, 18, 29, 254n59;
  *Defense of the Article on the Laboring
  Classes*, 19–20; *The Laboring Classes*,
  11, 19–20
Buck-Morss, Susan, 110
Burdett, Charles: *Chances and Changes;
  or Life as It Is*, 138–39; *The Elliott Fam-
  ily*, 115, 120, 129–30, 136–142; 272n60.
  *See also* it-narratives
Burn, James, 21, 156, 173–74

Cameron, Ardis, 36, 248
Capetillo, Luisa, 229
Carey, Mathew, 120–21, 126, 127, 270n27
Carroll, George, 85
Castañeda, Antonia, 223, 235, 237
Channing, Walter, 121
Chartists, 3, 11–12, 39, 251n1
Chávez-García, Miroslava, 237
Chernyshevsky, Nikolai: *What Is to Be
  Done?* 118
Child, Lydia Maria, 6, 27
Clark, Anna, 22, 64
class: and domesticity, 6, 9, 14–21, 24–25,
  46, 49, 114–15, 171, 188, 202, 251n4;
  as gendered, 1, 3, 6–8, 10–11, 23, 24,
  26, 86; and international division of
  labor, 220–21, 228; as racialized, 1,
  10–11, 30–31, 60–62, 153–55, 180–81,
  213, 219–21; and sexuality, 6–7, 11,
  14, 21–25, 45–48, 52–53, 63–66, 71,
  73–78, 86, 91, 97–112, 146–52, 155,
  187–88, 189–90, 196, 203, 221, 227–28,
  248–50. *See also* working-class women
Clay, Henry, 39, 77
clothing: female labor in production
  of, 30, 77, 117–18, 238–40, 243–44;
  importance in working-class women's
  culture, 76, 80, 92–93, 95–97; and

threat of class contamination, 119. *See also* Enstad, Nan; *Factory Girl, The* (Anon.); Steedman, Carolyn

Cobble, Dorothy Sue, 11

Cohen, Patricia Cline, 148

Collins, Jennie, 27–29, 115, 196

consumption: and factory women, 12–13, 76, 78–83, 92–93, 95–97, 187, 264n19; and female consumer activism, 138–39. *See also* clothing; factory workers; free produce movement; it-narratives

Cornell, Sarah Maria, 85

Crane, Stephen, 190

Davis, Paulina Wright, 50

*Defense of the Article on the Laboring Classes* (Brownson), 19–20

Defoe, Daniel, 121–22

Denning, Michael, 78, 80, 81, 84, 185–86, 218

dependency: and class discipline, 23–24; dangers of, examined in seduction narratives, 97–107; and feminine "virtue," 121–23; first-wave feminists on, 50; gendered and racialized in antebellum era, 4, 8, 15, 20, 21, 23, 158, 164, 166, 173, 188, 199; in seamstress fictions, 113–52; working-class women's critique of, 1–4, 8–9, 10–11, 24–27, 37–39, 52, 53, 172–79, 201–7, 213–18, 234–35, 238–39, 243–44

Dickens, Charles, 39, 46, 67, 185

domesticity: challenged by factory women, 21–24, 37–39, 52–54, 60, 63–64, 67–68, 96; contested in first-wave feminist writings, 48–51; as embraced by workingmen, 40–41, 257n37; and interracial female desire, 167–79, 184–84, 188; and middle-class gender norms, 6, 9, 14–21, 24–25, 46, 49, 114–15, 171, 188, 202, 251n4; and middle-class performance, 161–63, 167–79, 280n80; and pastoralization of domestic labor, 14–15, 46, 49, 161,

171, 258n57; reinforced in seamstress narratives, 113–16; and reproduction of cultural capital, 9, 49, 83, 106, 174; and sexual regulation, 14–15, 19–25, 37–39; as site of racialized class struggle, 21, 153–79; and whiteness, 38, 49, 115, 135, 154–56, 158–59, 168–79, 221–22

domestic workers: class resistance of, 1–4, 156–57, 168–79, 219–20, 237–45; compared to factory workers, 59, 155–57; excluded from definitions of the working class, 157–58; and racialization of service in antebellum era, 3–4, 6–7, 31, 153–79, 219, 228–29. *See also Aristocrat and Trades Union Advocate*; Collins, Jennie; *Hidden Hand* (Southworth); homework; *Our Nig* (Wilson); servants; Stewart, Maria W.; "Tales of Factory Life, No. 1" (Bagley)

Dorsey, Bruce, 129

Douglass, Charles, 40

Dreiser, Theodore, 122–23

Dublin, Thomas, 60–61

Du Bois, W. E. B., 158

Duggan, Lisa, 10–11

Eagleton, Terry, 67

Eastman, Mehitable, 54

education: middle-class definition of, 43; as object of working-class critique, 43–44; working-class autodidacticism 67, 251n6

*Ellen Merton, the Belle of Lowell* (Anon.), 101–3, 104, 105

*Elliott Family, The* (Burdett), 115, 120, 129–30, 136–42, 272n60

*Emily, the Beautiful Seamstress* (Bradbury), 148

Engels, Frederick, 39, 270n38; on "struggle for the breeches" in working-class family, 80, 188

English, William, 40; *Gertrude Howard*, 120

Enstad, Nan, 76, 81, 187

*Factory Girl, The* (Anon.), 90–97, 114

factory system: debates about, 39–40

*Factory Girl's Album*, 30, 51–2, 55, 62–66, 76, 131, 255n10, 258n59, 259n71, 262n115, 262n120, 262n112

factory workers: activism of, 10–11, 26, 39–40, 48, 51–72, 75, 83–86; and associationism, 52–53, 70, 74–75; as consumers, 66, 76, 80, 92–93, 95–96; critique of the "literary" 67–72; critique of sentimentality, 29–30; defined in opposition to domestic servants, 156–59; and discourse of slavery, 60–62, 74, 77–78, 85, 111–12, 155–56; as "factory Amazons," 40; in first-wave feminist writings, 48–51; on gendered "injuries of class," 57–58; and "labor feminism," 11, 52–53; and nonnormative sexuality, 37–39, 70, 75, 82–83, 256n15, 262n115; and "precarious whiteness," 36, 40, 61, 74, 77–78, 85, 101, 111–12, 155–56; as readers, 2, 78–83; redefining female "influence," 40; unsettled norms of feminine "dependency," 8–9, 10–11, 26–27, 37–39, 52, 53; and urban sociality, 76–78; on the working-class family, 62–66; in workingmen's writings, 40–48. *See also* Bagley, Sarah; *Book without a Title* (Tyler); *Ellen Merton, the Belle of Lowell* (Anon.); *Factory Girl, The* (Anon.); *Factory Girl's Album*; *Flora Montgomerie, the Factory Girl* (Anon.); *Lowell Offering*; Luther, Seth; *Mary Bean: The Factory Girl* (Anon.); *Mysteries of Lowell* (Bradbury); *Norton: Or, the Lights and Shadows of a Factory Village* (Argus) ; *Unravelling* (Graver); *Voice of Industry*

family wage: contested by working-class women, 9, 56, 58, 64–66, 264n11; endorsed by antebellum workingmen, 14, 38–39, 64; and normalization of domestic desire, 11, 14, 24, 36–38, 64–66,

116, 256n21, 269n12; and restriction of social sympathy, 19–20, 38, 98, 107. *See also* dependency

Fanuzzi, Robert, 8–9

Farley, Harriet, 47. See also *Lowell Offering*

Federici, Sylvia, 6

*Female Hunter, The* (Lobdell), 4–6, 7, 9, 12, 200, 252n14

feminism (first-wave): and associationism, 48–49; and the "bread question," 48–51; and working-class women, 48–52. *See also* labor feminism

Fern, Fanny (Sara Willis Parton): *Ruth Hall*, 113–14; "A Bit of Injustice," 123–24

*Flag of our Union*, 80

*Flora Montgomerie, the Factory Girl* (Anon.), 101

Folbre, Nancy, 49

Foner, Philip, 40, 259n71

Foreman, P. Gabrielle, 163, 166, 274n32

Foster, George, *New York by Gaslight*, 27, 34–35, 45, 81

Fourier, Charles, 7, 18, 29, 35, 48–49, 52. *See also* Brisbane, Alfred

*Frank Rivers; or, the Dangers of the Town* (Ingraham), 148–52

Fraser, Nancy, 114, 252n11, 268n87

free black workers, 6–7, 153–79; and urban white workers, 7, 164. *See also* *Hidden Hand* (Southworth); Hodes, Martha; *New York by Gaslight* (Foster); *Our Nig* (Wilson), Stewart, Maria; Truth, Sojourner; White, Shane

free produce movement (abolitionism), 138; and female consumer activism, 138–39; and it-narratives, 138; and labor reform, 138. *See also* Burdett, Charles

Freemont, Jessie, 162–63

Fuller, Margaret: on female "self-dependence," 39; on marriage, 63; *Summer on the Lakes*, 25

*Garies and their Friends, The* (Webb), 174
Gaskell, Elizabeth, 11–12
Gilmore, Michael T., 10
*Girls of Today*, 81
Graver, Elizabeth: *Unravelling*, 248–50
Graves, Mrs. A. J., 161
Greeley, Horace, 146
Greer, Jane, 81

Haag, Pamela, 87
Haas, Lisbeth, 232, 235–36
Hall, Stuart, 115, 181, 253n46
Halliday, Samuel B., 203, 280n66
Harris, Trudier, 154, 158
Harvey, David, 43, 87, 266n48
Hawthorne, Nathaniel, 265n30; *Blithedale Romance*, 23; *House of the Seven Gables*, 15–20
Hayden, Delores, 11
*Hidden Hand, The* (Southworth), 31–32, 153–56, 180–218; anti-sentimentality of, 183, 188, 190, 191–92, 193, 196, 198, 202, 209–11; cagey self-reflexivity of, 190–92; and the "excarceral," 217–18; and interpenetration of performance and print, 180–84; and labor feminism, 188, 207, 210, 218; lower-class interracial affiliations within, 154–56, 180–84, 213–18; and melodrama, 180–218; revision of melodramatic sexual scripts in, 203–13; stage adaptations of, 181–82; "struggle for the breeches" in, 188. *See also* Whiteley's Original Hidden Hand Company
Hobsbawm, Eric, 14, 214, 275n42
Hodes, Martha, on "mutability" of poor women's race identifications, 36, 38, 164, 252n19, 273–74n24, 275n44. *See also* precarious whiteness of poor and working-class women
homework, 119, 269n19. *See also* domestic workers; piecework; seamstresses
Hood, Thomas: influence on seamstress fictions, 124–30; and seamstress paintings, 125–26; "The Song of the Shirt," 124–28
*House of the Seven Gables, The* (Hawthorne), 15–20, 26, 203

"injuries of class," as gendered, 24, 58, 137, 254n72. *See also* Acker, Joan
Ingraham, Joseph Holt, 268n88; *Frank Rivers; or, the Dangers of the Town*, 148–52. See also Jewett, Helen
Isenberg, Nancy, 49
it-narratives, 138–39, 272n62

Jacobs, Harriet, *Incidents in the Life of a Slave Girl*, 6–7, 45, 118
Jameson, Anna, 35
Jameson, Fredric, 13
"Jesus and the Poor" (Lippard), 120
Jewett, Helen, 148, 152
Johnson, Paul, 54
Jones, Gavin, 10
Jones, Jacqueline, 162

Kaplan, Cora, 10, 75–76
Katzman, David, 158
Kelley, Robin D. G., 176
Kessler-Harris, Alice, 38, 256n21, 275n42
Kluge, Alexander, 10, 86

labor feminism, as fashioned by antebellum working-class women, 52–53, 63, 85–86, 118, 120, 142–46, 155–56. *See also* Cobble, Dorothy Sue; Orleck, Annelise
*Laboring Classes, The* (Brownson), 11, 19–20
land reform, 11, 221, 226–27
Lang, Amy Schrager, 10
Larcom, Lucy, 78
Lawson, Andrew, 263n137
Lazerow, Jama, 52
Lehuu, Isabel, 81–83, 183
LeSueur, Meridel, 29, 247
Levine, Lawrence, 183

Lhamon, W. T., 182
Libbey, Laura Jean, 80, 186, 265n28
Libretti, Tim, 84
*Lily, The*, 48–51
Linebaugh, Peter, 217–18
Lippard, George, 270n22; on seamstresses
    25, 120, 129
Lobdell, Lucy Ann: *The Female Hunter*,
    4–6, 7, 9, 12, 200, 252n14
Lorenzana, Apolinaria, 31, 220–23,
    234–42
Lott, Eric, 10, 168
"Lowell Factory Girl, The," 87
Lowell factory girl: and empire, 221–22;
    as national symbol, 11–12, 21, 55, 74,
    77–78, 248; and whiteness, 36, 61, 74,
    77–78, 101. *See also* factory workers
Lowell Female Labor Reform Association
    (LFLRA), 52, 55, 74, 254n61, 259n71,
    260n72, 260n84
*Lowell Offering*, 22, 47, 51–52, 62, 67–71,
    77, 93, 156–57, 254n66, 266–67n64,
    267n69, 281n10; debate over editor-
    ship of, 68–70. *See also* Bagley, Sarah;
    Farley, Harriet
Luther, Seth, 40–41, 257n34; *Address
    to the Working Men of New England*,
    41–48, 58, 60, 63, 68

*Madame Restell: An Account of Her Life*
    (Smith), 147–48
Malthus, Thomas, 24, 35, 81, 99, 100, 107
Martin, Angelique, 52
Marx, Karl, 36, 98; on textile workers, 30,
    115
*Mary Bean: The Factory Girl* (Anon.),
    103–5
McClintock, Anne, 114, 161
melodrama: and depictions of seam-
    stresses, 26, 117, 126–27, 129–44,
    165–66; and factory fictions, 72, 82,
    85–90, 103, 108, 111–12; and imagery in
    factory debates, 40; Peter Brooks on,
    87–88, 189, 213; and prostitute narra-

tives, 146–52; as working-class cultural
    form, 65, 86–87. *See also Hidden
    Hand, The* (Southworth)
Melville, Herman: "Tartarus of Maids," 8,
    73–74; and Shakespeare, 181
Michaels, Walter Benn, 16–18
Mitchell, Sally, 80
Monroe, Sarah, 117–18
Munroe, Ellen, 58
Montgomery, David, 3, 10, 270n24,
    270n30
"moral economy," 14, 18, 28–29, 65, 93,
    133, 176, 231, 253n47. *See also* Thomp-
    son, E. P.
Moretti, Franco, 122–23, 151
Murphy, Teresa, 91, 94, 260n81
*Mysteries of Lowell* (Bradbury), 33–34, 35,
    87, 107–12, 114, 148, 157, 191, 255n1
"Myth of Lowell," 35, 39, 43, 45, 56, 59, 71.
    *See also* "beauties of factory life"; Low-
    ell factory girl; "romance of labor"

*Narrative of Sojourner Truth*, 7, 29, 164,
    220
Neal, John, 43
Negt, Oskar, 10, 86
Newman, Simon, 85
*New York by Gaslight* (Foster), 27, 34–35,
    45, 81
New York Female Moral Reform Society,
    117, 127
*Norton: Or, the Lights and Shadows of a
    Factory Village* (Argus), 105–7

oral culture 27, 220; and class counter-
    memory, 2, 16, 29, 251n5; and class loss,
    29, 247–50; and working-class "ar-
    chive," 248, 183, 251n5. *See also* Collins,
    Jennie; orature; performance; Taylor,
    Diana; *testimonios*
orature, 183, 184, 220, 251n5, 277n2
Orleck, Annelise, 26, 52
*Our Nig* (Wilson), 27, 30–31, 153–79, 180,
    184, 188, 194, 229, 252n19, 272n57; and

black women's class resistance, 172–79; and class performance, 168–70, 173–79; dynamic of racial desire in, 163–79; as experimental text, 163–64; and precarious whiteness, 154, 156, 163–64, 171, 173, 176; and racialization of domestic labor, 154–56, 158–63, 167–76; redefinition of sympathy in, 178–79; and working-class seduction formula, 163–67

Owen, Robert, 23, 36

Padilla, Genaro M., 233–34
Paine, Thomas, 42
pastoralization of female domestic labor, 15, 154, 171, 258n57. *See also* aesthetics; Boydston, Jeanne
paternalism, 14, 24, 121, 125, 130, 134, 149, 188, 243, 262n113, 267n82, 273n10; working-class women's critique of, 14, 54, 56, 58–66, 69, 91, 94, 109, 112, 117
pauperism, 34, 50, 99–100, 120–21
Pérez, Eulalia, 31, 220, 223, 235–37, 242–46
performance: and class embodiment, 110, 130, 171–79; exchanges between print and performance cultures, 31, 77, 180–83, 220–21; importance in working-class culture, 30–31; inter-racial affiliations within, 3–4, 182. *See also* Bernstein, Robin; Bourdieu, Pierre; *Hidden Hand, The* (Southworth); Lhamon, W. T.; Lott, Eric; melodrama; oral culture; *Our Nig* (Wilson); Taylor, Diana; *testimonios*; White, Shane
Phelps, Aurora, 226
Phelps, Elizabeth Stuart, 47
piecework, 114–15, 132, 139–40. *See also* homework; seamstresses
popular fiction: and the bodily "low," 81–83; and fear of class contamination, 34–35, 82; figured as prostitute's body, 34–35, 82–83; and working-class

female subjectivity, 78–83, 186–87, 253n42, 264n19. *See also* aesthetics; Enstad, Nan; Greer, Jane; Lehuu, Isabel; sensationalism
Poovey, Mary, 14, 29, 120
poverty: in antebellum poverty discourses, 87, 98–100, 120–21; and female poverty narratives, 8–9, 27
precarious whiteness of poor and working-class women, 36, 156, 164, 171, 173, 176, 188, 213, 220, 245, 252n19, 255n10, 278n39. *See also* Hodes, Martha
"proletarian grotesque," 83–86, 90, 268n91. *See also* aesthetics
proletarian public sphere, and antebellum working-class women, 10, 86
prostitutes, 146–47; and female moral reform, 127–28; in urban sensationalism, 34–35, 80, 86, 98, 102, 106, 110, 146–52; see also *Frank Rivers; or, the Dangers of the Town* (Ingraham); Lehuu, Isabel; *Madame Restell: An Account of Her Life* (Smith); melodrama; popular fiction; sensationalism
Protestantism, 54; and female labor activism, 90–97. See also *Factory Girl, The* (Anon.); Murphy, Teresa

Rancière, Jacques, 86, 254n59
Robbins, Bruce, 12, 193, 228, 231, 273n10
Robinson, Alfred, 233, 234–35
Robinson, Harriet, 11–12, 26–27, 104
Roediger, David, 135, 158–9, 261n104
"romance of labor," 21, 45, 62, 73
Ruiz de Burton, Maria Amparo: *The Squatter and the Don*, 224–28, 229, 230, 231, 232, 282n28; *Who Would Have Thought It*, 220, 227–32
*Ruth Hall* (Fern), 113–14
Ryan, Mary, 63

Sánchez, Rosaura, 220, 222
Sanger, William, 147
Santamarina, Xiomara, 172, 274n29

Schocket, Eric, 10

Scott, Joan, 251n1

Seamstress, The (Arthur), 120, 126,
129–36, 137, 138, 139, 270n22

seamstresses, 30; African American slaves,
115–16, 118; contrasted with factory
workers, 30, 114–15; in *Emily, the
Beautiful Seamstress* (Bradbury); and
"feminine" dependency, 114, 116–17;
and free African American workers,
118; gothic power of, 119–20; in *The
Hidden Hand* (Southworth), 195,
210–11; labor activism of, 117–18;
Mexican American needleworkers,
238–40, 243–44; and "moralization"
of the working class, 24–25, 115; in
*Our Nig* (Wilson), 166; and plots of
decline, 113–14, 116, 120–24; 127–142;
portrayed by moral reformers, 117,
127–29; prominence in poverty writings, 120–21; in *Ruth Hall* (113–14);
"sentimental seamstress" as literary
type, 115, 124–42; in "The Song of
the Shirt" (Hood), 124–28; in "Stray
Leaves from a Seamstress" (Anon.),
142–46; in visual culture, 125–26; and
"whiteness," 115. *See also Seamstress,
The* (Arthur); *Elliott Family, The*
(Burdett)

seduction narrative: and antebellum
poverty discourses, 97–101, 120–21;
as antebellum working-class form,
38, 64–65, 71, 80, 85–112; and female
moral reform, 111, 127–29; and new
hostility toward poor mothers, 99–
100; parodied in *The Hidden Hand*
(Southworth), 211–13; and "precarious
whiteness," 107–12, 164–67; revision
of Richardsonian model, 86–87, 98;
and sensationalism, 97–112. *See also Ellen Merton, the Belle of Lowell* (Anon.);
*Emily, the Beautiful Seamstress*
(Bradbury); *Flora Montgomerie, the
Factory Girl* (Anon.); *Frank Rivers, or,*

*The Dangers of the Town* (Ingraham);
Haag, Pamela; *Mary Bean: The Factory
Girl* (Anon.); *Mysteries of Lowell, The*
(Bradbury); *Norton: Or, the Lights and
Shadows of a Factory Village* (Anon.);
Vicinus, Martha

sensationalism: and classed embodiment,
78, 83–86; links to political journalism,
34–35; and "proletarian grotesque,"
83–86, 90, 268n91; as working-class
aesthetic, 30, 33–35, 37, 41–48, 72, 76,
78, 81–86, 97–112, 152, 184, 186–87,
201, 264n19; and working-class female
desire, 8, 10, 13, 33–35, 76–78, 81–83,
86, 107–11, 148–52. *See also* aesthetics;
body; prostitutes; seduction narrative;
sexuality

sentimentalism: challenged in working-
class women's texts, 23, 29–30, 74–75,
80, 83, 109, 165–66, 174–75, 178–79,
183, 188, 190–93, 196, 209–11; and
"feminine" dependency, 23–25, 113–52;
as middle-class mode, 12, 14–15, 29–30,
34, 50, 63, 68, 70, 83. See also domesticity; *House of the Seven Gables, The*
(Hawthorne); seamstresses; sexuality;
sympathy

serial fiction, 185

servants: and feminist equation of wives
and servants, 49, 51; and intensity of
class feelings, 158, 167–79; middle-class
fear of class contamination by, 184;
and pastoralization of domestic work,
161–62; racialized in antebellum
era, 3, 135, 154–163, 219–21, 223, 226,
230–32; as readers of popular fiction,
79–80, 185; and slavery, 162–63, 187;
working-class women as, 1–4, 27–29,
49–50, 58, 59, 63, 74, 102, 107, 127–28,
148–49, 156–57, 192–93, 199, 200. *See
also* domestic workers; *Our Nig* (Wilson); Roediger, David

sexuality: and class, 6–7, 11, 14, 21–25,
45–48, 52–53, 63–66, 71, 73–78,

86, 91, 97–112, 146–52, 155, 187–88,
189–90, 196, 203, 221, 227–28; and
homoerotics of factory life, 70, 74–75,
76, 91, 95, 256n15; and interracial desire,
7, 34, 77–78, 168, 213–18, 229–30; and
middle-class domestic norms, 14–15,
19–25, 37–39; and working-class
sexual practices, 7, 23, 34, 62–66; and
working-class women's "excessive," nonnormative desires, 4–6, 34–35, 37–38,
70, 77–78, 81–83, 95–112, 146–52, 185,
203–13, 248–50, 262n115. *See also* aesthetics; bachelor; domesticity; family
wage; prostitutes; seduction narrative;
sensationalism

Shakespeare: and antebellum working-
class culture 3, 252n9; and Southworth,
181

"Sisterhood of the Green Veil" (Lippard),
129

Skidmore, Thomas: *The Rights of Man to
Property,* 15, 18–19

Slotkin, Richard, 23

Smith, Adam, 38, 138, 158

Smith, Charles: *Madame Restell: An
Account of Her Life,* 147–48

Smith, Henry Nash, 80

Smith, Stacey, 221

Southworth, E, D. E. N., 80; critical
response to, 82, 180, 190; literary depiction of seamstresses, 26; as "popular"
author, 181, 184–86; and working-class
female readers, 186–87; *Vivia,* 193–94.
*See also Hidden Hand, The*

Spillers, Hortense, 109

"Sporting men," 64. *See also Ellen Merton,
the Belle of Lowell* (Anon.)

*Squatter and the Don, The* (Ruiz de Burton), 224–28, 229, 230, 231, 232, 282n28

Stallybrass, Peter, 42, 83, 275n41

Stansell, Christine, 21, 24, 64, 66, 133,
162, 187, 205, 206, 211, 258n54, 262n113,
267n83, 270n38, 272n60, 273n10,
278n38, 280n73

Steedman, Carolyn, 10, 76, 92, 108–9, 157,
191, 203, 267n72, 280n65

Stewart, Maria W., 159–61, 170; "Lecture Delivered at the Franklin Hall,"
159–61; "Religion and the Pure Principles of Morality," 159

Stowe, Harriet Beecher, 16, 89, 146,
153–54

"Stray Leaves from a Seamstress"
(Anon.), 142–46; critique of female
moral reform in, 145–46; critique
of middle-class women's "sympathy"
in, 144–46; and idea of cooperative
industry, 144; and threat of class
contamination, 145; and threat of class
revolt, 144

Streeby, Shelley, 10, 82, 257n42

Sue, Eugène, 33, 107

sympathy: and abolition, 61–62; class
politics of, in antebellum era, 7, 12, 20,
28–30, 38, 48–50, 59, 62, 98, 105, 115,
124–27; as middle-class affect, 7, 20,
29–30, 38, 70, working-class women's
redefinition of, 28–30, 58–59, 61–62,
74–75, 178–79, 190, 211, 260n84. *See
also* associationism; Bagley, Sarah; Collins, Jennie; sentimentalism; sexuality

"Tales of Factory Life, No. 1" (Bagley),
156–57

Taylor, Barbara, 22–23, 48

Taylor, Diana, 183, 248

Ten Hour Movement, 63, 68, 256n24,
260n72, 260n81

*testimonios,* 31, 219–21, 225, 232–45;
as "archive" of Mexican American
working womanhood, 31, 220. *See also*
autobiography; Lorenzana, Apolinaria;
Pérez, Eulalia

Thompson, E. P., 54, 87, 157–58, 176

Tomlins, Christopher, 258n62

Tonna, Charlotte Elizabeth, 47

transatlanticism: and factory debates,
35–36; and labor reform, 11–12, 256n24

Trollope, Frances: *Adventures of Michael Armstrong*, 47

Truth, Sojourner, 7, 11, 49; *Narrative of Sojourner Truth*, 7, 29, 164, 220

Tyler, Martha W.: *Book without a Title: Or, Thrilling Events in the Life of Mira Dana*, 155–56

*Una, The*, 48–51. See also "Stray Leaves from a Seamstress"

*Uncle Tom's Cabin* (Stowe), 89, 181

United Tailoresses' Society, 117

*Unravelling* (Graver), 248–50

"Valentine Offering," 74–75

Vicinus, Martha, 87

*Voice of Industry*, 22, 30, 52, 54–63, 69–72, 93, 117, 259–60n71, 260n72, 264n3, 266n47

Ware, Norman 61

Warner, Michael, 83

Warner, Susan, 25, 210

Webb, Frank: *Garies and their Friends, The*, 174

*What Is to Be Done?* (Chernyshevsky), 118

Whiteley's Original Hidden Hand Company, 181–82

White, Allon, 42, 83, 275n41

White, Shane, 7, 153, 182

*Who Would Have Thought It* (Ruiz de Burton), 220, 227–32

Williams, Andrea, 164

Williams, Raymond, 12, 67

Wilson, Harriet, 27, 30–31, 153–79. See also *Our Nig*

working-class women: political activism of, 1–4, 8–9, 40, 51–72, 74–75, 117–19; as readers, 2, 12–13, 78–83, 185–87. See also autobiography; class; domestic workers; factory workers; popular fiction; prostitutes; seamstresses; servants

Wright, Fanny, 6, 56

Yeazell, Ruth Bernard, 123